Their of

*the text of this book is printed
on 100% recycled paper*

Theft of the Nation

THE STRUCTURE AND OPERATIONS

OF ORGANIZED CRIME IN AMERICA

Donald R. Cressey

HARPER COLOPHON BOOKS

HARPER & ROW, PUBLISHERS

New York, Evanston, and London

THEFT OF THE NATION: THE STRUCTURE AND OPERATIONS OF ORGANIZED CRIME IN AMERICA. Copyright © 1969 by Donald R. Cressey.

Printed in the United States of America. All rights reserved. No part of this book may be used or reproduced in any manner whatsoever without written permission except in the case of brief quotations embodied in critical articles and reviews. For information address Harper & Row, Publishers, Incorporated, 10 East 53rd Street, New York, N.Y. 10022. Published simultaneously in Canada by Fitzhenry & Whiteside Limited, Toronto.

First HARPER COLOPHON edition published in 1969 by Harper & Row, Publishers, Incorporated.

LIBRARY OF CONGRESS CATALOG CARD NUMBER: 68-15987

For Martha, Ann, and Mary

Contents

Preface

IN DESCRIBING America's era of Prohibition, Dean Jennings recently wrote, "The law was sick and dying, and no one cared. . . . Crime was just a harmless little game, and its heroes in almost every conflict were the gangsters who could outwit the villainous men with the badges."

The Prohibition era is gone, but organized criminals are more powerful than they ever were when their principal occupation was rumrunning and bootlegging. Their activities continue to be viewed as a harmless little game. But the game is neither harmless nor little. Organized criminals are gradually but inexorably stealing our nation. And still no one cares.

This book is an extensive revision of a report I prepared for the President's Commission on Law Enforcement and Administration of Justice. That report was written under conditions which can best be described as "desperate." Time pressures were such that important questions could not even be clearly formulated, let alone discussed. I viewed the report as a "first draft," and after it was published I spent a year collecting materials necessary to revising it.

The secrecy of organized criminals, the confidentiality of the materials collected by law-enforcement and investigative agencies, and the various filters through which both informers and investigators see organized criminals all pose serious problems for anyone who would write coolly and calmly about organized crime in America. The ongoing activities of organized criminals simply are not accessible to observation by the ordinary citizen, the ordinary reporter, or the ordinary social scientist. Even gaining access to some of the observations made by law-enforcement officers and investigative bodies requires "connections" such as appointment as a consultant to the President's Commission. It is not difficult to get information necessary to writing a gossipy exposé that "names names." The tough job is that of obtaining information about organization.

Upon being invited to work for the Commission, I was not at all sure that a nationwide organization of criminals exists. Discussions with my friends and colleagues indicated, and continue to indicate, that this skepticism is widely shared. I changed my mind. I am certain that no rational man could read the evidence that I have read and still come to the conclusion that an organization variously called "the Mafia," "Cosa Nostra," and "the syndicate" does not exist. Henry S. Ruth, Jr., Deputy Director of the President's Commission, invited law-enforcement and investigative agencies to submit reports on organized crime to the Commission. A summer spent reading these materials, exploring other confidential materials, and interviewing knowledgeable policemen and investigators convinced me that the following eight points are facts. An additional year of similar kinds of reading and interviewing supported my conviction. This book, like my report to the Commission, is above all an analysis and elaboration of these eight facts and the relationships between them.

1. A nationwide alliance of at least twenty-four tightly knit "families" of criminals exists in the United States. (Because the "families" are fictive, in the sense that the members are not all relatives, it is necessary to refer to them in quotation marks.)

2. The members of these "families" are all Italians and Sicilians, or of Italian and Sicilian descent, and those on the Eastern Seaboard, especially, call the entire system "Cosa Nostra." Each participant thinks of himself as a "member" of a specific "family" and of Cosa Nostra (or some equivalent term).

3. The names, criminal records, and principal criminal activities of about five thousand of the participants have been assembled.

4. The persons occupying key positions in the skeletal structure of each "family"—consisting of positions for boss, underboss, lieutenants (also called "captains"), counselor, and for low-ranking members called "soldiers" or "button men"—are well known to law-enforcement officials having access to informants. Names of persons who permanently or temporarily occupy other positions, such as "buffer," "money mover," "enforcer," and "executioner," also are well known.

5. The "families" are linked to each other, and to non-Cosa Nostra syndicates, by understandings, agreements, and "treaties," and by mutual deference to a "Commission" made up of the leaders of the most powerful of the "families."

6. The boss of each "family" directs the activities, especially the illegal activities, of the members of his "family."

7. The members of this organization control all but a tiny part of the illegal gambling in the United States. They are the principal loan sharks. They are the principal importers and wholesalers of narcotics. They have infiltrated certain labor unions, where they extort money from employers and, at the same time, cheat the members of the union. The members have a virtual monopoly on some legitimate enterprises, such as cigarette vending machines and juke boxes, and they own a wide variety of retail firms, restaurants and bars, hotels, trucking companies, food companies, linen-supply houses, garbage collection routes, and factories. Until recently, they owned a large proportion of Las Vegas. They own several state legislators and federal congressmen and other officials in the legislative, executive, and judicial branches of government at the local, state, and federal levels. Some government officials (including judges) are considered, and consider themselves, members.

8. The information about the Commission, the "families," and the activities of members has come from detailed reports made by a wide variety of police observers, informants, wire taps, and electronic bugs.

Bibliographical notes are at the end of the book. Since most of the notes refer only to the location of quotations and other pieces of information, I have not used superscript numbers; the citations are identified in the notes (pp. 325–342) by a key phrase. Most of the quotes appearing without citation are from interviews. Policemen with access to informants often quoted them to me. A few incidents have been slightly altered in the interest of anonymity. My objective is not that of identifying crooks who ought to be in jail. The objective is to show the effects of the fact that some crooks are organized.

I owe special thanks to Ralph Salerno, who until recently was with the Criminal Investigation Bureau of the New York City Police

Department. Mr. Salerno is an extraordinary teacher. He gave me lessons at all hours of the day and night in all parts of the country. I have swiped a few of his jokes and a lot of his stories.

I also am deeply grateful to other members of "the organized-crime gang" which developed as we worked together in Washington. These include Charles Rogovin, Director of the President's Commission Task Force on Organized Crime and now Assistant Attorney General of Massachusetts; Henry Ruth, Jr., Deputy Director of the Commission and now Professor in the University of Pennsylvania Law School; G. Robert Blakey, Consultant to the Commission and now Professor in the Notre Dame Law School; Robert L. Emrich, Consultant to the Commission and now the anthropological member of The Office of Law Enforcement Assistance; Henry E. Peterson, Chief of the Organized Crime and Racketeering Section of the United States Department of Justice; and Robert Herman, my research assistant and now a graduate student in political science at the University of California, Irvine.

The participants in the somewhat confidential Oyster Bay (New York) Conferences on Combating Organized Crime at first looked at me with a fishy eye but then unselfishly began contributing to my education. The originator of the conferences, Eliot Lumbard, then Special Assistant to Governor Rockefeller of New York, frequently walked with me in the woods and gave me lessons in elementary political science. My old friend Lloyd Ohlin got me started in "the organized-crime business," and a more recent friend, James Vorenberg, kept me going.

Harper & Row's Alfred E. Prettyman and Miss Jeannette Hopkins were so helpful that I dedicated my hand-wrought, three-stall, horse stable to them.

DONALD R. CRESSEY

Santa Barbara, California

"The racketeer is not someone dressed in a black shirt, white tie, and diamond stick pin, whose activities affect only a remote underworld circle. He is more likely to be outfitted in a gray flannel suit and his influence is more likely to be as far-reaching as that of an important industrialist. The American public may not see him, but that makes the racketeer's power for evil in our society even greater. Lacking the direct confrontation with the racketeer, the American citizen fails to see the reason for alarm. The reason, decidedly, exists. The financial cost of organized crime is not limited to the vast illicit profits of gambling or narcotics. When the racketeers bore their way into legitimate business, the cost is borne by the public. When the infiltration is into labor relations, the racketeer's cut is paid by higher wages and higher prices—in other words, by the public. When the racketeer bribes local officials and secures immunity from police action, the price exacted by corrupt law enforcement—incalculable in dollars—is paid, again, by the public. In short, organized crime affects everyone. It cannot be the concern only of law enforcement officers. It must be the urgent and active concern of every citizen."

ROBERT F. KENNEDY

Theft of the Nation

CHAPTER I

Trouble

The most flagrant manifestation of crime in America is organized crime. It erodes our very system of justice —in all spheres of government. It is bad enough for individuals to turn to crime because they are misguided or desperate. It is intolerable that corporations of corruption should systematically flaunt our laws.

LYNDON B. JOHNSON

IN THE UNITED STATES, criminals have managed to put together an organization which is at once a nationwide illicit cartel and a nationwide confederation. This organization is dedicated to amassing millions of dollars by means of extortion, and from usury, the illicit sale of lottery tickets, chances on the outcome of horse races and athletic events, narcotics, and untaxed liquor. Its presence in our society is morally reprehensible because any citizen purchasing illicit goods and services from organized criminals contributes to a culture of fraud, corruption, violence, and murder. Nevertheless, criminal organizations dealing only in illicit goods and services are no great threat to the nation. The danger of organized crime arises because the vast profits acquired from the sale of illicit goods and services are being invested in licit enterprises, in both the economic sphere and the political sphere. It is when criminal syndicates start to undermine basic economic and political traditions and institutions that the real trouble begins. And the real trouble has begun in the United States.

It is one thing to make a few dollars selling illegal lottery tickets, but it is another thing to achieve a monopoly on illegal gambling services by means of a simple weapon, a gun. It is one thing to bribe a policeman to overlook gambling, but it is another thing to dictate the actions of a state legislator or federal congressman or senator. It is one thing to amass a fortune by importing narcotics, but it is another thing to use this fortune to buy immunity from prosecution for murder. It is one thing to embezzle from union funds, but it is another thing to use a union to extort a small businessman's means of livelihood from him. It is one thing to beat up a loan-shark victim who is delinquent in his payments, but it is another thing to bribe city officials in order to get a liquor license or a construction contract. It is one thing to control gambling and most other illegal activities in a neighborhood, but it is another thing to demand, with a gun, a share of the butcher's profits, the baker's profits, the doctor's fees, and the banker's interest rates.

While organized criminals do not yet have control of all the legitimate economic and political activities in any metropolitan or other geographic area of America, they do have control of *some* of those activities in many areas. In some cities, all night-club owners must hand 10 percent of their income to a collector who stands in a corner of the establishment, figuratively speaking, shifting a gun from pocket to pocket or fingering the blade of a razor-sharp knife. In other cities, or areas of cities, all butchers must buy their meat, at inflated prices, from a man who, similarly, holds a deadly weapon in his hand. Some workingmen, especially unskilled laborers, do not know that they are members of a labor union—their employer pays their "dues" to a man standing in the doorway of factory or shop holding a bomb or, in the case of beauty salons, a box of live mice or a hive of honey bees. Equally important, members of crime syndicates have invested in every conceivable kind of legitimate business, and they completely control both small and large business firms, ranging from restaurants and trucking companies to international importing and distributing companies. They operate many of these businesses illegally, as the Kefauver Committee showed over fifteen years ago. They monopolize by force.

The men holding knives at the throats of American businessmen, whether these businessmen be engaged in illicit or licit enterprises, are not "independents." They work for someone who works for someone who works for someone. They have jobs to do. They are "organized." This means, among other things, that money extorted from night-club owners goes into the same coffers as the profits on narcotics importation and distribution. Moreover, the rulers of crime syndicates have strong interests in the governmental process and they are "represented," in one form or another, in legislative, judicial, and executive bodies all over the country. The residents of some political wards no longer have an effective vote—their governmental officials represent criminals rather than the law-abiding voters. Even the American citizens who are represented by honest elected and appointed officials have lost, to organized criminals, a few decibels of their democratic voice. The honest politician who must cope with a politician controlled by criminals loses some of his effectiveness. Organized criminals have gone beyond buying licenses to gamble from law-enforcement officers and minor city officials. They now are concerned with influencing legislation on matters ranging from food services and garbage collection to "invasion of privacy" (wire tapping, electronic surveillance, and computerization of criminal records) and the "defamation" of Italian-American hoodlums.

We recognize a danger. We cannot be sure of the degree of the danger any more than the observer of the beginnings of any other kind of monopoly can be sure of the degree of danger. If a large retail firm similar to the Atlantic and Pacific Tea Company lowers its prices to a level such that its small independent competitors happen to go bankrupt, that is free enterprise. If, after its competitors are forced out of business, the large firm raises its prices above those existing when it had competitors, thus forcing consumers to pay a tribute, that is exploitive monopolistic practice. By analogy, rulers of crime syndicates are beginning to drive legitimate businessmen, labor leaders, and other supporters of the ideology of free competition to the wall. They have established, by force, intimidation, and even more "legal" methods, monopolies in several relatively small fields such as distribution of certain kinds of vending machines, the supplying of linen to night clubs, and the supplying of some forms of labor. In some political arenas they have, as indicated, used force and fraud to monopolize the processes of democratic government. A "monopoly" on government is, of course, a dictatorship.

A former special attorney in the Organized Crime and Racketeering Section of the United States Department of Justice accurately has pointed out that "when organized crime embarks on a venture in legitimate business it ordinarily brings to that venture all the techniques of violence and intimidation which are employed in its illegal enterprises." Accordingly, consumers and taxpayers unknowingly pay tribute to the organized criminals who have entered legitimate business. This situation is more dangerous than was the situation in the 1920's and 1930's when the monopolies controlled by organized criminals were primarily monopolies on only the distribution of illicit goods and services. The real danger is that the trend will continue to the point where syndicate rulers gain such a degree of control that they drive supporters of free enterprise and democracy out of "business" and then force us to pay tribute in the form of traditional freedoms. Syndicate rulers are among the most active monopolizers in the American economy. On the occasion of his retirement from the Criminal Investigation Bureau of the New York City Police Department, one of the nation's few police experts on organized crime said, "Organized crime will put a man in the White House some day, and he won't know it until they hand him the bill." He might have said, alternatively, "*We* won't know it until they hand *us* the bill." Syndicate rulers are among the most active monopolizers of the democratic process.

Danilo Dolci, the Italian social reformer, has emphasized the potential danger of organized crime by pointing out that even now a "Mafia-client system" of politics operates under the label of democracy in much of the world we know best, the Western world. This is the system of politics in which a politician's clients buy votes for him with handouts of food, low-status jobs, a few pennies, personal recommendations, and "favors," or, alternatively, muster votes for him by threats of terror. This is the system in which the politician is able to obtain personal power and advantages in every possible combination because his clients are rewarded for procuring the votes of people whose collective interests lie in a direction very different from those of their governor. And this is the system of politics that America's syndicated crime rulers would with a vengeance substitute for an ideal participatory democracy. Dolci describes "the Western world" as follows:

The people in the industrialized zones have no effective political relationship, but rather some vague and distorted notions of current ideologies, while in the underdeveloped areas, what is being smuggled in under the guise of democracy, generally with complete success and immunity, is a genuine Mafia-client system. Under this system a large proportion of votes is acquired en masse through the purchase of newspapers (and newspapermen), television stations (and their staffs), and "politicians," or through all the many tried and tested techniques which range from ingratiating smiles to blackmail and intimidation—and this from the level of local administration to the highest levels of national government.

In other words, the goals and methods of public officials may not be as far from the goals and methods of our crime syndicate as we Americans would like to think. If syndicate rulers are permitted to achieve a monopoly on the democratic processes in the United States, we surely will regard as inevitable or even as "democratic" a world of ghettos, inequality, and discriminatory practices. Rather than steady movement toward total, continuous, and strategic commitment to the construction of a democratic world, there will be a throwback to a political system in which the strong increasingly come to agreements with the strong, powerfully increasing the ability of the strong to extract tribute from the weak.

It is difficult to determine the point at which antitrust action should be taken against the fictitious large retail firm noted in the example above. It is also difficult to determine the point at which the danger to American freedom posed by despotic rulers of crime syndicates is clear and present enough to justify strong defensive and retaliatory action. We are concerned because millions of Americans are, in hundreds of minor ways, already paying ransom to organized criminals. We do not mean the man who bets a dollar at 1 to 500 or 1 to 600 odds when the "honest" odds are 1 to 1000. We mean the housewife who must pay a few cents extra each day to have her trash hauled by a company controlled by criminals. We mean the teen-ager who pays a few cents more for a hamburger and a glass of milk because the vendor must buy his supplies from companies controlled by criminals. We mean the college student and the lawyer who must pay a few cents more for their books because they have at some stage been hauled by a truck operator who must, in order to maintain labor peace, buy his tires from a company controlled by criminals. We mean all the other citizens who are required to spend a quarter here and a dollar there because someone, somewhere in the chain from raw material to finished product, must pay a tribute to criminals. We also mean the taxpayer, the poor taxpayer, who must in the long run finance kickbacks to organized criminals and who must pay both his own taxes and a large proportion of the syndicate member's share of taxes. "If organized criminals paid income tax on every cent of their vast earnings, everybody's tax bill would go down, but no one knows how much." In the four-year period 1961–1965 the Internal Revenue Service assessed organized criminals almost a quarter of a billion dollars in taxes and penalties beyond the amounts paid by the criminals when they filed their income-tax forms. In 1965 the City and State of New York lost over $50 million in cigarette-tax revenues to cigarette smuggling by organized criminals. Further, since the smugglers paid no tax on the income derived from the sale of about $138 million worth of cigarettes, another tax source also dried up. These are insignificant amounts as the nation's budget and New York's budget go. They also are insignificant amounts of the tax burden citizens must bear because organized criminals cheat. The economic costs of organized crime to the ordinary citizen are similar to the economic costs of misrepresentation in advertising—each individual is damaged only a little, but collectively the citizenry pays plenty.

In some cases, of course, the monopolies started by organized criminals do not seem to hurt any individual's pocketbook. They might even reduce prices for a time, as does the fictitious retail firm mentioned above. The gambler whose bookie pays the same odds as does the race track feels no pinch if a part of the bookie's profits goes to an organization whose agents protect him from the police, and from themselves. A quarter in a juke box is a quarter in a juke box, whether the machine is owned by a crook or by my grandmother. The coins inserted in a cigarette vending machine release one package of smuggled cigarettes or one package of tax-paid cigarettes. If the dues and benefits in each of two union locals are the same, it costs me nothing if I pay my dues to a "paper local" owned by criminals rather than to a legitimate local.

The threat of organized crime to America is similar to the threat any potential monopolizer poses to a small businessman: "This man can hurt me." But there are differences, too. First, organized crime uses force and threat of force to obtain monopoly, while legitimate firms do not, at least not as often. Second, organized crime nullifies legitimate government more directly, and to a greater extent, than do other forms of monopoly. Business firms "own" elected and appointed officials, just as do criminal syndicates. The former attempt to nullify government by securing favorable legislation, the latter by this means *and* by obtaining immunity from the regulatory effects of legislation, including the criminal law. If a significant proportion of a society's rewards go to those who openly violate the law, and those who obey the law come to feel that criminal behavior pays more than honesty, we are in danger, even if the "leftovers" make us the wealthiest persons in the world. We agree with the President's Commission on Law Enforcement and Administration of Justice, which drew the following conclusion:

In many ways organized crime is the most sinister kind of crime in America. The men who control it have become rich and powerful by encouraging the needy to gamble, by luring the troubled to destroy themselves with drugs, by extorting the profits of honest and hardworking businessmen, by collecting usury from those in financial plight, by maiming or murdering those who oppose them, by bribing those sworn to destroy them. Organized crime is not merely a few preying on a few. In a very real sense, it is dedicated to subverting not only American institutions, but the very decency and integrity that are the most cherished attributes of a free society. As the leaders of Cosa Nostra and their racketeering allies pursue their conspiracy unmolested, in open and continuous defiance of the law, they preach a sermon that all too many Americans heed: The government is for sale; lawlessness is the road to wealth; honesty is a pitfall and morality a trap for suckers.

We also agree with Robert F. Kennedy who, when counsel for the Subcommittee on Investigations of the U.S. Senate Committee on Operations (McClellan Committee), became convinced that "if we do not on a national scale attack organized criminals, with weapons and techniques as effective as their own, they will destroy us."

CHAPTER II

From Mafia to Cosa Nostra

*The extraordinary thing about organized crime is that
America has tolerated it for so long.*
PRESIDENT'S CRIME COMMISSION

THE THREAT which organized crime poses to traditional American
economic and political freedoms can, interestingly enough, be determined by looking at Sicily as well as by looking at America. Because the Sicilian Mafia has been the subject of discussion and investigation, if not study, for almost a century, Americans can readily
learn more about it than they can about the activities of organized
criminals in their own country. While we are confident that American
organized crime is not merely the Sicilian Mafia transplanted, the
similarities between the two organizations are direct and too great
to be ignored.

For at least a century, a pervasive organization of criminals called
the Mafia has dominated almost all aspects of life—economic, political, religious, and social—in the western part of the island of Sicily.
This organization also has been influential, but not dominating, in
the remainder of Sicily and in southern Italy. In the early part of
this century, thousands of Sicilians and southern Italians became
American immigrants. The immigrants brought with them the customs of their homeland, and included in those customs are psychological attitudes toward a wide variety of social relationships. At
the same time, the immigration established an obvious and direct
route for further diffusion of the customs of Sicily to the United
States. Because the American farm land had been more or less
settled by the time the Sicilians and Italians arrived, they tended
to settle in the large cities of the Eastern seaboard, where they lived

together in neighborhoods. The fact that they lived together enabled them to retain for some time many of the customs of the old country, unlike, say, the Scandinavians who scattered through the upper Midwest. A certain "clannishness" contributed to the retention of the custom of "clannishness." Further, the custom of "clannishness" probably was accentuated by the move to a strange land.

In these early Sicilian and Italian neighborhoods, discussion of the workings of the Mafia and "The Black Hand" was commonplace. Violence was attributed to these organizations, and people feared the names. Men were shot on the streets but, out of fear, obvious witnesses refused to come forward. In Brooklyn, it became customary for housewives to say to each other, on the occasion of hearing the sounds of a murderer's pistol, "It is sad that someone's injured horse had to be destroyed." Fear was present, just as it had been in Italy and Sicily. No one can be sure that this fear was a product of the Old World Mafia, rather than merely the work of hoodlums who capitalized on the fear of the Mafia that existed back home.

During national Prohibition in the 1920's and early 1930's, the various bootlegging gangs across the nation were made up of immigrants and the descendants of immigrants from many countries. There were Irish gangs, Jewish gangs, Polish gangs, German gangs, Italian gangs, and many others. An organization known as "Unione Siciliana" was involved. Near the end of Prohibition, the basic framework of the current structure of American organized crime, to be described later, was established as the final product of a series of "gangland wars" in which an alliance of Italians and Sicilians first conquered other groups and then fought each other. During these conflicts the Italian-Sicilian alliance was called "the Mafia," among other things. There is no sound information about whether this "Mafia" was a branch of the Sicilian Mafia.

The Italian-Sicilian apparatus set up as a result of a 1930–1931 war between Italian and Sicilian criminals continues to dominate organized crime in America, and it is still called "the Mafia" in many quarters. The Federal Bureau of Narcotics has called it "Mafia" since the early 1930's, but the Federal Bureau of Investigation has denied the existence of an organization going by that name. While the Kefauver Committee in 1950 concluded that "there is a nationwide crime syndicate known as the Mafia," the Director of the FBI as recently as 1962 stated that "no single individual or coalition of racketeers dominates organized crime across the nation." Now the Director uses "Cosa Nostra" to refer to the "criminal fraternity" which others call "the Mafia":

La Cosa Nostra is a criminal fraternity whose membership is Italian either by birth or national origin, and it has been found to control major racket activities in many of our larger metropolitan areas, often working in concert with criminals representing other ethnic backgrounds. It operates on a nationwide basis, with international implications, and until recent years it carried on its activities with almost complete secrecy. It functions as a criminal cartel, adhering to its own body of "law" and "justice" and, in so doing, thwarts and usurps the authority of legally constituted judicial bodies.

We shall later discuss the various names given to the organization controlling organized crime. Whatever the "criminal fraternity" be called, there remains the question of whether it is the Mafia of Sicily and southern Italy transplanted to this country or whether it has arisen principally as the result of the response to a new cultural setting by hoodlum immigrants, some of whom happened to be Italian or Sicilian and thus knowledgeable about how to set up and control, by fear, an illicit organization. There are several reasons why this question is important.

First, it is a fact that almost all Italian and Sicilian immigrants, and their descendants, have been both fine and law-abiding citizens. They have unwittingly let criminals who are Italians or Sicilians, or Americans of Italian or Sicilian descent, be identified with them. Criminals of Italian or Sicilian descent are called "Italians" or "Sicilians," while bankers, lawyers, and professors of Italian or Sicilian descent are called "Americans." More Americans know the name "Luciano" than know the name "Fermi."

In early 1965 a group of New Yorkers formed an "American-Italian Anti-Defamation League," presumably to protect citizens of Italian descent from unwarranted attacks. From the beginning, however, it looked as though this association was designed to encourage respectable Italian-Americans to assist Italian-American criminals.

A law suit brought by the Anti-Defamation League of B'nai B'rith caused the association to change its name first to "American-Italian Anti-Defamation Council," then to "Americans of Italian Descent." In early 1968, the group decided to stress the constructive contributions of Italian-Americans, rather than to pursue its campaign of opposition to "ethnic slurs." However, Mrs. Mary Sansone, President of the Congress of Italian-American Organizations, was skeptical that the group's shift in official policy would help matters much. She said, "It's going to take them quite a while to clean up the mess of the group's first two years of existence."

Part of "the mess" arose because members of the association's Board of Directors made speeches on "How Italians Are Persecuted" and used the Organized Crime Report prepared by the President's Commission as an exhibit. The "mess" also arose in part from the selection, in 1966, of Frank Sinatra as National Chairman of the original group. This singer, actor, and entrepreneur was to help conduct "a campaign to discourage identification of gangsters in ethnic terms." Charles Grutzner, writing in *The New York Times,* pointed out that in 1963 the Nevada Gaming Control Board revoked Mr. Sinatra's license to operate a gambling casino because he had allowed a member of "the Mafia's national commission" to participate. This was Sam Giancana of Chicago. Mr. Grutzner also referred to a 1947 Havana meeting between Mr. Sinatra and Charles Luciano, whose organizational genius, and guns, helped create the current form of organized crime in America.

Ralph Salerno, an Italian-American, was formerly with the Criminal Investigation Bureau of the New York City Police Department, and in all his twenty years of police work he specialized in the detection of the affairs of the organization sometimes called the Mafia. In commenting on the American-Italian Anti-Defamation League and, more specifically, on the appointment of Sinatra, Mr. Salerno said:

I think the Italio-American community has been following the ostrich principle of putting its head in the sand and hoping the problem will go away. These twenty million fine, decent people have failed to disassociate themselves from about 10,000 wrongdoers who enjoy a blending in with the 20 million, so that when anyone points a finger at the wrongdoers they are able to say, "You are unfairly maligning 20 million good Americans."

Because his police work led to the arrest and public exposure of many criminals with Italian names and Mafia or Cosa Nostra membership, Salerno was frequently and severely criticized by Italian-American criminals. He was rarely defended by respectable, law-abiding Italian-Americans. On one occasion the brother of a defendant in a murder case against whom Salerno was testifying came up to him in a court corridor and said, "Why does it have to be one of your own kind that hurts you?" Salerno responded,

I'm not your kind and you're not my kind. My manners, morals and mores are not yours. The only thing we have in common is that we both spring from an Italian heritage and culture—and you are the traitor to that heritage and culture which I am proud to be part of.

If the American criminal organization, which is at once a criminal cartel and a confederation of criminals, is an importation from Sicily and Italy, it should be disowned by all Italian-Americans and Sicilian-Americans because it does not represent the real cultural contribution of Italy and Sicily to America. If it is an American innovation, the men of Italian and Sicilian descent who have positions in it should be disowned by the respectable Italian-American and Sicilian-American community on the ground that they are participating in an extremely undesirable aspect of American culture. This position was taken in 1963 by Paul P. Rao, Jr., the national President of the United Italian-American League, Inc. A few years later, Rao changed his position—apparently for personal reasons—and became a Director of the American-Italian Anti-Defamation League. But when the McClellan Committee received the usual complaints that its hearings were casting reflections on Americans of Italian ancestry, Mr. Rao, who was then New York City Tax Commissioner and a former Assistant District Attorney for New York County, came forward and said:

We regret that there have been some who have irresponsibly accused the Justice Department and the U.S. Senate subcommittee of maintaining a political smear against the Italo-Americans. . . . They who consider an exposé of racketeers dealing in narcotics, illegal gambling, prostitution, and murder as being ethnically prejudicial are either arguing illogically or are selfishly being motivated by their desire for personal publicity. We should not peremptorily dismiss the functions of the committee with diversionary cries of persecution and thereby mislead the millions of decent Americans of Italian origin who sincerely feel a personal obligation over the recent revelations, because of the coincidence of racial identification. We welcome the efforts of the committee to eliminate gangsterism, especially when involving individuals of Italian extraction. The public, however, fully realizes that other notorious names in the annals of the underworld clearly indicate that no ethnic group has a monopoly on crime. How can we eliminate criminal elements from our society if we are unenlightened as to their evil activities?

Second, many of the Sicilian and Italian peasants who emigrated to America did so precisely to escape Mafia despotism. During the early part of the current century, the Mafia dominated the economic, political, and social affairs of western Sicily, as it does today. Persons who defied the organization's leaders were injured, killed, or ruined financially. Some victims fled to the United States. These persons certainly did not bring the Mafia with them. Were they once more dominated? Are any of them, or their descendants, now members of an illicit crime syndicate?

Third, the Sicilian Mafia, like the American organization, was, and is, characterized by power struggles between individuals and factions. These struggles are most apparent when a top leadership position becomes vacant. Some of the losers in such struggles occurring in the early part of the century unquestionably fled to America. Further, in the late 1920's, Benito Mussolini, Fascist Premier of Italy, had the Mafia of southern Italy and Sicily hounded to the point where some of the members found it necessary to migrate, either to avoid official prosecution or to avoid "unofficial" liquidations and executions by the police. The number entering the United States, legally or illegally, is unknown. The rulers of the principal units of the American organization are now in their late sixties or early seventies. Many of them came to this country from Sicily or southern Italy early in the 1930's, and Burton B. Turkus, once an Assistant District Attorney in Brooklyn, has pointed out that the major business of one New York "Mafia" leader at the time "was in smuggling alien criminals who had been chased from Sicily and lower Italy." However, it might be a mere coincidence that the Italian-Sicilian domination of American illicit syndicates and the confederation integrating them began shortly after Mussolini's eradication campaign. The American "gangland war" and peace settlement which determined the present order of things also occurred in the early 1930's.

Fourth, if the American cartel and confederation is an importation from Italy and Sicily, and if it has retained its connections with the old country, then the strategy for eradicating it must be different from the strategy for eradicating a relatively new American organization. In other words, if "Cosa Nostra" is but a branch of the Sicilian-Italian Mafia, then its "home office" abroad must be eliminated before control will be effective. Some of the amateurs and independents now selling marijuana and LSD to American college students let it be known that their work is backed by a ruthless "Cosa Nostra" or "the syndicate." This myth gives power to persons having only a very slight relationship, if any, with Cosa Nostra. By the same token, some members of the American confederation propagate the legend that their organization is a branch of the old Sicilian Mafia. This legend also confers power on the persons who cultivate it. The legend helps perpetuate the notion that the current conspiracy is ancient and therefore quite impregnable.

Fifth, there is a tendency for members of any society or group to look outside itself for the cause whenever it finds itself confronted with a serious problem or, especially, with an evil. Any analysis of organized crime in America is affected, directly or indirectly, by this tendency. Even if all the evidence were to point to the conclusion that the American organization is merely a branch of a foreign organization, the person drawing the conclusion would in all probability be accused of "scapegoatism." As our discussion above indicated, even concluding that organized crime is dominated by Sicilians, Italians, and persons of Sicilian-Italian descent brings the accusation that the troubles of America are being tied to the back of an ethnic group, the scapegoat. Further, one who insists, as we did in Chapter I, that there *is* an organization of criminals in America risks being accused of assigning an assortment of evils and ills to a hidden, mysterious scapegoat. One who writes about organized crime risks being placed in the same category as flying-saucer fanatics and communist-conspiracy zealots, who know "they" are out there creating evils in our society even if we can't see them.

In some cases, "looking outside" means attributing problems to the characteristics of individuals rather than to the characteristics of the society or group itself. Our society tends, both popularly and scientifically, to view the criminal's behavior as a problem of individual maladjustment, not as a consequence of his participation in social systems. It is common to maintain, for example, that criminality is strictly an individual disorder which, therefore, can be treated in a clinic, just as anemia or syphilis can be treated in a clinic. An extreme position is that criminality actually is a biological disorder, treatable by modification of the physiology or anatomy of the individual through lobotomy, castration, interference with glandular functioning, or something else. The much more popular view is that criminality is an individual psychological disorder which may or may not have a strictly biological basis. The criminal may be considered as a person who is unable to canalize or sublimate his "primitive," antisocial impulses or tendencies; or he may be considered as expressing in criminal behavior some unconscious wish or urge created by an early traumatic emotional experience; or he may be considered as possessing some other kind of defective personality component. In any event, the implication is that crime and criminality are matters of the faults and defects of individuals, not of the society or group.

It is possible that attributing criminality to individual disorders is mere scapegoatism, permitting us to denounce the origins of crime without challenging any existing social conditions which we hold dear, and without assigning any blame to ourselves. James G. March and Herbert A. Simon have suggested, for example, that business managers tend to perceive conflict as if it were an individual matter, rather than an organizational matter, because perceiving it as an organizational problem would acknowledge a diversity of goals in the organization, thereby placing strain on the status and power systems. Similarly, in a family which has inadvertently but nevertheless inexorably produced a son's delinquency, it is convenient for the father to attribute the delinquency to "bad blood on the mother's side." For the same reason, the behavior of cold-blooded hired killers, and of the enforcers and rulers who order the killings, is likely to be accounted for solely in terms of the depravity or viciousness of the personnel involved, rather than in terms of organizational roles, including the roles of the victims. But during the last decade criminologists everywhere have been increasingly shifting to the position that criminality is "owned" by groups rather than by individuals and that, therefore, attributing it to individual disorders is either mistake of fact or scapegoatism.

In other cases, looking outside the society or group for the cause of an evil means looking to another society or group and heaping our sins on it. As Gus Tyler has said, "When such a scapegoat can be found, the culture is not only relieved of sin but can indulge itself in an orgy of righteous indignation." Recent work in the sociology of deviance has shown the great contribution to delinquency, alcoholism, homosexuality, and mental disorder made by the very agencies which attempt to deal with these phenomena. We will later discuss the fact that American society supports organized crime by demanding the right to purchase illicit goods and services. But if the Italian and Sicilian Mafia is responsible for organized crime in the United States, then documenting that fact and identifying the Mafia as the cause of our troubles is more science than scapegoatism. On the other hand, if the American cartel and confederation is a response to conditions of American life, documenting that fact is the critical problem. In a very real sense, then, deciding whether or not the American organization is a branch of the Sicilian one is a problem of deciding whether organized crime is "owned" by American society.

The problem of assigning a name to the American confederation of criminals is in part a problem of answering the five questions suggested above. If the American cartel and confederation had a specific name, like General Motors or the National Association of Manufacturers, then determining its formal organizational boundaries would be relatively simple. The fact is that no name used either by law-enforcement officials or by criminals aptly characterizes the society of organized criminals in the United States. In a series of conferences at Oyster Bay, New York, some of the nation's leading experts on organized crime struggled to find a name for the organization which operates organized crime in America, and as they did so they indirectly responded to the above questions by saying that the American confederation should not be confused with the Sicilian Mafia. The conference group reviewed the names commonly used by the public and by some members of the confederation. All of them were rejected.

"Mafia" was rejected specifically because it is a Sicilian term referring to a Sicilian organization, while many participants in the American conspiracy are not Sicilian. This ground for rejection is quite tenuous. After all, "Olivetti" refers to an Italian organization but all the participants are by no means Italian. The conference group really rejected the "Mafia" terminology in order to indicate their belief that the United States does not have a "branch office" of the Sicilian-Italian firm: "This name, for many practitioners, implies that the user is naive and expects that all organized crime was exported to the United States from Sicily."

The term "Cosa Nostra" was rejected because it incorrectly implies that all members of the conspiracy speak Italian and are of Italian descent. The term is used extensively in New York, and on the Eastern seaboard, but it is seldom heard in Chicago. Further, even in New York the term is often used only in a rather indirect sense. If a member introduces a second member to a third, he is likely to identify the stranger as *"amico nostro"*—"a friend of ours." He might even use English saying, "I would like you to meet a friend of ours." The key word, in any language, is "ours." If he says "a friend of *mine,"* the stranger remains a stranger. In telling the McClellan Committee of an incident occurring in his Atlanta prison cell, the Committee's star witness, a Cosa Nostra member, used this terminology, apparently without premeditation:

THE CHAIRMAN. Tell us what happened in the cell when you went back.
MR. VALACHI. I don't know if it was that day or the day after when the
the lights went out and he [Vito Genovese, a Cosa Nostra boss] said

he felt like talking that night. He says, he called Ralph Wagner, he said, "Come over, Wagner."

THE CHAIRMAN. Who is that? Ralph Wagner? Another member of the cell?

MR. VALACHI. An inmate but *he is not a friend of ours.* He is sitting down as though he is. If I did the same thing, I would have to run out of the cell—he is the boss. He sits down, *a guy that ain't a member.* I noticed that but I made believe I didn't notice it.

If two New York, Boston, or Philadelphia members hear of an event relevant to their operations, one might say, *"Questa è una cosa nostra,"* a phrase which is consistent with the usage of *"amico nostro."* What is said here is, "This is an affair of ours," not "I am a member of 'our thing' or 'our affair.' " Yet Italian criminals in the eastern part of the United States have corrupted the Italian, probably because they mix it with English. The bilingual ruler of an Eastern "family" of the organization was heard to say, "I am in La Cosa Nostra." He really could have remained silent. All the members, all the law-enforcement personnel dealing with organized crime, and most of the residents of his city know that he is the "boss" of the Sicilian-Italian apparatus in his area.

The following conversation is between a *"caporegime"* (sometimes called "captain" or "lieutenant"—see below, p. 114) and one of his subordinates. Members of Cosa Nostra had assaulted a federal law-enforcement agent. The guilty persons were known to the federal agency involved, but their whereabouts were not. The federal agents got in touch with the suspects' known associates in order to question them about the suspects' hiding place. After discussing the fact that the federal agents had "gone to every captain" and others, the two men used "Cosa Nostra" in the same casual way Valachi used "friend of ours." The conversation was recorded by means of an electronic "bug."

MIKE. Dirty cocksuckers. Now that they bring out everything, Pete, the Cosa Nostra is a wide open thing.

PETE. Yeah.

MIKE. It's an open book.

PETE. It's an open book.

MIKE. Pete, you know as well as I do, familiarity with anything whatsoever breeds contempt. We've had nothing but familiarity with our Cosa Nostra. . . .

PETE. It starts another trouble.

MIKE. If it brings up sides, what the hell are we supposed to do? I know only one thing, Pete. The Cosa Nostra is the Cosa Nostra. You just do what the fucking bosses tell you. I mean, you can't go and do what the captain even tells you.

Since *"amico nostro"* or, plural, *"amici nostri"* is used all over the United States, one is tempted to name the organization "The Society of Friends." The Quakers would complain, or sue, as the original Anti-Defamation League complained about, and successfully sued, the American-Italian Anti-Defamation League for using its name. One organized-crime investigator, disgusted with nit-picking efforts to find a linguistically proper name, remarked in exasperation, "Aw hell, we know it exists—let's just call it the Pizza Derby." A fellow law-enforcement officer objected, on the questionable ground that pizza is an American, not an Italian, dish.

The conference group noted that in Chicago the members sometimes refer to themselves as "the syndicate," sometimes as "the outfit," but these terms were rejected because they are local. Thus the Sicilian and Italian terms were rejected because they tend to stress the relationship to the "outside," while the Chicago terms were rejected because they do not stress this relationship.

"The organization" is sometimes used by members and, while this term does not imply anything about a relationship between the American organization and the Sicilian and Italian Mafia, it was rejected because it is "not very descriptive," meaning that it does not denote the relationship between the various branches in the United States.

It is significant that there is no plural form for "syndicate," or "organization," when these terms have a national referent. Neither is there, in the language used in the United States, any indication of the existence of more than one "Mafia" or "Cosa Nostra." While a criminal might on occasion talk about "the New York Cosa Nostra" or the "Philadelphia Mafia," or the "Boston syndicate," this usage is different from that in Sicily, where one "mafia" might be said to control the construction industry, another "mafia" the fruit markets.

Even rather local American terms, such as "the arm" (used in upstate New York), "the people" (used in the West), and "the mob" (used everywhere), have no plural forms. "The family" is sometimes used as a synonym for "Cosa Nostra," as well as to identify a geographically based unit under the control of one man. Thus, "I am in the family" refers to Cosa Nostra membership, while "I am in Carlo's family" refers to membership in the local section of "the family." This usage corresponds somewhat to the Sicilian usage of "Mafia" for reference to the entire organization and the usage of, say, "fruit-market mafia" for reference to a subdivision of the larger enterprise. There is no plural of the first usage of the American term ("the family"), but references to "families" in New York, Detroit, Philadelphia, and other cities are common. (For an illustration of the two usages in casual conversation between members, see p. 116 below.)

In Chicago, "outfit" and "organization" seem to refer to the local apparatus, which includes both Italians and non-Italians, while "syndicate" seems to refer to the amalgamation of all the "outfits" in the country. With reference to the Chicago scene alone, there is no plural of "outfit" or "organization." For example, Chicago language does not refer to various "outfits"—such as "Salerno's outfit," "the Rogovin outfit," or "Blakey's outfit"—as it once referred to distinct bootlegging gangs. In New York, "the mob" once referred to the entire collection, "of which the New York Mafia was but a part."

The Oyster Bay group accepted "confederation" as the best term. It should be noted that this term refers primarily to the organization of a *government*. The word "cartel" refers primarily to the organization of a *business*. The conference group concluded:

All of these terms are generally applied to a single loosely knit conspiracy, which is Italian dominated, operates on a nation-wide basis, and represents the most sophisticated and powerful group in organized crime. Practically all students of organized crime are agreed that this organization does not represent the total of organized crime, but there has been almost no attempt to name those organizations which constitute the remainder.

We are satisfied that "Cosa Nostra" is as good as any other term. While this phrase does not denote the fact that not all the persons engaged in organized-crime activities are Italian or of Italian descent, we shall later show that an Italian organization in fact controls all but an insignificant proportion of the organized-crime activities in the United States. While Cosa Nostra still tolerates some major operations by criminals of ethnic backgrounds which are not Sicilian or Italian, if one understands Cosa Nostra he understands organized crime in the United States.

Hank Messick, who has written extensively on organized crime, is convinced that Cosa Nostra is just a new name for Mafia, and he claims that a Jewish organization he calls the "Cleveland Syndicate" welcomed the use of the Italian name because it distracted attention from them:

> The income-tax investigation [of Las Vegas operations] referred to by the court was part of the "coordinated drive" on organized crime launched by Robert F. Kennedy when he became Attorney General. The campaign, while falling far short of its goal, achieved more in a short time than had ever been accomplished in the past. But before Kennedy resigned in 1964, the anti-crime drive had become almost an anti-Mafia crusade. Even J. Edgar Hoover informed the F.B.I. that there was a Mafia after all. For decades he had ignored it, but when Joseph Valachi gave it a new name, La Cosa Nostra, Hoover was able not to only admit its existence but claim his organization had known about it as far back as 1961. . . . For the Cleveland Syndicate, which hid behind the shadow of the Mayfield Road Mob for years, could not but welcome emphasis on La Cosa Nostra. Let the public and politicians assume Dalitz and Kleinman were nobodies. . . .

It is commonly assumed, as Mr. Messick does in the above, that the term "Cosa Nostra" is somewhat the invention of Joseph Valachi, who testified at great length, in short sentences, before the McClellan Committee in 1963. This is not the case. The FBI and other federal agencies in fact heard this term used many times before Valachi used it. In 1961 and 1962 they were spelling it "Causa Nostra." On page 60 we quote the 1963 testimony of Attorney General Kennedy, who said, "Because of intelligence gathered from Joseph Valachi *and from informants,* we know. . . ." He had the informants. There are five interlocking hypotheses concerning J. Edgar Hoover's grave concern over the operations of Cosa Nostra where he had shown little concern over the Mafia, whose operations were spelled out in fine print by the Kefauver Committee in 1951.

One hypothesis states that Hoover was jealous of Harry Anslinger, former Director of the Federal Bureau of Narcotics, who worried about the Mafia as long ago as the early 1930's. Since Mr. Anslinger insisted that the Mafia existed, the idea goes, Hoover denied its existence. This is probably the hypothesis employed by Messick in the quotation above—by giving the Mafia "a new name," Valachi saved Hoover's face, and enabled him to start investigating organized crime with great vigor. I doubt this hypothesis. J. Edgar Hoover is a cop as well as a politician. There are petty jealousies among cops, even top cops, but they tend to arise over the "credit" given for investigations and arrests, not over disputes about whether crime exists.

A second hypothesis is a variation of the first. It states that the Apalachin, New York, gathering of almost a hundred organized criminals in 1957 forced Hoover to recognize that a nationwide "criminal fraternity" exists (see page 57, below). He waited for "a new name" before taking any action.

A third hypothesis is that Attorney General Kennedy ordered Mr. Hoover to begin a drive on organized crime and he simply followed orders, as did the directors of other federal agencies. Since the information coming to him from informants indicated use of the "Cosa Nostra" terminology, he selected that title as the least desirable of many undesirable titles, as we have. From what I have read in the newspapers, however, Hoover has not been especially influenced by any of the "orders" given him by the many attorneys general who have come and gone during his long tenure. Further, as early as September, 1960, before Robert Kennedy became Attorney General, the FBI began to supply the Organized Crime and Racketeering Section of the Department of Justice with intelligence reports on four hundred of the nation's organized crime figures.

A fourth hypothesis is based on the fact that in 1961 and 1962 Congress passed laws giving the FBI jurisdiction to investigate organized-crime activities for the first time. These were the laws forbidding interstate travel for racketeering purposes, interstate shipment of gambling paraphernalia, and use of interstate communications for gambling purposes. Given jurisdiction, the idea goes, Hoover immediately got down to business. This hypothesis was suggested by Hoover himself. In 1966 he wrote:

Four and a half years ago, in September, 1961, the FBI was empowered to launch a concerted drive against the organized underworld. Some of us in law enforcement knew, of course, that syndicated gambling and other vices had been organized for a number of years. But there had been no effective Federal laws under which the FBI could proceed against these evils.

When the FBI was charged with investigative jurisdiction of the three interstate gambling and racketeering laws passed in 1961, it moved with deliberate speed to determine who was behind these nationwide underworld operations.

A fifth hypothesis is closely related to the third and fourth. In late 1960 and early 1961 the FBI and other federal agencies greatly stepped up their employment of wire taps and electronic bugs in organized-crime cases, and the hypothesis is that the sounds coming from these devices convinced Hoover that the United States was in grave danger. The "informants" mentioned by Attorney General Kennedy might have been bugs such as the one operating in the offices of the National Cigarette Service, Providence, Rhode Island, from March, 1962, until July, 1965 (see p. 120). On October 20, 1964, this bug revealed a Cosa Nostra "boss," Raymond S. L. Patriarca, saying that "in the event he is questioned about the Mafia or Cosa Nostra he is going to reply that the only Mafia he ever heard of is the Irish Mafia the Kennedys are in charge of. Patriarca will deny that he knew about La Cosa Nostra until Valachi mentioned it at the McClellan hearings."

Of the five hypotheses, the fourth seems to have the greatest likelihood of validity. It should be noted, however, that no amount of logical discourse can be as convincing as the sounds coming from wire taps and bugs. In fact, it is reasonable to believe that New York is said to have a more severe "organized-crime problem" than, say, Los Angeles, because, in part, New York law-enforcement agencies have been authorized to use bugs while the California agencies have not. Further, New York "families" of Cosa Nostra are said to be organized along lines different from Detroit, but the difference might lie simply in the fact that we have much better information, obtained by bugs and taps, about New York. If one never heard a criminal speak, and never talked with a noncriminal informant, he could hardly convince himself that *any* organization of criminals exists.

┄

Although the anthropological controversy about "diffusion versus independent invention" has largely been resolved, a look at the principal questions raised in the controversy shows that a cultural complex like organized crime could exist in both Sicily and America even if there had been no contact between the two nations. "In essence," explains Melville J. Herskovits, "the matter turns on the inventiveness of man; whether when in distant parts of the world we find similar artifacts or institutions or concepts, we must assume these to have been invented only once and diffused to the regions where they are observed, or whether we may deduce that they had originated independently in these several regions." The more extreme forms of "diffusionism" held that regardless of the distance or time between two cultural traits or complexes, these cultural elements had a single place or origin. Persons holding this view certainly would find great support in the fact that Italian immigrants used extortion to corner the New York artichoke market in the 1930's and that Italian immigrants used extortion to corner the tomato market in Melbourne in the 1950's. The appearance of the cultural trait in New York and Melbourne appears to be an obvious case of diffusion from Italy.

The matter is not so simple, however. Anthropologists also have noted that common needs and common conditions in widely separated societies will result in the invention of similar things, including ideas, even if there are no contacts between the two inventors. The "common conditions" may even be conditions of nature, which at once make for resemblances in cultural forms and limit these cultural forms. For example, anyone in need of a watercraft must fit the raw materials to the natural requirements of buoyancy and balance, with the result that the possibilities of variation in form from craftsman to craftsman, even if separated by great differences of time or space, are limited. Further, establishing that diffusion has taken place is not enough. A cultural trait or complex spread by diffusion might be accepted by one culture and rejected by another. It is accepted, in form modified by the needs and conditions of the receiving culture, only if that culture creates a "place" for it to appear. In the illustration used above, both New York and Melbourne necessarily established a place for monopoly by extortion to appear.

There is a remarkable similarity between both the structure and the cultural values of the Sicilian Mafia and the American confederation, as we shall show in later chapters. There have been extensive contacts between Sicilians and Americans. This does not mean that the Mafia has diffused to the United States, however. Whatever was imported has been modified to fit the conditions of American life. A place has been made for organized crime to arise in the United States, just as a place has been made for the Mafia in Sicily. Later we also will show that there is a significant similarity between the structure, values, and even objectives of prisoners and organized criminals, but there is no evidence that these cultural traits necessarily diffused from organized criminals to prisoners, or from prisoners to organized criminals. A man steeped in the traditions of organized crime can easily adjust to the ways of prisoners, and vice versa, possibly because the conditions producing the traditions of prisoners and of organized criminals resemble each other. Similarly, a man steeped in the traditions of the Sicilian and Italian Mafia can easily find his way around American organized crime, and the behavior of American criminals returning to Italy and Sicily has shown that the reverse is also true. As a matter of fact, if the problem of language were not present a man could with only slight difficulty move between the Sicilian Mafia and an American prison, leaving American organized crime out of the picture altogether. Further, it is highly probable that any active participant in, say, the Norwegian or French underground movement during the World War II occupation by the Nazis could move with ease in any of the other three organizations.

A few years ago an electronic bug recorded a casual conversation taking place in an automobile repair shop. One Cosa Nostra member told another how he and a third party had deliberately refrained from acknowledging each other's presence at a public event, in the interests of security. The same kind of conversation, and the same kind of security precautions, occur daily among prisoners, Mafia members, and members of underground movements.

WILLIE. Hey, you know who we seen the other night down at the track? You see, I had taken my daughter Saturday night to the trotters, you know. My daughter and my niece, Patricia. But Dom was coming in later. I got reservations next to—right *next* to—Aneill. They were ahead of us. Nothing. Nothing. The other guy was with his wife. He was with his sweetheart. He didn't look at me.

MIKE. Does he know you?

WILLIE. Yeah. He didn't look at me. I'll tell you the reason, Mike. There was a fucking guy there that looked more like the law than anything else in my, in my, in my life. I would bet on it.

While the members of Cosa Nostra, and its affiliates, have learned a thing or two from the Sicilian Mafia, this organization is indigenous to the United States. It does things "the American way." But because the objectives of Cosa Nostra are similar to those of the Sicilian Mafia, certain similarities between the two organizations become obvious. The potential danger of Cosa Nostra to the citizens of the United States can be observed by examining the tremendous degree of control the Mafia exercises in western Sicily. The Sicilian organization originated in peasant society, where face-to-face relations between neighbors predominated. It adapted, and it continues to adapt, as Sicily has become more industrialized and urbanized. At first it provided law and order where the official government failed to do so. It collected taxes, which were payments for protection against bandits. In the latter part of the nineteenth century, for example, one Mafia group governed a cluster of eleven mountain villages; the head and his assistants had a private police force of about 130 armed men. The leaders were well-established citizens, landowners and farmers, who supervised all aspects of local life, including agricultural and economic activities, family relations, and public administration.

Like contemporary rulers of Cosa Nostra units in the United States, the despots soon demanded absolute power. No one dared offend the chief's sense of honor. The lines between tax and extortion and between peace enforcement and murder became blurred, as they always do under despots. Today, "an overall inventory of Mafia activities leaves no doubt that it is a criminal organization, serving the interests of its membership at the expense of the larger population." Norman Lewis, among others, has shown that it has extended its influence from farms and peasant villages to the cities of western Sicily, where it now dominates commerce and government. It has a monopoly on almost all aspects of life. Mafia doctors get patients when other doctors do not, and only Mafia doctors can find vacant beds in overcrowded hospitals. Mafia lawyers have all the clients they can handle, and they have uncanny luck in winning cases. Mafia contractors get all the government contracts, even when their bids are higher than those of non-Mafia men, and despite the fact that they pay wages lower than the trade-union minimums. Mafia members, by tradition, do not run for seats in Parliament, but no man can get elected to Parliament—or anything else—without the support of "men of respect," also known as "men of honor."

Such corruption is not like "the bite" put on anyone doing business with Latin American civil servants. It is an *organized* bite, a feast by a society of cannibals. Sicily has given the Mafia a place. Both Luigi Barzini, a keen observer of the Italian scene, and Norman Lewis, a student of Mafia history, have given indications of the extent to which all economic, professional, political, and social life is dominated:

There are the cattle and pasture Mafie; citrus grove Mafie; water Mafie (who control scarce springs, wells, irrigation canals); building Mafie (if the builder does not pay, his scaffolding collapses and his bricklayers fall to their death); commerce Mafie; public works Mafie (who award contracts); wholesale fruit, vegetable, flower, and fish markets Mafie, and so forth. They all function more or less in the same way. They establish order, they prevent pilfering, each in its own territory, and provide protection from all sorts of threats, including the legal authorities, competitors, criminals, revenue agents, and rival Mafia organizations. They fix prices. They arrange contracts. They can see to it, in an emergency, that violators of their own laws are surely punished with death. This is rarely necessary. Most of the time the fact that they can condemn any man to death is enough to keep everybody toeing the line.

ᴓ ᴓ ᴓ

[By 1945] a great gathering of vulturine chiefs had collected to wet their beaks at the expense of farmers, whose produce they bought dirt cheap on the spot and carried to market in the Mafia's own beautifully decorated carts—or later, trucks. In the market only those whose place had been "guaranteed" by the Mafia were allowed to buy or sell at prices the Mafia fixed. The Mafia wetted its beak in the meat, fish, beer, and fruit businesses. It moved into the sulphur mines, controlled the output of rock salt, took over building contracts, "organized labor," cornered the plots in Sicily's cemeteries, put tobacco smuggling on a new and profitable basis through its domination of the Sicilian fishing fleets, and went in for tomb robbing in the ruins of the Greek settlement of Selinunte. . . . The Mafia gave monopolies to shopkeepers in different trades and then invited them to put up their prices—at the same time, of course, increasing their Mafia contribution. . . . The most obvious of the Mafia's criminal functions—and one that had been noted by the Bourbon attorney general back in the twenties of the last century— now became the normally accepted thing. The Mafia virtually replaced the police force, offering a form of arrangement with crime as a substitute for its suppression. When a theft, for instance, took place, whether of a mule, a jeweled pendant, or a motorcar, a Mafia intermediary was soon on the scene, offering reasonable terms for the recovery of the stolen object. . . . The Mafia intermediary, of course, wetted his beak at the expense of both parties. The situation was and is an everyday one in Sicily.

The public demand for protection against Sicilian bandits, and for other services not provided by the established government, created an illicit government which, in the long run, exploited all its members and ruled the very public that created it. The American demand for illicit goods and services has created an illicit government.

CHAPTER III

War, Peace, and Peaceful Coexistence

You are getting me all confused. It is like a Chinese chess game.

SENATOR KARL E. MUNDT

THERE IS a broad range of formal and informal organization among criminals. One kind of organization is simply a stabilized pattern of interaction based on similarities of interests and attitudes, and on mutual aid. "Street-corner" groups of delinquents are organizations of this kind. These groups have their own standards, attitudes, and public opinion, an effective system of communication, the shared danger of arrest and incarceration, the common experience of having lived in jail, and common attitudes about "outsiders." In other cases, "organization" means a particular set of roles that has come to be seen as serving express purposes by the persons playing the roles. Such organizations allocate specific tasks to members, limit entrance, and establish rules for their own maintenance and survival. As organizations move from the first form to the second form they become "formal" organizations rather than "informal" organizations.

"Formal" organizations have three characteristics. First, a division of labor is present. This means that there is occupational specialization, with each specialty fitting into the whole. Second, the activities of each person in the system are coordinated with the activities of other participants by means of rules, agreements, and understandings which support the division of labor. Third (as S. J. Udy, Jr., points out), the entire enterprise is rationally designed to achieve announced objectives.

These features are matters of degree. Among criminal organizations, the degree to which they are present affects the character of the crimes perpetrated. The geographically based Cosa Nostra "families" of criminals of Italian-Sicilian descent now operating in the United States fall on the "formal-organization" end of the continuum. Each "family" has formal positions for "boss," "soldiers," and other functionaries, to be described in Chapter VI, and each "family" has a position in the larger cartel and confederation call "The Family," "Cosa Nostra," or, simply, "organized crime." Members' organizational activities are tightly coordinated and controlled, not only by the structure itself, but also by a criminal code, the values and rules of which govern many of the interpersonal relationships in which members engage off the job.

Small working groups of criminal and delinquent gangs lie somewhere between the informal organization of street-corner groups and the formal organization of Cosa Nostra. They have divisions of labor based on the requirements of specific team operations, but controls over job responsibilities and daily activities are not as extensive or as precise as they are in Cosa Nostra. For example, the fundamental form of organization among pickpockets is the "troupe," "tribe," or "team" of two, three, or four members. The relationships between the men occupying the positions making up the troupe are "loose, ephemeral, and highly insecure," but there is organization nevertheless. The duties and responsibilities of each position are finely detailed. There is, for example, a position for a criminal whose duty it is to locate the prospective victim and distract his attention. A second position calls for a specialist skilled in actually removing the wallet from the victim's pocket. A third position requires skills in receiving the wallet from the man who took it. And a fourth position involves disposal of the stolen goods in legitimate, semilegitimate, or illegitimate channels. The men who fill these positions, even temporarily, are specialists. As in any legitimate organization, a variety of skills is required for effective operations.

"Organization," whether it be that of a working group of criminals, of a legitimate corporation, or of a criminal cartel, means rationality. As the third point (above) suggests, any organization worthy of the name is an apparatus rationally designed to accomplish announced objectives. Among small working groups of criminals, as among syndicated criminals, the objective is to perpetrate offenses which are relatively safe while at the same time profitable. Juvenile gangs, working groups of criminals, and Cosa Nostra all can be differentiated from less formal criminal groups by the fact that the members of the latter do not participate in a specialized set of positions rationally developed with an eye to efficiency and continuing operations.

In a casual conversation with an old friend who knew something about his past, a Cosa Nostra "soldier" reminisced about an occasion on which he had served his superiors by temporarily occupying an "executioner" position in a complex organization. As he reminisced, he inadvertently illustrated some of the differences between murder and *organized* murder. In the following excerpt from a bugged conversation, Mike shows, for example, that the men setting out to kill a designated victim constituted a group of specialists. They were a "working group" and the ties between them, so far as this job was concerned, were loose, ephemeral, and highly insecure. But Mike also indicates that this group's murderous behavior was integrated with the behavior of someone who had ordered the men to do the killing. Between the working groups and this man, apparently, were some people Mike calls "the guys." We may assume, further, that the behavior of the man giving the orders, and therefore of all the participants, was integrated with positions even higher than his, but the bug gave no indication of this. It is clear, however, that the working group of murderers was the lowest level in a hierarchy of positions rationally designed to perpetrate murder and other crimes.

When his gun jammed, Mike made sure that both the gun and the shell were retained by "the guys." He needed them "for proof" that it was not his fault that the execution did not come off. He had to "prove" to someone, presumably his boss and his boss's boss, that the gun jammed. This "soldier" also reveals that there apparently were at least four men whose activities were coordinated in this tough "piece of work." Mike and his "partner" were to do the killing and (probably) two other men each drove a car "up there." In Cosa Nostra terminology, the former are ordinarily called "hit men," while the latter are called "wheel men." Other evidence of rational organization also is apparent. Someone brought a hat from a "five and dime store" and delivered it to Mike, apparently as a disguise and as a replacement for his "peak cap." This man's work and Mike's work, thus, were coordinated. Mike does not even know the name of the man who handed him the hat—he refers to him as "a guy." He knows only that someone ordered him to wear a hat (an order which, in retrospect at least, he didn't like), and that someone else bought a hat and gave it to him. Mike attributes his failure to his defective gun, to the ill-fitting hat, and to his partner, not to himself. However, he does not blame the partner. He notes that when the hat fell off, the partner was disciplined enough to know that it might be incriminating evidence so he abandoned the murder and recovered the hat.

The conversation, like other bugged conversations, loses a great deal in transcription. As Mike recalls the attempted murder, his voice reveals considerable emotion. However, the emotion is neither the sadness of an efficiency expert recounting a failure nor the anxiety of a murderer recalling an attempted killing. It is the excitement, the fervor, of a big-game hunter telling about the big one that got away.

MIKE. Now, fucking Hugo, right after Kane, he had to remind me of that. I ought to rap him on his fucking head.

WILLIE. That's right. That had to do with— (Both laugh.)

MIKE. That dirty cocksucker. I'd kill this guy again. I'll get this cocksucker. Everytime I think—I think of this guy, I scratch.

WILLIE. Everytime you think of that, huh?

MIKE. I scratch. Everytime, I scratch. This—I think of him. This bothers the shit out of me.

WILLIE. Yeah.

MIKE. This bothers me. That guy's the luckiest fucking man on earth that morning.

WILLIE. Yeah. He was lucky. He was a lucky boy.

MIKE. Did you ever have a gun poked into your face like this?

WILLIE. No.

MIKE. Just like that. How many fucking times this cocksucker— I've asked a dozen fucking people and it's unheard of that a .38 snub jams up.

WILLIE. Jams up?

MIKE. And I told the guys, "I'm going to come back." I said, "Don't you dare throw these away. I want them for proof." I said, "Try them. They jammed up."

WILLIE. Of course.

MIKE. You know what they said? When I'm done, throw them away.

WILLIE. They did? If this was years ago you would see how fucking fast— (Inaudible). You would have to bring them to there. They said, "Have a fucking gunsmith examine them why didn't it go off."

MIKE. I proved it.

WILLIE. Well, you proved it. They didn't go off.

MIKE. Right in the chamber it jammed. It's unheard of. This fucking piece of work was the toughest. I don't give a fuck what anybody says. Freezing. Freezing. I was wearing double pants and underwear, and winter underwear.

WILLIE. Ice cold. Ice cold.

MIKE. Freezing.

WILLIE. Was that February or January?

MIKE. I don't know if it was February or January.

WILLIE. One of them two there. It was after the holidays.

MIKE. It was freezing up there. Right by the fucking water. And that wind was blowing and howling. I was scared. I was—

WILLIE. Shaking.

MIKE. Shaking. I couldn't catch this cocksucker. Finally catch him. The nerve of this guy. There's a guy that beat bullets.

WILLIE. He beat a bullet. That's right. He beat speed. He beat speed. Just like a guy pitching, throws a fast ball.

MIKE. It was this far from his back. I got out of the fucking car and I run. We had two cars and I ran after him like a fucking mad man. I tackled him. I fell into him. I was out of my fucking mind. I ran after him. The fucking hat went. I run into him and I tumbled all over.

WILLIE. I'm surprised you wear a hat, Mike.

MIKE. Huh?

WILLIE. I'm surprised you wear a hat, Mike.

MIKE. You got to wear a hat. You got to.

WILLIE. Hugo, he'd never wear a hat. Hugo, he'd never wear a hat.

MIKE. Oh, I didn't wear *my* hat. I wore a hat that I got from a guy who got it from a five and dime store.

WILLIE. Oh.

MIKE. I pulled it on. I jammed it on my head and— The day before I had a peak cap, and I didn't wear it. Huh, if I wore the peak cap, if I'd have wore the peak cap—

WILLIE. You would have run better. You would have run better.

MIKE. That's right.

WILLIE. You lost it. You have an inclination to. You're running and you think of your hat and you have your hands all over— (Inaudible.)

MIKE. I ran around the cars. That's when the hat—

WILLIE. That's when you went for your hat a little bit, too.

MIKE. Well, not only that. You see, my partner was smart enough. He was alert enough that when I lost my hat he fucked the work and he went for the hat. He wanted to recover the hat. Otherwise he'd be with me. While he was with me he could have helped me.

WILLIE. He would have been a goner, the guy.

The rationality behind the operations of working groups of criminals can be observed in three different contexts. First, the crimes committed by teams of criminals tend to be those whose nature makes it difficult to apprehend and prosecute the perpetrators. Second, the divisions of labor are such that all incumbents must be skilled in the use of techniques which in combination make the whole group's work safe and, therefore, profitable. Third, rational organization for safety and profit is indicated in some but not all working groups of criminals by the establishment of at least one position for a "corrupter" and one or more positions for "corruptees." The corruptee position is occupied by public officials who, for a fee, will insure that the group can operate with relative immunity from the penal process. It is as much a part of the criminal organization as any other position.

American syndicated crime is a system based on a further extension of this rational design for safety and profit. Although it is true that the division of labor in Cosa Nostra has been designed for the perpetration of crimes which cannot be perpetrated profitably by small working groups of criminals, let alone by criminals working outside an organization, the critical difference is not merely a difference in size. Small firms selling illicit goods and services must, if they are to capitalize on the great demand for their wares, expand by establishing a division of labor which includes positions for financiers, purchasing agents, supervisors, transportation specialists, lawyers, accountants, and employee-training specialists. The next rational move is consolidation and integration of separate divisions of labor into a cartel designed to minimize competition and maximize profits. Such a monopolistic move is, of course, a rational decision for peaceful co-existence. As such, it necessarily involves governmental considerations as well as business considerations.

🚩

The basic structure of the nationwide cartel and confederation which today operates the principal illicit businesses in America, and which is now striking at the foundations of legitimate business and government as well, came into being in 1931. Further, even the skeleton structure of the local units of Cosa Nostra, the "families" controlling illicit businesses in various metropolitan areas, was clearly established by a series of rational decisions made in 1931. These structures resemble the national and local structures of the Italian-Sicilian Mafia. As we have seen, however, our organization is not merely the Old World Mafia transplanted. As a matter of fact, the decisions made in 1931 wrested power from old-country Mafia "mustache Petes" and assigned it to "Young Turks" bent on doing things "the American way." An old man recently reminisced about the "old days." When he came to the United States from Sicily in 1922, at about age twenty, he was one of "the old-country ones that wore a mustache, carried a gun, and were really tough." In 1930 or 1931, he said, he changed his philosophy, "left the mustaches," and "went the American way." The social, economic, and political conditions of Sicily determined the shape of the Sicilian Mafia, and the social, economic, and political conditions of the United States determined the shape of the American confederation.

To use an analogy with legitimate business, in 1931 leaders of Sicilian-Italian organized-crime units across the United States rationally decided to form monopolistic corporations, and to link these corporations together in a monopolistic cartel. To use a political analogy, in 1931 local Sicilian-Italian units formed into feudal governments, and the rulers of these governments linked themselves together in a nationwide confederation which itself constitutes a government. Non-Italian units were fused into the cartel in 1934.

Feudalism was the system of political organization prevailing in Europe from the ninth to the fifteenth centuries. Basically agricultural, the system meant that a vassal held land belonging to a lord on condition of homage and service under arms. The relationship was a reciprocal one. The vassal deferred to the lord and in other ways paid homage to him; the lord, in turn, protected the vassal. The system was "hereditary" in the sense that the lord had custody of the vassals' heirs' property. Our word "attorney" comes from an old verb, *attorn,* which meant to transfer homage from one feudal lord to another, usually by consenting to the replacement of one lord by another. The structure of the Sicilian Mafia resembles that of ancient feudal kingdoms. The structure of the American confederation of crime resembles feudalism also, as it resembles the structure of the Sicilian Mafia. Like feudal lords and Sicilian Mafia chieftains, the rulers of American geographically based "families" of criminals derive their authority from tradition in the form of homage and "respect." They allocate territory and a kind of license to do business in return for this homage. Nevertheless, the feudal local governments formed in 1931, and the confederation between them, are American innovations.

It took a war to do it. Obviously, the current economic and political relationships between the Soviet bloc, including East Germany and East Berlin, and the American bloc, including West Germany and West Berlin, were for the most part determined by peace treaties and agreements pounded out in 1944 and 1945 by allies who possessed varying degrees of power, and who were suspicious and wary of each other. Obviously, Korea is geographically divided into two nations because a decision for peaceful coexistence, a decision to "end the fighting," was made in 1952. Just as obviously, the economic, political, and geographic relationships between organized-crime units in the United States were established, for the most part, by the peace treaties and agreements hammered out at the end of the Masseria-Maranzano war fought in 1930–1931.

This war, which is also known as the "Castellammarese war," has not been studied by the historians and social scientists who have dug out and recorded even the intimate personal thoughts of the principal leaders in other wars. We do not have a chronology of the battles, let alone interpretations of the reasoning involved in tactics, strategy, and peace agreements. The following account is not a "history." It is a sketch, based principally on the memoirs of one soldier, Joseph Valachi. The chronology of the killings of leaders is fairly accurate because it was verified by police records, but no one knows how many soldiers fought in the war, nor how many died. More important, the interpretations of motive given by Valachi are something like one would get had he asked me, a former sergeant, what President Roosevelt, General Chiang Kai-shek, Prime Minister Churchill, and Premier Stalin had in mind when they ordered my Air Force group into India and China in 1944. Further, Mr. Valachi's recorded memoirs are rambling and, at times, incoherent. The McClellan Committee devoted about a hundred pages to the war, but while Valachi (a Cosa Nostra member), Inspector John J. Shanley (Director of the Criminal Investigation Bureau of the New York City Police Department), and others were trying to explain the great significance of the war, the Senators were playing cops and robbers. They interrupted with enthusiasm whenever it appeared that Valachi might have detailed information about specific murders perpetrated at specific times and places by specific individuals, including himself. The Committee did not even discuss the peace agreements. But it is clear that the organizational experts who determined future relationships by means of arrangements for peace were Salvatore Maranzano and Salvatore Lucania (who later became famous as Charles Luciano, the name we shall use). These men established an apparatus which has persisted to the present. They had help, we should add, from non-Italian Prohibition gangsters who also had something at stake.

Everybody knows that during the period of national Prohibition members of rival bootlegging gangs killed each other with great frequency. It is only a slight exaggeration to say that these gangs—headed by men with all-American names like Madden, Capone, Torrio, Aiello, Flegenheimer (Schultz), Buchalter (Lepke), Shapiro (Gurrah), Kastel, Lansky, Siegal, Dwyer, Zwillman, Weiss, O'Banion, Moran, O'Donnell, and Diamond—settled everything with a bullet. They were constantly at war. Ethnically speaking, everybody worked for everybody, and everybody killed everybody. Near the end of the

Prohibition period, these gangs faced economic collapse because it was obvious that they would not be able to meet the competition from legitimate dealers in alcohol. They searched for new fields and found them, first, in gambling and extortion. They also faced a problem of survival. Just as legitimate businessmen sometimes face economic ruin when competition between them gets too stiff, the Prohibition gangsters faced the possibility of actual, as well as economic, extermination by each other. And just as legitimate business-men invent price-fixing agreements and other arrangements to avoid killing each other off, economically, by cut-throat competition, the gangsters attempted to come to a rational decision for peace.

Even during Prohibition, gang leaders made numerous, almost constant, attempts to "come to an understanding" so that the killings would stop. In 1930, Fred D. Pasley described a 1926 peace meeting between the leaders of the principal Chicago gangs. Peace was de-clared and the city was divided up geographically, with the lion's share going to the man with the most guns, Al Capone. The agree-ment lasted through two months. Then it was violated, and war broke out again when it became apparent that Capone was attempting to establish a "benevolent monopoly." The *Cleveland Plain Dealer* on December 6 and 17, 1928, reported a meeting of the "Mafia Grand Council of America." The Chicago police told the Cleveland police that this was a meeting of "captains of industry" to elect a national leader, a successor to Antonio Lombardo, a man Capone had seated as President of Unione Siciliana in November, 1925. Lombardo was murdered on September 7, 1928. The men attending the meeting were from New York, Chicago, Gary, Brooklyn, Tampa, Newark, Miami, and St. Louis. Two of them also attended the Apalachin, New York, conference in 1957.

In 1929, Giuseppe Masseria controlled the Sicilian-Italian organi-zation in New York, such as it was. A group of men called the "Castellammarese" (because they all came from the area along the Gulf of Castellammare in Sicily) rebelled against this control by what outside bootleggers called "The Italian Society." Salvatore Maranzano became leader of the rebels, and his group designated Peter Morello as "Boss of Bosses," a title which supposedly indi-cated absolute control over Mafia members. Both the Masseria group and the Maranzano group included men whose names are now familiar to all who follow newspaper accounts of organized crime. On the Masseria side were names like Luciano, Genovese, Costello, Terranova, Moretti, Adonis, Scalise, Anastasia, and Gambino. On the Maranzano side were Gagliano, Lucchese, Bonanno, Profaci, Magaddino, and others. Each of these groups contained at least two sets of men, but it is not clear whether each set constituted a "family" in the modern sense of the word. Masseria, whose men called him "Joe the Boss," dominated his set and one led by Alfred Mineo and Steve Ferrigno. Maranzano dominated his set and one led by Gaetano Reina. The Masseria group had rather weak alliances with non-Italian groups in New York, and the Maranzano group had close alliances with Sicilian groups outside New York.

On February 26, 1930, Mr. Reina, boss of one of the Maranzano units, was murdered by a member of the Masseria group. His deputy, Gaetano Gagliano, wanted to avenge this murder, and a conflict described by Mr. Valachi as both a "undeclared war" and "sneaking" broke out. It amounted to a series of assassinations, a feud. Gagliano recruited Valachi and others as assassins. He wanted new men, unknown to the Masseria group, so that the Masseria group would be unable to trace the vendetta to the Gaglianos. Gagliano was a diplomat who wanted peace—he recruited strangers to do his killing because his warmaking power was at that time no match for that of the Masserias, and because he was convinced that open war would break out if an assassination could be traced to his men. But while Gagliano was carefully insuring the peace, Masseria seized control of his unit and appointed a "puppet government," in the form of Joseph Pinzolo. (See chart on pp. 124–125.)

Maranzano, without the knowledge of Gagliano, on August 15, 1930, had his men murder the "Boss of Bosses," Peter Morello. Shortly afterward (on September 9, 1930), Pinzolo, the puppet governor of Gagliano's group, was shot by the Gaglianos, without the knowledge of Maranzano. Both assassinations, it developed, were made out of fear of Masseria's power. The Maranzano men, who were largely Neopolitans, had decided to exterminate all the Castellammarese hoodlums in the country. Many Castellammarese tried to surrender to Masseria, to "join up with him to save their lives," but

Maranzano decided to fight. Gagliano was not Castellammarese, but his life and his bootlegging business were in danger. Maranzano and Gagliano joined forces, forming an alliance as strange as the U.S.–U.S.S.R. alliance during World War II.

On November 5, 1930, Gagliano's men, with the knowledge of both Gagliano and Maranzano, executed both the leaders of one of the Masseria sets, Mineo and Ferrigno. The Masseria men learned, through this assassination, that the Maranzano group and the Gagliano group were working in common against them, with Maranzano as their general. Masseria declared war. "Now the war is nationwide; it is a declared, open war." Across the nation, those Castellammarese who had not already surrendered to Masseria, and some who had, went to the defense of Maranzano. Valachi testified that Gagliano spent $140,000 of his own money to finance the war; $5000 a week came from Mr. Magaddino, of Buffalo, a man who is currently the oldest member of Cosa Nostra's judicial and administrative body, "the Commission" (see below, p. 111). Joseph Aiello, a Chicago competitor of Capone's (a Neapolitan), contributed $5000 a week until he was killed, probably by the Capones, on October 23, 1930.

The war raged on in New York. In Chicago a similar war, or a battle in a general nationwide war, also was raging. There it involved the Capones, and the conflict was over control of Unione Siciliana, among other things. In Chicago, the "Unione" was in the early period of Prohibition engaged in a kind of piecework, sweatshop, alcohol-distilling enterprise. Hundreds of Sicilian immigrants were equipped with stills, and they sold their alcohol to the central organization. Five or six avowed "presidents" of this organization were killed between 1925 and 1931. The "Unione" broke with Capone in about 1924, but Capone seized control about a year later. Three men whom Capone seated successively as "president" were shot dead, one in late 1928 and two in early 1929. In 1927 Joseph Aiello offered $50,000 to anyone who would murder Capone, and at least four men, all from out of town, died trying to collect it. In the same year, Aiello tried to ambush Capone and the man he had established as president of Unione Siciliana, Antonio Lombardo. He was caught by the police, arrested, and detained at the detective bureau. Between twenty and twenty-five heavily armed Capone men surrounded the station, intending to lynch Aiello. The police broke it up. Upon his release, Aiello went into hiding and he remained in hiding until May, 1929, when Capone was jailed in Philadelphia. The 1930-1931 Chicago battles continued after Aiello was killed.

Presumably the war chest accumulated by Maranzano in New York was spent for matériel to be used on the New York front—guns, cars, fortresses—and for other expenses—transportation, support of soldiers' dependents, pensions for widows and orphans, living expenses for soldiers. Various peace feelers were sent to Maranzano by Masseria, who was losing. "He will give up anything he had if they will leave him alone. Maranzano refused." Maranzano had a personal grudge against a Masseria man, James Catania, and he vowed that he would not "make peace" until Catania was dead.

Catania was killed on February 3, 1931. Joseph Valachi, who was one of the murderers, recalled, "We were in war, Senator. . . . We were working as a team, just like any army would, you know." The Castellammarese and, presumably, other Sicilians, now jumped on the bandwagon, with the result that Maranzano had an army of about six hundred men under his command. Between forty and sixty of Masseria's men were killed. Masseria, still losing, retreated to a fortress, where he and his palace guard survived several sorties.

At this point, the Castellammarese war takes on an even closer resemblance to a war between nations. Noting that they were hopelessly outnumbered, or noting that Masseria would not solicit the help of non-Italian-Sicilian Prohibition gangsters, five of Masseria's key men—Luciano, Genovese, Terranova, Livorsi, and Straci—secretly surrendered to Maranzano. In exchange for their own safety, and profits, they agreed to execute Masseria, which they did on April 20, 1931. In Mr. Valachi's view, this killing ended the war: "Naturally, about five days after that there was peace. We closed this war." But not quite.

Maranzano called a meeting of four hundred to five hundred men, which Mr. Valachi claims to have attended. Maranzano explained to the group that Masseria and his men had been, in Valachi's words, "Killing people without just." He explained that the killings would now stop because he, Maranzano, was "the Boss of Bosses." He also established the notion that there would be bosses beneath him, each with an underboss and a *"caporegima,"* or "lieutenant," who, in turn, would have "soldiers" working for him. Maranzano did not invent this form of organization. He, or someone, lifted it bodily from the Sicilian Mafia (see belaw, p. 142). According to Mr. Valachi, Maranzano then "went out and explained the rules," namely, that henceforth there would be a rational, hierarchical, chain of command, with no individualistic, indiscriminate violence. He established his non-Castellammarese ally, Gagliano, as a boss. However, Maranzano ruled that anyone who had fought on his side in the war could remain with him. Valachi attorned from Gagliano to Maranzano and "the boys from the Castellammarese," as did two more of Gagliano's mercenaries. Luciano's betrayal of Masseria was rewarded with a position as a boss, and Genovese's reward took the form of underboss to Luciano. Others who had been traitors to Masseria or loyal to Maranzano were also rewarded with high positions. The six "families" now existing in the New York metropolitan area (one of the "families" is in New Jersey) were established. One boss thus established, Joseph Bonanno, remained a boss until 1964, when he was overthrown (see below, p. 152).

Shortly after the large meeting, Mr. Valachi says, a five-day banquet was held in celebration of the new "Boss of Bosses" and fifteen soldiers who had been with him from the beginning of the conflict (the Gagliano group). This also was a fund-raising affair for the fifteen men, who had been out of work for fourteen months. Contributions were made in the form of ticket purchases and, in the case of lesser lights, cash contributions. Over $100,000 was given to Maranzano in honor of his new position of leadership. Luciano contributed $6000, but it is not clear whether he attended the meeting.

Valachi received none of the money. After he had spent a few months casting broad hints in Maranzano's direction, his new boss explained that the money was needed for a "new war" because he could not get along with Luciano and Genovese. There are a number of versions of this inability to "get along." Valachi believes that Maranzano had hijacked some of Luciano's alcohol trucks. He also believes that Luciano and Genovese were not satisfied with the "boss of bosses" concept, which assigned subordinate status to them. Burton B. Turkus, Assistant District Attorney in Brooklyn during a 1940 crime probe, argues that another dispute, in the Amalgamated Clothing Workers' Union, played a decisive role. One faction in this union, he says, had hired Buchalter, Lansky, and Siegel as goons. The other faction approached Luciano for similar services but he declined because he did not want to fight his three friends. Maranzano took the job. Luciano and Genovese believed that this move was evidence of the inefficiency of the old-country ways of the "mustache Petes," and a bid for power as well. Our own hypothesis is that Luciano and Genovese aligned themselves with Buchalter, Lansky, Siegel, Shapiro, Capone, and others and told Maranzano that he was out of business; that a *coup d'état* had·taken place without bloodshed. This notion is not supported, however, by Valachi's statement that Maranzano showed him a list of ten or twelve enemies to be assassinated. Of the above names, only Capone's was included. With one exception, Flegenheimer (Shultz), the names were all Italian. At any rate, Maranzano refused to acknowledge the new power bloc. Accordingly, Luciano and Genovese ordered Maranzano and his chief supporters executed, perhaps to save their own skins. As Maranzano was setting Luciano and Genovese up for assassination, killers hired by them assassinated him, on September 11, 1931. Valachi testified that the killers were "four Jews." The hearings then went as follows:

THE CHAIRMAN. Now, you said some Jews killed him, is that right?

MR. VALACHI. The Jews, yes.

THE CHAIRMAN. Who were dressed as policemen?

MR. VALACHI. They had dressed as policemen, and they posed as policemen.

THE CHAIRMAN. Were they members of Cosa Nostra?

MR. VALACHI. No.

THE CHAIRMAN. How did they get into the picture?

MR. VALACHI. Well, they were very close with Charley [Luciano] and Vito [Genovese] at that time, and that is an allegiance group. Vito and Charley "Lucky," they were close to them.

THE CHAIRMAN. Do you get any information they were employed to commit this murder?

MR. VALACHI. Well, Senator, they seem to work together at times. You see they had trouble of their own later on, which I will explain, and Vito and Charley helped them when they had trouble among themselves. You see I am talking about Meyer Lansky.

THE CHAIRMAN. Kind of like swapping work. They would do something for one crowd and the other crowd then would help them out.

MR. VALACHI. I go into that later. [He was not given an opportunity to do so.]

The Maranzano slaying was not an isolated incident. It was part of the last major battle of a war. The day Maranzano was killed (September 11, 1931) has long been known as "purge day" in Cosa Nostra. On that day and the two days immediately following, some forty Italian-Sicilian gang leaders across the country lost their lives in battle. Most, if not all, of those killed on the infamous day occupied positions we would now characterize as "boss," "under-boss," or "lieutenant" (see p. 113 below). Perhaps it is for that reason that the "purge day" terminology emerged. In fact, Turkus maintains that September 11, 1931, marks the end of the Mafia in the United States. The organization he calls "Unione Siciliana" and which others call "Cosa Nostra" took over "The Italian Society." He argues that "the chief difference between the two lies in Unione's cooperation with other mobs, a characteristic entirely foreign to the clannish Mafia." It is quite possible that Turkus is correct. However, his nomenclature suffers from the fact that the losers of the war's last big battle were members of the Sicilian Castellammare group in New York, and Sicilian "greasers," "handlebars," and "mustache Petes" all over the country. If there was a "Unione," as distinct from a "Mafia," these men were in it. It also should be recalled that Masseria had been known as "Joe the Boss," making it conceivable that he was considered "the" Mafia leader by his followers. He also was, in the terminology of the time, a "greaser," "handlebar," or "mustache Pete." These terms meant, we think, that the person in question was an old-timer who did not believe in the "American way," the rational way, of doing business. Masseria was not against friendships, but "combinations" did not appeal to him. According to Turkus, his credo was, "An outfit runs on its own and knocks off anybody in the way." Perhaps Masseria was executed because he, like Maranzano, was an old-fashioned Sicilian, not because, as Valachi insists, Luciano and Genovese made a bargain with Maranzano. Genovese was not Sicilian. Neither was Capone, who in fact fought the "Unione Siciliana" in Chicago. Perhaps "Cosa Nostra" was invented to rid the organization of the Sicilian image created by both "Mafia" and "Unione Siciliana."

On purge day, panic swept the Castellammarese, who had lost both a boss and a self-appointed "boss of bosses." "All the guns are pointed at us," one of Valachi's old war buddies said. Valachi himself, having by this time learned a thing or two about war, again joined the winners. He shifted his allegiance to Genovese, who remained as Luciano's deputy and eventually succeeded him as "family" boss. Peace reigned. To end the killings and to prevent reprisals against victorious but war-weary soldiers, Luciano substituted for the "boss of bosses" position a *"consigliere* of six" made up of representatives of the five New York "families" and one New Jersey "family" established by Maranzano. This *consigliere* served as a local arbitration board and court. If for any reason one man wished to kill another, he had first to go to the *consigliere,* at the risk of being killed himself. The *consigliere* should not be confused with the "Commission," which has nationwide authority and which was a later invention. I suspect that the *"consigliere* of six" continues to operate in the New York area and that similar local boards operate in Chicago and Detroit.

The 1931 peace treaty destroyed the concept of an absolute national or even regional ruler, a "boss of bosses." However, in 1931 Luciano seems to have become "boss of bosses under the table," a title Valachi said Genovese held in 1963, when Genovese was in prison. Luciano "closed the books" on membership in Cosa Nostra, meaning that no new members could be admitted. The books remained closed until about 1954. They were then opened until about 1958, and they have been closed since that time. In 1964 informants were predicting that the books would open again in 1966 or 1967, but apparently this did not take place. A few members have been taken in during recent years, but only after a special dispensation was given, for each case, by the organization's ruling body, "the Commission." Luciano's concept of "membership" and its control amounted to a treaty on armies and armaments. The men designated as bosses in Luciano's new order of things agreed that no one of them would expand his unit's membership without the approval of the others. Included was a subsidiary agreement that membership in the Sicilian Mafia was no longer a sufficient qualification for membership in the American organization. This meant, of course, that one could not increase the strength of his "family" either by taking in new members or simply by importing trained soldiers.

The membership concept essentially froze armies and armaments at the state existing at the time of the treaty, thus giving an advantage to the Luciano "family," which has remained dominant ever since. "Arms" in Cosa Nostra includes soldiers, as is the case in all feudal governments. Both manpower and guns are needed for expansion, but any boss wishing to increase his power in relation to other "men of respect" must negotiate the expansion with them. First he must persuade the other bosses to agree to "open the books." Then he must persuade them to let him take in, proportionately, more members than the other "families" do. No boss has ever been significantly successful in such negotiations.

If one party to an armament agreement starts assembling arms in violation of the agreement, the other parties have two basic choices —war or an arms race. Cosa Nostra "families" have been involved in a "cold war" since 1931, and a few minor skirmishes have occurred as a result. But there has been no war between "families" since 1931. No arms race has occurred either, despite the fact that the treaty has been violated. In one case, at least, the skirmish following a treaty violation was short-lived: A "family" leader who took in members was assassinated, and his "family" was placed under the leadership of a man willing to acknowledge the dominance of the Luciano-Genovese "family." All the "families" have violated the spirit of the treaty by designating as "proposed" a number of men who will become members when the books are opened. Such a "proposed" receives the "respect," if not the profits, going to a member. If a weak international power "keeps its place," stronger powers may tolerate it, in part because conquering it might have as its consequence the formation of a coalition of powers against the conqueror. As we shall show later on, this principle probably is operating in the relationships between Cosa Nostra and non-Italian organized criminals, in the relationships between Cosa Nostra and the police, and in the relationships between America's twenty-four Cosa Nostra "families" themselves.

The 1930–1931 war and the 1931 peace treaty had immediate effects in most of the large cities of the nation. Unfortunately, no one has assembled any existing accounts of purge-day battles and the ensuing decision for peace in cities like Chicago, Detroit, and Philadelphia. Almost by accident, William Foote Whyte has given us an account of the situation in Boston, where he was engaged in a sociological study of an Italian neighborhood (which he called "Cornerville") in the late 1930's. In discussing the relationships between Cornerville and the rest of Boston, Whyte reported that "shortly before repeal" of Prohibition a "combination movement" in alcohol distribution reached its height in Boston. Leadership was vested in a man known as "the boss," just as was the case in other cities at the time, and just as is the case today. This boss was murdered "by some relatively unimportant gangsters," and his killing "seems to have grown out of a dispute unconnected with the monopoly."

The members of the combine were unable to agree upon a successor. Instead, they divided the field that the boss had controlled. The lessons in working together that had been learned by the combine members were to have a strong influence upon the subsequent organization of illegal activities in Cornerville. As the end of prohibition approached, the racketeers needed to find an alternative field into which to expand their activities. The policy racket seemed to provide this opportunity. Since bets of a dime, a nickel, and even a cent were taken, the racket appealed particularly to the poor man. At the height of prohibition profits, few of the top racketeers had paid attention to the exploitation of the numbers, but now many were beginning to see that small change would be worth collecting if it came in fast enough. A conference of all the leading racketeers in the territory was called one evening in a hotel in Eastern City [Boston]. At this meeting the syndicate for the control of the policy racket was formed, and means of conducting the business were agreed upon.

Whyte goes on to describe the career of a man who "took control of the policy racket in most of Cornerville, and became one of the members of the syndicate when it was formed to control the business throughout the city and in other towns and cities." This man came into power in "early 1931," shortly after a tough, "undisciplined" Sicilian gangster was murdered and shortly before the boss was murdered. The new leader participated in bootlegging, and he eliminated a gang of Irish competitors. He organized local gambling operations, which had been run by independent operators. The formation of the syndicate, according to Whyte, "brought about a reign of peace and order in the Cornerville rackets, which has lasted to the present day."

The McClellan hearing testimony of John T. Howland, Chief of the Bureau of Inspectional Services of the Boston Police Department, in 1963, confirmed Whyte's observations:

MR. HOWLAND. We feel that the organization in Boston is an unusually old one for the type of group. The last so-called gang war that happened in the area of Greater Boston happened in 1931, in December, when there was a gang fight in the city and some of the leaders of another group were killed. At that time, five of the members on this chart were all suspected of participating in that gang war, were arrested, and interrogated. There were indictments sought against some of them, but there was never any conviction. But five of those people were consorting together and were believed to be in an organization back in 1931.

THE CHAIRMAN. They probably gained control of the organization at that time.

MR. McNAMARA [Boston Police Commissioner]. That is right.

George C. Edwards, then Police Commissioner of Detroit, testified before the McClellan Committee that Mr. Valachi's history of the Maranzano-Masseria war supplied "a little confirmation of the nature of the warfare that went on in Detroit, about which we knew. But we knew nothing about the historical national aspects of that war until your hearings started. . . . We knew about the battles on the

Detroit front but we did not know about the front which extended nationally."

Cosa Nostra is currently dominated by a "Commission" made up of the heads of the most powerful "families." This body, which also is known by other titles, functions primarily as a judicial body. We will describe its operations later. It is different from the *"consigliere* of six" set up for the New York area by Charles Luciano. Its jurisdiction is the entire United States, the Bahamas, and parts of Canada. If each Cosa Nostra "family" is regarded as a "nation," the *"consigliere* of six" corresponds to NATO or the Common Market, while the "Commission" corresponds to the United Nations. Yet the exact date of the founding of this important body has not been determined. We know that a commission of nine was operating in 1940. Our hunch was that it was established in 1934, in connection with expanding the 1931 peace treaty so that it included the non-Italian units which helped Luciano betray Masseria and then conquer Maranzano. Hank Messick, a newspaperman knowledgeable in the area of organized crime, was cited earlier as stating that the term "Cosa Nostra" distracts attention from non-Italian organized criminals. He also argues that a "national association" of organized criminals was formed in 1934. It is conceivable that Cosa Nostra's "Commission" came into being at the same time, perhaps as a defense measure, among other things.

The date can be fixed with accuracy—not only because stool pigeons whispered about a meeting in New York or Atlantic City or Miami —but because certain things began to happen then and other things stopped happening. The country was divided into territories. Wars ended between regional groups, between religious groups, between national groups. Meyer Lansky was assigned Florida and the Caribbean. His partner, Bugsy Siegel, got the Far West, including Nevada. The Eastern Syndicate came into being along the Atlantic coast, and assignments were made according to racket as well as geography. Thus Costello got slots, Lepke got the garment industry, Luciano got narcotics and prostitution,

"Trigger Mike" Coppola got numbers, etc. Broadly speaking, the Cleveland Syndicate obtained the Middle West—outside of Illinois, of course, where the successor of Al Capone held sway. In lieu of that, the Cleveland boys were given Arizona by way of compensation. It might not have seemed a bargain at the time—"only sand and lizards," as one hood put it—but it had potential. For one thing, it bordered on Mexico.

Messick's information about the "national association" seems to have come from the book by Turkus, who reports that in 1934, at a meeting in a New York hotel, an Italian leader from Chicago proposed to leaders of both Italian and non-Italian groups that they all make up one "big outfit" or "one big combination." Turkus claims that Buchalter, Shapiro, Siegel, Lansky, Luciano, and other leaders all were either present or represented. The man initiating the proposal was Johnny Torrio, who was Capone's predecessor in Chicago.

It was quickly realized, of course, that no one of them would ever stand for one single boss—one czar over all. Each regarded himself as a big shot, and was fanatically jealous of his position. But it was explained how there could be central control based on cooperation, without sacrifice of individuality. A board, or, panel, of all the bosses themselves —that was the gimmick Johnny Torrio had in mind. Such a board could arbitrate intermob disputes by meeting and talking and deciding who was right and who was wrong. That was the key that finally convinced them. Each boss remained czar in his own territory, his rackets unmolested, his local authority uncontested. In murder, no one—local or imported—could be killed in his territory without his approval. He would have the right to do the job himself or permit an outsider to come in—but only at his invitation. In fact, no lawlessness, on an organized scale, could take place in his domain without his sanction and entire consent, unless he was overruled by the board of governors. And even then, he would have a say in the discussion. It was state's rights in crime. . . .

Soon, the criminal bands from beyond the East saw the strength in the union. The Brooklyn stool pigeons told us a second meeting was called in Kansas City, to hear from the Western executives. The Capone crowd from Chicago and the Kansas City mob liked the idea. Reports came from Cleveland and Detroit that the Mayfield Gang and the Purple Mob wanted in. In Boston and Miami, New Orleans and Baltimore, St. Paul and St. Louis—all flocked to the confederacy of crime, until it was nationwide.

We cannot say that Mr. Messick and Mr. Turkus are wrong. Perhaps such a meeting, or series of meetings, took place. It is conceivable, however, that what Turkus calls "a board or panel" is what today is called "the Commission," and that what he calls "the confederacy" is today called "Cosa Nostra." There are no non-Italians on "the Commission" or in Cosa Nostra. It is also possible that an arrangement for the arbitration of disputes between Italian and non-Italian leaders was made in 1934. However, so far as I have been able to determine, all the high-level "arbitration meetings" uncovered by law-enforcement agencies since 1934 (and before) were attended exclusively by Italians. Further, Turkus probably is right when he states, "Not one top boss in the underworld has been slain since 1934 unless the execution was sanctioned, approved, and, in fact, directed by the gang lords of the nation." But the "gang lords" doing the directing are and have been members of Cosa Nostra's "Commission." If non-Italian groups are in fact represented on a national "board" or "panel," they must cast their votes through an Italian. This would mean that they have been assigned something less than "equal say" and "equal power." There is no question that today some organized-crime units are led by men whose ethnic backgrounds are not Italian or Sicilian. Some of them have been operating since Prohibition days. But it is quite possible that these men are merely tolerated, not accepted as equals.

Real "arbitration" of disagreements occurs only when the parties involved are either men of good will or equals. American organized criminals cannot in any sense be described as men of good will. They fear one another. Neither are they equals. Even within Cosa Nostra, power goes to men with power. Collectively, the organization of Italians and Sicilians originally put together by Maranzano, Luciano, and Genovese is so powerful that no group of outsiders, and no combination of such groups, has been able seriously to threaten it. Moreover, when police have been bribed to let Cosa Nostra operate, any Cosa Nostra member whose illegal business is threatened by outsiders can call on the police for protection. Because Cosa Nostra has since 1931 had enough money and guns to put any competitor out of business, "arbitration" and all other forms of business "negotiation" are likely to take one of the two following forms: (1) "Get out of my territory or I will break your head." (2) "You give me (or "us" or "him") a piece of the action or you will wind up in the river." The matter is not one of arbitration. The problem is one of determining why the second form is used. The second form does not eliminate the outsider. It either keeps him as a partner or forces him to operate his illegal business in areas and in volume determined by the men with the muscle. For some reason, non-Italian groups are tolerated by an organization so strong and ruthless that it could within twenty-four hours dispose of all the non-Italian operators in the United States.

There are at least four plausible explanations of this tolerance, all of them based on the notion that the outsiders are somehow valuable to Cosa Nostra, valuable in ways we do not yet understand. The first explanation, which seems to be favored by law-enforcement personnel, describes the relationship in terms of ethnic stereotypes— Jews are the "smart financiers" for ignorant Italian leaders. This is a doubtful hypothesis, because financiers and investment counselors can be found in all ethnic groups.

A second explanation notes that the tolerance of outsiders stems from past favors done by those outsiders. It is widely believed that at the end of the Prohibition period, organized-crime activities on the Eastern seaboard were apportioned to specialists, with Frank Costello specializing in gambling, Luciano specializing in narcotics, numbers, and prostitution, Buchalter and Shapiro specializing in extortion, Siegel and Lansky (Suchowljansky) specializing in execution and "enforcement," and Zwillman specializing in "assorted New Jersey operations." It is significant that the only non-Italian survivor of this collection (which was called the "Big Six" despite the fact that at least eight men were involved) is Lansky. As Valachi said, "Anywhere Maier Lansky is, Vito Genovese is." Lansky is tolerated, the idea goes, because of the help he gave the Luciano group almost four decades ago. In Cleveland, a partnership (which Hank Messick calls "The Cleveland Syndicate") consisting of, at least, Moe Dalitz, Morris Kleinman, Sam Tucker, and Louis Rothkopf, began in the Prohibition era and has continued down to the present. For a time, at least, Lansky was a member of this partnership. There is no evidence of continuing partnership between this Cleveland group and the city's Cosa Nostra group.

Third, it is possible that non-Italians are tolerated because their leaders have the proper political connections. If I have a channel into the police department, city hall, or governor's office, you gain considerably if you become my partner. If you bankrupt me, or exterminate me, you do not have much to gain, and you might lose. China has the muscle necessary to bankrupt or capture Hong Kong almost any time she wants to do so. Perhaps Hong Kong is tolerated at least in part because the city's presence provides a communication channel with the West. Similarly, Cosa Nostra might tolerate the operations of non-Italians because of their "connections." "The Cleveland Syndicate," mentioned above, might be tolerated because it is politically dangerous to do otherwise.

A fourth explanation is simply an application of "the goose that laid the golden eggs" principle. Non-Italians are tolerated because it is profitable to do so. One does not, if he can help it, kill the man from whom he is extorting money or the man who owes him a large sum of money. Similarly, one does not kill off persons who are bringing in profits, as long as they don't cheat. Street-level workers in bet-taking operations, for example, operate under a kind of franchise from a Cosa Nostra member, with a portion of the profits going to a man who simply demands them and who, further, provides certain services such as immunity from arrest. On a higher level of operations, Mr. Lansky might be tolerated as a partner simply because he is an excellent businessman whose skills enable his partners to earn more money than they could earn without him. His old partner in murder, Benjamin Siegel, once said of him, "There is a guy who has a brilliant mind and for my money is one of the greatest organizers of his time." Specifically, toleration of Lansky probably rests on Cosa Nostra's need for expert knowledge about gambling, especially casino gambling. The genius of Cosa Nostra leaders is their tendency to exploit rather than to destroy. Securing a monopoly on organized crime activities by agreement rather than by feud is the essence of the "American way."

CHAPTER IV

Educating the Public

*If this blistering exposé doesn't arouse public anger,
I don't know what can.*

JOHN BARKHAM

SOME AMERICAN criminals, law-enforcement officials, political figures, and plain citizens know from experience that a nationwide cartel and confederation of criminals was established in 1931 and that it is more powerful today than it ever has been. Some of them have denied the existence of the apparatus because they are members of it. Others have denied its existence because they profit from it. As the Kefauver Committee concluded, "The money used by hoodlums to buy economic and political control is also used to induce public apathy." But honest officials have for over thirty years been trying to convince the American public that the nationwide apparatus does in fact exist. These men, who are mostly law-enforcement officers, prosecutors, and Congressional investigators, know that the activities of organized crime are threatening the foundations of American economic, political, and legal order. They see organized crime as a grave social problem, and they wish "the public" could be made aware of its own plight.

The Organized Crime Task Force of the President's Commission joined the ranks of these "social-problem perceivers." In devoting much of its volume to "educating the public," this group tried to create a social problem. The Task Force concluded, "Much of the public does not see or understand the effects of organized crime in society." This view was heartily accepted and published by the Commission because some Commission members, and some members of the executive staff, were part of the "uneducated" public. And this

54

despite the fact that tuition-free public education on this subject has long been available for the asking. In fact, information has been all but forced on our adult citizens, in the way reading and writing are forced on defenseless little children. But, continuing the analogy, considerable segments of the public remain illiterate. Perhaps we need new teaching techniques, or a whole new curriculum.

One of the earliest attempts to teach us that a nationwide crime apparatus exists was made by a defector. In a series of articles appearing in 1939, the former attorney for an illicit New York organization, a man who had occupied a position of "corrupter" for the organization, observed that a nationwide alliance between criminal businesses in the United States was in operation. J. Richard Davis in the early 1930's worked as an intermediary between a corrupt politician and the man who, by use of strong-arm methods, had seized control of all "numbers" gambling in New York County. In late 1936, after the district attorney had listened in on his telephone calls for four months, the politician was indicted. Mr. Davis disappeared. A tap was placed on his wife's home telephone. From this tap, it was possible to trace Davis and to convince him to cooperate in the prosecution of the politician, which he subsequently did. In exchange, he received a sentence of one year in jail, on his plea of guilty to a conspiracy to operate a lottery. While in jail he wrote an exposé of political corruption and crime in New York and also made the observation about the nationwide alliance. This was not the first time such an observation was made, but it dramatically foreshadowed statements which have been made in more recent years. The statement supports our conclusion that a nationwide organization for profit and peace was one outcome of the Masseria-Maranzano war.

When I speak of the underworld now, I mean something far bigger than the Schultz mob. The Dutchman was one of the last independent barons to hold out against a general centralization of control which had been going on ever since Charlie Lucky became leader of the Unione Siciliana in 1931. . . . The "greasers" in the Unione were killed off, and the organization was no longer a loose, fraternal order of Sicilian black handers and alcohol cookers, but rather the framework for a system of alliances which were to govern the underworld. In Chicago, for instance, the Unione no longer fought the Capone mob, but pooled strength and worked with it. A man no longer had to be a Sicilian to be in the Unione. Into its highest councils came such men as Meyer Lansky and Bugs Siegel, leaders of a tremendously powerful mob, who were personal partners in the alcohol business with Lucky and Joe Adonis of Brooklyn. . . .

It still numbers among its members many old-time Sicilians who are not gangsters, but anybody who goes into it today is a mobster, and an important one. In New York City the organization is split up territorially into districts, each led by a minor boss, known as the *"compare,"* or godfather. . . . I know that throughout the underworld the Unione Siciliana is accepted as a mysterious, all-pervasive reality, and that Lucky used it as the vehicle by which the underworld was drawn into cooperation on a national scale.

More than a decade after this statement appeared in a popular magazine of the time, many members of the public (and some law-enforcement officers) still had no notion that an illicit cartel both performed and controlled some types of crime across the nation. If they heard of "the Mafia," or "the syndicate," or "the outfit," or "the mob," or "the brotherhood," or "the *fratellanza,*" they did not believe what they heard, or did not believe it affected them. They had been shocked when in the late 1930's and early 1940's District Attorney Thomas E. Dewey and his special racket staff in New York City, and the honest members of the staff of District Attorney William O'Dwyer in Brooklyn, exposed a nationwide alliance of extortionists and killers. But by 1951 many of the same members of the public still had not read, or had forgotten, the hundreds of popular magazine articles describing "Murder Incorporated." Accordingly, they were again shocked and surprised when a second major effort to educate them occurred. The Kefauver Committee in 1951 was able to draw the following four conclusions from the testimony of some eight hundred witnesses who appeared before it.

(1) There is a Nation-wide crime syndicate known as the Mafia, whose tentacles are found in many large cities. It has international ramifications which appear most clearly in connection with the narcotics traffic.

(2) Its leaders are usually found in control of the most lucrative rackets in their cities.

(3) There are indications of a centralized direction and control of these rackets, but leadership appears to be in a group rather than in a single individual.

(4) The Mafia is the cement that helps to bind the Costello-Adonis-Lansky syndicate of New York and the Accardo-Guzik-Fischetti syndicate of Chicago as well as smaller criminal gangs and individual criminals throughout the country. These groups have kept in touch with Luciano since his deportation from this country.

In the next decade, investigating bodies were able to overcome some of the handicaps of the Kefauver Committee, which "found it difficult to obtain reliable data concerning the extent of Mafia operation, the nature of Mafia organization, and the way it presently operates." While *all* such handicaps will not be overcome for some years to come, there no longer is any doubt that several regional organizations, rationally constructed for the control of the sale of illicit goods and services, are in operation. Neither is there any doubt that these regional organizations are linked together in a nationwide cartel and confederation.

Some citizens were once again taken by surprise in November, 1957, when at least seventy-five of the nation's criminal-cartel leaders were discovered at a meeting at the home of Joseph Barbara in Apalachin, New York. They came from all parts of the country, and most of them had criminal records relating to the kind of offense customarily called "organized crime." At least twenty-three came from New York City or New Jersey, nineteen from upstate New York, eight from the Midwest, three from the West, and two from the South. At least two "delegates" were from Cuba, and one was from Italy. Because some of those in attendance avoided the police roadblocks, and because not all those captured were prosecuted, the places of residence of all the participants cannot be determined.

No one has been able to prove the nature of the conspiracy involved at Apalachin, but no one believes that the men all just happened to drop in on the host at the same time. Two of the men attending the meeting had met at a somewhat similar meeting of criminals in Cleveland in 1928. The Italian police in early 1968 revealed that some of them also attended an October, 1957, meeting in a motel at Castellammare del Golfo, near Palermo, Sicily.

Calling the Apalachin meeting, it turned out, was the most serious single mistake Cosa Nostra rulers have ever made. In the first place, discovery of the conference finally convinced some formerly skeptical government officials that a nationwide apparatus does in fact exist. A study of telephone traffic among the principals and their associates all across the nation revealed that there had been widespread interchange of telephone calls immediately prior to the meeting. For example, John Ormento, then alleged to be one of the nation's top dealers in narcotics, who was long a fugitive from justice as a result of a narcotics indictment for which he was subsequently convicted, had talked to other criminals in Cañon City, Colorado, in Dallas, and in Detroit just before he went to meet his friends at Barbara's estate. Senator McClellan concluded, "The telephone communications among these men just before the meeting gave conclusive evidence of the national scope and significance of this surreptitious conclave of the high and mighty in the underworld's secret domain." In the second place, these officials became convinced that law-enforcement intelligence is inadequate, that the procedures for studying the organization controlling the sale of illicit goods and services in the United States are inadequate, and that the procedures for disseminating hard facts about organized crime to law-enforcement agencies and the public are inadequate.

New methods for obtaining information were soon introduced on the federal level—principally in the form of "informers" who were in fact wire taps and bugs. The information thus obtained has been extraordinarily helpful in developing background information relevant to successful prosecutions of individual members of Cosa Nostra. But there have been few changes in the methods used to analyze the intelligence information obtained. Even the Apalachin conference did not stimulate law-enforcement agencies to hire anthropological and sociological experts on the social organization of secret societies, or even to hire business-administration experts knowledgeable about social organization generally. Federal agencies alone in 1967 applied $22,355,000 to combating organized crime ($8,600,00 of this amount was spent by the FBI), but not one dime went to research and development. Equally important, no new devices for educating the public were invented. Instead, we were treated to a barrage of popular articles saying, in effect, that a bunch of respectable-looking "hoodlums" and "gangland figures" had met in upstate New York. Organized crime is too important to be left to policemen, prosecutors, and sensationalists.

One response to the discovery of the Apalachin meeting was increased investigative action by the United States Attorney General, the Federal Bureau of Narcotics, the Federal Bureau of Investigation, the Internal Revenue Service, and several state and local agencies. In 1954 the Department of Justice had formed an Organized Crime and Racketeering Section to encourage a concreted drive against the leading organized criminals identified by the Kefauver Committee. However, efforts to institutionalize an antiracketeering intelligence program were hindered by lack of coordination and interest by some Federal investigative agencies, including the FBI. In 1958, after the Apalachin meeting, an Attorney General's Special Group on Organized Crime was created to gather information about, and to prosecute, the Apalachin conferees. This group's functions were soon assumed by the existing Organized Crime and Racketeering Section. In late 1960 the FBI began to supply the Section with regular intelligence reports on the country's major organized-crime leaders. But with only seventeen attorneys and with minimal intelligence information from other federal agencies, the Organized Crime and Racketeering Section could hardly be effective. In 1961 the Section was expanded in what has come to be called an "organized-crime drive." By 1963 there were sixty attorneys in the Section, and regular intelligence reports on organized crime were secured from twenty-six separate federal agencies.

Beginning in about 1961, the investigating agencies began to receive intelligence information about the existence of the criminal confederation now commonly labeled "Cosa Nostra," a large-scale criminal organization complete with a board of directors and a hierarchical structure extending down to the street level of criminal activity. In a third major effort to "educate the public," the McClellan Committee in 1963 portrayed this syndicate to a nationwide television audience. Once again, a considerable number of citizens had forgotten, or had never heard, the information on organized crime presented to them over a period of thirty years. They were shocked

and surprised when they heard Joseph Valachi, an active member
of the confederation, describe the skeletal structure of the organization, its nationwide operations, and its membership. The testimony
of Valachi and supplementary information obtained from bugs, taps,
and informers enabled the Attorney General, Robert F. Kennedy,
to testify as follows before the Committee:

> Because of intelligence gathered from Joseph Valachi and from in-
> formants, we know that Cosa Nostra is run by a commission and that
> the leaders of Cosa Nostra in most major cities are responsible to the
> commission. We know that membership in the commission varies between
> nine and twelve active members and we know who the active members
> of the commission are today.
>
> We know, for example, that in the past two years, at least three
> carefully planned commission meetings had to be called off because the
> leaders learned that we had uncovered their well-concealed plans and
> meeting places.
>
> We know that the commission makes major policy decisions for the
> organization, settles disputes among the families, and allocates terri-
> tories of criminal operations within the organization.
>
> For example, we now know that the meeting at Apalachin was called
> by a leading racketeer in an effort to resolve the problem created by
> the murder of Albert Anastasia. The racketeer was concerned that
> Anastasia had brought too many individuals not worthy of membership
> into the organization. To insure the security of the organization, the
> racketeer wanted these men removed. Of particular concern to this
> racketeer was that he had violated commission rules in causing the
> assault, the attempted assassination of Frank Costello, deposed New
> York rackets boss, and the murder of Anastasia. He wanted commission
> approval for these acts—which he received. . . .
>
> Such intelligence is important not only because it can help us know
> what to watch for, but because of the assistance it can provide in de-
> veloping and prosecuting specific cases. . . . Thus we have been able
> to make inroads into the hierarchy, personnel, and operations of or-
> ganized crime. It would be a serious mistake, however, to overestimate
> the progress Federal and local law enforcement has made. A principal
> lesson provided by the disclosure of Joseph Valachi and other informants
> is that the job ahead is very large and very difficult.

Now, more than five years later, and over ten years since the
Apalachin meeting, the job ahead is still "very large and very diffi-

cult." While law-enforcement officials now have detailed information about the criminal activities of individual men who are participating in illicit businesses and illicit governments, knowledge of the structure of their confederation remains fragmentary and impressionistic. Perhaps it is for this reason that both the Chief Justice of the United States and the President of the United States recently tried their hands in an attempt to educate the public about the danger of organized crime.

In March, 1967, Chief Justice Earl Warren surprised many of the delegates to the First National Conference on Crime Control (a conference called by the President) when he selected "organized crime" as the topic of his address. Although Mr. Warren appeared before the Conference on rather short notice, there were hundreds of other topics on which he could have addressed the delegates. A month or two after the Conference, I had an opportunity to ask him why he had chosen this topic despite the fact that the President's Commission had allocated such a small proportion of its resources to it. He replied that he thought the Commission had not paid enough attention to the topic, that he wanted to emphasize its importance. In his address, the Chief Justice asked whether we are "sufficiently concerned to dig below the surface to discover the reasons for crime and then to face up to the situation notwithstanding it may be costly or even embarrassing to do so." He pointed out that organized crime "strikes at the vitals of society," "produces great wealth," and "gathers power as it goes along." He concluded: "Organized crime can be stopped because it is a direct assault upon the community in which it thrives, and no crime syndicate can openly defy the law in any of its money-making activities if the community is determined that it shall not exist." He went on to observe, however, that communities are not always eager to eradicate organized crime, or even to slow it to a faltering walk. In the first place, the government officials whose duty it is to fight organized crime are sometimes corrupt and, thus, part of the organization. In the second place, "powerful business interests which are considered above reproach" are sometimes responsible for organized-crime conditions. The Chief Justice reported that while he was a prosecuting attorney he had tried to close down organized prostitution in his city, but his efforts were strenuously resisted by bankers, real estate dealers, and retail furniture dealers, all of whom increased their profits by dealing with the prostitute organization at rates higher than those available from honest citizens and legitimate business organizations.

President Johnson did not mention organized crime in his address to the same Conference. Nevertheless, during his years in office the President tried to educate the public about the criminal organization. In his 1965 message to Congress on crime, he directed attention to the phenomenon of organized crime and then promised, "I am calling on the Attorney General, the Secretary of the Treasury, and the other heads of the federal law-enforcement arms to enlarge their energetic effort against organized crime. The Department of Justice will submit legislative proposals to Congress to strengthen and expand these efforts generally." No significant legislative proposals appeared, however, so a year later the President, a former teacher, tried to improve his teaching techniques by becoming more explicit. In a March, 1966, "Special Message on Crime" he pointed out that organized crime is "the most flagrant manifestation of crime in America" and held that its existence is "intolerable." (See the quotation on p. 1.) In a White House press release dated May, 1966, the President renewed his educational efforts. He pointed out that organized crime "constitutes nothing less than a guerrilla war against society," and then went on to say:

Most damaging of all are the efforts of racketeers to seek protection against honest law enforcement by corrupting public officials. Such evil strikes at the heart of democracy. It corrupts individual officials. It breeds a general contempt for law. It saps public respect for law enforcement.

To remedy this "evil," the President issued the following directive:

I am today calling on each federal department and agency engaged in the war on organized crime to redouble its efforts. I am today directing the Attorney General, our chief law-enforcement officer, to direct the Government's renewed drive against these corporations of corruption.

At about the same time, the President issued a "Memorandum for Heads of Departments and Agencies Participating in the Federal Organized Crime Drive." In this memorandum he said, "Organized crime constitutes one of the most serious threats to a peaceful and prosperous society," and he asked each of the department heads (1) to review its current organized-crime drive programs and present status reports to the Attorney General, (2) report periodically to the Attorney General on the progress of organized-crime investigations, and (3) "establish direct lines of liaison with the Department of Justice to enable the Attorney General to carry out his responsibility for directing this program."

Apparently the only persons to receive the full impact of these messages were those law-enforcement personnel and criminal-justice personnel who already knew about the dangers of organized crime. They received the message with enthusiasm, believing that the "organized-crime drive" inaugurated by Attorney General Kennedy with the support of President Kennedy would be revived. Nothing significant occurred.

In early 1967 the President again took a stab at "educating the public." After he had received the Report of his Commission on Law Enforcement and Administration of Justice, he once again called attention to organized-crime activities. On May 6, 1967, he presented a "Crime in America" message to Congress, saying about organized crime that he was "determined to extend our efforts to root out this poisonous element from our society." He promised to increase the number of organized-crime personnel in the Department of Justice, and he directed the Acting Attorney General, Ramsey Clark, "to establish a special program to offer state and city officials assistance in setting up effective plans to combat organized crime."

In these public statements the President was, it appears, attempting to teach us that organized crime is a significant social problem that deserves immediate attention. Yet the President at first failed to educate even his own Attorney General. Two weeks after the President issued his "Crime in America" message, Mr. Clark stated his conviction that organized crime is only a "tiny part" of the entire crime picture, though an important one. However, in November, 1967, the Attorney General said he was going to inaugurate the program which the President had, in his "Crime in America" message, directed him to establish. On the basis of recommendations made by the President's Commission, seven centers of Cosa Nostra activity were to become the targets of special "strike forces" made up of investigators from the Treasury Department's Alcohol and Tobacco

Tax Division, the Bureau of Narcotics, the Bureau of Customs, the Internal Revenue Service's Intelligence and Audit Divisions, and the Labor Department's Racketeering Division. This federal operation, which does not meet the President's request that technical assistance be given to states and cities, is coordinated by the Criminal Division of the Justice Department. No mention was made of any possible coordination with work of the Federal Bureau of Investigation. The forerunner of this idea probably was a "strike force" or "task force" which operated with some success (thanks to a knowledgeable live informer) in the Buffalo area during the autumn of 1966. The FBI did not become part of the Buffalo "strike force" but FBI agents did work with the group, and FBI cases were involved.

During the summer and autumn of 1968, just before the elections, Mr. Clark apparently began to get the President's message. He inaugurated his own mild campaign to educate the public. His annual report for 1967–1968 contained a barrage of statistics indicating that increased activity against organized crime had resulted in increased numbers of indictments and convictions. He wrote a newspaper column saying, among other things, "Many find it difficult to believe there is organized crime, but its existence is confirmed by history, experience and reason." An Associated Press dispatch released on September 4 quoted him as saying that organized crime "has corrupted American life for decades." The Attorney General also reported that strike forces had been sent to three "centers of organized crime," and soon would be sent to other centers. He requested a budget sufficient to enlarge the Organized Crime and Racketeering Section staff from about 100 to about 160, including twenty attorneys for strike forces. He even quoted J. Edgar Hoover as saying that 1967 "marked one of the most effective all-out drives against organized crime in the history of law enforcement."

Too many Americans heed the opinion that organized crime is only a "tiny part" of the crime problem. As Henry Ruth, Deputy Director of the President's Commission, recently wrote, "The limited perspective which most of the public and its governmental servants possess about organized crime is perhaps the severest detriment to the construction of a strong countereffort." Since the time of the Apalachin meeting, and especially since the McClellan Committee hearings, law-enforcement personnel have shown conclusively that "families" of criminals of Italian and Sicilian descent either operate or control the operation of all but a tiny part of the illicit businesses in large American cities—including gambling, usury, and the wholesaling of narcotics. They have identified the persons playing the various occupational roles in each of these "families," and they have conclusive evidence that the "families" are linked together in a nationwide cartel and confederation. Nevertheless, some government officials, some social scientists, and some plain citizens remain unconvinced.

There seem to be three interrelated factors involved in the prevailing indifference or even skepticism of many citizens.

First, information on organized crime has, by and large, been presented to the public in a haphazard and sensational manner. Policemen dealing with organized crime say the public is misled by the tendency of mass media to play "cops and robbers" and "gang busters" whenever organized crime is mentioned. The police are well aware of the sensationalism present in televised Congressional hearings involving unsavory characters, in newspaper accounts calling organized criminals "muscle men," "gorillas," and "meat hooks," and in books and popular-magazine articles with titles like "The Mafia Menace" and "The Menace of the Mob." If a Congressional hearing is televised as a cops-and-robbers story, it has no more effect than a routine fictitious cops-and-robbers story—what some of us in the Far West are beginning to call an "Eastern." Housewives watched the televised Kefauver Committee hearings and McClellan Committee hearings as they did their ironing, all the time cheering, we hope, for the good guys. But when the glare of publicity was off, the housewives turned to other soap operas and cops-and-robbers stories, perhaps planning that tomorrow they would return for the next episode. No legislative hearing on organized crime has been conducted as an inquiry, a "study," rather than as an exposé or a trial.

The ineffectual and even misleading cops-and-robbers presentation of organized-crime affairs is also apparent in the language used to discuss them. Television personnel and members of Congressional investigating committees, like newspapermen, find it virtually impossible to depict organized criminals as anything but gangsters who prey principally on each other. For example, there are few televised news stories, televised Congressional hearings, or newspaper accounts in which Mr. Lucchese is called "Thomas Gaetano Lucchese" or Mr. Ricca is called "Paul Ricca." The writer always displays his "inside knowledge" about how things *really* are in "the mob" by using first name, corny "alias," and last name. Even the President's Commission could not resist this form when discussing Louis "Lepke" Buchalter, Emmanuel "Mendy" Weiss, and John "Big John" Ormento. Such language sets Cosa Nostra members apart, as if they were romantic and not very harmful Damon Runyon characters. "Thomas Lucchese," when he was alive, could possibly have been someone who was corrupting my labor union, but "Three-Finger Brown" could only have been a somewhat fictitious gangster in a cops-and-robbers story.

Similarly, Chicago newsmen almost always call usury "the juice racket," and this terminology lets the reader believe that the activity has nothing to do with him or the safety of his community. The criminals' terminology is also apparent when the word "scam" is used to describe bankruptcy fraud. Most of us can understand the seriousness of the crimes of usury, bankruptcy fraud, and bribery, but we have a hard time realizing that it is our friends and neighbors, not "gangsters," who are, in the long run, the victims of "the juice racket," "the scam racket," or "the fix." We have an even more difficult time realizing that it is our friends and neighbors, not "gangsters," who are conducting "the juice racket," "the scam racket," and "the fix."

Probably of even more relevance to any prevailing skepticism about the operations of organized crime is the fact that the murder of a Cosa Nostra member by men acting under orders from the boss of the victim's "family" is invariably described by the mass media as a "hit" or "gangland slaying." Such terminology gives the impression that gangsters like Al "Scarface" Capone and Earl "Hymie" Weiss are still fighting for territory. Like the title of Dean Jennings' recent book, *We Only Kill Each Other: The Life and Bad Times of Bugsy Siegel,* such terminology also gives the impression that killings of organized criminals have nothing to do with respectable members of society. But they do. A large proportion of such murders are executions of members who have secretly left the criminals' camp to join the forces of law, order, and decency. Calling the murder a "hit" makes it all but impossible for the reader to realize that his own welfare is involved. Control of a community's economic and political affairs by an organization of criminals is a serious matter, certainly as dangerous as would be control of these affairs by Communists. The probability is high that any Cosa Nostra member executed by his superiors has, for any of a number of reasons, been serving as an American spy, in much the way citizens of enemy nations sometimes work as American spies. The public will not be "educated" about organized crime until it understands that organized criminals prey on the economic and political order, not on each other. We must understand, further, that there is no longer any "underworld" of organized criminals. The penetration of business and government by organized crime has been so complete that it is no longer possible to differentiate "underworld gangsters" from "upperworld" businessmen and government officials.

Second, there is a proclivity in our society, even among social scientists, to view criminality as an individual matter rather than as an organizational matter. As we indicated earlier, the criminal's behavior is usually viewed, both popularly and scientifically, as a problem of individual maladjustment, not as a consequence of his participation in social systems. Consistently, the law-enforcement process has been, by and large, designed for the control of individuals, not for the control of organizations. Only in exceptional cases, such as those involving price-fixing or other monopolistic practices, are organizations put on trial. In making a similar point, the economist Thomas C. Schelling has said:

At the level of national policy, if not of local practice, the dominant approach to organized crime is through indictment and conviction, not through regulation, accommodation, or the restructuring of markets and business conditions. This is in striking contrast to the enforcement of antitrust or food and drug laws, or the regulation of industries affecting the public interest.

Since it is the duty of law-enforcement agencies to put individual organized criminals in jail, they necessarily must be more concerned with collecting evidence that will lead to trials of individuals than with evidence about the relationships between criminals or about the structure and operations of illicit organizations. Accordingly, law-enforcement personnel are only rarely efficient "educators of the public," so far as criminal organizations are concerned.

"Organized-crime intelligence" is a relatively new concept. Special intelligence programs dealing with organized crime have been established in only a handful of jurisdictions. And even in units established in police departments and prosecutors' offices to do intelligence work, there has been an understandable confusion of the procedures essential to organized-crime investigations and those essential to organized-crime intelligence. In the former, the objective is to detect which individuals are committing crimes, and to present to courts the evidence pertaining to crimes committed. In the latter, one objective is to do broad "background studies" of organized crime, in the way the CIA studies Cuba, Russia, and China. In intelligence work, there is concern for the activities of individuals, but there also is concern for the past, present, and predictable operations of the organization to which the individuals belong. Since the police traditionally have been oriented to criminal investigation rather than to intelligence, it is not surprising to find that the "organized-crime files" of intelligence units are generally indexed only as to persons. Thus, in these files one can look up "Smith" and find that Smith is engaged in usury and other organized-crime activities. The investigator might, alternatively, be able to turn to a "usury index," which lists the name of Smith and the names of other usurers in the community. But he is not likely to find in the files of law-enforcement and prosecuting agencies any analyses of the economics of usury, of the relationships between the incidence of usury and the financial policies of legitimate lending institutions, or of the correlation (if any) between the incidence of usury and the "need" for usury on the part of gamblers, legitimate businessmen, and the poverty-stricken. Because the "organized-crime files" of criminal justice agencies must be arranged with a view to prosecuting individuals, these agencies find it difficult to educate the public to the effect that "the problem of organized crime" is in fact quite different from "the problem of juvenile automobile theft." Perhaps it is for this reason that Chief Justice Warren, in his address to the First National Conference on Crime Control, carefully distinguished between "organized crimes" and "individual crimes."

Third, the confidential nature of much information plagues any law-enforcement agent, criminal-justice administrator, or anyone else who would "educate the public" or even supply raw data to persons who would try to organize and analyze it for tactical or strategic intelligence purposes. One element in both good police investigative work and good intelligence work is silence. Further, when a case is before a grand jury or in the process of trial, disclosure of information by the government could well result in dismissal. Libel and slander suits, and even political reprisals, are likely to threaten any policeman, prosecutor, or investigator who tells what he knows or thinks about organized criminals. At a meeting of law-enforcement officers and criminal-justice personnel in 1967, Henry Peterson, Chief of the Organized Crime and Racketeering Section of the United States Department of Justice, commented, "I know to a moral certainty that in the upper echelons there is an amalgamation between the International Longshoremen, Teamsters, and Cosa Nostra." Mr. Peterson was immediately bombarded in the press, where apologies were demanded by members of all three organizations. He never elaborated on his statement, despite the fact that such an elaboration would be a significant lesson in "the education of the public." An elaboration might in fact be critical to the legal order of our nation, in an indirect way, because it is the Brotherhood of Teamsters that would unionize our police departments.

There is a great difference between knowing something and proving it in a court of law, and law-enforcement officers working in the organized-crime field are quite reluctant to reveal anything they cannot reasonably expect to prove. They are deeply concerned with the injustice of any "character assassination" which might stem from any gossip or half-baked facts in their files, even if the potential victim is a known murderer or a notoriously corrupt legislator. When discussing the infiltration of Cosa Nostra members into legitimate business, one federal official said, "As sure as I'm sitting here, two banks in New York City are controlled by hoodlums." But when he was asked why the government does not take legal action against them he responded, "It's one thing to know it; it's quite another to prove in court a violation of law." There is not the slightest doubt that the federal official knew the names and criminal histories of the "hoodlums" controlling the banks. Had he revealed them, he might have more efficiently "educated the public," but in doing so he might have violated the law. Part of what is known about organized crime has been learned by means of wire taps and bugs, and disclosure of some of the information obtained in this way is, unfortunately for public education, against the law.

If "the public" is to be educated about the evils and dangers of organized crime, the curriculum must be changed. Members of the public—and policemen, prosecutors, and legislators as well—must learn to think in terms of the complex interrelationships among criminals, and between criminals and others.

In many respects, the organization of organized criminals is like the organization of police departments, and the relationship between this organization and others is like the relationship between, say, the New York Police Department and others. One can readily see the need for policemen to obey the orders given them by men above them in the police hierarchy. One can readily see the need to keep much police data out of the hands of criminals, and the need for coordination of the activities of both individual policemen and of police departments.

It is more difficult to appreciate the fact that there exists in the United States a confederation of criminal organizations which is very similar in structure and even in values (honor, respect, obedience, manliness, honesty) to the confederation of police departments. The Apalachin meeting, after all, was not much different from a meeting of the International Association of Chiefs of Police. What a chief of police tries to do with, to, and for the patrolmen in his department is not too different from what a Cosa Nostra boss tries to do with, to, and for his "soldiers." And in both cases the boss or chief and the lower-echelon men alike are readily replaceable—they occupy positions that are coordinated with other positions, and when they leave their positions other men are recruited to fill the vacancies. That is what "organization" means. When a policeman retires there is no necessary effect on the structure, the organization, of his department, even if the *operations* of his department might be slightly hampered for a very short time by loss of his expertise. Similarly, when a Cosa Nostra member is incarcerated there is no necessary effect on the structure of the criminal fraternity. The behavior of a Cosa Nostra member is "owned" by his organization, and the behavior of a policeman is "owned" by his organization, just as the behavior involved in speaking the English language or the French language is "owned" by groups rather than by individuals.

CHAPTER V

Demand, Supply, and Profit

The underworld is what it is largely because Americans are too moral to tolerate human weakness, and because they are too great lovers of liberty to tolerate the tyranny which might make it possible to abolish what they prohibit.

WALTER LIPPMANN

THE AMERICAN confederation of criminals thrives because a large minority of citizens demands the illicit goods and services it has for sale. As Walter Lippmann observed at the end of the Prohibition era, the basic distinction between ordinary criminals and organized criminals in the United States turns on the fact that the ordinary criminal is wholly predatory, while the man participating in crime on a rational, systematic basis offers a return to the respectable members of society. If all burglars were miraculously abolished, they would be missed by only a few persons to whose income or employment they contribute directly—burglary insurance companies, manufacturers of locks and other security devices, police, prison personnel, and a few others. But if the confederation of men employed in illicit businesses were suddenly abolished, it would be sorely missed because it performs services for which there is a great public demand. The organized criminal, by definition, occupies a position in a social system, an "organization," which has been rationally designed to maximize profits by performing illegal services and providing legally forbidden products demanded by the members of the broader society in which he lives. Just as society has made a place for the confederation by demanding illicit gambling, alcohol and narcotics,

72

usurious loans, and a cheap supply of labor, the confederation has made places, in an integrated set of positions, for the use of the skills of a wide variety of specialists who furnish these goods and services. Organized crime cannot become a social problem until a much broader segment of society perceives that the cost of the services provided is too high.

It is true, of course, that criminals who do not occupy positions in any large-scale organization also supply the same kinds of illicit goods and services supplied by the confederation. Perhaps a large proportion of the persons demanding illicit goods and services believes that they are being supplied by criminals who are unorganized and who, for that matter, are not very criminal. The existence of such a widely held belief would account for the fact that the public indignation which becomes manifest at the time of an exposure of the activities of members of the confederation—such as a Senate hearing, an Apalachin meeting, an execution of an informer—is sporadic and short-lived. A gray-haired old lady who accepts a few horse-racing bets from the patrons of her neighborhood grocery store is performing an illegal service for those patrons, just as is the factory worker who sells his own brand of whiskey to his friends at the plant. Law violators of this kind do not seem very dangerous and, if treated in isolation, such persons cannot be perceived as much of a threat to the social order. Accordingly, they tend to be protected in various ways by their society. The policeman is inclined to overlook the bookmaker's offenses or merely to insist that they not occur in his precinct, the judge is likely to invoke the mildest punishment the legislature has established, and the jailer is likely to differentiate such offenders from "real criminals."

We do not argue that such "mom and pop" kind of catering to the demands of the community is necessarily insidious, though by no means do we condone it. What is insidious is the fact that the providers cannot be individual entrepreneurs for long. "Gambling" cannot be perceived as a social problem until it is widely understood that bookmakers and lottery operators are organized to insure that *making* bets is gambling but *taking* bets is not. The nature of the bookmaking business is such, as we will show later, that bookmakers must join hands with others in the same business. Other illicit businesses have the same character. Nowadays, moreover, free enterprise does not exist in the field of illicit services and goods— any "mom and pop" kind of small illicit business soon takes in, voluntarily or involuntarily, a Cosa Nostra man as a partner.

By joining hands, the suppliers of illicit goods and services (1) cut costs, improve their markets, and pool capital; (2) gain monopolies on certain of the illicit services or on all of the illicit services provided in a specific geographic area, whether it be a neighborhood or a large city; (3) centralize the procedures for stimulating the agencies of law enforcement and administration of justice to overlook the illegal operations; and (4) accumulate vast wealth which can be used to attain even wider monopolies on illicit activities, and on legal businesses as well. In the long run, then, the "small operation" corrupts the traditional economic and political procedures designed to insure that citizens need not pay tribute to a criminal in order to conduct a legitimate business. The demand, and the profits, are too great to be left in the hands of "mom and pop" operators. As the Kefauver Committee reported about the demand for gambling services, "The creeping paralysis of law enforcement which results from a failure to enforce gambling laws contributes to a breakdown in connection with other fields of crime." Organization, not gambling or usury or narcotics distribution or labor racketeering or extortion or murder, is the phenomenon to worry about.

Despite the fact that most forms of gambling are illegal in most parts of the United States, a significant proportion of American citizens want to gamble. They spend about $5 billion annually betting legally at race tracks and an unknown amount gambling legally in Nevada. Estimates of the amount bet illegally each year range from $7 billion to $50 billion. While it is impossible to determine the calculations on which such estimates are made, there is a consensus among law-enforcement officials that illegal betting on horse races, lotteries, and sporting events totals at least $20 billion a year. Cosa Nostra members take about one-third of the gambling gross as their share, so if that gross is in fact $20 billion they acquire some

$6 to $7 billion annually. In 1967, the United States spent about $30 billion on the Vietnam war. The total American budget for foreign aid is about $2 billion annually. The $6 or $7 billion going into the hands of organized criminals each year is not all profit. From this amount must be deducted the costs of doing business, such as wages, rent, bribery, and armaments. Neither can it be assumed that this amount is divided equally among the five thousand or so members of Cosa Nostra. But the profits are huge enough to make understandable the fact that any given member of Cosa Nostra is more likely to be a millionaire than not.

In most large American cities, the opportunity to gamble is provided by Cosa Nostra. Members of this organization do not themselves own and operate all the illegal betting and lottery enterprises, but those they do not own they control, or provide with essential services. The organization profits, thus, in three ways. It provides an enterprise for which there is a great demand and, accordingly, for which customers are willing to pay a high price. It secures, by direct intimidation and extortion, a portion of the profits of any competitors who attempt to meet part of the demand. And it provides, in exchange for a portion of profits, reinsurance ("lay-off") services, which any man taking bets needs if he is to avoid being a gambler.

Later we will show why a personnel hierarchy organized into at least six steps is essential to providing betting services for a community. Someone takes the gambler's bet and gives the money, usually via a runner, to a second-echelon person in charge of a district. From the district office the money goes to a main officer, where a third-echelon worker calculates the pay-offs. Profits then move upward through complex channels to the head of the entire city set up. This man is usually called a "boss," but he might be known to the readers of the sports page, or even of the society page, as a "sportsman." The "sportsman" ordinarily does not own the entire operation, in the way a retail merchant may own several branch stores. Instead, he allocates franchises on a territorial basis, something like a Southern landowner allocates land to sharecroppers.

There are distinct advantages in "sharecropping" a bookmaking or lottery business, as compared with trying to make it alone. In the late 1950's the independent bookmakers of Suffolk County (eastern Long Island), New York, were "organized" by a Cosa Nostra clique. Put simply, representatives of Cosa Nostra boldly demanded 50 percent of the profits of all the bookmakers in the area. Behind the takeover were threats of maiming and murder, but the independents soon learned that at least six economic advantages accrued from casting one's lot with "the outfit." In the first place, a "sportsman" or two provided absolute backing for all bets so that the independent operator no longer needed either to gamble or to reinsure his bets through a "lay-off" operation. In the second place, this backing permitted each independent operator to handle more bets, with the result that each bookmaker actually made a bigger profit while on a 50–50 basis with Cosa Nostra than he had made when he controlled his own illicit business. Third, the bookmakers no longer found it necessary to do so much running around the streets taking bets. They merely provided regular bettors with New York City telephone numbers. After the bettors had called in their bets and had them recorded in a rather elaborate set of books, the bookmaker needed only to go around and collect the money or, in a minority of instances, pay off. Fourth, the bookies themselves no longer had to handle many telephoned bets, thus making it more difficult for the police to determine by wire tapping what was going on. Fifth, the bookies had legal services and men with "connections" available to them, so that the risk of conviction, even when arrested, was decreased. Sixth, squabbles with other bookmakers were minimized—under the new arrangement, each man was assigned exclusive rights to a specified territory.

It is possible that a seventh advantage accrued also. In 1960 Commissioner Charles R. Thom of the Suffolk County Police told the New York State Commission of Investigation that centralization of police forces led to centralization of criminal forces:

It is somewhat startling to learn that the syndicates are particularly happy with the consolidation of the nine police departments into the Suffolk County Police Department, as they feel that protection is easier to arrange through one agency than through many. The intensive campaign against gamblers instituted by this Department commencing January 1 had the astounding side effect of solving the recruitment problems of the syndicate, as our drive successfully stampeded the independents into the arms of the syndicate for protection, and the syndicate can now pick and choose those operators they wish to admit.

🚩

The usury business, usually called "loan-sharking" or "shylocking," consists simply of loaning money at rates higher than the legally prescribed limit, commonly 20 percent per week. No one knows how much revenue organized criminals earn each year from usury. Dollar for dollar, it is a better business than taking bets, but citizens gamble more dollars than they borrow from usurers. It is safe to say, as the President's Commission did, that the business is in "the multibillion-dollar range."

It is not necessary that usury be organized, in the way it is necessary that bet-taking be organized. Any criminal can play. But the criminal who would play must have three things not available to most criminals—customers, capital, and a method of collection. The members of the Cosa Nostra organization that provides illegal gambling for a community possess these three things. For that reason, a large proportion of all contemporary usurers are members of Cosa Nostra or are backed by them. One New York City usurer made a loan of a million dollars in the morning and another loan of a million dollars in the afternoon of the same day. Another man by means of usury increased his net worth from $500,000 in 1960 to $7,500,000 in 1964.

Usurers provide a service which is sorely needed, especially by gamblers and by others whose financial problems arise from a bit of shadiness. Many victims of usury operations are compulsive or eager gamblers who have borrowed from loan sharks in an attempt to recoup gambling losses. While they are not conspirators in the usury operation, they are compromised as conspirators in the gambling activity. As the former Director of the Chicago Police Intelligence Division has said,

The same degree of complicity usually applies to a businessman who wants to borrow money quickly, and for reasons best known to himself doesn't want anyone to know about the loan. Oftentimes the mere making of such a loan violates ethical standards of his business or social affiliations. When such is the case, the co-conspirator factor indirectly applies and such businessmen rarely become complainants if they can manage to repay the loan.

Some years ago I did a study of embezzlers and found, among other things, that embezzlement is generally an attempt to solve an unsharable financial problem, a problem which the trusted person is ashamed of because it was created by some illegality, immorality, or "foolishness" which he is reluctant to admit to others. Because the trusted person's problem is unsharable, the sources of legitimate loans available to him are cut off. Some trusted persons solve their unsharable financial problems by embezzling. Perhaps others find the solution in the usurious loans available from loan sharks. But this embezzlement-preventing function of usury is not all gravy. In some embezzlement cases the unsharable financial problem is indebtedness to a loan shark.

The corruptive influence of Cosa Nostra loan-sharking recently came to the surface in New York City. In the summer of 1968 James L. Marcus, the city's former Commissioner of Water Supply, Gas and Electricity, and one of Mayor Lindsay's close advisers, pleaded guilty to taking a bribe in return for awarding an $835,000 city contract. Mr. Marcus had resigned his high position in December, 1967, a few days before a federal grand jury returned an indictment charging that he had received a $16,000 share of a $40,000 kickback on a contract to clean a Bronx reservoir. The indictment charged that when Marcus awarded the contract he was acting under the direction of Antonio Corallo, whom the McClellan Committee, the FBI, U.S. Attorney Robert M. Morgenthau, and the New York Police Department have described as a Cosa Nostra underboss. In July, 1968, Mr. Corallo was sentenced to three years in prison for conspiring to bribe Marcus, and in September Marcus was sentenced to fifteen months for his part in the conspiracy.

Mr. Marcus was in financial trouble even before he went to New York's city hall. His London-based Conestoga Investments firm, whose business was that of bringing borrowers and lenders together, seemed to swallow up all the money he poured into it. Two Conestoga investors complained to the district attorney about the way Marcus was handling the company's money. A well-placed friend of one of Marcus' business partners recommended the financial services of Corallo, a man who was, among other things, a loan shark's loan shark. Corallo was a well-known criminal. In 1941 he served time for narcotics trafficking, and in 1962 he was sentenced to two years in prison for bribing a judge to fix a fraudulent bankruptcy case. Shortly after his release in 1965, he departed for England, where he hoped to invest Cosa Nostra money in recently legalized gambling casinos; but Scotland Yard, alerted by the FBI, refused to let him into the country. He had been publicly identified by various law-enforcement and investigating agencies as a labor racketeer and a strong-arm enforcer in the garment industry. Thomas Lucchese, boss of the Cosa Nostra "family" Corallo belonged to, became seriously ill with a brain tumor in the summer of 1966 (he died in July, 1967), and the newspapers reported that Corallo was slated to move up to the vacant position. Nevertheless, Marcus went to Corallo for help. According to Sandy Smith and William Lambert, writing for *Life,* Corallo immediately offered Marcus $10,000 "to ease the pressure from his more urgent creditors," and within a few days lent him $40,000. Marcus made interest payments totaling about $14,000 in less than a year.

A Manhattan grand jury in May, 1968, handed up an indictment accusing Michael Bonfondco of criminal usury, and Marcus was named as one of Bonfondeo's victims. Marcus allegedly borrowed $5000 from Bonfondeo in October, 1966, and settled with him on December 15, 1967, three days before his resignation as Commissioner and three days prior to his indictment. Mr. Marcus was said to have paid $5000 interest on this loan, at an annual rate of 104 percent. Two other victims mentioned in the indictment were said to have paid interest at the annual rate of 260 percent. It was not made clear whether the alleged $5000 loan to Marcus was completely independent of the $40,000 he is said to have borrowed from Corallo. In either case, the interest payments could only have contributed to, not solved, Marcus' financial problems.

Smith and Lambert insist that Corallo deliberately made the loan to Marcus as a means of corrupting him. There is no sound reason to doubt this theory. "Favors," not a mere $14,000 a year in interest, seemed to be Corallo's objective. One favor he received for his efforts was the awarding of the reservoir contract, complete with its

kickback clause. There were additional "favors." Marcus was indicted three times by New York authorities in connection with
other conspiracies, and he pleaded guilty in each case. In a statement made before passing sentence on Marcus, the presiding judge
commented that the "reservoir fix was not an isolated affair." The
reservoir conspiracy, he said, was part of a broader plot for "the
infiltration of sinister elements into government."

In July, 1968, the millionaire contractor who made the $40,000
pay-off was sentenced to a two-year prison term for his part in the
conspiracy. At his trial he testified that he paid the $40,000 as a
"finder's fee" because he was afraid his construction business would
be ruined by strong-arm Cosa Nostra tactics if he did not. The pay-off
was demanded by a man he had known as a "labor consultant" for
twenty-five years: "I knew he was connected with the Cosa Nostra.
He was a muscleman who wouldn't hesitate to put the arm on an
individual. I knew if he gave me a command I would adhere to it.
His word was law." The contractor went on to say he knew the
"labor consultant's" reputation as an extortionist and reported he
knew there would be "union trouble" if he did not pay—"a slowdown
of the drill runners, the laborers, the engineers."

To my knowledge, no analysis of the economics of usury, including
analysis of the kinds of customers loan sharks have, or how much or
how often each type of customer borrows, has ever been completed.
The first study of this kind is being undertaken by John Seidel, a
graduate student at Harvard. Many victims of usury operations are
compulsive or eager gamblers. Others, like James Marcus, are ordinary businessmen with financial problems arising from activities
that are on the margin between honesty and dishonesty. Still others
are working men who need a few dollars to carry them over to next
pay day.

Any self-respecting illegal gambling casino or dice game has a
resident loan shark. If a regular customer who has gone broke
wants to make one more pass of the dice or wants to look at one
more poker hand, the loan shark will finance the gamble for him,
usually at only 10 percent interest—for twenty-four hours. If the
gambler wins, he repays his financier on the spot. If he loses, he
has borrowed the lost money from the loan shark and must repay

it within twenty-four hours. Fair enough. As security for the loan, the gambler puts up his body.

The pattern is the same among other types of loan-shark customers. Sometimes owners of small businesses borrow to save their skins when legitimate channels of credit are closed. Narcotics addicts borrow to purchase heroin. Loan sharks borrow from loan sharks in order to finance their loan sharking. Factory workers who lose money to the resident bookmaker discover that the resident bookmaker is also a resident loan shark. The bookmaker-usurer will be glad to loan them money not only to cover gambling losses but also for such legitimate needs as rent, medical bills, and beer. Like other victims of loan sharks, factory workers put up their bodies as collateral.

The interest rates are not constant. Usurers get whatever interest they can get. The commonest loan is the "six for five," which means that next Saturday you pay me six dollars for each five I hand you today. It comes to 20 percent per week. For $400, you pay $80 per week each week until such time as a lump payment of $480 is made. You leave an envelope containing $80 with a tavern owner each Saturday. The payments are due exactly at noon on Saturday, and if you come in at 12:15 at the end of the first week, you owe me another week's interest—on $480, not on $400.

Interest rates can be as low as one percent a week, and as high as 150 percent per week. The variation depends on four conditions—the relationship between the lender and borrower, the intended use of the money, the size of the loan, and the repayment potential. Some loan sharks service a neighborhood in the way a barber or shoe repairman services it. Their "six for five" interest rates on loans made to community residents do not fluctuate much. Even when their capital (often borrowed from a bigger loan shark) diminishes, they do not raise their rates. Loans are viewed as having a price rather than an interest rate, and the price tends to be steady, just as the neighborhood barber's or shoemaker's prices tend to be steady. This type of loan shark often doubles as a bookmaker. Other loan sharks specialize in financing gamblers, at interest rates not lower than 5 percent a week—260 percent a year. Still a third type, occupying higher Cosa Nostra echelons, loan large sums, at rates of one or 2

percent per week, to other loan sharks and to rather affluent businessmen. Such a man is an especially important figure in the Cosa
Nostra organization because he channels the syndicate's proceeds
from bet-taking and narcotics into highly profitable circulation. He
is known in police and Cosa Nostra circles as a "money mover."

The boss of one Cosa Nostra "family" is said to have given a
half-million dollars in cash, divided five ways, to five of his lieutenants for Christmas. The only obligation of each man was to repay him
$150,000 within a year. Despite the strings attached to the Christmas
presents, the lieutenants were delighted. They knew that $100,000 in
capital would much more than double itself in the usury market
place within a year. The gesture was something like that of an honest
grandpa giving each of his honest descendants a legitimate loan of
$100,000 and asking them to repay it at an annual interest rate of
only one percent. The difference is this: In Cosa Nostra if you invest
so unwisely that you are unable to repay, grandpa might kill you.

Usurers have "collectors" as their assistants. These men do not
send dunning letters. One Chicago collector likes to refer to himself as "The Leg Breaker." Murder, however, is frowned upon by
usurers. Loan sharks go to great lengths to avoid killing the goose
that lays the golden eggs. They execute debtors only when those
debtors trespass against them, or when they believe it is time to set
an example or two for all debtors and potential debtors. The usurer
is not likely to insist on payment of the principal unless he himself
is indebted to a usurer.

Interest is another matter. The loan shark's objective is to take
every dime the borrower can lay his hands on, and he often suc-
ceeds. We shall see later that some of the legitimate businesses owned
by Cosa Nostra members were collected as payments on usurious
loans. The New York State Commission of Investigation in late 1964
showed that 121 of the "high-echelon members" of the five New
York City Cosa Nostra "families" were engaged in loan-sharking.

The interest on any loan of $10,000 is high enough to drive a
prosperous businessman into bankruptcy. At 20 percent interest per
week, such a loan costs $104,000 a year. After the borrower has
been bled white, two sequential courses of action are taken. First,
he is told to get more money. To stress the seriousness of this re-

quest, the usurer is likely to ask leading questions about the routes the borrower's children take to school, or about the shopping and social habits of his wife. These thinly veiled threats often send the borrower to father-in-law, uncle, and grandpa for all the money they possess. But if the borrower's desperate fund-raising campaign fails to produce more money, the usurer hires a goon to hang the borrower out a hotel window by his legs, to break his arms, to kick him in the stomach, or to take similar action. Collectors usually work on a commission basis, receiving half the amount of interest they collect.

In Philadelphia, a jeweler with a penchant for gambling was the valued client of a local usurer because he repaid his loans punctually. The jeweler introduced two of his friends to the usurer, not knowing that he thereby was automatically guaranteeing their interest payments. But the friends missed a few payments and took off for California, leaving the jeweler liable for their debts and interest. Four goons showed up at the jeweler's store and glared at him. The jeweler even cashed bad checks to pay his friends' loans, but he couldn't make it. He was invited to visit the usurer, and he accepted the invitation. Upon his arrival, the four goons—"one looked like King Kong"—put him in his own car, drove him through an alley, beat him on the head with a club, stopped the car, took him to the back room of a restaurant, beat him with a blackjack, returned him to the car, and knocked out two of his teeth with a whiskey bottle. They then put him in the trunk of his car and drove around for about a half-hour. After more beating with the blackjack, he was again taken to the basement of the restaurant, handcuffed to an overhead pipe in a walk-in refrigerator, and punched in the stomach by all four men, working in a relay. Then he was released, but without his car. He took a taxi to a hospital where he was informed, the next day, that the $2,000 car would pay $500 worth of the debts and that if he didn't sign over the title, he would owe the usurer $100 a week interest. When he went home that night, he called his girl friend, who told him she had received two threatening telephone calls, one of them saying, "If [borrower] don't pay the loan we'll cut off your teats and send them to him in a box."

When he is certain that no more money can be squeezed out of his victim, the usurer generously "stops the clock," meaning that interest is no longer compounded on the indebtedness. Sometimes the clock is stopped for an indefinite time—until the borrower "gets back on his feet"—but more frequently it is stopped for a specified period of time, such as a year. After this respite, the clock starts ticking again, as do the window hangings, the arm breakings, and the beatings.

Indebtedness to a usurer, thus, literally places one in the clutches of criminals, as when the creditor hangs the debtor out a hotel window by his legs. To avoid such physical experimentation, the debtor sometimes gets into the clutches of criminals in a more figurative way. A young employee of a stockbroker speculated unwisely and illegally. His accounts became short about $20,000. He scraped together part of this amount, then borrowed the remainder from a usurer, at interest of 20 percent a week. He was able to pay the interest and repay the capital without incident. Believing he had a good thing going, he repeated this pattern three times within the next year. While he was in the process of paying off his fourth loan, he discovered that one of his friends was in a predicament similar to that arising from his own first shortage. He did him the favor of referring him to his usurer, who generously agreed that one percent of the interest paid by the friend would apply to the young man's loan, provided the young man guaranteed payment of his friend's principal and interest. This arrangement was so agreeable that the young man soon brought in a second friend, who was granted a usurious loan under the same conditions. But it developed that neither of the friends could keep up the payments on their loans, and then the trouble started. When the young man went to the loan shark to talk the matter over, a goon punched him in the stomach. The loan shark and the goon told him they would kill him if all the debts were not settled. A few weeks later he was forced into an automobile, driven to a secluded spot, and hit over the head with a blackjack. Eventually the loan shark stopped the clock, but by now the young man had lost his job and was financially desperate. The loan shark and his backers (whom he called "the boys uptown" and who were Cosa Nostra figures) ordered him to dispose of some stocks that had been stolen in a recent burglary. Fortunately, the young man went to the police instead. Cosa Nostra involvement in three areas of crime—burglary of the stock, usury, and selling the stolen stock—was achieved by excellent organization, which worked to the great disadvantage of the young stockbroker's assistant.

In a similar case, a lawyer was so indebted to a usurer that he agreed to become a bookmaker in order to repay the debt, and in order to avoid having his arms broken. A famous sports broadcaster, hopelessly indebted to a loan shark, ended up steering his affluent associates to a crooked dice game in order to earn a percentage of their losses, to be applied to his indebtedness. On a less elaborate level, in a scheme to get a liquor license, a usury victim let the usurer use his name as a front. He was paid $100 a week for this service, but he never saw the money—it went as partial payment of the interest on the usurious loan. A New York City hairdresser won credits against his indebtedness to a loan shark by revealing which of his customers might be likely targets for jewel thieves. The loan shark, in turn, passed the information on to other members of his Cosa Nostra "family."

When a man borrows from a usurer, he confers a kind of moral superiority on the usurer and all his associates. Loan sharks know that a borrower comes to them because he is in a vulnerable position, and this vulnerability is translated into moral weakness. The usurers' ensuing position of moral dominance enables them to make the borrowers seem like the villains in the drama. The victims themselves contribute to this conception of moral superiority-inferiority by acknowledging the usurers' "moral right" to collect the indebtedness by use of force. After all, the borrower puts his body up as security for his loan. Perhaps it is the conferred moral superiority of usurers which makes it rather easy for them to convert borrowers into criminals.

The assumption of moral superiority is apparent in the following transcript of a tape-recorded conversation between a borrower and a collector. The latter is not content simply to try to collect money, or even to punch the borrower in the belly. He must reduce the borrower to a subhuman status, "proving" to him that he is not worthy of the company of morally superior men who are willing to assist him—at usurious rates of interest—and who really dislike punching him in the belly. "Jack" is a legitimate businessman who borrowed

$3500 from a loan shark to meet the end-of-the-month bills confronting his small company. The agreement was to pay $175 a week for twenty weeks, after which the principal would be due. This comes to 100 percent for twenty weeks, or about 260 percent per annum. The business failed, and Jack was unable to keep up his payments. The usurer gave the collection contract to a Cosa Nostra collection specialist. Jack then made the mistake of asking another Cosa Nostra member to intercede with the collector. The man agreed, for a fee of $1000. But Jack couldn't pay this debt either, so it was assigned to "Dom," still another Cosa Nostra collector, who pressured Jack to pay him $25 a week for about twelve weeks. Dom then became the collector for the original loan shark, for the usurer's collector, for the man that interceded, and for himself. In desperation, Jack went to the police, agreed to the bugging of his room, told Dom he was leaving town, and waited (with policemen in the next room) for Dom to arrive.

DOM. Son of a bitch. (Inaudible. Sound of door closing.) What are you doing here?

JACK. What am I doing here?

DOM. What are you doing?

JACK. Look. Look. One minute.

DOM. I told you I don't want no part of this activity. I was here earlier. I want to convince you that——— I told you, I tried to convince you. (Inaudible.) I don't give a shit what you do now. I'll meet you downstairs. (Inaudible.) I'll meet you by your car. [Dom is looking for a bug.]

JACK. You won't find one. You won't find one. That's all I got to say.

DOM. He's doing the right thing by you.

JACK. What do you mean, he's doing the right thing? He isn't doing the right thing. He isn't doing the right thing.

DOM. What's on your mind, Jack? Why this bullshit? Why?

JACK. Look, I can't take any more of this. (Inaudible. Both talking.) I can't take any more of this.

DOM. What you fucking around with the guy for? Grab eighteen hundred? You ain't even a fucking man, do you know that? You ain't even a man. (Both talking.)

JACK. All I'm doing is paying out and paying out through my nose.

DOM. What are you paying? What are you paying?

JACK. I paid you. I paid everybody. (Both talking.) Paid everybody.

Dom. What have you paid? Paid the Court?

Jack. I paid you. I paid the Court. I paid everybody.

Dom. How much money you got left?

Jack. I'm not giving no money any more, Dominic. I'm not going to give any money. I can't. I'm going away. I'm taking off. I'm leaving. I'm not giving any more money. I've had it. I need the money. I'm taking off and I'm leaving everything.

Dom. What do you accomplish? What do you accomplish, Jack?

Jack. What do I accomplish?

Dom. Yeah.

Jack. I get rid of everything. (Both talking.) I'm giving money on all sides.

Dom. Did you take this money? Did you take this fucking money?

Jack. Not from you. (Both talking.) I didn't take it. Not from you I didn't take it.

Dom. Who'd you take it?

Jack. I didn't take it from (inaudible) neither. The money I'm paying you I didn't take it from you.

Dom. Who'd you take it, Jack? The money I'm taking from you?

Jack. I didn't take it from you. You didn't take it out of your pocket.

Dom. Who did you take this money from?

Jack. Who'd I take it from?

Dom. Who'd you take it from?

Jack. I didn't take it from anybody. I didn't take the money from you.

Dom. Who'd you take it from?

Jack. The money I'm paying you, I didn't take it from you.

Dom. Am I shaking you down in other words you're telling me? Am I shaking you down?

Jack. Well, aren't you? Aren't you?

Dom. You say I'm shaking you down? I'm shaking you down? I'll bust your fucking mouth. I'm shaking you down? You prick. I'm shaking you down?

Jack. Look, Dom, cut it out now.

Dom. Cut it out? What you mean, cut it out? You made a fucking patsy out of me, you cunt.

Jack. I didn't make no patsy out of nobody.

Dom. What you mean, you didn't make no patsy out of nobody?

Jack. What kind of patsy did I make?

Dom. (Inaudible.) You were trying to fuck me from the beginning. Those were your intentions from the beginning. Those were your intentions from the beginning.

JACK. Nothing was my intentions. Just circumstances brought it around. I'm not paying no more. I can't pay no more.

DOM. You ain't leaving. You ain't leaving. I'm telling you, you ain't leaving, Jack. (Both talking.) I want you to raise your hand to me. I want you to raise your hand to me because I'll knock you fucking dead. (Inaudible.) I'll let you go back to work.

JACK. Cut it out now.

DOM. Cut it out? Give me my—— how much money you got?

JACK. I'm not giving no money out.

DOM. You ain't leaving this fucking town. Just forget about it. No matter where the fuck you go, I'll find you. (Both talking.) Because you are hard on. (Inaudible.) Because you are fucking hard on.

JACK. I'm leaving. I'm leaving.

DOM. You can't be good to a cuntlapper like you because you are fucking hard on. You—— for eighteen hundred dollars. I don't give a fuck. You can keep the eighteen hundred and go and blow the fucking thing.

JACK. I ain't paying no more money to nobody.

DOM. For eighteen hundred dollars you're running away from your fucking wife and kids. You are a real cuntlapper.

JACK. It's not eighteen hundred dollars. It's a lot of money—a lot of money—and I ain't got it and I ain't going to pay anymore. I'm not going to pay any more. I've had it. I've had it. I'm up to my ears in debt from all sides. I'm paying. (Inaudible.)

DOM. You ain't paying nobody.

JACK. I paid you, didn't I?

DOM. What did you pay me? Seven hundred dollars. At twenty-five dollars a week.

JACK. All right. That's it.

DOM. Didn't I go along with you? Give you a fucking break?

JACK. Well, I—well, I can't pay anymore. I owe the city. I owe this guy. I owe that guy. (Inaudible.) As far as I'm concerned, I'm just waiting now to take off.

DOM. You ain't taking off, Jack. You may take off if I call a fucking ambulance. Maybe you take off in a fucking ambulance. That's the only way you're taking off.

JACK. I'm gonna leave. I'm leaving town one way or another. (Sound of Dom assaulting Jack.) I've just had it, Dominic. That's all. I've just had it. I can't pay any more.

DOM. What you want to do? What you want to do now? What do you

want to do? I tell you, you ain't leaving. What do you want to do?
What do you want to do? What do you want to do now?

JACK. Look, Dom, you're not going to accomplish nothing by beating
me up. You know that. You're not going to accomplish nothing.

DOM. The money.

JACK. There's no money. I don't have it with me. I got it in my car.
I got the money in my car.

DOM. Well, go downstairs and get the fucking money.

JACK. I'm not going out of here with you, Dominic. I'm not leaving.

DOM. I'll carry you out.

JACK. You're going to have to then. You're going to have to carry me
out. (Pause while Dom telephones his supervisor for instructions,
mostly inaudible.)

JACK. I've got a million things here. They're investigating me. Every
goddam thing. I don't want it any more. I don't want the damn thing
any more. I don't want no part of it.

DOM. I don't give a fuck if you go and fuck yourself.

JACK. Nobody cares. I don't care either. I don't care either at the moment. What's going to happen? Someone going to knock me down?
That's. (Telephone rings and Dom answers it. Inaudible.) I can tell
you, there's no more blood from a stone. That's it. That's it. I earn,
I earn money and all I do is pay it out. I pay it out.

DOM. Tell me who you are paying it to?

JACK. I pay the city. I pay you. I'm gonna pay that bank. You know that
they're not all paid off yet. (Inaudible.) I got to pay you. Everybody.
Everybody is on my neck. Everytime I turn around, I'm paying somebody money. (Inaudible.) I'm taking off and I'm running. That's all.

DOM. Not with my fucking money you ain't. Who do you—who the
fuck you think you are?

JACK. Dom, it isn't your money I'm taking. I'm not taking your money.
It's not you took money out of your pocket for me. Did you take
the money out of your pocket for me?

DOM. Hey, stool pigeon.

JACK. What's that got to do with you?

DOM. You took plenty of money from me. And you took plenty of
money from them. (Both talking.) What do you want to do? What
do you want to do? What do you want to do? Tell me what you want
to do, Jack. I do anything you want to do. (Inaudible.) Do whatever
you want to do. You had eleven hundred, you had eleven hundred
dollars that you paid. That's seven hundred plus eleven. I don't even

want the seven hundred. It's going back to fucking Joe, your cousin. That's where it's going. I don't want nothing. (Both talking.) I don't give a fuck. (Inaudible.) He wouldn't have gave you that fucking money if I wasn't there, and what do you want to do, Jack? What do you want to do, Jack?

JACK. He knows what I mean. Joe knows what I'm doing. Joe knows what I'm doing. Whether he knows it or not.

DOM. Now give me my fucking money. Three hundred dollars more you owe me personally.

JACK. I don't owe you any money.

DOM. I say you owe me three hundred.

JACK. I don't owe you any money, Dominic.

DOM. Jack, I say you owe me——

JACK. I don't owe you—— (Both talking.)

DOM. I say you owe me three fucking hundred. Now I want my fucking money. (Sound of Dom assaulting Jack.) Or, I'll put you down the fucking hill. Give it to me. Give it to me.

JACK. I don't have it. (Sound of Dom assaulting Jack.) Owwwwww.

DOM. I've been fucking nice to you. You prick, you give me my fucking money.

JACK. Look, I don't have it. I don't have your money.

DOM. You don't have it?

JACK. I spent it on an airline ticket.

DOM. It's downstairs in your fucking car.

JACK. No. I gave it to the airlines.

DOM. You didn't spend no seven hundred dollars on a fucking airplane. You ain't going to Europe, you prick, you. I want to be nice to you. I told you forget about everything. I want nothing. Go back to work. Don't leave town. No. You gotta fuck around like the little cuntlapper that you are. (Inaudible.)

JACK. Look, I gotta run because of this and a million other things. (Inaudible.) I'm not going to—— I'm not going to take this any more. (Sound of Dom assaulting Jack.)

DOM. Jack, don't. Don't stop me, Jack. Please don't let me—— (Sound of assault and of door being forced open.)

POLICE OFFICER. Turn around. Turn around and hit the wall.

Generally speaking, Cosa Nostra usurers have learned that a borrower who is hopelessly in debt should be used, not killed or even maimed. Usurer's victims are increasingly becoming the "inside men" in a wide variety of crimes. Even if they manage to repay their loans by means of crime, their troubles do not stop. After a man has agreed that the alternative to being killed or injured is to commit crimes whose proceeds will be used to repay an indebtedness, he finds that he really has agreed to commit crime in order to insure his own safety. The indebtedness has nothing to do with it.

Some of the businesses that look like legitimate loan companies are merely fronts for usury operations. The employees of these fronts serve principally to locate needy persons who look like good loan-shark victims. But the institutions themselves serve to mask the illegality of the usurer's operations. They are loan sharks' loan sharks, lending to usurers huge sums which they, in turn, have obtained from legitimate banks. It is a short step from illegal usury—with its efficient system of extortionate enforcement—to legal money lending, especially through factoring. Among other things, a "factor" provides money to business firms in exchange for the signing over of accounts receivable, which the factor then collects. Factors also make loans against other collateral, however. In late 1963 Frank Sacco, described by United States Attorney Robert M. Morganthau as a "Cosa Nostra associate," was indicted in New York on a charge involving the theft of stock certificates. An article in the *Wall Street Journal* reported that Mr. Sacco was the sole owner of two legitimate factoring firms in New York City. Factoring, like loan-sharking itself, is an excellent device for invading legitimate businesses. Mr. Morgenthau, for some time a highly successful prosecutor of organized criminals, described the process as follows:

A hoodlum will lend a businessman money at high rates. If the businessman is unable to pay up, he soon finds himself with a new partner. The hoodlum will take over part, or most, of the business and retain the respectable businessman as a front.

Someone estimates the cost of everything. The McClellan Committee estimated that the drug addicts in the United States spend about $350 million a year for heroin. The Committee estimated, further, that narcotics importers and wholesalers had a standard income of about 6 percent of this gross, something like the stockholders of a public-utilities corporation. This puts the profit of a few Cosa Nostra members, who are in the business of importing and wholesaling narcotics, at about $21 million annually.

Members of Cosa Nostra do not hustle a hundred dollars here and a hundred dollars there selling heroin to dope fiends. The profits in this retail operation are too low, and the risks are too great. Transactions with addicts are handled by independent "dealers" (the word "pusher" is rarely used on the street) who work like dogs to keep up their own habits or, consistently, their own cool style of living. Dealers make a dollar wherever they can find it. They usually have a few "holes" (women) whoring for them, and they might fence stolen property now and then. In fact, they might even steal the property before they fence it. Some own apartment houses or other income-producing property that doesn't take too much time away from their hustle. Such street-level narcotics dealers are indispensable to Cosa Nostra. Later we will show that they play roles which might be considered parts of the organization. However, the dealers rarely are members of Cosa Nostra.

Gambling money moves upward from the street through at least six levels of a personnel hierarchy. Narcotics move downward through the same hierarchy, except that they are not ordinarily handled by the street-level workers serving as bookmakers and lottery-ticket salesmen. Narcotics retailers do not work on the sharecropper plan utilized by bookmakers and lottery operators. Because the heroin business involves a commodity rather than a service, it operates like a legitimate importing-distributing-wholesaling-retailing business. Each member of the personnel hierarchy buys and then sells. The street-level dealer is an independent businessman who purchases at wholesale prices and sells at retail prices. He might or might not be required to buy from a specific wholesaler, at risk of his life. If the dealer, or anyone else in the heroin industry, doesn't have enough money to finance his purchases, he can always borrow from a usurer. Narcotics operators are good usury risks because drug addicts desperately need the product they have for sale.

At the top are importers of multi-kilo lots. At the next level are "kilo men," who handle nothing less than a kilogram of heroin at a time. A kilo man makes his purchase from an importer-supplier and receives delivery from a courier. He dilutes the heroin by adding three kilograms of milk sugar for each kilo of heroin. The product is then sold to "quarter-kilo men" and then to "ounce men" and then to "deck men," there being further adulteration at each stage in this process. Eventually, street dealers dispense it in five-grain packets called "bags" or "packs" or "balloons." The cost to the consumer is in excess of three hundred times the cost of the original kilo.

Use of the "kilo man" term varies from community to community. Sometimes it refers to all the men working at the three highest levels in the business organization—the importer, the man who buys from the importer, and the man to whom it is sold in bulk lots. This *third* man, rather than the second man, sells the drug to the "quarter-kilo men." In the San Francisco area, the "kilo man" terminology is rarely used, but the level of what is called "the big-time dealer" is about the same as that of "kilo men" in other cities. The "big-time dealer" buys heroin in pound lots, delivered by "runners" (couriers), who bring it from Los Angeles, at $3500 to $4000 per pound. The "big-time dealer" adds about 94 to 98 percent milk sugar to the heroin and sells it to a "piece man" at $250 an ounce. The "piece man" sells in ounce lots to a "spoon man," who cuts the ounces and sells to a "bag man," who in turn may divide the "spoons" into $10 "balloons" (¼ to ½ gram). Most street-level dealers handle "big bags," or "spoons," of about 2 grams and costing from $40 to $60, depending on the percentage of heroin. In the course of a year, a dealer may slide up and down the scale from "pieces" to "balloons," but Alan G. Sutter has shown that the prestige rests with the "piece man," and organizational positions for "piece men" persist, as do the other positions, even if they are vacated by specific dealers.

A major portion of the heroin used in the United States comes originally from Turkey. The heroin traffic is organized like an hourglass, with ten to fifteen Cosa Nostra members occupying the center section. The top section consists of hundreds of Turkish farmers, each of whom produces a small crop, and dozens of processors who refine the raw material first in Syria and Lebanon and then in southern France and Italy. The bottom section of the hourglass consists of the "piece men" or "quarter-kilo men" and all the street-level salesmen beneath them. The farmer in Turkey gets about $35 per pure kilogram of opium, and the addicts of New York pay about $225,000 for this much unadulterated heroin.

The bookmaker or lottery operator might be required, at risk of his life, to split his gross with a Cosa Nostra clique. Members of Cosa Nostra, thus, rely on control of a large number of local bookmaking and lottery operations for their huge profits. However, the heroin business is not, on the retail level, organized like bookmaking is. Territory is not allocated, financial backing is not provided, and protection from arrest and imprisonment is not offered, let alone guaranteed. That is why dealing in heroin on the street is so much riskier than taking bets. Dealing is not riskier than bookmaking simply because the penalties for selling heroin are greater than the penalties for taking bets; the difference lies in the fact that the dealer has no organization behind him. A member of the Cosa Nostra "family" operating in a city might require that heroin dealers in his area buy from him or die, but once the dealer buys his drugs from the syndicate he is on his own. He does the best he can.

The importation and wholesale distribution of narcotics takes huge amounts of cash, like usury. Just anyone cannot get into the business. Even without the risks of imprisonment, the illegal business is risky enough. Fortunes are lost whenever a big shipment of narcotics is confiscated by customs agents or other law-enforcement officials. About 20 percent of the attempted flow is confiscated. Perhaps a shipment is hijacked now and then, as truckloads and shiploads of alcohol were hijacked during the period of prohibition, but I have never heard of such an event occurring at the importation or wholesaling levels. The demand for heroin is great, and the fact that heroin is illegal makes it horribly expensive. For persons who are willing to risk imprisonment, who have enough capital to finance huge purchases, and who have enough additional capital to carry them through huge but temporary losses stemming from confiscations, the profits are enormous. Cosa Nostra members have these characteristics. Other persons also have them, of course, and for that reason Cosa Nostra has competitors in the narcotics importation and wholesaling business, especially on the West Coast.

Because American business and industry has been extensively unionized, industrialists and businessmen seek black-market labor. Cosa Nostra meets this demand, and frequently cheats the business-men who make it. Fraud, extortion, and bribery are the basic crimes involved when Cosa Nostra members work as labor brokers. But these same crimes, plus income-tax evasion, are the foundations of all the organizations' activities. In order to differentiate Cosa Nostra's activities in the labor field from its activities elsewhere, law-enforce-ment personnel some years ago began using the term "labor racketeer-ing" to refer to the former. Unfortunately, this term directs our at-tention away from the fact that all Cosa Nostra operations are, basic-ally, racketeering. It is quite appropriate to speak of Cosa Nostra involvement in "usury racketeering," "business racketeering," and even, in the case of monopolizing illegal bet-taking businesses, "rack-eteering racketeering." All involve extortion of the kind used by Lord Clive, founder of the British Empire in India, who in his youth formed a gang of fellow delinquents to collect tribute from shop-owners who did not wish to have their windows broken. All take organization.

Four fundamental operations are involved when Cosa Nostra members become labor brokers. Three of the operations, in their many variations, are provided as a service to greedy, crooked, or shady businessmen who have created the demand for a cheap supply of labor. In the fourth kind of operation, the Cosa Nostra member steals from his own union.

First, real unionization of some businesses is prevented by pre-tending, for a fee, that the shops are unionized. Nine men riding in two convertible-topped automobiles parked by the door of a sand-wich shop. Two Cosa Nostra men walked into the shop. One handed the proprietor a business card and said, "You got to sign up with this union, right now." The proprietor, who had only four employees, replied, "I can't give you the answer right now." The second Cosa

Nostra member was a bit persuasive: "Listen, you better sign, otherwise we know where you live." The man signed, but his employees never were really unionized. The employer paid their "initiation fee" and he regularly paid their "dues," all of which were simply pay-offs to the two men. He was never asked for a list of his employees, and the employees had no idea that they were union members. Since he paid his employees wages lower than the rates set by legitimate unions, the apparent extortion turned out to be a pretty jolly affair for all except the workers.

For a larger business, $5000 a year is a cheap price for a nonunion "unionized" shop. One trucking firm is so well known to be controlled by Cosa Nostra that it is called a "mob's barn." The company is "unionized," but the workers do not get union wages. There is no "union trouble" in this company.

Second, in a variation of the first operation, employees are made members of fictitious "paper locals" which have been established in part to help greedy employers reduce labor costs. In the "sweetheart-contract" operation, a Cosa Nostra member for a fee writes a labor contract that cheats the workers out of wages and benefits they could legitimately obtain at the bargaining table. For example, most union contracts specify the names of the holidays to which the employees are entitled—New Year's, Christmas, Easter, Fourth of July, Rosh Hashonah, Passover, Washington's Birthday, Thanksgiving Day. But "sweetheart contracts" might restrict employees to only one or two holidays a year. In one such contract negotiated by the stupid Cosa Nostra president of a paper local, the only holiday granted to a work force made up exclusively of Catholic Puerto Ricans was Passover. A man who could neither read nor write was vice president of one fictitious Cosa Nostra local.

A company that manufactures chairs suddenly stopped manufacturing the cushions for the chairs. It began to purchase them, instead, from a newly formed company which was owned by a Cosa Nostra member. Shortly thereafter, a new union local was formed, and the son of the cushion company's owner became president of it. The union then "organized" both the chair company and the cushion company. About a dozen friends and relatives of the cushion-company owner were put on the payroll of the chair company.

In a beautiful double cross, two Cosa Nostra members acting as business agents for a real union local agreed to let a shopkeeper pay them fees for a highly favorable contract. But later they went back for more. They told the shopkeeper that they had never reported the fraudulent contract to the local, then handed him a new contract with a different local, and demanded another pay-off. The shopkeeper paid, but he reported the matter to the district attorney, who convicted the two men of extortion, despite the fact that the shopkeeper's hands were by no means clean. But the district attorney never was able to find the second local, which simply disappeared. Its address was the same as that of a Cosa Nostra leader's office, but no union records could be found.

Fictitious locals are business properties. A low-level Cosa Nostra member engaged in gambling, usury, and narcotics financing simply purchased, for $30,000, a small-town union local from a Cosa Nostra boss. Later he sold a part interest in the local to a friend.

Third, employers are threatened with labor strife or mayhem if they do not pay under-the-table fees to the Cosa Nostra members heading union locals, "paper" or otherwise. This, of course, is the outright extortion called "labor racketeering." It need not be, however. One man paid a union to picket his competitor, believing that the competitor wouldn't be able to pay them off because he had already done so. He was wrong. The competitor paid the officers of the local a higher fee, and they picketed the originator of the plot.

It is not at all unusual for a Cosa Nostra union official to engage in a mild form of extortion by demanding that his relatives be put on the company payroll. In another thinly veiled form of extortion, some Cosa Nostra union "leaders" demand that the employing company hire them as "labor consultants." One company avoids paying some of its income taxes by overpaying one of its suppliers and then secretly taking the overpayment back. It uses the same scheme to bribe the president of a union local. Thus, it overpays a Cosa Nostra member for merchandise supplied by him. This man, in turn, passes the overpayment on to a second Cosa Nostra member, who is president of the local.

Cosa Nostra members have effectively used the National Labor Relations Board as part of their pressure for extortion. One man stated his "paper local's" terms to a shopkeeper, who refused them. The crook threatened to report him to the NLRB for unwillingness to negotiate, which is an unfair labor practice. As a variant, a Cosa Nostra union leader struck a company so that his brother, owner of a competing company, would get more business.

While some Cosa Nostra men get rich by threatening strikes or slowdowns if businessmen do not pay under-the-table fees, others make a nice living by offering their services in the settling of "labor disputes" of this kind. In April, 1968, *The New York Times* reported that a grand jury had indicted the vice president of Spartan Industries—of which the billion-dollar E. J. Korvette chain of discount stores is a wholly owned subsidiary—for perjuring himself in testimony about such an arrangement. The indictment said the vice president had made a move for labor peace by seeking the aid of three hoodlums, two of them reputed Cosa Nostra leaders. In return for the help of the three "labor consultants," companies formed by them were to be given contracts to provide Korvette's with basic services such as window washing and garbage collection. The vice president was to share in the profits of the companies. Specifically, the indictment charged that the vice president had committed perjury when he told a grand jury he had never asked a reputed lieutenant in a New York Cosa Nostra "family" to help him persuade an unidentified labor union official to "lay off" in his demands. The case has not yet come up for trial.

Fourth, funds are stolen or otherwise obtained illegally from union funds or from union pension and welfare systems. This varies from the simple fraud of putting one's wife on the payroll to overpaying a consultant for services rendered. Funds are commonly embezzled by sending large checks to lawyers for nonexistent services. One local borrowed money from its own welfare fund, then used the money to buy Cadillacs for each of its Cosa Nostra officials. Two union locals jointly "purchased" a Cosa Nostra member's summer home for $150,000 but never used it. One union official bought a great deal of jewelry at one store with embezzled union funds. He was reported to the police by an irate union member who happened to notice the purchase and said, "Something crooked must be going on as no one pays full retail prices for jewelry, especially union officers who have many contacts."

The industries which seem to be most susceptible to shakedowns and to connivance between employers and union officials are those employing unskilled or only semiskilled labor. Significantly, it is the unions serving such industries that are most likely to be controlled by Cosa Nostra members. Many of the New York companies engaged in housewrecking are nonunion, and even the companies having union contracts hire nonunion personnel on occasion. There is a saving of some $2.50 per hour per man, and this difference permits the dishonest company to underbid the honest companies, even when the dishonest company must pay an illegal fee to a corrupt union official. Cosa Nostra members seek control of the officers of union locals so they can get a share of the pay-offs. "Control" may be secured legitimately, by helping an officer win a union election. More frequently it is achieved illegitimately, by outright extortion from an honest or dishonest official.

The American demand for illicit goods and services produces huge Cosa Nostra profits, which are then invested in legitimate enterprises and in politics. Robert F. Kennedy made the following statement while he was Attorney General of the United States: "What is at least disturbing—and for me insidious—is the increasing encroachment of the big businessmen of the rackets into legitimate business." Cosa Nostra members have been, and are, acquiring and operating legitimate enterprises, ranging from Las Vegas casinos to huge corporations, to butcher shops, to restaurants and bars. Moreover, some of them have deposited huge sums in Swiss banks, and they draw on these fruits of crime whenever they want to buy or corrupt another large piece of America. Carmine Lombardozzi, a New York Cosa Nostra leader, once obtained control of a Wall Street brokerage house, and used it fraudulently to sell stock to the public.

The business interests of the men attending the 1957 meeting at the estate of Joseph Barbara in Apalachin, New York, probably are representative of the kinds of legitimate businesses which have been acquired by organized criminals everywhere. It should be noted, however, that no one has learned the extent of the concealed business interests held even by the Apalachin conferees. Besides their illicit businesses, at least nine of them were in the coin-machine business; sixteen were in the garment industry; ten owned grocery stores; seventeen owned bars or restaurants; eleven were in the olive-oil and cheese importing business; nine were in the construction business. Others were involved in automobile agencies, coal companies, entertainment, funeral homes, ownership of horses and race tracks, linen and laundry enterprises, trucking, waterfront activities, and bakeries. According to Peter Andreoli, Assistant District Attorney for New York County and a top-ranking expert on the investigation and prosecuting of organized criminals, the host of the meeting was the operator of the Endicott, New York, branch of the Canada Dry Bottling Company; Dominic Alaimo of Pittson, Pennsylvania, was co-owner of the Hogan Dress Company and was a committeeman of Local 8005 of the United Mine Workers of America; Russell Bufalino owned the Penn Drape and Curtain Company in Pittson, Pennsylvania; Joseph Bonanno of Brooklyn and Tucson was the owner of the Colorado Cheese Company of Trinidad, Colorado; Roy Carise of Buffalo owned a restaurant in that city; Paul Castellano of Brooklyn owned the Emcie Markets, a chain of six stores; Vito Genovese was treasurer of County Line Steel Corporation in Amityville, New York, and had an interest in the Erb Strapping Company in New York; Joseph Profaci owned the United Uniform Corporation, the G & P Coal Company, the Carmella Mia Packing Company, and an olive-oil business.

There are four possible combinations of legitimate-illegitimate acquisition and legitimate-illegitimate operation of businesses, and Cosa Nostra members participate in all of them. Some businesses are legitimately purchased with the fruits of crime and operated legitimately. Others are legitimately purchased with the fruits of crime and operated illegitimately. A third possibility involves illegitimate acquisition and legitimate operation, while the fourth alternative is to acquire a business illegitimately and then to operate it illegitimately. No outsider knows which of these four types is dominant. There is a tendency to look at Las Vegas, where until recently the profits from illegal bet-taking and other crimes were secretly invested in certain legitimate casinos which were operated illegally (at least so far as income-tax payments are concerned), and then to assume that all businesses owned by Cosa Nostra members are operated illegally. It is quite possible, however, that most of the legitimate businesses owned by Cosa Nostra members are operated legitimately, at least most of the time.

Thus it should not be concluded that all the Cosa Nostra members investing in legitimate business are "compleat crooks." One incentive for entering legitimate business is the hope of becoming respectable. Although members see "nothing wrong" with their activities, they nevertheless are sensitive to public criticism. One Cosa Nostra ruler who is pretty much of a monster indicated great concern because, in his opinion, the newspapers portray him as a monster. No one knows what proportion, if any, of the members enter legitimate business and then settle down to a legitimate life. It is known, however, that top-level men have "retired" to respectability in the suburbs. William Foote Whyte tells the story of the drive of one low-level member to become respectable:

Joe the Wolf started out as a bodyguard for a prominent gang leader. He had frequent clashes with the law. Once, when a gangster was shot, Joe the Wolf was caught running away from the scene of the crime. He was tried for murder and acquitted. For some time after that Joe was picked up by the police whenever a gang murder had been committed. He complained that he was being hounded. His activities were changing. He made money in the numbers and acquired some legitimate business interests. He played up the respectable side of his career and discouraged the use of his nickname. He refused to allow his daughter to go out with racketeers. She married a man of a respectable family who was engaged in a legitimate business. The elaborate wedding reception attracted a large gathering, including many local businessmen and prominent politicians. Newspaper accounts of the affair described the bride's father as a "well-known sportsman." Although Joseph Lupo is still known to corner boys as Joe the Wolf, he has traveled far toward respectability since his early days.

One Cosa Nostra "family" owns at least $300 million in real estate, and these holdings do not seem to be operated with much more dishonesty than that characterizing other large real-estate operations. Another Cosa Nostra clique offered to lend money to a legitimate corporation on condition that a Cosa Nostra man be appointed to the board of directors and that a nominee selected by the clique be given first option to purchase if there were any outside sales of the company's stock. This offer seems little different from any offer that might be made by a quite legitimate clique with large amounts of capital. Moreover, ownership of businesses is easily concealed, and Cosa Nostra members own many enterprises that have "front men" operating them in a respectable manner. I have no idea who really owns most of the stores where I do business. As Andreoli has said:

Racketeers, primarily concerned with providing an outlet for illegitimate money, concealing it from the taxing authorities and, at the same time, making a profit, acquire undercover ownership of legitimate businesses. A front man acts for the true owner. He is usually not in any way connected with the criminal acts of his principal. He may not even be aware of his principal's criminal activities. Complete control over the front man is maintained. Actual ownership is most difficult to trace and it is impossible to determine how extensive is this kind of infiltration of legitimate enterprises.

It is not unusual for Cosa Nostra members to acquire a small business in payment of a gambling debt. Frequently, however, there is an intermediate step involving a usurious loan to pay the gambling debts. When a small businessman is unable to meet the exorbitant interest payments on a usurious loan he has floated to pay a gambling debt (or to take care of other needs), he finds himself with a partner, usually a silent one. The criminal partner's percentage of the profits might be paid to him merely by adding his name, or the name of his brother-in-law, cousin, or friend, to the company payroll. It might be paid by requiring the original owner to buy some of his supplies, at exorbitant prices, from a company owned by the criminal partner. The "supplies" so purchased might, in fact, be fictitious. Such practices open up new avenues of extortion for the silent partner.

In one case, a restaurant owner who could not make the payments to a loan shark on a gambling debt found that the usurer had declared himself a partner in the business. The silent partner placed his own man in the restaurant as manager. Soon thereafter the real owner learned that he could purchase coal only from a company owned by Cosa Nostra members, at above-market prices. Then he had to turn over the hat-check concession to persons designated by his Cosa Nostra partner. Linen services, food, and other products soon had to be purchased from companies owned by the partner's Cosa Nostra "friends," the term used to designate members of the organization. He was told what entertainers to engage, and he was ordered to hire a Cosa Nostra "labor consultant." He was compelled to furnish free food and drink to parties of Cosa Nostra members who padded into his restaurant.

Occasionally, a legitimate business is acquired simply by walking in and announcing, "I am your partner." It is not uncommon for the criminal establishment to take a small percentage, say 10 percent, of the gross income of all the retail businesses of a certain kind in a community. For example, every bar owner in a midwestern city pays 10 percent of his gross to Cosa Nostra criminals whose representatives simply tell them that they or their business will be harmed if they do not do so. The New York Court of Appeals—the state's highest court—recently reported out an extortion case of this kind:

Irving Holtzman was an executive of several corporations engaged in the distribution and operation of coin operated equipment whose enterprises reached into four of the five boroughs of New York City as well as Nassau and Suffolk Counties. In recent years Mr. Holtzman's business ventures grew and prospered to such an extent that the self-appointed "family" of sharers in the prosperity of honest businessmen determined that the time had come for Mr. Holtzman to share his wealth—"to give up a piece" of his business.

Sometime during the early part of June, 1964, a concerted effort was commenced to extort $25,000 from Mr. Holtzman as well as a 25% share of his business interests. As the arrangement was explained to Mr. Holtzman, "If at the end of (a) week you have $1 left, we take 25 cents and you keep 75 cents."

Mr. Holtzman, unmoved by the "family's" generosity and shaken by an assault on his wife by certain members of the "family," described to him as "animals," contacted the Nassau County police.

During the month of June the police, with the consent of Mr. Holtzman, through the use of wiretaps and bugs, recorded numerous conversations of Mr. Holtzman and Salvatore Granello, known to his "family" and "animals" as Sally Burns. These recordings clearly established the existence of an extortion conspiracy on the part of Granello, Dino Conte and others.

As Mr. Holtzman's adamance persisted through June, the "family" apparently became more anxious. On the morning of June 30, 1964, Mr. Holtzman's daughter, Mrs. Ronald Billings, then pregnant and residing in Plainview, received a call which, from its contents, could only have been made by one of the "animals." Mrs. Billings was advised that "if your father doesn't cooperate we'll come to Sylvia Lane (Plainview) and kick your * * * * pregnant belly in."

A refinement of this "pure extortion" technique involves selling merchants something they do not need, or selling them a needed product at above-market prices. For example, in 1958 Joseph Di Varco, better known as Joey Caesar, was in the business of selling glass-washing machines to Chicago bars and taverns. According to the Chicago Crime Commission, Di Varco also was a "North Side syndicate boss." His salesmen were easily placing the machines in North Side bars by using the simple but convincing sales pitch, "Joey Caesar wants you to buy this machine." Earl Johnson, Jr.—formerly a Special Attorney in the Organized Crime and Racketeering Section of the United States Department of Justice—has emphasized the fact that the whispered name of a Cosa Nostra boss often will inspire as much fear in the hearer as brandishing a loaded revolver in his face. Newspapers and other media sometimes inadvertently contribute to a boss's power by indicating that he is to be feared. For example, Johnny Carson, the television master of ceremonies, once or twice a year mentions the Mafia, then apologizes for doing so, saying something like, "I had better watch out." Sometimes he tells a "joke" about Cosa Nostra's involvement in ruthless extortion and murder.

It is only a short step from such crude extortion to a 50–50 partnership, and then to 100 percent ownership. Loan sharks have taken over ownership of businesses ranging from optical supply stores to night clubs to brick companies. The two partners in a New York furniture store were asked by a member of Cosa Nostra for a percentage of their profits. They ignored the request and one partner was subsequently beaten up. Foolishly, they then asked another member of Cosa Nostra for advice and, even more foolishly, followed his suggestion that they seek assistance from still other Cosa Nostra members. A member of the Profaci-Magliocci-Colombo "family" agreed to provide protection, but it was not long before he announced that he was a partner in the business which, at that time, had a fully paid inventory of $60,000. One of the partners was compelled to sell his half-interest for $10,000, while the other received $5000 for half his share. The new partners then milked the firm by selling all its assets. This was followed by a serious fire. The insurance claim for the fire loss was settled for $105,000.

Businesses which are acquired either legitimately or illegitimately are sometimes disposed of illegitimately. A common method of such disposal is through bankruptcy fraud, also known as "bust out" and "scam." In the short-range version of this game, the Cosa Nostra member conceals the transfer of ownership from the company's creditors and thus is able to operate on the former proprietor's credit rating. He orders merchandise, sells it at a loss, and declares bankruptcy. In the long-range version, called "rehash" in Chicago, Cosa Nostra members use some of their own capital. After acquiring a business, they make a number of large bank deposits, usually through "front men," in order to establish their credit rating. They then buy merchandise in huge quantities from a number of suppliers—first for cash, then on fifteen-day credit, then on thirty-day credit, then on whatever the creditors will bear. They make payments for all goods regularly and on time, and steadily increase the size of orders. Then, usually just before a holiday, huge orders are placed. Once the goods arrive, the "bust-out" occurs. The merchandise is sold for cash, sometimes at less than wholesale prices, to discount houses under control of "friends of ours" or to other somewhat-less-than-honest businessmen who are willing to buy at cut-rate prices without asking too many questions. The creditors are left with substantial claims and a bankrupt business with no assets. If the creditors look like they will complain too loudly, they are threatened with murder. During the summer of 1968, New York police arrested fourteen men said by Brooklyn District Attorney Aaron E. Koota to be engaged in systematic fraud of this kind, and to be "directed by powerful Mafia leaders." Mr. Koota said the organization, which had fourteen retail outlets in the metropolitan area, opened one store for business on April 28 with a cash deposit of $30,000 in a Brooklyn bank. By the end of June large orders, covered by checks, went out to Playtex, Proctor and Gamble, Westinghouse, and other suppliers. In all, merchandise worth $500,000 was ordered just prior to the July 4th weekend. All the checks bounced. When police investigated, they found that the company had moved to a new location and assumed a new name.

Bankruptcy fraud was not invented by Cosa Nostra, but the organization has perfected the operation, and about a half-billion dollars a year goes to Cosa Nostra as profits from it. On March 4–5, 1961, about three hundred automobiles (purchased on credit) were sold by a Chicago Ford agency at much less than cost, but when creditors started bankruptcy proceedings, only $5,000 could be found. Some of the cars showed up in the possession of syndicate members, friends and associates. One of them, a Thunderbird, was driven to Las Vegas, where the driver "delivered it to a well-known singer and entertainer and was registered in the name of a record company owned by him."

In late 1967 an important member of a New York Cosa Nostra "family," John Dioguardi, was sentenced to five years in prison and fined $10,000 for the bankruptcy of Consumer Kosher Provisions, Inc., a former Brooklyn meat-processing company. The government contended that after the bankrupt company was milked dry, Mr. Dioguardi set up a new company, First National Kosher Provision Company. The assets of the new company, the Assistant United States Attorney said, consisted of $33,000 worth of equipment and meat taken from the bankrupt company. There were 152 creditors with claims totaling $300,000, but Dioguardi and two other defendants (one of them Dioguardi's cousin) left them less than $3000. The President's Commission reported on a similar, but more profitable, case as follows:

Another tactic was illustrated in the recent bankruptcy of a meat-packing firm in which control was secured as payment for gambling debts. With the original owners remaining in nominal management positions, extensive product orders were placed through established lines of credit, and goods were immediately sold at low prices before the suppliers were paid. The organized criminal group made a quick profit of three-quarters of a million dollars by pocketing the receipts from sale of the products ordered and placing the firm in bankruptcy without paying the suppliers.

The principal operations of organized criminals are not independent of each other. Bet-taking, usury, narcotics distribution, labor fraud and extortion, corruption of government, and control of legitimate businesses all go together. Legitimate interests serve as an outlet for the vast amounts of money acquired illegitimately and also provide a tax cover. With the aid of lawyers and accountants, some of who have done a tour of duty as employees of the Internal Revenue Service, members of Cosa Nostra now insure that it is extremely difficult to catch them in income-tax evasion. Ownership of legitimate enterprises creates an aura of respectability. Moreover, by investing in legitimate businesses the profits of illicit businesses, the member is able to make his money, which is the fruit of crime and therefore contraband, earn more money. When the contraband money is invested in legitimate businesses, it is almost impossible to trace it to its criminal source.

Ownership of a legitimate business and labor fraud frequently go hand in hand. When a business is owned by Cosa Nostra, the employees are likely to be required to be members of a union owned by Cosa Nostra. However, in some instances they are denied union representation completely. When the business is unionized by a Cosa Nostra union, the employees work for less money than they otherwise could earn, are entitled to fewer holidays, and are cheated out of welfare funds. John Dioguardi obtained a charter from an Auto Workers Union in the Midwest, organized a number of "paper locals" with his friends as officers, then used the locals as instruments of extortion and for the sale of "sweetheart contracts" to greedy or dishonest employers anxious to keep their employees' wages as low as possible. Later this same Dioguardi, together with Anthony Corallo, attempted to gain control of Joint Council 16, the governing body of the Brotherhood of Teamsters in New York City. Meanwhile, Dioguardi acted as a "labor consultant." On one consulting job, he and two labor-union officials offered to guarantee labor peace to a manufacturer for payment of a $30,000 bribe. A wire tap, installed pursuant to a court order, disclosed this scheme, with the result that all three defendants were ultimately convicted.

Senator McClellan has pointed out that Dioguardi and Corallo were supported in their attempts to gain control of Joint Council 16 by James Hoffa, later head of the International Brotherhood of Teamsters:

It was quite evident that this was done in order to back Hoffa's climb to power in the International. Dio [Dioguardi] and Corallo had brought forty hoodlums into the labor movement with them—men with records of 178 arrests and 77 convictions for crimes that included theft, narcotics trafficking, extortion, conspiracy, bookmaking, stinkbombing, assault, robbery, accessory to murder, forgery, burglary, and other felonies. It was during the hearings on the New York "paper locals" that Hoffa had his longest and most astonishing losses of memory, when he was forced to sit and listen to tape recordings of phone calls between himself and Dioguardi concerning their collusive drive to capture Joint Council 16. In one Committee session, Hoffa pleaded loss of memory a total of 111 times.

CHAPTER VI

The Structural Skeleton

The habit of hearing charges promiscuously bandied to and fro, but seldom probed to the bottom, makes men heedless.

LORD BRYCE

SINCE 1963, when Joseph Valachi testified before the McClellan Committee, there has been a tendency to label America's nationwide criminal cartel and confederation "Cosa Nostra" and then to identify what is known about Cosa Nostra's division of labor as the structure of "organized crime" in the United States. I have followed this tendency, believing that the Cosa Nostra organization is so extensive, so powerful, and so central that precise description and control of it would be description of all but a tiny part of all organized crime. But this tendency has its attendant hazards.

In the first place, calling the entire apparatus "Cosa Nostra" might lead to continuing misplaced skepticism about whether a dangerous organization of criminals exists in fact. Individual citizens do not necessarily find that their local bookie, lottery operator, or usurer is of Italian or Sicilian descent. When "Cosa Nostra" is used as a synonym for "organized crime," these citizens might, then, believe that their local criminal purveyor of illicit goods and services has nothing to do with organized crime. The term directs attention to membership, rather than to the power to control and to make alliances. It should be understood that Cosa Nostra is the inner core, and that the only phrase adequately describing Cosa Nostra positions plus positions occupied by outsiders (of various national, ethnic, and religious backgrounds) is a rather clumsy one: "nationwide criminal cartel and confederation."

In the second place, using "Cosa Nostra" as a capitalized noun implies that the economic and political structure of this secret society is as readily identifiable as that of associations such as the Elks, the Los Angeles Police Department, or the Standard Oil Company. This is obviously not the case. We know very little. Our knowledge of the structure which makes either Cosa Nostra or "organized crime" organized is only a little bit better (thanks to taps and bugs) than the knowledge of Standard Oil which could be gleaned from interviews with gasoline-station attendants.

Detailed knowledge of the formal and informal structures of the confederation of Sicilian-Italian "families" in the United States would represent one of the greatest criminological advances ever made, even if it were universally recognized that this knowledge was not synonymous with knowledge about all organized crime in America. Since we know so little, it is easy to make the assumption that there is nothing to know anything about.

But we do know enough about the structure of Cosa Nostra to conclude that it is indeed an organization with both formal and informal aspects. When there are specialized but integrated positions for a board of directors, presidents, vice presidents, staff specialists, works managers, foremen, and workers, there is an economic organization. When there are specialized but integrated positions for legislators, judges, and administrators of criminal justice, there is a political organization. Like the large legitimate corporations which it resembles, Cosa Nostra has both kinds of positions, making it both a business organization and a government. Further, Cosa Nostra exists independently of its current personnel, as does any big business or government. Business, government, and Cosa Nostra go on despite complete turnover in the personnel occupying the various positions making up the organization. If a president, vice president, or some other functionary resigns or dies, another person is recruited to fill the vacant position. No man is indispensable. Organization, or "structure," not persons, gives Cosa Nostra its self-perpetuating character.

As the former Attorney General's testimony before the McClellan Committee indicated (see p. 60), the highest ruling body in Cosa

Nostra is the "Commission," sometimes called the "High Commission," the "Grand Council," the "Administration," *Consiglio d'Amministrazione,* the "Roundtable," or the "Inner Circle." This body serves as a combination board of business directors, legislature, supreme court, and arbitration board, but most of its functions are judicial, as we will show later. Members look to the Commission as the ultimate authority on organizational disputes, and each Commission member is sometimes called a "chairman" or an *"avvocato"* (advocate, counsel). The Commission is made up of the rulers of the most powerful "families," which are located in large cities. At present, eight such "families" are represented on the Commission, but the number of commissioners usually varies from nine to twelve. Thomas Gaetano Lucchese, head of a New York "family," died in 1967. For a time, it looked as though leadership of his "family" was to be taken over by his deputy, Anthony Corrallo. However, Corrallo was arrested before he was "raised"—which is the Cosa Nostra term used to refer to selection as a member of the Commission. Three of the eight "families" currently represented on the Commission are in New York City, one in Buffalo, one in Newark, and one each in Philadelphia, Detroit, and Chicago.

The Commision is not a representative legislative assembly or an elected judicial body. Cosa Nostra "families" in cities such as Baltimore, Dallas, Kansas City, Pittsburgh, and Tampa do not have members on the Commission. It is probable, however, that the "families" in these and other areas have a specified Commission member, usually a regional neighbor, looking after their interests. The members of the Commission do not regard each other as equals. There are informal understandings which give one member authority over another, but the exact pecking order, if there is one, has not been determined. The Commission is not a recent invention. We have already reported that on December 6 and 7, 1928, the *Cleveland Plain Dealer* described a Cleveland meeting of "The Mafia Grand Council," which Chicago police called a meeting of "The Captains of Industry." A "Grand Council" of nine men was operating in 1940, and federal agencies knew for certain in 1959 that the ruling body of Cosa Nostra was a Commission made up of nine to twelve men. The Apalachin conference was a meeting of Commission members and their lieutenants.

In some sections of the country, the next level of authority, below the Commission, is a "council" made up of the more experienced members of each "family" in a particular geographic area. New York, Detroit, and Chicago (at least) have councils. The patriarch of the council may be called a "Don" or "chairman," and he might or might not be a member of the Commission. Council members are elected by the council. When a council member dies, the council chooses a new member from the men in his "family." The New York body is sometimes called a "council of six" (see p. 145), sometimes, more mundanely, a "grievance committee." In Detroit, the Don is sometimes called "elected boss" or "chairman of the board," and the council is sometimes named the "high court." It has three members, called "elder statesmen," one from each of the three principal Detroit groups, which might be three distinct "families." Sam Giancana of Chicago was until recently both a Commission member and the Don of the Chicago Council or "Board." This policy-making Board has five members, each with his own territory—usually coinciding with a number of Chicago police districts.

Beneath the Commission and councils are at least twenty-four "families," each with its "boss." The wealthiest and most influential "families" operate in New York, New Jersey, Illinois, Florida, Louisiana, Nevada, Michigan, and Rhode Island. The "family" is the most significant level of organization and the largest unit of criminal organization in which allegiance is owed to one man, the boss. The number of members in a "family" varies from about 800 to about 20. The largest of the twenty-four known "families" operates in New York City and adjacent New Jersey cities. Only occasionally do members say "I am in Cosa Nostra." But it is commonplace for them to make statements such as "I am in Carlo's family," or "That damned Bonanno family has got to be watched." Italian words are used interchangeably with each of the English words designating a position in the division of labor. Rather than "boss," the words "il capo," "don," "capofamiglia," and "rappresentante" are used. Moreover, the term "family" is not used in all communities. In Kansas City the apparatus is called "The Clique." Similarly, each Milwaukee member is affiliated with one of three cliques which, collectively, might or might not constitute a "family."

The boss's primary function is to maintain order while at the same time maximizing profits. Subject to the possibility of being overruled by the Commission, his authority is absolute within his "family," geographical area, and any sphere of influence which does not bring him into conflict with another boss. He is the final arbiter in all matters relating to his branch of the confederation. Some bosses are members of the Commission. Each boss who is not a Commission member probably has his designated *avvocato* on the Commission.

The members of a "family" are likely to believe that they elect their own boss, but this is only vaguely the case. The "family" ordinarily submits the name of the man of its choice to the Commission, but the Commission makes the final decision. When a boss, Thomas Lucchese, became seriously ill during the summer of 1966, law-enforcement personnel knew that there would have to be a meeting of the Commission, or some subcommittee of it, in order to designate a successor. They followed men for over three months, until they were finally led to the meeting in a Queens (New York) restaurant, La Stella (see p. 190).

Each boss knows each of the other bosses personally. Accordingly, each "family" is interrelated with every other "family." Alliances and agreements are usually formal, but sometimes they are merely based on the mechanism of "respect" the bosses have for each other, and the fear they have of each other. The boss also initiates any alliances or other arrangements necessary for living in conditions of peaceful coexistence with any nonmember organized criminals permitted to operate in his community. In Boston, for example, the boss (who lives in Rhode Island) until recently permitted an Irish group to conduct lottery and bookmaking operations in one section of the city, probably because the profits lost were not worth the bloodshed necessary to drive the Irishmen out of business. The Commission rejects or ratifies any treaty or other arrangement which a boss might make with non-Italian groups.

Beneath each boss of the larger "families," at least, is an "underboss," or *"sottocapo,"* appointed by the boss. This position is, essentially, that of executive vice president and deputy director of the "family" unit. The man occupying the position often collects information for the boss. He relays messages to him, and he passes his orders down to the men occupying positions below him in the hierarchy. He acts as boss in the absence of the boss.

On the same level as the underboss there is a position for a "counselor," or adviser, often referred to as *"consigliere,"* or in slang, *"consuliere."* The person occupying this position is a staff officer rather than a line officer. He is likely to be an elder member who has partially retired after a career in which he did not quite succeed in becoming a boss. He is appointed by the boss, but he gives no commands or orders. He is something of a neutral adviser to all "family" members, including the boss and underboss. The counselor also is a historian. Consistently, his advice is based on precedent, frequently reflecting the wishes of the boss, of whom he is a close confidant. He therefore enjoys considerable influence and power. Although the counselor has no subordinates reporting to him, he is given a piece of the action of many members, in return for his counsel.

Also at about the same level as underboss is another staff position, "buffer." The top members of the "family" hierarchy, particularly the boss, avoid direct communication with the lower-echelon personnel, the workers. They are insulated from the police. To obtain this insulation, commands, information, money, and complaints generally flow back and forth through the buffer, who is a trusted and clever go-between. However, the buffer does not make decisions or assume any of the authority of his boss, as the underboss does.

To reach the working level, a boss usually goes through channels. For example, a boss's decision on the settlement of a dispute involving the activities of the "runners" (ticket sellers) in a particular lottery game passes first to his underboss and buffer, then to the next level of rank, which is "lieutenant," "captain," "head," *"capodecina," "capo-regime,"* or, simply, *"capo."* This position, considered from a business standpoint, is analogous to works manager or sales manager. The person occupying it is the chief of an operating unit. The term "lieutenant" gives the position a military flavor, and it once was the rule that one could not go to an underboss or boss without the lieutenant's approval. This rule changed in the early 1960's. Each boss now has at least two or three "soldiers" who report directly to him and who are answerable only to him. Although *"capodecina"* is translated "head of ten," there apparently is no settled number of men supervised by any given lieutenant. All lieutenants in a "family" are of equal status, no matter how many men each supervises. The number of such leaders in a "family" varies with the size of the "family" and with the specialized businesses the "family" conducts. Each lieutenant usually has one or two associates who work closely with him, serving as messengers and buffers. They carry orders, information, and money back and forth between the lieutenant and the men belonging to his regime. They do not share the lieutenant's administrative power.

Beneath the lieutenants there might be one or more "section chiefs" or "group leaders." Messages and orders received from a boss's buffer by the lieutenant or his buffer are passed on to a section chief, who also may have a buffer. A section chief may be a deputy lieutenant. He is in charge of a portion of the lieutenant's operations. In most "families," however, the position of lieutenant and the position of section chief are combined. In general, the larger the regime the stronger the power of the section chief. It is advantageous, in the interests of security, to cut down the number of individuals who are directly responsible to any given line supervisor.

About five "soldiers," "buttons," "button men," "good fellows," "wise guys" (meaning "right guys"), or just "members" report to each section chief or, if there is no section chief position, to a lieutenant. The number of soldiers in a "family" varies from about twenty to over six hundred. The lieutenant and the men reporting to him are sometimes called a "clique," "circle," or *nostra brigata,* but each of these terms also is sometimes used as a synonym for "family." In Chicago, the terms "soldier" and "button" are not frequently used. There, a "street man" or "operator" reports to a "district man" (who is either a button or a lieutenant), who reports to an "area man" (probably a lieutenant but possibly boss or underboss), who reports to the Chicago Council, whose chairman reports to the Commission. When Giancana was Chicago Boss, some district men reported directly to him.

In our second chapter we transcribed a recording of a bugged conversation between two Cosa Nostra members who were lamenting the fact that federal agents were learning a great deal about the structure and operations of the organization. In that conversation, a soldier (Mike) used the titles "boss" and "captain" in discussing Cosa Nostra with Pete, who is his own captain (see p. 18 above). Pete, it develops, was especially upset because he feared that the law-enforcement officers would embarrass his daughter, a nun, if he did not reveal what he knew regarding the whereabouts of the men who had assaulted a policeman. In a conversation about this potential embarrassment, Mike and Pete again made references to structual terms such as "family," "boss," and "head."

MIKE. He was told specifically—

PETE. To come and see me?

MIKE. You're a *captain*. No, they don't want to come to you. They don't want to come to you to embarrass you with your daughter.

PETE. Who did they tell that to?

MIKE They told that to Freddy.

PETE. Yeah.

MIKE. They don't want to embarrass you. Three of them called. To him. They said, "We don't want to go to Petey Pumps, we don't want to embarrass him with his daughter."

PETE. They already did.

MIKE. They already went to you—er—this week—this is the bullshit.

PETE. Yeah.

MIKE. They don't want to give no—in other words, they are telling you they don't want to embarrass you. In other words they won't go to the convent. Well, I say, right now they are giving you the zing. "You want us to go to the convent? You want us to embarrass you? Well then, see that the right thing is done."

PETE. Yeah.

MIKE. Actually what it boils down to, they're looking to use a stick. "But now we'll go on midnight raids. We'll do this. We'll do that. We'll do the other thing. *You're a captain.* You belong to Carlo's *'family'*—(a man yells in the background and Mike yells back, "Hey, Dope, cut it out.")—You belong to *'the family.'* "

PETE. Well, previous to that he hands me Carlo's picture. "You know him?" I said sure I know him. "How long you know him?" I know him twenty, thirty years. ["Carlo" is boss of a New York "family."]

MIKE. They didn't expect you to say nothing.

PETE. "Can you tell us anything about him?" The only thing I could tell you about him is that he is a businessman, been in business all his life. Brought up four kids. They had a good education. They're all in business. They all went to college and—married—a profession. I said, what else could you ask for? He's got a very nice family. See, over there what they do—they want to get a message through. I mean get a message through someplace. There's no question about it. (Inaudible. Both talking.)

MIKE. They want to put the heat on you, me.

PETE. Yeah.

MIKE. Because here is the proof of it. They've gone to every *captain*.

PETE. Yeah.

MIKE. And they call them *"captains."* One guy said *"foreman."* And the other guy said *"caporegime."* I mean, they're going right to each *head*. To the *head* of everybody they're going to. But for them to say this, when he told me this, I said, Jimmy, I think he already saw them.

PETE. Yeah.

MIKE. I think he already saw them, I said. Now to put the heat on him to go to his daughter, I said, this don't make no sense to me. I said, where the fuck does this come into the picture? Now they don't want to embarrass you.

PETE. What are they going to embarrass me for? What can they do? Go up there?

MIKE. Well, God forbid. They can't—they can't throw her out.

PETE. No.

MIKE. They couldn't throw Albert's brother out. How they going to throw her out?

PETE. Nah. They can't throw her out.

MIKE. Embarrassment, that your daughter is a nun. I mean, Jesus Christ. It's supposed to be an honor.

PETE. They can't do nothing. They won't do nothing.

A soldier might operate an illicit enterprise for his boss on a sharecropping basis, or he might "own" the enterprise and pay homage to the boss for "protection," the right to operate. All soldiers in good standing are guaranteed a livelihood and need not fear encroachment on their illicit operations by other soldiers. Further, they are guaranteed assistance in overcoming any threatened competition from non-members. They also are promised various social-security benefits such as near immunity from arrest and, when immunity cannot be maintained, bail, legal assistance, and unemployment compensation in case they go to jail. In short, blackjacks, bribery, and guns are used to protect soldiers and all other Cosa Nostra members from anyone who might want to harm them physically or harm their business, whether the business is licit or illicit.

It is not absolutely essential that a soldier or any other member engage in illegal activities, but each soldier must report to his lieutenant at least once a month, whether or not he has anything to report about. Some members have retired from active crime, but one can leave the organization only by death. Theoretically, one could be boss of a "family" and not engage directly in illegal activities. None of the twenty-four known bosses has chosen this course. The boss alone has the power to admit members, but he can do so only within limits set by the Commission, with the permission of the Commission, and at times designated by that body. "Suspension" of membership (but not stripping of membership) has been used as a punishment for swindling another member and for excessive indebtedness to another member.

Partnerships between two or more soldiers, and between soldiers and men higher up in the hierarchy, including bosses, are common. The partnership could be in a usury operation, a dice game, a specific lottery, a specific bet-taking establishment, a vending-machine company, or any other enterprise, legal or illegal, making it possible to turn a fast buck. Most soldiers, like most upper-echelon "family" members, have interests in more than one business.

"Family" membership ends at the soldier level. All members are of Italian descent. Members once had to be Italian by birth or by parentage on both sides of the family. This specification has, in one or two cases, recently been relaxed so as to admit men whose mothers are not of Italian descent. Similarly, a few men have been allowed to retain active membership despite the fact that they married women of non-Italian descent.

Membership in the Italian-Sicilian Mafia does not automatically make one a member of the American organization. This might not have been the case before World War II, but now even a Sicilian Mafia member must be recommended for membership. In the old country, a man could not be a soldier (or a member of any rank) if his father were also a member. The idea was to avoid a blood line that would work to the disadvantage of men not in that line. Some American "families" follow this principle, some do not. Albert Anastasia, late boss of a New York "family," was the first of the American bosses to give up this taboo. Vito Genovese and Joseph Profaci followed it, but Thomas Lucchese and Joseph Bonanno did not. At least two current "families," both of New York, do not follow it. Although the sons of some bosses cannot be members of their father's "family," they might be members of their father-in-law's "family." There are no restrictions on the membership of other male relatives. In one "family," brothers are boss and lieutenant. There are complaints that the lieutenant takes advantage of his brother's power, just as there were complaints that Attorney General Kennedy took advantage of President Kennedy's power.

About five thousand men are known members of "families" and, hence, of the cartel and confederation which is Cosa Nostra. But beneath the soldiers in the hierarchy of operations are large numbers of employees, sharecroppers, franchise holders, and commission agents who are not necessarily of Italian descent. These are the persons carrying on most of the work "on the street." They have no buffers or other forms of insulation from the police. They are the relatively unskilled workmen who take bets, answer telephones, drive trucks, and carry messages. Bet-taking and usury are not confined to members of Cosa Nostra, but almost all the successful nonmember bet-takers and usurers either sharecrop for members or front for them. My guess is that 95 percent of all the bookies and lottery operators in the United States are either soldiers or nonmembers who are sharecropping for soldiers. In Chicago, for example, the workers in a major lottery business operated in a Negro neighborhood were Negroes; the bankers for the lottery were Japanese-Americans; but the game, including the banking operation, was licensed, for a fee, by a Chicago "family" member. The entire operation, including the bankers, was more or less a "customer" of the Chicago branch of Cosa Nostra, in the way any enterprise operating under a franchise is a "customer" of the parent corporation. In this area, as in many others, the "small fry" were Negroes and the "big sharks" were Cosa Nostra men.

The above sketch of the authority structure of Cosa Nostra is based on a variety of sources, most of them having their roots in information released at the time of the 1963 McClellan Committee hearings, including the testimony of Joseph Valachi. But the sketch based on this information was recently validated by publication of only ten FBI summaries of the sounds coming from a single electronic bug. Moreover, these summaries gave detailed information about functions and operations as well as structure. The FBI calls such summaries "airtels." On May 19, 1967, *The New York Times* reported that Ramsey Clark, Attorney General of the United States, had asserted that electronic eavesdropping is "neither effective nor highly productive." This was a variation on his assertion, made in November, 1966, that the FBI had been wasting its time in eavesdropping activities. By genuine coincidence, the day after Mr. Clark was reported to have minimized the effectiveness and productivity of bugging, *The Providence Journal* published the ten airtels. In doing so, the *Journal* inadvertently showed that the Attorney General was, to use a phrase used in another connection by the Kefauver Committee, "pathetically in error."

From March, 1962, until July, 1965, the Federal Bureau of Investigation maintained, for purposes of strategic intelligence, an electronic bug in the office of National Cigarette Service, Providence, Rhode Island. Raymond L. S. Patriarca, boss of the New England Cosa Nostra "family," was one of two partners in the National Cigarette Service, a vending-machine company. Every few days the FBI agents would summarize the tape-recorded conversations and send the summaries to FBI headquarters and various branch offices. In a hearing as to whether the fruits of the microphone surveillance had tainted a federal court case of income-tax evasion against Louis Taglianetti, the government prosecutor provided defense counsel with the records of the surveillance. *The Providence Journal* reported that the defendant's attorney invoked the Jencks Act, which provides that in any federal criminal prosecution a defendant is entitled to examine and use any government statement or report relating to the testimony of a government witness, and if it contains matter which does not relate to the testimony of the witness, the government shall deliver the statement or report to the judge, who examines it privately and removes the material not relating to the witness's testimony before directing the government to deliver it to the defendant. However, the American Bar Association's *Standards Relating to Electronic*

Surveillance implies that the government voluntarily disclosed the airtels so that Taglianetti might have an opportunity to establish that the tax case against him was the fruit of unlawful electronic surveillance. The question of who shall decide what parts of a transcript of an electronic surveillance shall be revealed to a defendant—the government prosecutors, the judge in chambers, or the court in an open adversary proceeding—is now before the United States Supreme Court. It is possible that the judge in the Taglianetti hearing examined all the FBI's summaries of its bugging tapes, and then ordered the government to give Taglianetti specific records of conversations in which he was involved. At any rate, the material furnished to the defendant became public. It was this material that was published by *The Providence Journal* on May 20, 1967. The published summaries certainly represent only a small fraction of the complete FBI record. Yet they are so revealing that Cosa Nostra members, and especially Raymond Patriarca, probably wish they had not been introduced as an exhibit in defense of a rather insignificant Cosa Nostra figure.

To the uninformed reader, these airtels seem relatively meaningless. But, as G. Robert Blakey of Notre Dame's Law School aptly observed in his testimony before a United States Senate Committee during the summer of 1967, "To make them pregnant with significance, it takes only a little familiarity with the nature of organized crime. . . . When you have this familiarity, the impact of these few airtels is staggering." The "little familiarity" needed to understand the airtels is merely an elementary knowledge of Cosa Nostra's authority structure, from Commission to soldier. Professor Blakey carefully analyzed the ten airtels. From words coming out of the mouths of Cosa Nostra members themselves, speaking in a context in which there was no reason to lie or be evasive, it may be concluded that the following, slightly adapted from Blakey's analysis, are facts. The figures in parentheses are the dates on which the facts came through the hidden microphone.

1. There is an organization called "Cosa Nostra." (10/19/64 and 10/26/64)
2. The organization is headed by a "Commission." (10/20/64 and 10/26/64)

3. The organization is divided into "families." (9/13/63 and 10/26/64)
4. "Families" are headed by "bosses." (9/13/63 and 10/26/64)
5. "Families" are staffed by "underbosses," *caporegime,* and "soldiers." (9/13/63, 1/25/65, and 10/26/64)
6. The Commission appoints the boss. (9/13/63 and 10/26/64)
7. The Commission must approve new members. (9/13/67)
8. The Commission settles disputes and can rule "families" in the absence of a boss. (10/26/64 and 9/13/63)
9. The Commission holds hearings and takes votes. (10/26/64)
10. A "family" boss engages in at least the following kinds of internal organizational affairs:
    a. He grants or withholds permission to operate illegal businesses. (1/25/65)
    b. He rules on dividing the profits of illegal businesses. (1/25/65)
    c. He arranges bail. (4/16/63)
    d. He arranges for the operation of illegal businesses during incarceration. (10/31/63)
    e. He orders members to fulfill their personal obligations. (10/26/64)
    f. He orders members to fulfill illegal business obligations. (3/11/63)
    g. He worries about his image among upcoming members. (11/4/63)
11. A "family" boss engages in the following relationships with, and methods of insulation from, the world outside Cosa Nostra:
    a. He influences decisions of the state attorney general (1/25/65), high-ranking state police officials (11/4/63), licensing authorities (1/25/65), paroling authorities (4/17/63), probation authorities (1/28/65), and sentencing authorities (10/31/63).
    b. He keeps informed of the serious crimes of his associates. (3/14/63, kidnapping; 10/19/64, murder)
    c. He shows concern for scientific investigation. (4/17/65)
    d. He avoids using phones that might be tapped. (1/25/65 and 10/31/63)
    e. He declares "martial law." (1/25/65)

12. Members are called "friends of ours" (1/26/65), are brought into the organization in a ceremony (9/13/63), and transfer from "family" to "family." (9/13/63 and 10/20/64)
13. Members are ordered to kill. (10/26/64)
14. Members are involved in the following illegal activities:
    a. Gambling. (3/11/63, 11/4/63, and 1/26/65)
    b. Usury. (10/20/64 and 1/25/65)
    c. Bribery. (1/25/65 and 10/26/64)
    d. Perjury. (1/25/65)
    e. Fraud. (1/25/65)
    f. Extortion. (1/26/65)
    g. Kidnapping. (3/15/63)
    h. Murder. (10/19/64, 1/28/65, 10/26/64, and 1/25/65)
15. Members are involved in the following legal activities:
    a. Gambling. (9/13/63)
    b. Labor unions. (1/29/65 and 2/17/65)
    c. Race tracks. (10/20/64, 10/27/64, and 1/25/65)
    d. Vending machines. (10/19/64 and 1/25/65)
    e. Liquor. (3/9/63)
16. Some "families" have over 150 members, and a "family" of 120 members is "small." (10/20/64)
17. The Cosa Nostra organization is nationwide, and extends into Canada.
    a. Providence.
    b. Chicago. (9/13/63)
    c. New York. (9/13/63)
    d. Baltimore (11/4/63)
    e. Washington, D.C. (11/4/63)
    f. New Jersey. (10/20/64)
    g. Boston. (1/25/65)
    h. Miami. (3/15/63 and 1/25/65)
    i. Philadelphia. (1/25/65)
    j. Canada. (10/20/64)

From the information in the airtels, one cannot rightfully generalize about the nature and the extent of interaction between Cosa Nostra members in various cities. But the bug did make clear that Patriarca (who on March 25, 1968, was sentenced to five years in

MASSERIA GROUP

BOSS

GIUSEPPE MASSERIA

Murdered April 20, 1931 by unidentified killer of Maranzano Group.

JOSEPH CATANIA

Murdered Feb. 3, 1931 by Salvatore Shillitani, and Nick Capuzzi and "Buster" from Chicago (not further identified).

BOSSES

**ALFRED MINEO
STEVE FERRIGNO**

Both murdered Nov. 5, 1930 by Girolamo Santuccio and Nick Capuzzi and "Buster" from Chicago (not further identified).

BOSS OF

PETER MORELLO

SALVATORE MARANZANO

SUCCESSION OF GAN

BOSS

SALVATORE C. LUCANIA

Deported 1946. Died Jan. 26, 1962.

UNDERBOSS

VITO GENOVESE

Fled to Italy in 1934 to avoid prosecution for murder.

CHEE GUSAE (Phonetic)

Died natural causes approx. 1936-37.

FRANCESCO SAVERIA (Costello)

Attempted murder May 2, 1957 when deposed by Vito Genovese.

BOSS

VITO GENOVESE

Returned to U.S. from Italy in 1946. Convicted on narcotics conspiracy violation on April 17, 1959. While in Federal Penitentiary the control of group is vested in:

BOSSES

PHILIP & VINCENT MANGANO

Philip — murdered at direction of Albert Anastasia, April 19, 1951. Vincent deposed at direction of Anastasia, missing and presumed dead since 1951.

BOSS

ALBERT ANASTASIA

Murdered Oct. 25, 1957. Conspiracy between Carlo Gambino, Joseph Biondo and Vito Genovese.

UNDERBOSS

FRANK SCALISE

Murdered at direction of Albert Anastasia, June 17, 1957.

BOSS

CARLO GAMBINO

UNDERBOSS

JOSEPH BIONDO

ACTING BOSS	UNDERBOSS	CONSIGLIERE
THOMAS EBOLI	GERARDO CATENA	MICHELE MIRANDA

CHART OF "CONFEDERATION FAMILIES"
1930 TO 1965

MARANZANO GROUP

BOSSES

Murdered Aug. 15, 1930 by "Buster" from Chicago (not further identified).

Murdered Sept. 11, 1931 by hired killers including Sam Levine for Vito Genovese and Salvatore Lucania (Charles Luciano).

BOSS
SALVATORE MARANZANO

UNDERBOSS
ANGELO CARUSO

BOSS
GAETANO REINA
Murdered Feb. 26, 1930 by unidentified killer of Masseria Group.

UNDERBOSS
GAETANO GAGLIANO

BOSS
JOSEPH PINZOLO
PLACED IN GAGLIANO GROUP BY MASSERIA
Murdered Aug. or Sept. 1930 by Girolamo Santuccio for the Gagliano Group.

CONTROL AFTER MARANZANO

BOSS
GIUSEPPE PROFACI
Died of natural causes in 1962.

BOSS
GIUSEPPE MAGLIOCCO
Died of natural causes in 1963.

UNDERBOSS
SALVATORE MUSSACHIO

BOSS
JOSEPH COLUMBO

UNDERBOSS
CHARLES MINEO

BOSS
JOSEPH BONANNO
Deposed in 1964.

UNDERBOSS
CARMINE GALANTE

BOSS
FRANK LA BRUZZO
Invalidated by the "Commission" in 1965.

UNDERBOSS
JOHN MORALE

BOSS
GASPARE DI GREGORIO

UNDERBOSS
PETER CROCIATA

BOSS
GAETANO GAGLIANO
Died of natural causes in 1953.

UNDERBOSS
GAETANO LUCCHESE

BOSS
GAETANO LUCCHESE

UNDERBOSS
STEFANO LASALLE

Adapted from *Combating Organized Crime*, a report of the 1965 Oyster Bay, New York, Conferences on Combating Organized Crime; pp. 26–27.

prison and fined $10,000 on his federal-court conviction of con-spiracy to murder) had close relationships with Cosa Nostra leaders in New York City. Among those with whom Patriarca had direct or indirect dealings during the period under electronic surveillance were about a dozen men whose Cosa Nostra positions have been identified by U.S. Senate investigating committees: Joseph Bonanno, then boss of one of the New York "families"; Vito Genovese, boss of a second New York "family"; Thomas Eboli, acting boss of the Genovese "family" after Genovese was imprisoned; Thomas Lucchese, then boss of a third New York "family"; Carlo Gambino, boss of the fourth New York "family"; and Salvatore Mussachio, underboss in New York City's fifth "family," which until 1962 was headed by Joseph Profaci and now is headed by Joseph Colombo. Patriarca also had direct or indirect dealings with John Biele, a lieutenant in the Vito Genovese "family"; Eddie Coco, a lieutenant in the Thomas Lucchese "family"; Anthony Corallo, another lieutenant in the Luc-chese "family" and a strong contender for the position of boss when Lucchese died; Sam Rizzo, lieutenant in the Stefano Magaddino "family" of Buffalo; and Patsy Erra, enforcer for Mike Coppola, a lieutenant in the Vito Genovese "family."

The authority structure sketched out above constitutes the "organi-zational chart" of Cosa Nostra as it is described by its members. Three things are missing. First, there is no description of the many organizational positions necessary to actual street-level operation of illicit enterprises such as bookmaking establishments and lotteries. As indicated earlier, some of the positions in such enterprises are oc-cupied by persons who are not Cosa Nostra members. Second, and more important, the structure described by members of the cartel and confederation is primarily only the "official" organization, such as that which might be described by the organizational chart of a legitimate corporation. Cosa Nostra informants have not described, probably because they have not been asked to do so, the many "un-official" positions any organization must contain. To put the matter in another way, there is no description of the many functional roles performed by the men occupying the formally established positions making up the organization. Third, the structure as described by members is the structure of membership roles, not of the relationships between members and indispensable outsiders like street-level workers, attorneys, accountants, tax experts, and corrupt public officials.

In the business of taking bets on the outcome of horse races and other contests, dozens of specialized positions—occupied by well-trained craftsmen, executives, financiers, and bookkeepers—are essential. There are at least six levels of operating personnel in such enterprises, and each of these levels except the lowest one is occupied by persons with a corresponding status in the "family" structure of Cosa Nostra. A soldier, for example, is likely to hold a position in one of the lower levels of a bet-taking establishment, while a boss or commissioner is likely to hold a position in one of the higher levels.

The gambler wishing to place an illegal bet on the outcome of a legitimate horse race usually gets in touch with a man occupying a "solicitor" position, one of the many positions making up the structure of the illegal betting organization. There are three types of solicitor positions. All three types may be subsidiary to a single "bookmaker" position. Occasionally a bookmaker also occupies the position of solicitor, and the street name for what I call "solicitor" is, in fact, "bookmaker." The two positions are distinct, however, even if one man fills both of them. Ordinarily, a solicitor serves a bookmaker, in exchange for a percentage of the profits or in exchange for a straight salary. The person playing the role of "stationary solicitor" accepts bets at a fixed location, such as a newsstand, store, office, house, or factory floor. Gamblers go to him. A few stationary solicitors operate "horse rooms," where wagers are accepted on each race just before it is run, as at the track. Horse rooms tend to be small operations because the solicitor, who also functions here as bookmaker, has no opportunity to reinsure his bets. We shall see that, accordingly, he must live in hope that his patrons will bet approximately like the bettors at the track will bet. He gets by because most bettors, at the track or elsewhere, simply bet on the "favorites" selected by morning newspapers and racing forms. The returns on the gambler's investment are small when a "favorite" wins.

Men occupying the position of "traveling solicitor," or "walking solicitor," go to the bettors. Each traveling solicitor has a rather fixed route, which takes him through office buildings and factories. He, like the stationary solicitor, is likely to think of himself as a bookmaker, and he is popularly, but erroneously, called a "walking bookmaker," or "walking book." He issues small slips of paper on which bets are recorded, keeping a duplicate copy which he later turns over to the bookmaker. The solicitor may set limits determined by the bookmaker: "I'm a ten-dollar man" means that his bookmaker is a small operator who permits him to take bets no greater than ten dollars.

The third type of street-level position, "telephone solicitor," is occupied by men who simply advertise their telephone number to bettors. Men occupying the position of "runner," which is similar to the position of traveling solicitor, go out of the telephone room to collect the bets and make the pay-offs. Unlike the traveling solicitor, however, the runner takes no bets. Each customer of a telephone solicitor has an account, and some of them are permitted to settle up on a weekly or monthly basis. Solicitors take bets at the odds appearing in the "morning line" provided as a public service by metropolitan newspapers and racing forms to "sportsmen" all over the nation. These odds are approximate. They are based on prognostication of racing outcomes by so-called "sports writers" or racing-form handicappers. The odds actually paid to men holding winning tickets depend on the pattern of the legitimate betting at the track where the race is run. Race results, and the amount of the pay-off for the persons betting on winners, are announced, in the late afternoon, by radio stations and newspapers. However, bookmakers usually put ceilings on the amounts they will pay off. In Philadelphia, for example, bookmakers consistently pay odds no higher than 20 to 1 on winners, no matter what the pay-off on the same horses at the track.

The bookmaker position is at the second level in the organizational hierarchy of bet-taking enterprises. Men occupying this position have title to a neighborhood, which they divide up among their solicitors. It is not unusual for a bookmaker to employ six to ten telephone solicitors and a similar number of runners, who rarely are members of Cosa Nostra. The bookmaker, sometimes called a "handbook operator," or "handbook," ordinarily is in business for himself, as a sharecropper for his Cosa Nostra boss. If he is not his own solicitor, he can expect a little trouble from the solicitors who gather bets for him. These men, like the bookmaker, are cheats. Sometimes they book the bets solicited, rather than handing them in or calling them in to the bookmaker. In Chicago, this system for cheating the bookmaker is called "holding the cream," presumably because the solicitor holds back those bets which he believes are sure losers. If the bookmaker, who is likely to be a soldier in a Cosa Nostra "family," suspects that all bets are not being turned in, he notifies his lieutenant, who, in turn, might call out a man to occupy the position of enforcer. The solicitor loses his job, and his head is broken as a deterrent to others. Unauthorized soliciting of bets in a bookmaker's bailiwick is also severely frowned upon. Four Cosa Nostra "executioners," under orders from an "enforcer," called on an unauthorized solicitor-bookmaker in one city, telling him that henceforth he was to call all his bets to a specified telephone number. When he failed to do so, he was beaten up on three different occasions. He finally saw the light, and henceforth was permitted to "knock down the business," meaning that he got 25 percent of the profits (or losses) on the bets he called in. As in usury, Cosa Nostra finds it sound fiscal policy to keep the victim bringing in money.

The bookmaker does not gamble. His profits are established by the same procedures as are the profits of the legitimate track operators, who deduct 15 to 20 percent of the gross before calculating the amount to be paid on any winning horse. For example, suppose that only two horses are running in a race and that five hundred persons each bet $2 on Number 1 and five hundred persons each bet $2 on Number 2. Assuming that in this state the track operators are allowed to keep 20 percent of the gross, the five hundred persons who bet on the winning horse would share $1600 between them, for a pay-off of $3.20 for each $2 invested. The matter is not this simple because about eight horses run in each race and because gamblers can bet that a given horse will come in first, or second, or third. But the essential point is that the money bet on losers, less a percentage, is used to pay off the persons betting on the winners. The 15 to 20 percent of the gross deducted by legitimate track operators goes for taxes, expenses, and profits. The bookmaker pockets the entire 15 to 20 percent, less salaries or commissions for solicitors and runners, less a percentage paid to a "family" member for a license to operate or for the cost of reinsuring some bets, less unspecified sums (sometimes a percentage) for corruption of police and political figures, and less small amounts of "employee welfare funds" to be used for bail and attorney fees in time of need. His personal profit, after these expenses are paid, runs about 10 percent of his gross. A run-of-the-mill bookmaker in New York City grosses about $5 million per year; a small-town bookmaker who acts as his own solicitor has about $5000 a year left after he pays his winners, his police chief, and his Cosa Nostra "protectors."

There are three conditions under which the bookmaker cannot lose: (1) he pays track odds; (2) the proportion of all money bet with him on winners is the same as the proportion of all money bet on winners at the track; (3) the proportion of all money bet on losers with him is the same as the proportion of all money bet on losers at the track. Bookmakers usually have little choice about the first condition— gamblers insist that they pay track odds because doing so keeps them somewhat honest. But the last two conditions do not always obtain. That is, the bookmaker's customers do not always bet, collectively, like the persons at the track do. Were this situation allowed to go uncorrected, on any given day the amount bet with the bookmaker on losing horses might not be enough to pay off those of his customers who have selected winners. The bookmaker would then have to dig down into his wife's household funds or, God forbid, down into the funds he has been saving up for a gambling holiday in the Bahamas. This will never do.

Suppose that while the thousand race-track aficionados were betting their money as indicated in the oversimplified example given above, sixty bettors gambling with a bookmaker each bet $2 on Number 1, and forty bettors each bet $2 on Number 2. Should Number 1 win, the bookmaker would have only $160 (after deducting his 20 percent) to divide among the sixty holders of winning tickets, for a pay-off of only about $2.70. Unless odds different from those at the race track had been announced in advance, a hue and cry would be raised in the late afternoon when the local radio "sportscaster" announced that the winning horse had paid $3.20. If the bookmaker paid $3.20 to each of his sixty holders of winning tickets, it would cost him $192, leaving him only $8 (4 percent) for the day's work. Considering his overhead, this would mean a loss. Moreover, under this kind of arrangement the bookmaker would be engaged in gambling, to which he and everyone associated with him is opposed.

Another arrangement must be made. If the bookmaker can make the proportions of his "outs" and "ins" (losers and winners) correspond with the proportions of "outs" and "ins" at the track, he can merely deduct his 20 percent like the track does. And the closer he can get to the track proportions of "outs" and "ins," the closer he gets to an "automatic" 20 percent gross profit. As a first stab at accomplishing this trick, he juggles the odds a bit. For example, he might have announced in advance that he never pays more than 20 to 1 on a horse, even if the track pays 30 to 1 or even 40 to 1. These "house odds" help a little, but not much. He finds a better solution to the problem in reinsuring some of his bets, just as a casualty-insurance company reinsures a risk that is too great for it to assume alone. This takes him to a man occupying a position in the third level of the bet-taking hierarchy, the "lay-off man," who is likely to be a lieutenant or an underboss in the "family" hierarchy. Persons occupying this position are bookmakers' bookmakers.

Stated simply, the bookmaker places with the lay-off man a bet equal to the amount of his "overload," which is the amount needed to pay off winners minus the amount bet on losers. Even those bookmakers who pay off at their own preannounced odds, rather than at the odds paid by the track, must lay off the overload in order to minimize risks. In the oversimplified hypothetical arrangement mentioned above, for example, the bookmaker would deduct twenty of the sixty Number 1 bets from his pool, giving them to the lay-off man. His pool then contains $80 bet on the winning horse and $80 bet on the losing horse. He can't lose. He has what gamblers call a "middle," which is another name for a sure thing. He deducts his 20 percent ($32) and pays $3.20 to each of the holders of winning $2 tickets. Moreover, the lay-off man gives him a percentage of the profits, usually 50 percent, on all bets he calls to him. The lay-off man pays a percentage to a Cosa Nostra boss for the privilege of doing business, and he has other expenses. It is obvious that men occupying this position need larger bankrolls than do bookmakers. Lay-off men take bets exclusively from bookmakers and exclusively by telephone. Each bet is recorded in the bookmaker's name, and the account is settled at the end of each week or each month. The few bookmakers who do not have the 50–50 arrangement must pay a fee for each bet made with the lay-off man. The establishment administered by a lay-off man is likely to be called a "clearinghouse," "master book," or "lay-off room."

But it should be noted that the lay-off man, like the bookmaker, might be confronted with an unbalanced relationship between his "outs" and his "ins." Since he also, like the bookmaker, is interested in a 20 percent gross return (before expenses) on his investment rather than in gambling, he seeks the services of a man occupying a position at the fourth level of the bet-taking hierarchy, "large lay-off man," or "big lay-off man." Large lay-off men accept lay-off bets from all the lay-off men in a large metropolitan area. The operation here is like that of a city or county clearinghouse.

There is no known special name for the positions at the two highest levels of the bet-taking corporation. The men occupying these positions are also called large lay-off men. One type services all the metropolitan large lay-off men in his state or region, operating a kind of intrastate clearing house. Another set of positions is occupied by large lay-off men who service the state men, serving as a national clearinghouse. One large lay-off man operating at the national level works out of Chicago. Others live in Las Vegas and other cities. A large lay-off man who lives in Las Vegas but who operates on a nationwide basis takes in about $20 million a year, and his annual profit is about 4 percent of the gross, or $800,000.

By means of the lay-off procedure, the proportions of "outs" and "ins" bet with each bet-taker can be made to balance each other or to resemble the proportions of "outs" and "ins" bet at any given track on any given horse race. When the thousands of bets made by off-track gamblers all over the country are filtered up to the large lay-off man operating on a nationwide basis, the statistical biases in betting which occur in any given local bookmaker's shop cancel each other out. In other words, when the number of bets is large, the probability is high that the proportions bet on losers will offset the proportions bet on winners, as at the track. This can be readily seen in betting on athletic contests. Bookmakers nowadays handle bets on baseball games, football games, basketball games, and boxing matches as well as horse races. In central New York State, in fact, only about 40 percent of the bookmaking business is concerned with horse racing. When the New York Yankees play the

Los Angeles Dodgers in the World Series, everyone patronizing a bookmaker in New York wants to bet on the Yankees and everyone in Los Angeles wants to bet on the Dodgers. If, in this situation, New York should win, the New York bookmakers would lose their shirts, and if Los Angeles should win the Los Angeles bookmakers would lose their swimming pools. But if the bookmakers in the two cities can pool their business, they have a "middle." Neither set can lose, for then the statistical biases stemming from a desire to bet on one's home team balance each other off. The money bet on the loser can be used to pay off the persons betting on the winner, minus a percentage. In sports betting, the various levels of lay-off men function to set various local and regional betting biases against each other. In horse-race betting, they function to insure that all bookmakers operate as one nationwide bookmaker whose customers bet just like the gamblers at the track setting the odds. This solitary nationwide bookmaker, who handles both sports bets and horse-race bets, is Cosa Nostra.

But Cosa Nostra also cheats. In sports betting it cheats by bribing athletes, generally by means of an organizational position for a "corrupter," to be described below. In horse-race betting it cheats by "fixing" the outcome of races. No reasonable man bets on trotting races nowadays because it is so easy to bribe the drivers. It also cheats in horse-race betting by means of a set of positions rationally designed for cheating and ordinarily occupied by employees of national-level large lay-off men. If, just before a horse race, it looks like there is some possibility that the persons occupying positions for national-level large lay-off men might lose huge sums because their books are out of balance with the legitimate books at the track, they employ the services of a man occupying a position called "come-back man." The men occupying this position function in such a way that the legitimate track bettors themselves reinsure the bets taken by large lay-off men. The come-back man is an "odds changer" who stands by at the race track. Just before each race, he or his assistant opens a telephone line to a representative of the syndicated large lay-off men. When the latter's books are out of balance with those at the track, the person serving in the position of come-back man is instructed to bet large amounts (say $50,000) on specific horses, thus making the track odds the same as they would be if based on the proportions bet with the large lay-off men on each of the horses. Miss Virginia Hill, a favorite companion of organized criminals in the 1940's, was employed as a come-back man.

The division of labor necessary to conducting a successful illegal lottery closely resembles the structure essential to profitable bet-taking. Lottery games are called "numbers," "policy" (from *"polizza,"* the Italian word for the lottery ticket), or, in Spanish-speaking communities, *"bolita."* The basic idea is simple enough. The player bets that he can guess which three-digit number, like 2-7-9, will come up in an agreed-upon tabulation such as the total of all money bet at a race track on a given day. Players could once bet pennies and nickles, but today a quarter usually is the minimum, and $1 bets are the rule. Regular $10 bets are accepted in some locations, and some lotteries have no limit on the size of bets. The gambler has one chance in a thousand to guess right. If he does guess correctly, he gets paid at odds of about 500 to 1, and certainly not higher than 600 to 1, leaving a nice margin of profit. There are variation bets, such as a "boxed" or "combination" number, where one bets on 2-7-9 but, at the same time, on 2-9-7, 7-2-9, etc. It is also possible to play a "bleeder" (last two numbers only) at odds between 60 and 80 to 1, or a "leader" (first number only) at odds between 5 and 8 to 1. In "single action," which is popular in Harlem, the player bets on, say, 2-7-9 and then also bets, at odds of about 8 to 1, that the first number will be 2 or the second number will be 7 or the third number will be 9. The odds are reduced on popular numbers. For example, 0-5-7 would in the Heinz pickle factory be a "cut number." "Repeaters," "triples," or "trips" such as 4-4-4 are always cut numbers. A number like 5-6-7 might be cut only during May, 1967, and 1-2-3 might be cut on December 3 of every year.

Two or three different lotteries are run each day in large cities. Pittsburgh has four "houses," as its citizens call their illegal lotteries: Old Stock, New Stock, Early Race, and Late Race. In the Old Stock lottery, the three lucky digits are determined by the totals of the daily New York Stock Exchange transactions—the last digit in the figure representing total stock advances is selected as the first number, the last digit in total declines is selected as the second, and the last digit in the total of unchanged stocks is selected as the third number. The New Stock "house" is similar, but winners are determined by the digits fifth from the right in the numbers reporting total volumes of stock trading of various kinds. Early Race and Late Race numbers are determined by adding the total amounts bet in the horse races run at a given track on that day. For example, in Early Race the "leader" is the first digit to the left of the decimal point in the total of all money bet on the first five races.

"Policy" is like the Pittsburgh lotteries except that one can bet on a single number or any combination of numbers up to five digits. The normal "gig" is a three-digit bet. Some cities still use a "Treasury Number," which is the final digits of the United States Treasury cash balance. In this lottery, as it is played in Syracuse, New York, the player does not select his number. For a fixed sum he receives a printed ticket which is pasted or stapled so that the five-digit number cannot be seen until after the purchase has been made. There is more profit in Treasury Number than in other lotteries because the odds are less favorable to the bettor. Occasionally, a lottery with numbers determined by throws of dice, the spin of a fortune wheel, or draws from a hat crops up. In Chicago, *bolita* is run this way. But such systems are so susceptible to fraud that people play them only if they are very stupid or if there is no relatively honest place to gamble.

The person who sells the lottery ticket to the bettor holds a position called "writer," "policy writer," "pick-up man," "walking writer," or "runner." The duties of the men in this position resemble those of stationary solicitor and traveling solicitor. Usually the writer works in a fixed location, called a "spot," where he is free from arrest except in most unusual circumstances. A spot may be a tenement hallway, a newsstand, an elevator, a bar, a grocery store, or a street corner. In New York in 1960, each of the three police patrolmen serving a day-time shift collected $2 from each spot daily. Higher-ranking policemen had their own bag men, who called at each spot weekly or monthly and collected much more than a mere $2 per day. The total minimum payment for "police protection" was about $2500 monthly per spot. Ninety spots in one section of Harlem alone paid police about $2,500,000 a year. A writer working on a spot sells about $1000 worth of bets a day, six days a week, so the police were taking about 10 percent of the gross. In Buffalo, New York, writers collectively sell about $7 million worth of illicit lottery tickets a year; this amounts to about $11 for each of Buffalo's citizens.

Writers ordinarily get a percentage of all the money they take in. This ranges from 10 to 25 percent, depending upon the city. New York writers get 25 percent of the gross from their employers, and winning bettors hand them 10 percent of the amount of each winning ticket. Some writers work for a salary, but even when they are on salary, some kind of commission usually is paid them. In 1938 the salaried writers in Chicago went on strike and got their salaries increased from $30 to $35 a week. Nowadays, the writer usually works on a "cash basis," meaning that each day he turns all the money over to a supervisor, who later pays him for any hits his customers have had, plus his commission. An occasional writer may be permitted to "go on the gamble" rather than take a commission on the gross. If he works under this arrangement, he shares the risks on the numbers he writes, and he receives a share of the profits. To "go on the gamble" is not much of a gamble because, as indicated, the pay-off is 600 to 1 or less on a 1000 to 1 chance. A writer "on the gamble" must have sufficient capital to pay off lucky hits of large bets. If he doesn't, he may find it necessary to borrow from a usurer, which is not a businesslike way to try to accumulate a fortune.

A "field man," or "controller," who is likely to be a Cosa Nostra soldier, supervises about ten writers, who turn the day's slips and money over to him. He watches the writers for dishonesty, and in time of need he assists them by paying court fines, attorney fees, bail bonds, etc. The field man and his bookkeepers and messengers are likely to be called a "turn-in station," or "substation," even if they conduct their business in an automobile. In some cities, writers turn over their money and slips to a central location called a "drop." The "drop man," who might be a lunch-stand owner or simply a housewife, is a paid employee who merely receives packages. Another paid employee, "pick-up man," takes the packages to the field man. Field men, like writers, ordinarily work on a commission basis, usually 10 percent of the amount of bets sold by his writers.

A "manager," "owner," or "banker," often a Cosa Nostra lieutenant, receives the slips and money from each of the field men. Some
managers have up to sixty or seventy field men working for them, but
eight or ten is customary. The manager does business at a fixed location called the "main office," "bank," or "wheel headquarters." Each
branch of the policy-lottery business, especially, is likely to be called
a "wheel," which is the operating unit in which the money bet by
losers is used to pay off the holders of winning tickets. Each wheel
has a name, and religious terms are sometimes used—"The United
Sacred Heart Society" or "The Saint Anthony Society." The profits
on "The Silver Wheel" are not used to pay off the winners in "The
Saint Anthony Society" even if the latter on a given day has so
many "hits" that its operators are scrounging around for ready
cash. The two wheels may, in fact, use different systems for determining the lucky number. One man may own more than one wheel,
however. If a wheel or bank is "independent," in the sense that it
is operated by nonmembers of Cosa Nostra, the owner must permit
a Cosa Nostra soldier or lieutenant to check his "ribbon" (adding-
machine tabulation) of each day's play so that the Cosa Nostra boss
can be sure he is getting his cut, usually one percent "off the top."
In some cities, even soldiers and lieutenants are "independents," who
give their boss a percentage of the gross for the privilege of doing
business in his territory. A manager who believes that he cannot
handle all the bets coming in on a given day may lay off some of
them with the same lay-off men that service bookmakers.

When the day's slips and receipts have been turned over to the
manager, he sets a crew of about six employees to work on them. I
do not know the special terms used, if any, for each of these occupational specialities. Someone tabulates the amounts bet with each
writer and, indirectly, with each field man. Someone determines
which slips are winners. Someone serves as payroll clerk for all the
commission agents and employees working for the manager. Someone
hands winning slips and a bundle of money to a messenger (usually a
man who also serves as a writer) who goes out and "drops drawings"
(distributes winnings) to field men, who distribute them to writers,
who distribute them to lucky bettors.

The men in the top executive positions of lottery enterprises are the same men who are in the top executive positions of bookmaking enterprises. Accordingly, cheating should be expected, and it occurs. Attempts to rig the number are not uncommon. One crude system is to flood the area of a wheel with "dream books" and "numerology books" suggesting that a specific number be played on a given day, and then to cut that number severely. More efficiently, customers are encouraged by means of "dream books" to bet on a certain number and then the source of the winning number is controlled so that the heavily played number cannot come up. Even when a number is heavily played "naturally," that number may be eliminated from the possibility of coming up.

In one famous New York case, two of the three numbers were being released in advance of publication by dishonest employees of a newspaper, and the third was being selected by the lottery owners and inserted at the appropriate place in the totals released by the legitimate Cincinnati Clearing House. Knowing the first two digits, the operators studied the day's tickets to find out which third digit following these two digits had the lowest play for the day. The New York District Attorney heard, on legal wire taps, the following conversations, in which one man informed another that the desired third digit was 6: "You got a date at six." The man receiving the information would then call the Cincinnati Clearing House. One conversation went as follows:

"Bill there?"
"Bill speaking."
"Charlie wants to see you at six."
"I'll be there. Goodbye."

A detective went to Cincinnati and found that each day a distinguished, white-haired man, the Secretary of the Clearing House, was taking the telephone call around noon in an empty directors' meeting room. The Secretary, who was a pillar of respectability and who had succeeded his father in the office of Secretary, then released the desired figure. The lottery operators had a crock of gold spilling into their laps, but they were able to corrupt the Clearing House official for only $1000 a month. The Secretary was fined $1000 and sentenced to six months in jail. The Cosa Nostra lieutenant to whom all the rigged information was given escaped punishment.

꘍

Businessmen and managers know that identifying a position as that of, say, "vice president" is rather meaningless unless there is a description of what the person occupying the position actually *does*. And what he does is a response to an "unofficial" position he occupies at the same time he occupies the "official" one—he might be "expediter" or "troubleshooter" or "psychotherapist" as well as vice president. In Cosa Nostra, we have seen, persons occupying the soldier membership position may also hold a working position like usurer's collector, bookmaker, or field man. A lieutenant, underboss, or boss might also be usurer, lay-off man, large lay-off man, or manager. Or a man might "officially" be a soldier, lieutenant, or underboss (so far as membership is concerned) while at the same time "unofficially" holding a position designed to contribute to the entire "family" operation, not just to the family's bet-taking business. The buffer position is of this kind. This position has been identified by the New York policemen who watch Cosa Nostra operations, not by the members themselves. Because it is not on their own "organizational chart," lower-level "family" members might completely overlook it, just as a stock clerk in a legitimate company might overlook the fact that the person serving as vice president also plays the role of "troubleshooter." Later we will discuss a series of functional Cosa Nostra positions which do not fit in the hierarchy of positions ranging from commissioner to soldier. "Corrupter," "corruptee," "enforcer," and "executioner" are positions of this kind. They are occupied for temporary periods, even fleetingly, by men who also occupy an "official" position in a "family," such as soldier, and an "official" position in an economic enterprise, such as field man.

"Boundary problems," among other things, can be examined by consideration of unofficial functional positions. For example, I am confident that, from the perspectives of the Italian-Sicilian participants, "the organization" to which they belong does not extend to persons who are not members of a "family." But I am not at all confident that the solicitors, writers, pick-up men, and others who participate in the operation of illicit businesses, and who might or might not be Italian, consider themselves outside "the organization," even if they know they are not in Cosa Nostra. They frequently refer to Cosa Nostra members merely as "financial backers." The person serving as a corruptee—a dishonest policeman or politician, or the former Secretary of the Cincinnati Clearing House—is not likely to consider his position an essential part of "the organization," but it is, nevertheless. Similarly, the lawyers, accountants, and tax experts who serve Cosa Nostra leaders occupy positions which are essential to making the whole thing go.

The skeletal Cosa Nostra authority structure we have outlined is by no means the structure of the organization providing America with illicit goods and services. Even the skeleton has more bones than those we have described, as our comments on unofficial positions suggest. The structure outlined is sufficient to demonstrate, however, that a confederation of "families" exists and that the way the confederation is organized affects the way illicit businesses are conducted. Investigating agencies have, since the 1957 Apalachin meeting, documented the fact that the complete apparatus is tightly knit enough to have a corporate chain of command. Bugs and wire taps have helped. In one ten-minute conversation between a New York lieutenant and one of his soldiers, all the following titles were used at least once: "Cosa Nostra," "the administration" (for Commission), "the boss," "the old man," *"capo,"* *"caporegime,"* and "family." Moreover, the names of the men occupying the major Cosa Nostra positions have been known for at least five years. It will be some time before the investigating agencies will be able to depict the numerous functional positions making up the complete structure of the organization whose authority structure has been sketched out. Some aspects of structure can be deduced from studies of function; details can be learned only by close observation of the interactions between participants.

CHAPTER VII

Origins of the Authority Structure

In America, the traditional Mafia has evolved into a relatively complex organization which perpetuates selected features of the older peasant organization but subordinates them to the requirements of bureaucracy.

ROBERT T. ANDERSON

THE AUTHORITY STRUCTURE we have outlined for Cosa Nostra resembles the structure of the Sicilian-Italian Mafia. This resemblance does not, however, lead to the conclusion that our confederation is merely the Mafia transplanted to new soil. As we indicated in Chapter II, even when cultural elements are borrowed, they undergo changes, often of a fundamental nature, in response to the different cultural, social, and psychological surroundings to which they are introduced. "Cultural elements do not transfer mechanically as units from one ethnic setting to another so that their pathways of distribution are marked by persisting identities. Rather, diffusing elements are likely to undergo complicated changes of form and meaning as they enter new cultural settings." Invention calls for combining elements or traits. The process is no different when one or more of the elements are borrowed from another cultural setting than it is when all the elements come from the same cultural setting.

The structure and values of the Sicilian Mafia could readily have been invented in the United States, independently of any contact with Sicily, just as they have been independently invented by prisoners and members of underground movements in many parts of the world. But we know that there have been extensive contacts between the United States and Sicily. Nevertheless, the things borrowed had to be "Americanized" in much the way the immigrants themselves became Americanized. A man whose grandfather came to America from England is by far more "American" than he is "English." By the same token, any importation from Sicily two or three generations ago also is by now far more "American" than it is "Sicilian." The importation of Italian and Sicilian culture traits, including high evaluation of relationships within the extended family, provided a fund of elements on which to innovate. Thus, while the American confederation may be a "lineal descendant" of the Mafia, as Anderson has demonstrated, the similarities have definite limits set by the social and cultural setting of the two organizations. The confederation in the United States has responded to the changing technology and bureaucratization in America, and the Sicilian Mafia has responded to similar changes in the Sicilian cultural setting. Organized crime thrives in Sicily because for years there has been a place for it to thrive there. America has more recently made a place for organized crime. By examining the organization which has been occupying the Sicilian place, we can learn a great deal about the organization occupying the American place.

The early Sicilian Mafia groups were kin groups, with a hierarchy of authority relevant only to family affairs—the patriarch and his heirs. By the turn of the current century, each group had a chief and his assistants and a concept of "membership," which admitted "men of honor" even if they were not relatives. The face-to-face family-like group changed in the direction of a business organization.

A book published in 1900 indicates that one Mafia group, at least, had a structure almost identical to the structure of American "families," reported above as described by members of Cosa Nostra. This group, founded in about 1870, consisted of about 150 members, who seized control from the more traditional, family-oriented Mafia in a Sicilian town. Units were soon established in neighboring towns and villages. The head of the whole organization was called a *capo,* and each jurisdiction was under the direction of a *sottocapo.* Each *sottocapo* in turn had an assistant, the *consiglio direttivo.* Membership meetings were held to judge members charged with breaking the code of the group. Robert T. Anderson, commenting on the bureaucratization of the Mafia with the development of a hierarchical structure of authority, carries the description of the structure up to the council or, possibly, commission level: "The problem of succession to authority continues to be troublesome. Journalists tend to designate one or another chief as the head for all of Sicily. A high command on this level does not seem to have developed beyond irregular councils or autonomous *capi*."

The similarity to the skeletal structure characterizing Cosa Nostra in the United States is obvious. Even more important to an understanding of the American organization is awareness of the roots of the "family" concept as it is used by Italian-Sicilian criminal units in the United States. In Sicily, the family tie is the strongest social relationship known. The island has been ruled by Greeks, Carthagenians, Romans, Goths, Arabs, Phoenicians, Normans, Germans, Frenchmen, and Italians. One consequence of this political domination by outside governments, each with its peculiar set of rules, was an extreme emphasis on family relationships. The individual must subordinate himself to his family, a stronghold in a hostile and unpredictable land. "Mamma" is a central expression in the language of the island.

Sicilian villages are united by the fact that marriages are seldom made outside the community, making the village itself an extended kinship group. At the turn of the century there was a strong preference for cross-cousin marriages, despite the fact that such marriages were prohibited and therefore rare. Second cousins and third cousins did marry, and more frequently than in Italy. Additional ties were, and are, secured by religious rites such as that of godparenthood.

Because the Mafia began in rural villages, a clear line between the criminal band and the extended family could not be drawn. It cannot be drawn even today. Luigi Barzini has noted:

The first nucleus of the Mafia is the family. Some families have belonged to the "*società degli amici*" from time immemorial, each father leaving the domain to his eldest son as naturally as a king leaves his kingdom to his heir. A father always takes part in confidential negotiations with the eldest son at his side. The latter never speaks. He looks, listens, and remembers everything, in case the older man were suddenly killed. Some new families emerge from nothing. Like all new people, they must struggle with the older families, survive, and slowly assert themselves. As the years go by, they accumulate henchmen, vassals, and property, establish solid relations with landowners, businessmen, politicians, policemen and other Mafia families. Their rank is determined, at first, by the number and fearlessness of their male members and, later, by the number of useful connections they establish. In one village several Mafia families can coexist as long as they do not compete in the same field of activity: each of them must work its particular sector and all of them must be ready to unite against a common threat.

Barzini goes on to describe how powerful families in the same district agreed to peaceful coexistence, first by forming a stable union known as a *"cosca,"* then by establishing a *"consorteria"* with other units of the same kind, and then by constructing the societywide Mafia, a kind of underground movement. The word *"cosca"* comes from a corruption of the dialect term for artichoke—a composition of separate leaves forming a solid unit. But the alliance is not an alliance of equals. One family gathers lesser families around it, and the leader of the supreme family is the head of the *cosca*. All families pursue identical or closely related activities, and the leader of the *consorteria* is everybody's leader. There is no election. One family becomes dominant, and its head becomes the ruler of all:

Many *cosche* pursuing identical or similar activities often join an alliance called *consorteria*. The group also recognizes one *cosca* as supreme and its leader as everybody's leader. This happens spontaneously, almost gradually, when the *cosche* realize that one of them is more powerful, has more men, more friends, more money, more high-ranking protectors and relations than any of the others, could do untold damage to anybody defying its will and could benefit all those who collaborate and submit. All of the *consorterie* in Sicily finally form the *onorata società*, or the Mafia. It is, as has been said, a fluid and incoherent association with vague boundaries.

There are all sorts of degrees of affiliation: a family may operate as a unit without necessarily joining forces with other families, a *cosca* may carry on its business for years without joining other *cosche*, and a *consorteria* of *cosche* may dominate its territory independently of the island association. A sort of Mafia patriotism, however, unites all members; they know they owe all possible support to any *amico degli amici* who needs it, for whatever reason, even if they have never heard of him, provided he is introduced by a mutual *amico.*

Gaetano Mosca, writing in the *Encyclopedia of Social Sciences,* also uses the *"cosca"* terminology—indicating, however, that the relationships between *cosche* were not always characterized by sweetness and light. The early *cosche* engaged chiefly in cattle rustling, extortion, and kidnapping for ransom. Accordingly, the relations between neighboring *cosche* might be cordial but were more likely to be "so antagonistic that difficulties would have to be settled by shooting. The great majority of mafist murders grew out of rivalry between *cosche* or members of one *cosca."*

One could well substitute for the Mafia term *"cosca"* the term "council," as that term was used in the last chapter. Mr. Valachi, in his testimony before the McClellan Committee, used *"consigliere* of six" to describe the council coordinating the six New York area Cosa Nostra "families" of criminals. He could have said *"cosca."* The *consorteria* of Sicily bears a striking resemblance to the alliance represented by the Commission of America. And in America as in Sicily, the alliances between "families" are not alliances of equals. Further, the supremacy of one family and the leadership of its head are recognized by American criminal "families" everywhere, and especially in New York. The peace treaty ending the American interfamily war fought in 1930–1931 abolished the previous system of "boss of all bosses," replacing it with the New York *"consigliere* of six" and, eventually, the Commission. Nevertheless, the ruler of one of the six "families" established in the New York area by the treaty became dominant. Mr. Valachi testified, "They eliminated the boss of all bosses, but Vito Genovese is a boss of all bosses under the table."

Mr. Genovese was in 1959 convicted on a narcotics conspiracy charge. He has been in prison since that time, and in his absence Thomas Eboli is serving as "acting boss" of his "family." This "family" has been the most powerful of all twenty-four American "families" since 1931. Its first boss was Charles Luciano, who served from 1931 to 1946, when he was deported. Luciano was succeeded by Francisco Salverio (Frank Costello), who, in turn, was suc-

POSITIONS IN A COSA NOST[RA]

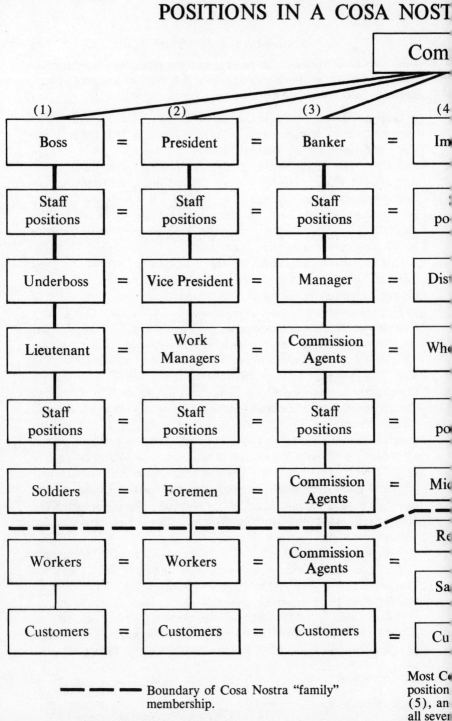

	Com[mission]		
(1)	(2)	(3)	(4
Boss =	President =	Banker =	Im
Staff positions =	Staff positions =	Staff positions =	po
Underboss =	Vice President =	Manager =	Dis
Lieutenant =	Work Managers =	Commission Agents =	Wh
Staff positions =	Staff positions =	Staff positions =	po
Soldiers =	Foremen =	Commission Agents =	Mi
Workers =	Workers =	Commission Agents =	Re
			Sa
Customers =	Customers =	Customers =	Cu

━ ━ ━ Boundary of Cosa Nostra "family" membership.

Most C[osa Nostra] position[s] (5), an[d] all sever[al]

"FAMILY" ORGANIZATION

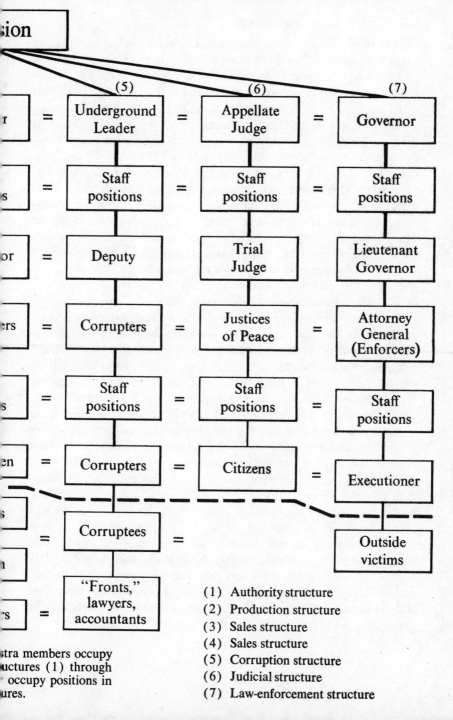

		(5)		(6)		(7)
r	=	Underground Leader	=	Appellate Judge	=	Governor
s	=	Staff positions	=	Staff positions	=	Staff positions
or	=	Deputy		Trial Judge		Lieutenant Governor
rs	=	Corrupters	=	Justices of Peace	=	Attorney General (Enforcers)
s	=	Staff positions	=	Staff positions	=	Staff positions
en	=	Corrupters	=	Citizens	=	Executioner
s		Corruptees	=			Outside victims
n						
rs	=	"Fronts," lawyers, accountants				

(1) Authority structure
(2) Production structure
(3) Sales structure
(4) Sales structure
(5) Corruption structure
(6) Judicial structure
(7) Law-enforcement structure

tra members occupy
uctures (1) through
occupy positions in
ures.

ceeded by Genovese, who had been Luciano's underboss in early years but who lived in Italy from 1934 to 1946 in order to avoid prosecution for murder. It has not been clearly established that Costello was more than acting boss for Luciano. Neither is it clear that Genovese became boss, rather than acting boss, until Luciano's death. Despite the fact that Genovese is in prison, he remains as boss, and his group—which has about eight hundred members—continues to be called the "Genovese family." It has lived peacefully, even if in a state of tension, with the other New York "families" since 1931. There have been numerous assassinations and two serious armed conflicts in the New York area since the decision for peace. However, these conflicts—one of them called the "Gallo-Profaci war"—have been intrafamily affairs, concerned principally with a "family" ruler's need to protect himself from his underlings, or with problems of succession to the throne. None of the "families," in New York or elsewhere, established after the 1930–1931 war have been made up exclusively of Sicilians or Sicilian-Americans.

The 1931 decision for peace in the New York area was accompanied by a decision for peaceful association between all Italian-Sicilian "families" in the United States. Yet groups of these "families" did not, outside New York, Chicago, and Detroit, form into *cosche,* or councils. Except in these three large cities, the type of structure found in the Sicilian Mafia cannot be used in the United States, partly for reasons of geography. It is only about forty miles from Castellammare del Golfo to Palermo, but it is a thousand miles from Buffalo to Kansas City. Face-to-face interaction is impossible. Further, at the time of the peace treaty there were not, in Baltimore, Boston, Buffalo, Philadelphia, or other cities enough illicit businessmen to make up more than one "family," or else one family leader had dominated the arrangement almost from the beginning and was able to maintain his singlehanded grip on the reins of power. Whatever the cause, there now seems to be only one "family" in each Cosa Nostra city outside Chicago, New York, and, possibly, Detroit. It is conceivable, however, that even in cities like Baltimore and Buffalo the arrangement is something like that of a *cosca* and that we consider the unit a "family" only because our police intelligence agencies have not uncovered the real arrangement.

The current structure of relationships between American "families" also has been affected by the balance of power existing at the end of the 1930–1931 interfamily war. We have seen that the conditions of the peace treaty favored the Luciano-Costello-Genovese-Eboli "family," which has had a powerful seat on the Commission from the beginning. More important, conditions at the end of the war determined who was *not,* subsequently, going to have power. Simply stated, there were no clear-cut powerful "families" in Western cities at the time arrangements were made for mutual respect and cooperation between "families" across the nation, and this condition has affected the distribution of organized criminals in the United States ever since. In 1931 the perspective of criminals, like the perspective of most legitimate businessmen and politicians, was that anything west of Chicago or south of Philadelphia was unimportant. Las Vegas wasn't even there. On the island of Sicily, the Mafia, considered as a loose alliance of *consorterie,* dominates the west but not the east, for reasons not yet explored. In the United States, the confederation is not as dominant in the West as in the East because at the critical period of decision-making there was no one in the West to make decisions. Because of conditions on the American scene, then, the entire Cosa Nostra apparatus in the United States is more like that of a *cosca* than like that of a *consorteria* or a Mafia. Were it not for the councils in New York, Detroit, and Chicago, the American structure could in no sense be said to go beyond the *cosca* level. Since *consorterie* are essential units in the structure of the Sicilian Mafia, it also could be enthusiastically argued, then, that there is no Mafia in the United States.

Now that the Western cities overlooked in the 1930's have become economically and politically important, they have been designated "open areas," or "open territory," by Cosa Nostra's Commission and its non-Italian allies. Nevada is the best example of open territory. Until Howard Hughes started buying Las Vegas casinos, anyone could operate there, and almost everyone did. Bosses of several different Eastern "families" have been partners in many of Nevada's "gaming rooms," as residents of the state like to call them. Chicago, like Nevada, is designated an "open area." However, this city is not "open" in the sense that Las Vegas was "open." It is controlled by a boss, and outsiders cannot just move in. There is no clear-cut hierarchy in any of the cities in Western states. Los Angeles and San Francisco do not have powerful monopolistic "families" of Cosa Nostra, despite the fact that certain men with Italian names have repeatedly been identified as involved in illegal bet-taking, lotteries, usury, and bankruptcy fraud. The Los Angeles police have repelled a number of attempts to invade the "open territory" of their city.

Unlike Las Vegas and Los Angeles, Chicago was by no means economically and politically weak in the early 1930's. At the time of the treaty, various Italian-Sicilian groups of great wealth and power had to be accommodated, as did groups of non-Italian syndicated criminals. The Chicago area is "open" only in the sense that some of these groups still must be accommodated. Perhaps it is for this reason that the term "Cosa Nostra" is not extensively used in Chicago. Texas and Florida are similar to Nevada. However, Tampa has its own "family," and the Miami territory (which includes the Bahamas) has long been controlled by a New York–Miami partnership. At least two New York "families" and a Detroit "family" have interests in Miami. Cosa Nostra members from all over the United States take their winter vacations in Miami, and a few have retired there, just like real people.

But despite the geographic variations, the basic organized-crime unit in both the United States and Sicily is the "family." It is conceivable that in America this arrangement began as a defense against imagined predators, as it began as a defense against real predators in Sicily, and then developed into a rationally devised division of labor for conducting illicit businesses. The evidence from current studies is that the cultural training of Italian and Sicilian immigrants equipped them to see persons in power as exploiters who should not be trusted. We know, further, that legitimate businessmen are now paying tribute to hoodlum "labor-relations experts," who don't know Samuel Gompers from Shirley Temple, because these same businessmen once asked the hoodlums to protect them from labor strife. Perhaps there were other predators that also needed to be controlled. It is likely, however, that the "family" arrangement was more or less a "second thought" in America, arising in response to intergroup warfare rather than in response to a need for protection against bandits. Whatever the cause of the American development, the arrangement now closely resembles the relationship between individual Sicilian families and the Sicilian Mafia.

There are differences, however. The main differences between the American Cosa Nostra and the Sicilian Mafia have arisen principally because greater distances separate American "families," already discussed, and from three other conditions in the United States. These are (1) the short period of time since the major thrust of the Italian-Sicilian immigration, (2) fragmentation of the native extended family by migration to the host country of only a part of that family, and (3) location of the immigrants in the urban areas of a rapidly industrializing nation rather than in the rural areas of an agricultural nation.

The identification of family boundaries and Mafia unit boundaries in Sicily took centuries to develop. A duplicate organization in the United States would necessarily have had to develop since the turn of the century. There simply has not been time to develop in America the close-knit family relationships characterizing Sicilian peasant villages. Moreover, the extended families of Sicily did not move in a body to the United States. Parts of many families, including a disproportionate number of males and young adults, joined the emigration. Even in the Sicilian neighborhoods of American cities, the traditional Sicilian family affiliations could not be the primary basis of social interaction as they were at home. One device for establishing family relationships and, thus, restoring personal security, was creation of fictive families. I do not know the extent to which this device was used by respectable immigrants and their descendants. I know that it was, and is, used by organized criminals.

In Sicilian Mafia families it became necessary or convenient in about 1920 to supplement and extend family ties by taking in members who were not relatives. The conditions of immigration made it necessary for American "families" of organized criminals to *begin* with this arrangement. Membership in a "family" was extended to those Italians as well as to those Sicilians who demonstrated willingness to be dominated by a despot, even if not related to him by blood or marriage. Similarly, fictive kinship ties were extended to persons associated directly or indirectly with "family" members in religious ceremonies—godparents, godchildren, best men at the weddings of sons or nephews, classmates in a confirmation ceremony, brothers-in-law, brothers of sisters-in-law, brothers of sons-in-law or of sisters of sons-in-law, etc. While such alliances, like arranged marriages, are commonly used in peasant societies as means for extending the influences and increasing the wealth of a family, in the United States they were essential to *establishing* the criminal "family" rather than extending it. Later we will show that the need for technological experts in modern criminal operations has made it necessary for syndicate leaders to reconsider traditional membership criteria. A "family" might soon include men who are members because they are accountants and lawyers, not because they are related by blood or even by religious ceremony or residence of ancestor in Sicily or Italy.

It is true, however, that genuine family relationships play an important part in determining one's status in American "family" units. One cannot move very high in the organization unless he is somehow related to the boss. Further, intermarriages between the sons and daughters of confederation members are common, and there are a few cases in which there have been three generations of alliances through marriage. The Detroit family seems to be especially old-fashioned and "Sicilian" in this respect. One New York lieutenant who attended the Apalachin meeting has three older sisters, all married to men who also participated in the conference.

The "family" fiction helps keep peace within "families" and be-between "families," but it also creates problems. Perhaps the greatest of these is the procedure for succession. Because the family is not real, the "father" cannot leave his domain to his eldest son, or even to a relative close to him in the organization. Yet the "family" concept makes it impossible to establish an orderly procedure for selecting successors from among nonrelatives. When in October, 1964, the long-time boss of a New York "family," Joseph Bonanno, disappeared on the eve of a scheduled appearance before a federal grand jury, armed conflict broke out between the 250 or so members of his group. The FBI believes that Bonanno was kidnapped on orders from the Commission because he had been plotting the murder of two other New York bosses, Mr. Gambino and Mr. Lucchese. Apparently there had been some hard feelings between the New York City groups, and between the Bonanno "family" and the Magaddino "family" of Buffalo, because of disagreements about the smuggling of narcotics from Canada. As early as September 13, 1963, Raymond L. S. Patriarca of Providence was overheard, on the FBI bug described on pp. 120–126, commenting to the effect that a "family" (presumably that of Bonanno) had been put under the control of the Commission:

Patriarca then told Tameleo to tell Joe (possibly Joseph Lombardo of Boston) that the boss and underboss in New York are out; that right now that "family" is under the Commission. Patriarca did not know who they were going to make as boss of this "family" as they have not picked the person as yet. He specifically warned Tameleo to give this information to Joe and Joe alone; if he want to tell anyone else, that is his business. (9/13/63)

About a year later, on October 20, 1964, Patriarca again discussed the Bonanno group. (It should be noted that Bonanno was kidnapped on October 21, 1964.)

Patriarca told Modica that the word had come down that no one was to do any business with any of Bonanno's group because of the fact that he (Bonanno) failed to show up at a Commission hearing when ordered to do so. . . . Ray [Patriarca] stated that Joey, whom he described as the guy with Carlo, called him a few weeks ago and said that Carlo wanted to see Patriarca on Thursday, but Patriarca was unable to make the trip. He told Joey to call Friday if Carlo (Gambino) wanted to see him on Friday or thereafter. He has not received a call from Joey since that time. Nick stated that he met Carlo's brother Joe on the street the other day and Joe told him that Bonanno's group was pulling away from him (Bonanno). He stated that Mike Zepella (phonetic), who is with Bonanno, "turned in the other thing" with 63 or 65 guys and they expect more. Vito, the one in jail, was described as the muscle man for Lelow (phonetic). It appeared to the informant that Lelow is the top guy of the Bonanno group in Canada. Lelow, according to Nick, took his side (probably Bonanno's) and "does not want to know anything." Everyone else is coming along and the number is now up to approximately 150 (who have apparently defected from Bonanno). Nick made the statement that Profaci had the smallest group, namely 120. According to Patriarca, Bonanno has a lot of people on account of his (Bonanno's) father. The individual who started the ball rolling in connection with the defection from Bonanno was Gasper. He went to Joe Bonanno and said to him, "Why don't you straighten this out?" And when Joe Bonanno did not comply with the orders, apparently from the Commission, he was the first to defect and they all followed. (10/20/64)

ⁱ *ⁱ* *ⁱ*

An individual believed to be Danny Raimondi's father contacted Patriarca. Raimondi questioned Patriarca about the fate of Bonanno. Raymond [Patriarca] explained that he was called to New York three weeks ago, during which the fate of Bonanno was discussed. They decided that Bonanno was no longer a boss or Commission member. They also put out the word that nobody is to have any business dealings or associate with any members of the Bonanno group. A week later, Patriarca received another call from New York to attend another meeting. However, prior to the time he left Providence, this meeting was canceled for some unknown reason. It was Patriarca's opinion that Bonanno was not killed by any member of the opposing faction. He pointed out that, if the opposing faction wanted him killed, they would have done so at the time they grabbed him on Park Avenue, as is the case in most killings of this type, particularly when there are witnesses, such as the lawyer, around. He pointed out that they were taking a chance in kidnapping Bonanno and killing him later and could not see why it would serve any purpose to kidnap him first. Because of this, he believes that Bonanno is still alive and that he, Bonanno, engineered the alleged kidnapping. He pointed out that he is not sure of this, but it is only his opinion. Raymond [Patriarca] stated that he spoke to the group in New York in behalf of Raimondi and told them that, because his son is "with him," meaning Patriarca, they should not cause him, Raimondi, any harm. Raimondi pointed out that Gus Marino (phonetic) was thrown out, apparently by the Bonanno group. Raimondi is a member of the Bonanno family. Patriarca further pointed out that, when Bonanno did not appear before the Commission when requested on eight or nine different occasions, he was given one additional chance. Instead of Bonanno himself appearing, his son appeared, but they told him that they did not want to talk to the son, but the father. Raymond explained that about one-half of Bonanno's group have turned themselves in to the Commission. He pointed out that even Bonanno's relation by marriage who was on the Commission voted to throw Bonanno out of Cosa Nostra. This Commission member was described as being from Detroit. Raimondi mentioned the name of Caruso and stated that Larry (probably Gallo) was going "there" Thursday again. Informant did not know the significance of this statement. Raymond [Patriarca] pointed out that he wanted no fighting among this group and stated that Bonanno was the cause of his own downfall, because he was so greedy. (10/26/64)

Mr. Bonanno's lawyer, who was with him at the time of the kidnapping, later said that two men with guns shoved Bonanno into an automobile. One of them said, "Come on Joe, my boss wants to see you." The police believe that Bonanno was released a few days later, after promising to surrender his leadership. But he remained in hiding until May 17, 1966, when he walked into a federal courthouse and gave himself up. Mr. Bonanno had designated his brother-in-law, Frank LaBruzzo, as boss and named his son, Salvatore Bonanno, as counselor. The Commission did not accept Bonanno's recommendations. In January, 1965, a subcommittee of this body, meeting at a restaurant in Cedarhurst, New York, selected Gasperino DiGregorio as boss of the Bonanno "family." This is the "Gasper" mentioned near the end of the October 20, 1964, FBI airtel reprinted above.

Mr. DiGregorio is a brother-in-law of Stefano Magaddino, who is boss of western New York, the Ohio Valley, and parts of Canada. Mr. Magaddino also is the oldest member of the Commission. DiGregorio was best man at Joseph Bonanno's wedding, and he is godfather to Salvatore Bonanno. He was born in Castellammare Trapani, within five miles of Bonanno's childhood home in Castellammare Del Golfo, some forty miles from Palermo. Both men were born in 1905. DiGregorio lives modestly in West Babylon, New York, and has a garment factory in Brooklyn. He has no police record. At the time of his disappearance, Bonanno had a fantastically high income from bet-taking, usury, and narcotics importation. He has a home and extensive real-estate holdings in Tucson, Arizona, dairy interests in Wisconsin, a share of the legal gambling in Haiti (allegedly), and investments in both legal and illegal businesses in Canada. Three months before the kidnapping, in fact, Bonanno sought Canadian citizenship, perhaps because he was in trouble of some kind in New York City. His attorney told a Canadian immigration hearing that Bonanno "loves this country" and had an interest in three Canadian companies, G. Saputo & Sons, Cremerie Stella, and Cremerie Costenza, all makers of Italian cheese specialties. According to Charles Grutzner, organized-crime expert for *The New York Times,* "The Mafia is said to dominate the pizza trade in Montreal's large Italian community through controlling prices of cheese specialties." The Bonanno "family" has for decades had other interests in Montreal, which is a bet-taking lay-off center, where United States bookmakers and lay-off men reinsure their bets.

After Joseph Bonanno disappeared, the younger Bonanno and several of his father's lieutenants refused to recognize DiGregorio's leadership, claiming that Magaddino had dictated to the Commission that his brother-in-law should have the position. Salvator Bonanno made a bid for the leadership himself, and he mustered a group that believed he should be boss. On January 28, 1966, Salvatore, who reportedly is rather stupid and eccentric, met in the Ridgewood section of Brooklyn with some of his followers to assess his strength. The DiGregorio faction heard of the meeting and attacked. Twenty shots were fired at the Bonannos, but none of them found a human mark, leading the police to believe that the sortie was an attempt to frighten Salvatore into abandoning the role of the pretender to the throne. About one hundred neighbors were questioned by the police, but all but one said they had seen and heard nothing. Salvatore Bonanno and six others received thirty-day jail sentences for refusal to answer questions put to them by a Brooklyn grand jury. When they were released from jail they were again indicted for contempt when they refused to testify before the grand jury.

When Joseph Bonanno came out of hiding in May, 1966, he began a campaign to wrest control from DiGregorio, and a sidewalk war began. In April, when DiGregorio was summoned for questioning about the Ridgewood shooting, he suffered a heart attack and stepped down from the leadership. He had been similarly stricken a year earlier when subpoenaed to appear before a federal grand jury. Some law-enforcement officials believe that DiGregorio was unable to control the "family" business and that consequently he was deposed by the Commission, which then invited the elder Bonanno to come out of hiding and tried to restore power to him. Others believe that Bonanno simply refused to give up his power, and continued to direct his "family" affairs from his "retirement" residence in Tucson. But DiGregorio, with the backing of Stefano Magaddino, designated Paul Sciacca as Boss. Peter Magaddino, a cousin of Stefano Magaddino's, was in November of 1966 caught by Montreal police in the company of Salvatore Bonanno and other Bonanno men. The New York police said Peter Magaddino had been a member of Stefano's Buffalo "family" but had had a falling out with his cousin.

Mr. Sciacca does not have the stature to command the "respect" of his "family" members, and the battle for succession to the throne has continued. There have been numerous casualties on both sides, including five murders. The first casualty was Frank Mari, who was wounded by gunshot fire in July, 1966, apparently as a reprisal for the DiGregorio raid on the Ridgewood meeting. The shooting frightened some of the DiGregorio crowd into shifting back to Joseph Bonanno. Among those killed later were three former Bonanno lieutenants who had defected to the DiGregorio group. Bonanno's Tucson home was bombed during the summer of 1968, as were the homes of two other Cosa Nostra leaders residing in Tucson. Perhaps these bombings were a warning that the Commission *really* intends to take over the Bonanno "family." By failing to back up its original decision to remove Joseph Bonanno as boss, the Commission has placed the obedient heeders of its decision in danger of life and limb. The vacillating character of the Commission's decisions in this case might be due to Bonanno's status as a Commission member, and to his quarrels with other members.

Because membership in a "family" is not restricted to relatives, membership theoretically can be allocated by individual bosses. But induction of members by a boss increases that boss's strength relative to that of other bosses. Unless membership is controlled, the "family" fiction therefore threatens conditions of peaceful coexistence.

Cosa Nostra adopted the fictive "family" system, but consistently, it also adopted centralized control, by the Commission, of membership criteria and of "family" sizes. The organization works like Phi Beta Kappa, whose national officers control membership both by setting the criteria local chapters must use for admission of individual students and by ruling on which university and college campuses may establish a chapter of the fraternity. The Ku Klux Klan has a similar arrangement.

As indicated earlier, "the books are closed" is used in Cosa Nostra to indicate that a new member cannot be admitted by any boss, without specific approval by the Commission, and the books have been closed for over a decade. One motive for the assassination of Albert Anastasia, boss of a New York "family" from 1951 until his death in 1957, was the fact that he had expanded the membership of his group while the books were closed. This action was in violation of the 1931 peace treaty and, thus, threatened to shake up the entire pattern of political deterrence. Yet in the autumn of 1963, Raymond Patriarca of Providence was able to induct a new member into his "family." The FBI bug in the office of the National Cigarette Service revealed the following:

Patriarca is going to New York with Henry Tameleo and they are going to make Nick or Chick a member of the "family" Wednesday night, 9/25/63, at the Roma. The reasons they are going to make Nick on Wednesday night is "in case they want to make peace Thursday." If they did, he indicated that he (Patriarca) would be tied up trying to effect the peace. [Perhaps this refers to the Bonanno bunch.] Patriarca has obtained permission from the Commission to make Nick because it was an emergency and pointed out that if it were not an emergency, the Commission would not recognize him as a member. He obtained the permission from Tony (last name unknown) to make Nick a member and the ceremony is to take place at 4:00 P.M. on 9/25/63. . . . Patriarca instructed Tameleo to go to Boston and tell Jerry Angiulo what is going on and the Commission has OK'd the making of this kid (Nick). Patriarca is going to turn Nick over to an individual, whose name the informant could not ascertain, or "Whoever they put in Chicago." . . . Raymond [Patriarca] said that the other 24 guys are not made, but the informant did not ascertain the significance of this. . . . He also told Tameleo to tell Joe that the kid will be made at 4 o'clock on September 25. (9/13/63)

A new "family" will be able to develop in the United States only if a nucleus of men can gain control of some small criminal activity and then, over a period of years, gradually "accumulate henchmen, vassals, and property" and slowly "establish solid relations with landowners, businessmen, politicians, policemen, and other . . . families."

Although the fictitious "family" creates problems, it also helps maintain Cosa Nostra exclusiveness. It is an important integrating mechanism, useful to maintaining the identity, cohesion, secrecy, and snobbishness of the membership organization dominated by the Commission. Some members of the upper socioeconomic class in the United States use the same mechanism, and for the same purposes. In New England, at least, it is common for persons of high status to refer to each other as "cousin," even if there is no blood relationship between them. The pretense of blood relationship serves to maintain exclusiveness in the upper classes. Newly rich persons, certainly including all the millionaires of Cosa Nostra, are unable to gain upper-class status simply because they are not one of the fictional blood relatives, the "cousins." The "family" figure performs the same function for Cosa Nostra. A man who suddenly makes a million dollars in a dice game or some other criminal operation cannot become "one of us" in Cosa Nostra, any more than a man who suddenly makes a million dollars betting at the race track can become "one of us" in the upper classes. He is not in the "family." Securing a place in an organized crime "family" is as difficult as securing membership in upper-class society—it takes time to accumulate the necessary "respectability" and "connections." Should an upper-class person violate this principle by taking newly rich persons into the membership of his "cousins," he is likely to be "cut" by his friends. In organized crime, the word is "hit," the synonym for murder.

🖤

Earlier we indicated that common needs and common conditions both make for resemblances in cultural forms and limit these cultural forms. This "law of limited possibilities," as it was called by the anthropologist Alexander Goldenweiser, who formulated it, gives valuable insight into the fact that there is a condition of peaceful coexistence and cooperation between Mafia families in Italy and Sicily, and a similar condition of peaceful coexistence and cooperation between the various organized-crime syndicates in the United States, whether these syndicates are organized as "families" or something else. Professor Goldenweiser's "law" could even be extended to the politics of international diplomacy. There are three important similarities between the needs and the conditions which produced the Sicilian "honored society" and the conditions which produced the American criminal confederation.

First, the closer the geographic proximity, the greater the need for defenses which will permit "family" survival. One such defense is armament, another is a peace treaty or an attitude of respect. In narrow geographic areas, territorial claims are likely to overlap, making conflict inevitable. Wasteful feud or war, followed by rational peace treaties which draw boundaries, are the result, although the "war" step is not inevitable. Boundaries can be geographical, but they also can relate to activities. Each unit can be bound to participate in only one principal kind of activity, as in Sicily. Or, as in New York, all units can be bound to a specified share of the profits from numerous activities, the share being established by the degree of power at the time of the treaty. In simple terms, it is efficient for criminal bands of about equal strength living in close proximity to maintain their common strength against a common enemy (legitimate government) by maintaining the peace, whether these bands are in New York or in western Sicily.

Second, the greater the similarity of the product or service provided by the criminal "families," the greater the likelihood of a confederation between them. The focus here is on business rather than on political diplomacy or strength to wage war. It is economically advantageous for similar businesses to cut costs by avoiding duplication and by forming trade associations which limit the amount and kind of competition. Criminal businesses providing similar or identical products require the same contacts, the same suppliers, and the same kinds of skilled workmen. Further, the corrupt official who issues "licenses" for illicit businesses in a territory may demand that the favors asked of him and the payments made to him be centralized so as to avoid detection and misunderstanding, thus stimulating cooperation.

Third, alliances of groups in widely separated geographic areas are stimulated when the groups deal in goods or services which, by their nature, require coverage of large territories, and the use of common carriers or communication systems. A "family" taking bets in one city has arrangements with police and politicians which would be difficult for a traveler from a distant "family" to establish, even if the local "family" would permit him to operate in its territory. But both "families" must use the services of national-level large lay-off men, high-level financiers, and a wide network of information and communication services. For example, the importation and distribution of narcotics requires elaborate alliances and connections. Such alliances in the narcotics business have been established among American "families" and between American "families" and Sicilian syndicates. Alliances also have existed on an international level between Americans and Canadians, Americans and Italians, Americans and Frenchmen, Americans and Turks, Americans and Lebanese, and others. In a campaign to break up such alliances, Charles Siragusa, formerly deputy director of the Federal Bureau of Narcotics but at the time working as a United States agent in Italy and Greece, once seized 800 pounds of narcotics and arrested a dozen persons in three countries—Turkey, Lebanon, and Syria—all in twenty-four hours.

Many other conditions which are common to Sicilian villages and American urban life could be described. The above sketch supports the notion that the structure of American organized crime is similar to the structure of the Sicilian Mafia not merely because of the Sicilian ancestry of some American criminals, but more importantly because the functions performed by the two organizations are similar. There is no question, of course, that experience in a Sicilian Mafia would be of great advantage to anyone setting out to devise a structure for the operation and control of illicit businesses in the United States. The well-trained officer of a foreign army can be of great assistance to any newly established African nation which has made a place for an army in its political and economic structure.

CHAPTER VIII

The Code

*The carrying out of our recommendation for imme-
diate, comprehensive, and scientific nationwide inquiry
into organized crime should make possible the development of an intelligent plan for its control.*

WICKERSHAM COMMISSION, 1931

IT WAS SUGGESTED in Chapter II that the owners and managers
of the big American enterprise selling illicit goods and services must
be governors as well as business executives. The illegal character of
the American crime cartel turns that cartel into a confederation, a
governmental organization as well as a commercial organization. The
authority structure of Cosa Nostra "families" and of the relationship
among Commission, councils, and bosses is the structure of a government as well as of a business. Even the title used by the participants
for two principal positions in Cosa Nostra's division of labor—lieutenant (captain) and soldier—are governmental titles rather than
business titles. The government which is Cosa Nostra is superimposed
on the operations of any specific illegal business owned or operated
by Cosa Nostra, often with drastic results. For example, a soldier
working as a field man in a policy wheel is rewarded if he increases
profits, and his income goes down when profits go down. But while
he functions, hopefully, as a profit-maker in his field-man role, he
never ceases to be a soldier. He must obey as well as produce. Should
he disobey the boss, he is likely to be punished or murdered, even if
his disobedience brings in greater profits.

The fundamental basis of any government, legal or illegal, is a
code of conduct. Governmental structure is always closely associated

with the code of behavior which its members are expected to follow. The legislative and judicial processes of government are concerned with the specification and the enforcement of this code, whether or not it is clearly set down in rules precise enough to be called "law." A behavioral code, such as the Ten Commandments, becomes "law" only when it is officially adopted by a state, a political organization. Yet the distinction between a state and other organizations such as a church, an extended family, or a trade union is quite arbitrary. As E. Adamson Hoebel's study of American Indian groups has shown, the distinction is most difficult to maintain when attention is turned to societies where patriarchal power is found. The problem can be illustrated by gypsies, who have no territorial organization and no written law, but who do have customs, taboos, and a semijudicial council which makes decisions about the propriety of behavior and, on the basis of these decisions, assesses damages and imposes penalties. The problem also can be illustrated by the "families" of Italian-Sicilian criminals in America, and by the confederation they have formed. Behavior in these "families," like behavior of members of the Sicilian Mafia, is controlled by a government which is substituting for the state, even if the code being enforced can in no sense be considered "criminal law" or "civil law."

We have been unable to locate even a summary statement of the code of conduct used in governing the lives of Cosa Nostra members. There are no "hard data" on governmental structure, but there are no data at all on "the law" of the organization. Because the code of conduct for Cosa Nostra members is unwritten, the files of law-enforcement and investigation agencies, even those whose principal function is assembling intelligence information on organized crime, cannot contain information even remotely comparable to the information available to even the most unenthusiastic student of the American criminal law. There are no statutes to memorize, no Supreme Court decisions to analyze, no law-review analyses to ponder, and no textbooks to provide answers for examination questions. Further, informants are only rarely available for interview, so one cannot locate the organization's "criminal law" in oral codes, as anthropologists do when studying "primitive law." Merely observing the everyday interactions of Cosa Nostra members with each other, with other criminals, or even with noncriminals would provide clues about any special code of conduct they have formulated, but there is no way to observe such interactions in detail. Cosa Nostra cannot be infiltrated. For observation of everyday interactions we must rely on unreliable informers and on remote and impersonal electronic bugs.

These facts of life pose a serious methodological problem for one who would learn something about the norms, values, and rules of organized criminal society. We propose to "solve" the problem in two separate ways. First, we can move from the unknown to the known by deriving social-psychological facts from sociological facts. That is, we can deduce information about norms and codes by analyzing social structure. Second, we can assume that there are similarities in the codes of groups whose places in the broader conventional society are essentially the same. Specifically, we can logically assume that there are similarities in the behavioral codes of groups whose consent to be governed by a legitimate government is given only grudgingly, and for a price. The relationship of prisoners to their governors, the relationship of the populations of contemporary occupied nations to their military governors, and the relationship of Sicilian peasants to numerous occupying governors all resemble the relationship of Cosa Nostra to government officials in the United States. Concretely, "the code" of prisoners can logically be used as an aid in the formulation of "the code" of norms governing the gross conduct of Cosa Nostra members and other organized criminals.

The road from observations of social structure to generalizations about a code of conduct is a rocky one. We can take a clue from the "logic of archaeology" (and of history and geology), but that logic is not without fault. When sociologists and other scientists are unable to test the reliability and validity of observations, they are likely to conclude that no observations have in fact been made. But over the years archaeologists have created information and manufactured data by reasoning that knowledge about inaccessible affairs can be obtained from consideration of affairs accessible to study.

A. R. Radcliffe-Brown has described this approach as one of the methods for reconstructing cultural history, although he is quite critical of it. From bones, pots, tools, and other artifacts dug up by archaeologists, and from analysis of the relationships of these objects to each other, conclusions are drawn about the religious, political, and economic affairs of extinct cultures. Intelligence agencies, of course, use the same kind of reasoning. Strategic intelligence consists, in part, of making a lot out of a little.

If this kind of inferential process is applied to the problem at hand, we can use knowledge about the structure of Cosa Nostra to create information and manufacture data about behavioral norms. It is true, of course, that our knowledge of structure is as yet quite fragmentary and restricted. Nevertheless, specification of the details of all the positions in a division of labor is not essential to an understanding of the main features of a behavioral code. For example, consideration of only one position in the Cosa Nostra structure, that of enforcer, enables one to create information about complex governmental processes and a set of "laws." The enforcer position is "unofficial," in the sense that it appears on no member's chart of Cosa Nostra's hierarchical authority structure and in no description of the division of labor constituting an illicit business. Yet all observers of organized crime agree that the position exists. Moreover, analysis of only one Cosa Nostra murder would establish that it exists, even if most observers insisted that it did not.

The enforcer position, like others, is not to be confused with the person occupying it. The position is more often unoccupied than occupied. The man who moves into it and behaves in terms of its duties and obligations might occupy it for only a few days and then never occupy it again. On the other hand, he might so efficiently fulfill the rights and duties of the position that he becomes a specialist in fulfilling them. Any person occupying the position of enforcer makes arrangements for injuring or killing members and, occasionally, nonmembers. The person occupying the position does not order the maimings or murders, and he does not injure or kill anyone. He performs functions analogous to those performed by a prison warden or the prison official who makes the arrangements for imposing the death penalty. This means that the position must necessarily be integrated with a number of others, including a position for the person actually doing the killing or maiming (executioner), and a position for the person (boss, underboss, commissioner) giving orders to, and participating in "understandings" with, the person occupying the enforcer position. Moreover, since these positions, like the enforcer's functions, are political, they must necessarily be coordinated with other political positions and functions of a legislative, adjudicative, or law-enforcement character. The enforcer position is necessarily one of a subset of positions existing within a broader division of labor designed to maximize organizational integration by means of "just" infliction of punishments on wrongdoers. The presence of an enforcer position in a division of labor must, in other words, be taken as evidence of the presence of complementary governmental positions, leading to our conclusion that Cosa Nostra is a government as well as a business.

The presence of an enforcer position in a division of labor also can be taken as evidence that members of the organization have created some functional equivalent of the criminal law, from which all government officials derive their authority and power. Whatever the content of this set of "law," the presence of the enforcer position signals the fact that it has been designed to minimize the degree of conflict and to maximize the degree of conformity among members. But any set of "law" designed for this purpose must necessarily stress loyalty, honesty, rationality, respect for leaders, and patriotism, and we may therefore assume that such norms are stressed in the society of organized criminals. Informants hypothesizing about a boss's motives for ordering the injuring or execution of "family" members affirm that the behavioral code of Cosa Nostra emphasizes these norms. This field man had his arms broken because he was not turning in all the bets he collected, that lieutenant was executed because he tried to unseat the boss, this underboss was executed because he became psychotic and it was feared that he would betray the group in the course of his insane mutterings, and that soldier was executed on orders from his boss and the Commission because he defied the boss's orders to stop invading the bookmaking territory owned by another boss.

The presence of an enforcer position in a division of labor also signals the fact that punishments are to be imposed "justly," in a disinterested manner. Since punishments are imposed in this manner in order to maintain the consent of the governed, we may assume that the relationships among organized criminals are to a great extent determined by rules and expectations which insure that the consent of the governed is not lost. When justice prevails, the norms that govern the resort to adjudication serve to reduce conflict because they establish regularized expectations about the way disagreements will be settled. American society's laws making larceny a crime punishable by imprisonment are reflected in children's playground behavior with respect to bats, balls, swings, and roller skates. And Cosa Nostra's "laws" making disloyalty (informing) a capital offense are reflected in everyday tight-lipped and cautious conversations, in fish-eyed facial expressions signifying arrogance, ignorance, and innocence, and in gestures of deference and "respect." Because American society supports the law of larceny, incidents requiring judicial prosecution for larceny arise only occasionally. And because Cosa Nostra society supports the "law of loyalty," incidents requiring the services of men acting as enforcer and executioner also arise only occasionally.

Stated in reverse, the principle is that regularized expectations concerning the way disagreements will be settled are also the norms used in the adjudicative process. The presence of an enforcer position in Cosa Nostra's division of labor, then, enables us to conclude that the day-to-day interactions of organized criminals are directed by norms which are also used in the adjudication process. The existence of an adjudication process signals, in turn, the existence of a legislative process. "The law" must somehow be established before it can be enforced, whether it be established by royal decree, by democratic vote, or by some combination of fiat and ballot.

Since there is such a striking similarity between the structure of the Italian-Sicilian Mafia and the structure of the American confederation of criminals, it should not be surprising to find great similarity in the values, norms, and other behavior patterns of the members of the two organizations. As mentioned earlier, any organizational structure, at least in its governmental aspects, is related both to its objectives and to the kind of code of behavior members are expected to follow. The code of behavior of the Mafia and the code of behavior of American organized criminals, in turn, are likely to be similar because both organizations are outlawed. Two succinct summaries of the Sicilian Mafia code of *"omertà,"* or "manliness," specify the focal concerns of members. The first statement was made in 1892, the second in 1900.

(1) Reciprocal aid in case of any need whatever. (2) Absolute obedience to the chief. (3) An offense received by one of the members to be considered an offense against all and avenged at any cost. (4) No appeal to the state's authorities for justice. (5) No revelation of the names of members or any secrets of the association.

✿ ✿ ✿

(1) To help one another and avenge every injury of a fellow member. (2) To work with all means for the defense and freeing of any fellow member who has fallen into the hands of the judiciary. (3) To divide the proceeds of thievery, robbery, and extortion with certain consideration for the needy as determined by the *capo*. (4) To keep the oath and maintain secrecy on pain of death within twenty-four hours.

The two statements differ very little. One spells out the dictatorial character of the government and the other mentions criminal activities. These variations could well be the consequence of the perspectives of the two summarizers, rather than differences in codes themselves. Both statements indicate that the Mafia creed asks the members for loyalty, honor, respect, rationality, secrecy, honesty, and, above all, consent to be governed, which in this case means consent to be executed. Except for the last item, these are the attributes of honorable men everywhere, and even honorable men agree, as a part of their citizenship, to the death penalty for traitors. Gus Tyler only exaggerated slightly when he said the rules very well might have been written for the Three Musketeers (one for all and all for one), for the Industrial Workers of the World (an injury to one is an injury to all), for the Irish Republican Army, for the Mau Mau, for the Hatfields or the McCoys, or for delinquent gangs struggling over "turf" or waging a battle against officialdom. The code expresses hostility toward the authority in power while at the same time recognizing the need to acknowledge its might.

Despite the clear evidence that the Sicilian Mafia has a structure similar to that of any rationally devised bureaucracy, authorities are not convinced that the organization was, or is, much more than an informal agreement to abide by the behavioral code. Gaetano Mosca reports that a Sicilian-Italian dictionary of 1868 defines the Mafia as a neologism denoting any sign of bravado, a bold show, while a dictionary of 1876 defines it as a word of Piedmontese origin somewhat equivalent to "gang." Thus, in the nineteenth century the term was defined both as an attitude and as a group of men. This pattern has been carried forward by Luigi Barzini, who says that in one of its meanings the word should be spelled with a lower-case "m," while in the other meaning the word should be capitalized.

The lower-case mafia is a state of mind, a philosophy of life, a conception of society, a moral code, a particular susceptibility, prevailing among all Sicilians. They are taught in the cradle, or are born already knowing, that they must aid each other, side with their friends and fight common enemies even when the friends are wrong and the enemies right; each must defend his dignity at all costs and never allow the smallest slights and insults to go unavenged; they must keep secrets, and always beware of official authority and laws. . . . a Sicilian who does not feel these compulsions should no longer consider himself a Sicilian. . . .

Mafia, in the second and more specialized meaning of the word, is the world-famous illegal organization. It is not strictly an organized association, with hierarchies, written statutes, headquarters, ruling élite and an undisputed chief. It is a spontaneous formation like an ant-colony or a beehive, a loose and haphazard collection of single men and heterogeneous groups, each man obeying his entomological rules, each group uppermost in its tiny domain, independent, submitted to the will of its own leader, each group locally imposing its own rigid form of primitive justice. Only in rare times of emergency does the Mafia mobilize and become one loose confederation.

The notion that the Mafia is more of an attitude than an organization was also taken by Premier Mussolini's Chief of Police, Cesare Mori, who was in charge of the drive against the Sicilian Mafia in the 1920's:

The Mafia, as I am describing it, is a peculiar way of looking at things and of acting which, through mental and spiritual affinities, brings together in definite, unhealthy attitudes men of particular temperament, isolating them from their surroundings into a kind of caste. It is a potential state which normally takes concrete form in a system of local oligarchies closely interwoven, but each autonomous in its own district.

In this short statement, there are at least six words or phrases ("caste," "potential state," "concrete form," "system," "oligarchies," "autonomous") which refer to structural or organizational aspects of the Mafia, not to attitudes. This kind of oversight could occur in two ways. First, many writers are not aware that there can be organization without written rules, formal procedures, and organizational charts similar to those of a governmental bureau or department. Second, police must necessarily be more interested in capturing individual criminals than in worrying about the structure of organizations. Since attitudes belong to individuals, while "hierarchies" belong to organizations, even Mussolini's prefect of police overlooked some of the evidence he needed to help him in his organized-crime drive. A number of men with common attitudes, a hierarchy of authority and power, a system for accepting or rejecting applicants, and a system for policing the behavior of the participants is an organization, even if the goals are not precisely stated. Formal fraternal organizations invent positions, roles, and rituals in order to maximize the commitment of the members, and in that way they develop attitudes of brotherhood and kinship. The Sicilian Mafia started with brotherhood and kinship and developed the structure necessary to a government and business organization as well as to a fraternity.

The snippets of information I have been able to obtain about the code of conduct and the enforcement machinery used in the confederation of American organized criminals have convinced me that there is a striking similarity to the code of conduct and enforcement machinery governing the behavior of prisoners everywhere. This is no coincidence. The governments which prisoners have devised for regulating their own conduct are, like the government of Cosa Nostra, responses to official governments that are limited in their means for achieving control objectives. Further, there is a remarkable similarity between the Cosa Nostra code, the code of the Sicilian Mafia, and the code of underground resistance groups operating in occupied nations in wartime. All four groups stress (1) *extreme loyalty* to the organization and its governing elite, (2) *honesty* in relationships with members, (3) *secrecy* regarding the organization's structure and activities, and (4) *honorable behavior* which sets members off as morally superior to those outsiders who would govern them. The characteristics which the norms of the four groups have in common do not necessarily establish that the four have been in contact with each other. The norms said by Paul J. Gillette and Eugene Tillinger to characterize the Ku Klux Klan resemble the norms said by Tan Jee Bah to characterize certain criminal societies in Singapore, but these groups have never been in contact. But neither are the similarities completely accidental. In order to maintain their status as governors of illegal organizations, the leaders of the four types of organization must promulgate and enforce similar behavioral codes.

All four illicit organizations are products of a situation in which an official and dominant government has lost or has failed to obtain the consent of the governed. Accordingly, similarities in the basic values shared by members of each organization could have arisen without contact between the organizations. Sicilians lived under conditions very similar to "occupation" for about a thousand years. Various conquering forces lost the Sicilians' consent to be governed, and the Sicilian peasants learned to evade the government in power. Equally important, they learned to devise substitutes for providing the services ordinarily provided by official governments, and these substitutes eventually became the Mafia. During World War II, Norwegian, French, and Polish underground members, among others, were dedicated to harassing the Nazis and to easing the pangs of occupation; they could not call on the Nazis for the administration of justice or for other governmental services. Efficiency and even survival itself depended upon loyalty and secrecy. Prisoners are held against their will in an authoritarian setting; we shall see that they, too, withdraw their consent to be governed by their official governors.

The Cosa Nostra case is not so simple, for America is in no

sense occupied by an alien government. Yet the similarity is there, for on matters pertaining to the purchase and sale of the illicit goods and services on which organized crime thrives, the consent of a large minority of the governed is withheld. Cosa Nostra is not now dedicated to escaping all the demands of civilized government. It is as yet dedicated only to maintaining immunity from the official criminal-law process, especially in the areas in which respectable citizens demand illicit goods and services, just as was the case with underground groups during World War II. Jan Karski has effectively argued that the Polish underground was dedicated to providing the Polish people with Polish economic, political, and social institutions. Even the Ku Klux Klan developed as an underground resistance movement of Southern whites against the Reconstruction government —and has been dedicated to providing a way of life which the regional majority wanted. Perhaps it is this similarity to unofficial underground governments that stimulates law-enforcement officers to refer to American organized criminals as an "enemy." While this appellation is correct, in view of the fact that there is organized defection from the rules of the governing body, it is incorrectly used as a rallying cry for prosecution of organized criminals. If organized criminals could be handled as enemies in time of traditional wars, rather than as citizens with the rights of due process, they could have been wiped out long ago.

Nevertheless, it is not concern for due process in its pure form which permits organized crime to thrive in the United States. The late Professor Herbert Bloch showed, as have many others, that the American confederation thrives because a large minority of citizens demand the illicit goods and services it has for sale. The unofficial governments found among Sicilian peasants, among the participants in underground movements, and among prisoners are signs that even a strong government might be limited in its means for achieving its control objectives. The unofficial government which is Cosa Nostra suggests that our strong government is similarly limited. A prison administrator is admonished to control inmates, but he is limited in what he can do to, with, and for inmates by the values of his society and by the need for inmate help in production, maintenance, and even security tasks. In occupied countries, the alien government must try to maintain security measures which will minimize the chances that it will be overthrown, but at the same time it cannot use security measures so strict that the natives cannot perform at least the minimal tasks necessary to economic production and social order. *All* the loyal citizens cannot be incarcerated or shot. There must be "compromise"—sometimes indistinguishable from corruption—on the part of the official government.

American government officially wants organized crime eradicated, but it limits itself by respecting the wishes of a large minority which demands the "right" to purchase illicit goods and services, and by following traditional concepts of due process in trying to prosecute the sellers of these goods and services. In this game, everyone wins. Those who insist, for example, that gambling be outlawed win by displaying the evidence, in the form of an antigambling statute, of opposition to gambling. Those who insist on gambling, gamble in spite of the statute. And those who have the capital and the muscle necessary to meet the competition can provide the illicit gambling services and reap huge profits because they are protected by the very morality which got the antigambling statute passed in the first place.

Because their transactions are outlawed, the big illicit businesses which have grown up to meet the demands of the public cannot be internally regulated by law. The executives of Cosa Nostra cannot routinely call upon the legitimate government for protection from underlings, from competitors, or even from robbers and embezzlers. If their firms are to survive, they must protect themselves. Moreover, they must show concern for unemployment-compensation plans, retirement pensions, and procedures for adjudicating civil disputes. All these substitutes for the services ordinarily provided by government have been devised by the leaders of the American confederation. In devising them, the leaders have transformed their business organization into an illicit government which resembles the illicit governments represented by the Sicilian Mafia, by underground movements, and by alliances of prisoners.

Enforcing "the law" of this private government involves further violation of our criminal laws, and not just the laws outlawing the sale of illicit goods and services. Crimes of violence and murder are committed for the purpose of maintaining "legal" order in the illicit government which is the confederation. The wealth acquired from millions of two-dollar bets made daily with what might appear to be "mom and pop" bookies is protected by perpetration of the most horrendous crimes known to man. The wealth thus protected and the coercive power amassed to protect it are then used to corrupt the very legal and economic order which gives the two-dollar bettors their freedom.

Of the four types of unofficial and illegal government, most is known about prisoners' government. For at least twenty years researchers have been documenting the tenets of prisoners' behavioral codes, and they have shown that there is close similarity between the code used in one prison and the code used in another. I shall use knowledge about the code of prisoners as a source of information about the Cosa Nostra code which, as indicated, is not directly observable. One summary of the many descriptions of life in a wide variety of prisons has suggested that the chief tenets of the inmate code can be classified roughly into five major categories. Elsewhere I have shortened and rewritten this summary as follows:

First, there are those maxims that caution: *Don't interfere with inmate interests*. These center on the idea that inmates should serve the least possible time while enjoying the greatest possible number of pleasures and privileges. Included are directives such as *never rat on a con; don't be nosy; don't have a loose lip; keep off a man's back; don't put a guy on the spot*. Put positively, *be loyal to your class*, the cons.

A second set of behavioral rules asks inmates to refrain from quarrels or arguments with fellow prisoners: *don't lose your head; play it cool; do your own time; don't bring heat*.

Third, prisoners assert that inmates should not take advantage of one another by means of force, fraud, or chicanery: *don't exploit inmates*. This injunction sums up several directives: *don't break your word; don't steal from cons; don't sell favors; don't be a racketeer; don't welsh on debts. Be right*.

Fourth, some rules have as their central theme the maintenance of self: *don't weaken; don't whine; don't cop out* [plead guilty]. Stated positively: *be tough; be a man*.

Fifth, prisoners express a variety of maxims that forbid according prestige or respect to the guards or the world for which they stand: *don't be a sucker; skim it off the top; never talk to a screw* [guard]; *have a connection; be sharp.*

Prison inmates as a group do not give the warden and his staff their consent to be governed. By withholding this consent and developing their own unofficial government, they accomplish precisely what prison officials say they do not want them to accomplish— illegally obtained status symbols, power, and an unequal share of goods and services in short supply. Organized criminals, like prisoners, live outside the law, and in response to this outlaw status they, like prisoners, develop a set of norms and procedures for controlling conduct within their organization. John Irwin and I have shown, in fact, that the five general directives making up the prisoners' code are characteristic of the code of good thieves everywhere. Specifically, the chief tenets of this thieves' code as it is found among organized criminals can be summarized and briefly illustrated as follows:

1. *Be loyal to members of the organization. Do not interfere with each other's interests. Do not be an informer.* This directive, with its correlated admonitions, is basic to the internal operations of the Cosa Nostra confederation. It is a call for unity, for peace, for maintenance of the *status quo,* and for silence. Generally speaking, the decision for peace which followed the 1930–1931 war was based on this directive. Although a lieutenant or boss may order a soldier to commit crime, a soldier cannot commit crime on his own, without the approval of his superiors. To do so might be to interfere with another member's interests. If the member of one "family" has a business in the territory of another "family," as sometimes happens, he is expected to inform the boss of the second "family," so he can keep a helpful eye on the business. If a member leaves his home territory for "business reasons," he must supply his superior with an itinerary. The need for secrecy is obvious. Until about ten years ago, members were forbidden to speak to law-enforcement agents; now they may speak to them when practical, but too many conversations will surely arouse suspicion. A lieutenant talking to two soldiers about the value of secrecy made the following comment in order to

illustrate his point: "They blew up his car. Nobody knows about it. Another guy they shot up. Nobody knows about it. Other shootings. Nobody knows about it."

2. *Be rational. Be a member of the team. Don't engage in battle if you can't win.* What is demanded here is the corporate rationality necessary to conducting illicit businesses in a quiet, safe, profitable manner. Violence involving other Cosa Nostra members and stealing from members is to be avoided. Controversies are to be settled by means of a rational judicial process set up for that purpose (see p. 207). The directive extends to personal life. Like a prisoner, the man occupying even the lowest position in a "family" unit is to be cool and calm at all times. This means, for example, that neither a soldier nor any other member is to use narcotics, to be drunk on duty, to get into fights, to have an affair with another member's wife or (if married) with the sister or daughter of a member, or to do much of anything without first checking with his superiors. The underboss of a New York "family," accompanied by a soldier, passed a law-enforcement officer on the street. The soldier spat on the policeman. The underboss apologized profusely and, presumably, took punitive action against his worker. The soldier was not, in the language of inmates, "playing it cool." The boss of a different "family" at one time temporarily stopped all lottery operations in his city because the business was drawing the attention of the police to the even more lucrative criminal activities of the organization. As Tyler has observed:

In this era of the "organization man," the underworld—like most institutions that prosper within an established culture—has learned to conform. Its internal structure provides status for those who would plod along in workaday clothes. In its external relations, it affects all the niceties of a settled society, preferring public relations and investment to a punch in the nose or pickpocketing.

3. *Be a man of honor. Always do right. Respect womanhood and your elders. Don't rock the boat.* This emphasis on "honor" and "respect" helps determine who obeys whom, who attends what funerals and weddings, who opens the door for whom, who takes a tone of deference in a telephone conversation, who rises when another walks into a room. Later we will show that emphasis on honor

actually functions to enable despots to exploit their underlings. It is the right and duty of every member to question every other member's conduct, even that of a boss or underboss, if he suspects that the other man is not "doing right." He also is duty-bound to come to the defense of all others—on the principle that an offense against one is an offense against all.

4. *Be a stand-up guy. Keep your eyes and ears open and your mouth shut. Don't sell out.* A "family" member, like a prisoner, must be able to withstand frustrating and threatening situations without complaining or resorting to subservience. The "stand-up guy" shows courage and "heart." He does not whine or complain in the face of adversity, including punishment, because "If you can't pay, don't play." In his testimony before the McClellan Committee, Joseph Valachi reported that juvenile delinquents appearing in police stations or jails are watched and assessed to determine whether they "stand up" to the police, this behavior being taken as a sign that they possess the "manliness" so essential to membership in Cosa Nostra. More recently, a soldier used "stand-up kids" in an attempt to praise the qualities of the members of his lieutenant's regime. This soldier is "Mike," whose conversations on pp. 18 and 116 above showed concern for an FBI investigation:

They are telling them everything. Who's Cosa Nostra. What's the picture here. Who the bosses are. Who's the bosses? These are kids that don't know nothing. They are schooling them. They are telling them up and down the line what everything is here. They are actually exposing the whole fucking thing to innocent kids. (Inaudible.) Innocent kids. Exposing the whole thing. "He's a captain." (Inaudible.) And so forth, I said. Good. Your kids now, you know, are all stand-up kids. They're going to bring a guy in that is not a stand-up kid, and— . They are going to tell them not a word.

5. *Have class. Be independent. Know your way around the world.* Two basic ideas are involved here, and both prohibit the according of prestige to law-enforcement officials or other respectable citizens. One is expressed in the saying, "To be straight is to be a victim." A man who is committed to regular work and submission to duly constituted authority is a sucker. When one Cosa Nostra member intends to insult and cast aspersion on the competence of another, he

is likely to say, sneeringly, "Why don't you go out and get a job?" Second, the world seen by organized criminals is a world of graft, fraud, and corruption, and they are concerned with their own honesty and manliness as compared with the hypocrisy of corrupt policemen and corrupt political figures. A criminal who plays the role of corrupter is superior to a criminal who plays the role of corruptee.

Vague, general, and overlapping as the tenets of the code are, they form the foundation of the legal order of the confederation. One's standing in the status hierarchy of Cosa Nostra depends in part on his ability to bring in profits, in part upon his not being caught violating the code. Serious violators of the prohibitions against informing and against interfering with another criminal's interest are killed. Since conformity to or deviation from the code is so important in the lives of family members, it is probable that argot terms have been developed for various kinds of conforming and deviating behavior. I am not familiar with any such argot terms which are unique to the confederation, however. "Stand-up guy," "rat," "fink," "stool pigeon," and variants of these terms are used, but these terms are not significantly different from those used by the members of other systems, legal and illegal. A campaign slogan used by a Nevada governor with reference to himself was: "He is a stand-up guy."

Both Samuel M. Strong and Clarence Schrag have suggested that groups characterize members in relation to the problems, lines of interest, and focal concerns of the group, and then attach distinctive names to these types. Since the problems, focal concerns, and lines of interest of prisoners and members of the criminal confederation are almost identical, it would not be surprising if the distinctive names attached to some types of organized criminals were not similar to the distinctive names attached to some types of prisoners. Before turning to an examination of the functions the code has in the governing of confederation members, I would like to suggest that investigators with access to criminals' conversations should be able to find among confederation members the three principal deviant roles found among prison inmates. Preliminary examination indicates that these roles are indeed present among organized criminals, despite the fact that I have heard no argot terms for them. I am convinced that the functions the code serves for the confederation will not really be understood until the relationships among the three informal roles are understood.

Prisoners who exhibit highly aggressive behavior against other inmates or against officials are likely to be called "toughs," "hoods," "gorillas," "ballbusters," or some similar name, depending on the prison they are in. The terms are all synonyms, and they refer to men likely to be diagnosed as "psychopaths," who hijack their fellow inmates when the latter are returning from the commissary, who attack guards and fellow inmates verbally and physically, who run any kangaroo court, who force incoming inmates to pay for cell and job assignments, who smash up the prison at the beginning of a riot. Precisely the same type is found among organized criminals. "Dutch Schultz" (Arthur Flegenheimer), one of the last Prohibition gangsters to hold out against "The Italian Society" that formed just prior to the 1930–1931 war, exemplified this type. The following description of a murder committed by Flegenheimer was written by his lawyer, corrupter, and money mover. It reveals the "tough," or "gorilla," character of both the murderer and his victim:

Dutch Schultz was ugly; he had been drinking and suddenly he had his gun out. The Dutchman wore his pistol under his vest, tucked inside his pants, right against his belly. One jerk at his vest and he had it in his hand. All in the same quick motion he swung it up, stuck it in Jules Martin's mouth, and pulled the trigger. It was as simple and undramatic as that—just one quick motion of the hand. The Dutchman did that murder just as casually as if he were picking his teeth. . . . Julie was the bigmouthed ape who ran the restaurant racket for Schultz. He had two big labor unions terrorized and in two years he had shaken down $2,000,000 from the eating places in the Broadway section, including Jack Dempsey's. Once I had seen Julie with his bare hands beat up a man horribly. . . . Julie was saying that he had stolen only $20,000 and the Dutchman was insisting he had stolen $70,000 and they were fighting over the difference.

Currently, "toughs" in criminal syndicates are likely to occupy an enforcer or executioner position. Enforcers, as we have seen, carry out punishments, including executions, ordered by a judicial authority which has some legislative basis for its action. The process of "carrying out" a judicial order does not require that the penal administrator personally inflict the punishment or perform the execution. In Cosa Nostra, a variety of positions for executioners have been designed for this purpose. One type of executioner "sets up" the victim, another does the actual killing, and other types make lesser contributions. The men who occupy these positions resemble the prisoners called "toughs" both when they are performing their duties and when they are off duty.

In Cosa Nostra, as in prison, the man who plays the role of the "tough" is both an asset and a threat to other types of leaders. He is a leader because he stands above the ordinary run of soldiers or buttons, and he is an asset because he readily follows order to control by "muscle." But the fact that he controls by "muscle" also makes him a threat to whoever uses him. Raymond V. Martin, former Assistant Chief of Brooklyn South Detectives, has described the "Gallo-Profaci war" that developed in 1961–1962 when a faction of "toughs" in a Brooklyn "family" tried to overthrow their leaders because they believed they were being cheated. One of the Gallo brothers was described in 1959 as "chief enforcer and goon for the hood-dominated Local 266 of the Teamsters Union" after he had assertedly held a knife at the throat of a businessman who had permitted another union to install a pinball machine in his bar.

The style of the modern Cosa Nostra "tough" is revealed in the following conversation between two soldiers and their lieutenant. The men are angry because they believe that discipline in Cosa Nostra is breaking down, and because they have evidence that even some members ("friends") are being induced by police officials to become informers. Assassination is their solution. In the soliloquy, Mike proposes that the organization return to a former system of interrogating and testing each member to insure loyalty. He indicates his willingness and the willingness of his lieutenant, Pete ("Petey Pumps"), to undergo such a screening process.

MIKE. I said it two years ago. You got to go deep in the fucking holes and make new tunnels. That's what we gotta do.
PETE. Underground?

MIKE. Underground. Underground and reorganize and come up. And leave a couple of fucking bodies on every fucking corner. And every fucking stool pigeon we got a line on. There hasn't been any of that. I don't want to be vicious. I don't want to be bloodthirsty, but, Pete, you talk to people and they're not afraid no more. They're looking to defy you.

PETE. Yeah.

MIKE. They actually are looking to defy you. So, you don't want to say—say Jesus Christ, you don't want to be known as a bloodthirsty guy. Where is all this going to get us now? Guys walk in. They want to spit in your face. I mean every—not every third guy, but *every* guy that walks in to the station house or FBI office is given an opportunity to be a rat. So, he's got a house, he's got a business, he's got a few dollars. He's facing twenty years. So shit, "Nobody's going to know about it, I'm going to live."

LARRY. We got a lot of no good cocksuckers there. There's even a fucking guy. One, one *friend* over there that we think—

MIKE. I know. I know all about it. This cocksucker. Nice fellow (Inaudible.) In the head. You know where I want to put him, don't you?

LARRY. This is *ours*. This cocksucker. I got to take this cocksucker, this dirty motherfucker.

MIKE. You know where you got to put him? You know what I told Pete? You got to pick a lamppost. He's got to put the— hang him on the lamppost. You understand? You got to cut his prick off. You got to put it in his pocket and you got to give him a nice slash and leave him up there. That's what you got to do. That will serve notice to every fucking rat stool pigeon what's gonna happen when and if he finks.

LARRY. Mike, we gotta lota garbage.

MIKE. You can't leave them and you can't bury them. Bury them. You can't—

LARRY. Nah. You know what I told 'em? You know what I told 'em? I said, "Look, let's fuck around—let's fuck this shit. They know everything. Now fuck them. Let 'em see what we'll do. Then let them go fuck themselves." What are they gonna do? Go and hide? Fuck them. To let them go, they gonna break their mother's cunt. Go break the Rock of Gibralter. They got a better chance. What are they gonna break? They gonna break their sister's cunt.

MIKE. The ones they were gonna break, they broke down already. The rats they already broke down. It goes back to the same thing we said yesterday. The ego's been deflated. We took their prestige away. Now,

I have an old proverb: "If I can't fight you, I join you." This is what we have to do then. Then we got to retrench ourselves. Now, we got to get wise to ourselves. We got to go deep, deep, deep, deep. Like you said yesterday what you did with your bookmaker. You took from here and you put it to there. That's what we got to do now. We have to do what we should have been doing. We had a meeting one time: "Who did you bring there? Who was he? Where was he born? How was he born? What is he doing right now?" Every fucking friend should be screened. I wouldn't give a fuck. Pete, have you got anything to hide? I got nothing to hide. Whoever was my godfather? What am I doing? He's got to come and he's got to ask me what I'm doing, and how I'm doing, and where I'm doing it, and I got to tell him. Every skipper's got to bring a fucking report on any fucking man that belongs to him, and if he feels the least bit of doubt he's got to show it, and he's got to screen him, and each skipper has got to get two or three guys. Screen out Mike Scandi. Yeah. Screen out Petey Pumps and— We got to do that. Like I said, I don't want to be bloodthirsty. Leave a couple of fucking heads hanging on a fucking pole. The stool pigeons that are flouting it in our face, they'll think twice. They'll think fucking twice before going over to the Law. *Friends or no friends*. They seem to say the same thing: "What are they going to do to me? They aren't going to hurt me." They're getting deals out of it. They're coming out and telling you that they put a fucking fort around Gallo. Gallo gave them the fucking information. Whether it's true or isn't true we have our own ways of finding out.

A second type of prisoner role is identified in prison argot as the "merchant," "peddler," or "con politician." Prisoners playing this role do favors for their fellow prisoners in direct exchange for favors from them, or for payment in cigarettes, the medium of exchange in most prisons. Many if not most of the "favors" involve distribution of goods and services which should go to inmates without cost—the "merchant" demands a price for dental care, laundry, food, library books, a good job assignment, etc. Thus the "merchant," like the "tough" or "gorilla," actually exploits other inmates while seeming to help make prison life easier for them.

Cosa Nostra also has positions for "merchants" who make their way in the world by manipulating and "dealing" with their fellow criminals. One criminal occupational position occupied by "merchants" is that of usurer. While these persons lend money at usurious rates to respectable victims outside the confederation, they also take advantage of their fellow criminals' misfortunes by helping and assisting them, at usurious rates. Prison inmates make a distinction between the "real man" or "right guy" (to be discussed below) who might "score" for food occasionally, and the "merchant" who sells stolen food on a "route." The man who "scores" may distribute part of the loot to his friends, with no definite obligation to repay, but the man with the "route" gives nothing away. The loan shark (sometimes called a "shylock," a "shy," or a "shell") is, by analogy, the man with the "route." He is out to make money wherever he can make it. Since usurers stand by to lend money to gamblers in need, and since organized criminals are frequently gamblers in need, usurious loans often are made to members of the organization. In hearings on loan-sharking held by the New York State Commission of Investigation, Ralph Salerno, then Sergeant of Detectives in the Criminal Intelligence Bureau of the New York City Police Department, testified, in effect, that the organized criminal's need for the services of the loan shark makes it possible for the loan shark to exploit him:

It is a demonstration of power. You have something which, I think, is unique in criminal fields in loan-sharking to a height and to a degree in their own criminal circles that I have never seen duplicated anywhere. It seems to be an unwritten law that even if you are a criminal, even if you are a top guy, you always pay the shylock. . . . You borrow money, you pay it back. . . . [The members of the Gallo brothers' clique] weren't afraid of the shylock. But they didn't know when they might need him again. So they very diligently paid the shylock.

The buffer position in Cosa Nostra "families" also is a position for a "merchant." As we indicated earlier, men occupying the position of buffer are carefully selected and highly trusted by the boss or by a lieutenant. The main duty of the buffer is to be aware of all the operations of his immediate superior and to keep that superior officer informed, while at the same time keeping him insulated from police and prosecuting attorneys. In practice, however, this duty requires him to gather information about his fellow criminals and to report his findings to a man who has the power of life and death over the underlings. Accordingly, in return for "favors" he allocates "favors," such as interviews with the boss or lieutenant, which in a different system the lower-status worker would be able to get for himself, free of charge.

The "right guy," or the "real man," is the third principal type of inmate role identified in prison argot. Men who play this role are the highest status men in any prison. This is no accident, for the prisoner's code of behavior summarized above is really the code of a "right guy," the epitome of the "good prisoner." Because the "right guy" in prison closely resembles the "stand-up guy" in confederated crime, it also may be said that the Cosa Nostra code summarized above is the code of the "stand-up guys" who have the highest status in the hierarchy of a "family" and in the complete confederation. The author of a book published in 1930 used the "right-guy" phrase in reference to organized crime. In describing Al Capone's affection for a restaurateur, one Tony the Greek, Fred D. Palsey commented as follows:

Needless to say, Tony was another who esteemed Capone as "a right guy." He was of the species known as Capone fans, which numbers thousands in Chicago. He liked nothing better than to spin yarns of Capone's big-heartedness.

If the boss or underboss of a "family" were asked to describe an ideal underling, or if a soldier were asked to describe an ideal boss or underboss, each probably would use the "big-heartedness" phrase. He also would use many of the other phrases used to describe the "right guy" in prison. The following is one such description. I quote at some length because in the next chapter I will show how the "right guys" of organized crime, the bosses and underbosses, use the "right-guy" code to protect themselves from both the police and underlings.

A *right guy* is always loyal to his fellow prisoners. He never lets you down no matter how rough things get. He keeps his promise; he's dependable and trustworthy. He isn't nosy about your business and doesn't fall all over himself to make friends either—he has a certain dignity. The *right guy* never interferes with other inmates who are conniving against the officials. He doesn't go around looking for a fight, but he never runs away from one when he is in the right. Anybody who starts a fight with a *right guy* has to be ready to go all the way. When he's got or can get extras in prison—like cigarettes, food stolen from the mess hall, and so on—he shares with his friends. He doesn't take advantage of those who don't have much. He doesn't strong-arm other inmates into punking or fagging for him; instead, he acts like a man.

In his dealings with the prison officials, the *right guy* is unmistakably against them, but he doesn't act foolishly. When he talks about the officials with other inmates, he's sure to say that even the hacks with the best intentions are stupid, incompetent, and not to be trusted; that the worst thing a con can do is give the hacks information—they'll only use it against you when the chips are down. A *right guy* sticks up for his rights, but he doesn't ask for pity: he can take all the lousy screws can hand out and more. He doesn't suck around the officials, and the privileges that he's got are his because he deserves them. Even if the *right guy* doesn't look for trouble with the officials, he'll go to the limit if they push him too far. He realizes that there are just two kinds of people in the world, those in the know skim it off the top; suckers work.

If there were no violations of the Cosa Nostra code, everyone would be a "stand-up guy," or, to use the prisoner's term, a "right guy." For this reason, the bosses, underbosses, and other high-status men promulgate both the code and its corollary, the notion that all members should be "stand-up guys" like themselves. Were the code never violated, there would be no informers and few loose lips, with the result that the illicit government's operation would be a complete mystery to the police and other representatives of legitimate government. Further, if every member were a "stand-up guy" or a "right guy," the captain would never be a threat to the underboss, and the underboss would never be a threat to the boss. That is not the case. The code is violated, obviously, by men acting the role of "tough" and the role of "merchant," for they are exploiting fellow criminals and thereby interfering with their interests.

The fact that a code of conduct calling for loyalty, secrecy, rationality, honor, and resistance is violated, even frequently, does not mean that it is unimportant in the control of conduct. Our legitimate "code" regarding the right to private property has been put into the precise form of the criminal law, and the "code" as well as the law is violated whenever a larceny is committed. Nevertheless, this "code" determines, directly or indirectly, a broad range of social interactions among both honest and dishonest citizens. The important problem for one who would understand a society or group guided by a code is not that of determining whether the code is violated but that of determining the code's function in the preservation of order.

CHAPTER IX

Some Functions of the Code

This phantom of government enforces its own law, carries out its own executions, and not only ignores but abhors the democratic processes of justice which are held to be the safeguards of the American citizen.

KEFAUVER COMMITTEE

THE CODE of honor and silence which asks every member of Cosa Nostra to be a "stand-up guy," and which underlies the entire structure of the criminal cartel and confederation, performs the same important function that the "rule of law" once performed for absolute monarchs—it protects the personal power of the rulers. Although implementing the ideal of "a government of law, not of men" is now viewed as basic to protection of man's freedom from tyrants, the idea was once used for maintaining the conditions of tyranny. One who displeased the monarch by revolting against him in the name of democracy was taking the law into his own hands. As democracy developed, so did the prohibitions against *ex post facto* legislation, ideas about the right of revolution, and similar systems of government by the law of the people rather than by the law of the monarch. Whether or not a "government by law" insures basic freedoms to a greater degree than does a "government by men" depends upon who makes, and enforces, the law. In Cosa Nostra, the rule of law is the rule of a despot.

Although the code of organized criminals is purportedly for the protection of "the people," it is administered and enforced for the protection of each boss. Since the boss of a "family" has the most to lose if the organization is weakened through an attack by outsiders, he enthusiastically promotes the notion that an offense against one is an offense against all. Moreover, this same principle protects the boss from his own underlings. The principle gets transformed so that it deals with matters of safety rather than matters of offense—the safety of all depends upon the safety of each. Since each conforming member is guaranteed a livelihood without fear of encroachment by other members or by nonmembers, each member must be "protected." This transformation, of course, authorizes the boss to take extreme measures to insure his own safety by crushing any plot or potential plot against him by his underlings. The principle also encourages informing. Despite the code's admonition to be tight-lipped, one is guilty by association if he does not report that a member has injured him or another member. By promulgating the idea that "We are all equals in matters of defense," the boss makes lower-status workers his "boys," who henceforth are dependent upon his paternalism. Organized criminals frequently refer to some subordinate, who might be fifty years old, as "the kid." A boss who can establish that he will assist his followers when they have been offended or when they are in need has gained control over these men. They become indebted to him. They are obligated to reciprocate, in the name of "honor" and "loyalty," thus enhancing his privileged position. The saying is, "If you don't respect the boss, no one will respect you."

Those aspects of the code which prohibit appealing to outside authorities for help and justice also serve to concentrate power in the hands of the few and, hence, to enable leaders to exploit followers. The ruler of an organized-crime unit, whether it be an entire Cosa Nostra "family" or a thirty-man lottery enterprise, has three classes of enemies—law-enforcement officers, outsiders who want his profits, and underlings. The code protects him from all of them.

Of the three groups, the law-enforcement agencies seem to be the least threatening. We will show later that police actions against organized crime are hampered by lack of enthusiasm on the part of the governments which support the police, by lack of coordinated intelligence information, and by a commitment to due process of law. Each "family" has been rationally organized to take advantage of these conditions and, thus, to insulate the boss and underboss from the law-enforcement processes. The bosses promote a code of honor which makes it extremely difficult to get members to bear witness against the bosses, a code of honor which is enforced by the death penalty. At the same time, the bosses themselves rarely violate the statutes prohibiting bookmaking, usury, extortion, assault, and murder. Their offenses are *conspiracy* to commit crimes of these kinds. While "conspiracy to commit a crime" is itself a crime, proving a conspiracy for legal purposes usually requires a confession on the part of one of the conspirators, a witness. Law-enforcement officers must stand around unable to prove what they know, namely that bosses are partners in almost every kind of crime ever committed. While bosses obtain immunity from arrest and prosecution by promoting a code giving them the right to kill any member who serves as a witness against them, they also order their lives so as to take full advantage of the legal safeguards guaranteed by the Constitution. Similarly, they control their "families" on the basis of information provided by a network of informers, wire taps, and electronic bugs, but they voice righteous indignation when they discover that a police officer has tapped one of their telephones or bugged one of their offices.

The immunity of the bosses from arrest and prosecution gives them great power. They brag that they have a "rabbi," a "beard," a "cousin," or a "front" in city hall or in the police department, and that this corruptee will insure that no one who sticks with them will be seriously hurt by the forces of law and order. Accordingly, even a thirty-day jail sentence imposed on a boss creates consternation in the streets. Such a sentence demonstrates that the procedures for insuring immunity have broken down. If the police can bust Joe the Boss, how can Joe the Boss keep promising immunity to me, a soldier? Cooperative work between the FBI, the Illinois Crime Commission, and the Chicago Police Department, with consequent arrests and incarcerations, has, in fact, recently created a considerable degree of consternation on the streets of Chicago. One leader got so spooked that he punched an innocent stranger in the mouth, believing him to be a policeman who was following him. The job of Chicago boss is so risky, because of police surveillance, that no one is killing anyone to get it. It was only a little more than a decade ago (in 1956) that Sam Giancana and other "Young Turks" sprayed some shots around the front door of the then boss, who took the hint and resigned—giving to Giancana his seat as boss, his seat as chairman of the Chicago council, and his seat on the Commission. But while Giancana was in 1965–1966 serving a one-year jail term for perjury, there was talk about who would be his replacement in the three positions. Sam Battaglia finally was persuaded to serve as acting boss, and he continued in that capacity after Giancana, apparently discouraged, disappeared upon being released from jail. But in May, 1967, Battaglia was found guilty of extorting $48,500 from a construction firm.

Trouble at the highest level of Chicago's "outfit" does not mean that organized criminals no longer have great influence in the city. In most cities, police power is no match for the power of the bosses. Displays of tremendous Cosa Nostra power are shown on occasion, even in Chicago. As long ago as 1927, when a group of Italian "around-the-world-fliers" visited Chicago, Al Capone was selected to be a member of the official greeting party. Officials explained that they thought Capone's presence would prevent possible anti-Fascist demonstrations, implying that Capone could maintain order where police officials could not. Similarly, in the summer of 1966 the director of New York City's Youth Board asked two Cosa Nostra soldiers, Albert and Lawrence Gallo, to help halt racial violence in the East New York section of Brooklyn. The implication, of course, was that Cosa Nostra could keep order where the police and social workers could not. Earlier, as a matter of fact, a member of the Genovese group had demonstrated his power as a peacemaker in a role as ally of the police. When members of CORE were picketing the Mulberry Street police station, which is located in the "Little Italy" section of Manhattan, neighborhood Italian-American boys congregated to taunt and throw rocks at them. One of the Genovese men went to the area and made a two-word, heart-warming, appeal to the neighborhood boys' sense of social justice: "Go home." The boys went home. John J. Cassesse, President of the New York Patrolmen's

Benevolent Association, commented that the use of the Gallo brothers by city officials sapped the morale of the police force:

I can just see what will happen. It's this way. When a police officer goes up to some juveniles who have been misbehaving and tells them to quiet down and move along, what will they say to him? "You're not the boss around here, Mr. Gallo is." When you single people like that out, you make them tin gods in the neighborhood—people known for their habitual lawlessness.

Cosa Nostra bosses also on occasion demonstrate their power by displaying their immunity to arrest. When a subcommittee of the Commission met in a New York restaurant in 1966 to select a successor to a boss, the police broke up the meeting (see p. 113). But what criminal charge could be pressed against these nice old gentlemen gathered together for a bit of food and wine in an Italian restaurant? The police took them into custody as "material witnesses" but could find no grounds for arresting them. Defiantly, most of the members of the group returned to the restaurant the next evening and finished the meal. The newspapers carried a picture of the men hoisting a toast to the plainclothesman standing by helplessly.

There is a story about electronic bugging that also demonstrates the relative helplessness of the police. A Cosa Nostra official whose office was bugged was overheard confessing, to an associate, his part in a murder. A few days later he discovered the bug. Still later, in a street-corner encounter with a police official known by the bugged criminal to have access to transcripts of conversations obtained by bugs, the Cosa Nostra figure revealed that he had found and destroyed the bug. He then surmised that the policeman must have heard the confession. Blank stare by the policeman. The criminal then said something like the following before walking off: "Until Tuesday, even Joe (the associate) didn't know that. Now he knows it, and you know it. I'll see you around." He said, in other words, that he knew the rules regarding admission in court of evidence obtained by wire taps and bugs was such that he was immune from prosecution for murder.

The police are disorganized. There is a striking lack of coordination and cooperation among police departments on organized-crime matters. And even within single police departments there is little coordination and cooperation. Most policemen are ignorant of organized-crime activities. They therefore are indifferent to the problems of policemen trying to deal with them. The well-qualified director of the Intelligence Division of Chicago's Police Department was recently transferred to a routine post that paid $4000 a year less than he had been earning; the most charitable interpretation of a new police commissioner's motives in ordering this transfer is that he made the move out of ignorance. Perhaps the commissioner was unaware of the pressing need for coordination and continuity in the city's struggle to keep from being *completely* corrupted by organized criminals.

Ignorance also could have been a dominant factor in the motivation of a New York policeman who accepted a Cosa Nostra soldier's invitation to work for him as a gun expert. He wound up agreeing to make dumdum bullets for the soldier, knowing that they would be used to kill men who were informing federal agents about Cosa Nostra activities. The charitable interpretation is possible, despite the fact that the policeman, in a bugged conversation, advised the soldier that his colleagues from precincts "Six-Two" and "Six-Four" had been talking about the soldier. The policeman also might have merely been ignorant when he failed to note that a "hot" gun is one that has killed someone. Charitably interpreted, his question about whether two guns were "hot" was a question about whether the guns were stolen. But the question threw the soldier into a funk because he knew that a "hot" gun is also one that has been used in a murder. The policeman did not agree that local policemen "like it" when a federal informer is killed; to him, "it doesn't make any difference." The following is a transcription of a conversation taking place in an automobile repair shop. When the conversation was revealed, the policeman was suspended by his department. However, an indictment against him was dismissed when the taped conversation (called an "overheard" by police intelligence officers) was suppressed because it had been obtained in violation of Constitutional law.

POLICEMAN. Colt. Colt. There has to be a name. Colt Cobra.
MIKE. Yeah.
POLICEMAN. Can I make a phone call? I'll let you know tomorrow.
MIKE. This fits in there. Now wait a minute now. They're both the same. Identical. There's a "P" on the side. Does that mean anything?

POLICEMAN. I don't know.

MIKE. Both the same. Identical. One bullet fits in this one and won't fit in that one. It goes up to here. It won't go no further. This fits in the other one.

POLICEMAN. Different shell. You know, you got different guns. Different guns. Different caliber. One is a—most probably a special and one is a positive. They take two different shells. This is positive and the other one I gave you is special.

MIKE. If I bring in the two pieces—

POLICEMAN. Bring them in. I'll look at them.

MIKE. Will you make dumdums for me? I haven't got the casings for the other one.

POLICEMAN. Huh?

MIKE. I haven't got the casings for the other one.

POLICEMAN. But this you got to have.

MIKE. I got the casings for the one but I haven't got the bullets for the other gun. This one—

POLICEMAN. Yeah.

MIKE. No bullets for the other one. The casing fits.

POLICEMAN. But you got no dumdums. You get square cutters.

MIKE. I don't give a fuck as long as it blows a hole in him this big.

POLICEMAN. Yeah. It will go in there and come out here. You can put your fist through a fucking hole that big.

MIKE. You like the way we set up the federal stool pigeons?

POLICEMAN. What do you mean, "stool pigeons"?

MIKE. Stool pigeons.

POLICEMAN. Oh. That's what you're after, stool pigeons?

MIKE. Yeah. Only stool pigeons.

POLICEMAN. Oh yeah?

MIKE. Nobody else. Only stool pigeons. I mean, like, the cops like stool pigeons when they go, especially if they're federal stool pigeons, right?

POLICEMAN. Nah. You're kidding. How many days have I seen and have I heard—

MIKE. I said the cops—

POLICEMAN. Yeah?

MIKE. New York policemen—

POLICEMAN. Yeah?

MIKE. Like it when a federal stool pigeon is hit.

POLICEMAN. Nah. What difference does it make? To me it doesn't make any difference.

MIKE. There's a big difference. I'll tell you why. A New York cop—
(telephone rings)—detective or police department doesn't like a
federal stool pigeon. (Inaudible.) Because he'd stool on anyone. (Inaudible.) I never do it. I walk. They listen to me. I know it. I walk.
I need a what-you-call-it guy. A phone guy.

POLICEMAN. You ought to check your phones.

MIKE. (On telephone.) Hello. Big S. He's very busy. You want him?
Rich? Do you want him? All right, wait, I'll go get him.

POLICEMAN. Who's that? Richie?

MIKE. You understand? You see, they want him to be theirs. When
they're working for the feds, they don't talk to you and me because
when something blows federally, the city's got the something. The city
guys get burned.

POLICEMAN. Nah.

MIKE. Sure they do. (Yells to employee.) Hey, Rich, your son is on
the phone.

(Four days later, the policeman returns to the repair shop.)

POLICEMAN. Was anybody down to see you from the Six-Two or Six-
Four?

MIKE. They came yesterday.

POLICEMAN. Oh, because—

MIKE. The guys from the Seven-O came over.

POLICEMAN. Oh. But I heard something. I didn't know what they mentioned. I just heard "Mike Scandi," "Scanfeld," or something. I don't
know what.

MIKE. Charlie says, "Mike, they came. They—they wanted you, but you
weren't here. We already called in and told him you weren't here. He
said, 'Forget about it.' "

POLICEMAN. Oh, because I didn't know.

MIKE. They're looking for somebody else. (Sound of paper being un-
wrapped. Inaudible voice.) No, I got them right here. That's what
I'm reaching for. Here's two of them. Understand? Now, you'll find
that the one fits one and won't fit the other. I didn't bring the what-
you-call it. I didn't bring the (stutters)—the—the—bullets.

POLICEMAN. Are these hot?

MIKE. No. What hot? Hot? They're stolen. What are they hot? There's
only a number. There's nothing else on it. There's nothing on that.
There's only a number on that. You can touch it with your fucking
hands.

POLICEMAN. I'm not worried about that. This looks like a .32. A little difference. That's NP .38 Colt. NP cartridge. .38 Colt NP cartridge. I'll have to check it.

MIKE. Well, go ahead then. You got to take 'em.

POLICEMAN. I can't take 'em.

MIKE. Sure. I want to make sure that you get—that you make them dumdums. Or them whereabouts—whereouts—where-evers—whatever you call them. I mean, after all, you can find them. I can't find them. These. Here. You could have picked them up any place, right?

POLICEMAN. Right. Good idea. Right. It will be a little while before you get them.

MIKE. Hey, don't tell me that.

POLICEMAN. It will be a week or so before you get them.

MIKE. Oh no. C'mon. I mean—hey—er—forget it then.

POLICEMAN. Er—

MIKE. Oh no. No.

POLICEMAN. Tomorrow I won't have a chance. But I'll try the day after.

MIKE. Hey, Lenny.

POLICEMAN. On Friday or the day after.

MIKE. Lenny, don't—don't tell me that any more. My right arm, you're taking my right and left arm now.

Attorney General Robert F. Kennedy illustrated vividly and simply, if inadvertently, the relative power of Cosa Nostra and the police. In discussing the "fear of reprisals" that prevents Cosa Nostra informers from coming forward, Senator Edmund S. Muskie of the McClellan Committee asked the Attorney General how long he could give protection to an individual who testifies against Cosa Nostra members. The Attorney General responded as follows:

We have taken steps, Senator, to even move people out of the country. We have provided them positions and work in areas where nobody will really have any contact with them. We have arranged to move their families and have their names changed. I think we have procedures now where, if an important individual comes forward and is willing to testify, that we can give him that kind of protection.

In other words, the Attorney General ironically said, if Cosa Nostra decides on reprisals the combined American state and local police forces, working with the FBI and other federal agencies including the Army, Air Force, Navy, and United States Marines, cannot do much about it. The American citizen must be stripped of his identity and, in extreme cases, shipped off to foreign soil. The President's Commission cited this testimony and then commented, "When the government of a powerful country is unable to protect its friends from its enemies by means less extreme than obliterating their identities, surely it is being seriously challenged, if not threatened." Yet this Commission itself acknowledged the relative power of Cosa Nostra as compared with police forces when it recommended:

> The Federal government should establish residential facilities for the protection of witnesses desiring such assistance during the pendency of organized-crime litigation. After trial, the witness should be permitted to remain in the facility so long as he needs to be protected. The Federal Government should establish regular procedures to help Federal and local witnesses who fear organized-crime reprisal, to find jobs and places to live in other parts of the country, and to preserve their anonymity from organized-crime groups.

My hunch is that we will not have to worry about this procedure for long. Cosa Nostra bosses are becoming so powerful that they might soon abandon the extreme measures customarily used in their attempt to maintain organizational integration and their own immunity from arrest and prosecution. If, like the man overheard confessing a murder, they know that the police are quite powerless to prove their conspiracies in court even when there is a witness to the conspiracies, they won't bother to kill the witness. "I know I did it, he knows I did it, and you know I did it. Would you care to write a letter to Ann Landers?"

More threatening than police are competitors, sometimes called "Indians" by the members of the establishment. Puerto Rican groups in New York and Mexican-American groups in Los Angeles are now giving the confederation a little competition, especially in the narcotics business. By and large, however, competition from outsiders is sporadic, unorganized, and short-lived. Significantly, there is little competition from the quarter where one would logically expect it to come from—the customers, especially poor Negro customers. The direct victims of Cosa Nostra and of all organized criminals are the urban poor, especially members of minority groups. Numbers lotteries and bookmaking businesses thrive on the dollars of unskilled Negroes, not on bets placed by the rich, the educated, the well-housed, the well-employed. Similarly, the American drug addict is likely to be poorly educated and unskilled, and a member of a disadvantaged ethnic minority group. And it is the urban poor, the factory worker, and the marginal Negro businessman, not the affluent suburbanite, who frequently is so desperate for a loan that he seeks out a usurer. Congressman Joseph M. McDade of Pennsylvania summarized as follows his views and the views of twenty-two of his Republican colleagues in the House:

The warlords of this cycle of poverty and crime are the organized-crime racketeers. If their activities could be curtailed, the growing crime rate would be dramatically reduced, and the War on Poverty might have a better chance to succeed. . . . The urban poor are the victims of organized crime in at least three ways. First, it is their precious money which provides the basic income for organized crime's growing network in "legitimate" business. Second, when the rate of street crime rises, as the victims of organized crime seek the quick money they need to meet the demands of organized crime, street crime is perpetrated against all segments of society, including the urban poor. . . . But it is the final price paid by the urban poor which may in the long run be the most insidious cost of organized crime. That price is society's lack of respect for law, order, and authority—the by-products of corruption.

In an address to the National Civil Liberties Clearing House, Congressman McDade followed up these points by saying, "We are losing ground in the war on poverty because organized crime takes from the urban poor far more money than the government puts in." He quoted the Reverend Martin Luther King as follows:

The most grievous charge against municipal police is not brutality, although it exists. Permissive crime in ghettos is the nightmare of the slum family. Permissive crime is the name for the organized crime that flourishes in the ghetto—designed, directed, and cultivated by the white national crime syndicates operating numbers, narcotics, and prostitution rackets freely in the protected sanctuaries of the ghettos. Because no one, including the police, cares particularly about ghetto crime, it pervades every area of life.

One reaction to the fact that urban Negroes and other urban poor people are the direct victims of organized crime is resolution to eradicate the evil. This is the reaction of Congressman McDade, who said, "We believe that one part of the answer to improved conditions for the urban poor must be a war on organized crime—and a war on organized crime is inseparable from a war on local police corruption." But another reaction is a recommendation that organized crime be reorganized in such a way that Negroes, not Cosa Nostra, be permitted to monopolize organized-crime activities in Negro ghettos. This, apparently, is the reaction of the Congress of Racial Equality which, at its 1967 annual convention, held at Oakland, California, adopted the following resolution: "Blacks should take control of the operation of vices in their community, should turn them into economic enterprises, and should eliminate those most harmful to the psychological health of the community." This threat to control by the Cosa Nostra establishment apparently was not considered very dangerous by the editors of the *Washington Daily News,* who buried the story on the obituary page of their July 5, 1967, issue. On the other hand, perhaps the relative strength (with reference to organized crime) of Cosa Nostra and CORE is such that reporting the resolution on the obituary page is symbolic of things to come. In late 1967 *The Wall Street Journal* reported that a black man has a better chance of being elected mayor of Selma, Alabama, than moving into "the big money with the Syndicate." The victimized and affronted Negro can hardly go to his local human relations commission with a charge that Cosa Nostra is not an equal opportunity employer.

A third reaction, falling between the first two extremes, asks that Negroes' opportunities to profit from illegal gambling be equal to those of whites. A few years ago Adam Clayton Powell, who was then United States Representative from Harlem as well as a minister, charged that New York police discriminated against Negroes by arresting a greater proportion of independent Negro lottery operators than Italian lottery operators. He did not expect that numbers gambling would stop. He therefore asked only that discriminatory arrests of Negro criminals stop:

> I am against numbers in any form. But until the day when numbers is wiped out in Harlem—I hate to say this from the pulpit—I am going to fight for the Negro having the same chance as the Italian.

Congressman Powell went on to charge that arrests were being made in an attempt to protect the Italian organization from Negroes who were trying to conduct lotteries independent of it:

> At this time, no arrests have been made in East Harlem, the center of Italian and syndicate activity. Until action begins in that area and higher up, it is apparent that . . . arrests are an attempt to embarrass the Negro community while continuing the policy of allowing the higher-ups to go scot-free.

Later, the Congressman declared that "every Negro lottery operator in Harlem had been put out of business," and he estimated that Harlem Negroes "spend $5,000,000 a year to support Italian and Jewish policy bankers." The estimate was far too low. *The New York Times* estimated at the time that the *profit* from numbers lotteries in Harlem after winners and employees had been paid, was approximately $1 million per *month*.

Congressman Powell is not alone in his belief that organized criminals call on the police for help in dealing with competitors. Competition among Cosa Nostra members has been reduced by fair-trade agreements, by arbitration and pseudojudicial procedures, and by a code which prohibits one member from interfering with the business of another. But other means also are used to reduce competition within the group, and it is these means which are used to reduce competition from the outside. One of them is assassination and the threat of assassination. Another is the coercive power of the legitimate government—the illegal activities of competitive outsiders are reported to the police. It is not necessary that one be honorable with respect to outsiders. If the police hit a bet-taking operation often enough, no one is willing to bank-roll it. Frequent raids are devastating even if no convictions are obtained, because the cost of bribery goes so high that no one can afford it. I am not going to invest with you unless you can guarantee pretty good protection of my money. Moreover, bookmakers and writers nowadays rarely give the bettors receipts for their bets, a measure designed to avoid detection. Accordingly, when a bookmaker or writer is arrested, his fine-feathered customers rush to his supervisor claiming they had winning bets. This can be costly. Similarly, when the records of a usurer are confiscated and the usurer incarcerated, all sorts of six-for-five debtors claim that they owe nothing. This is risky business, however. Men have been killed for trying it.

William Foote Whyte, the sociologist, commenting on the state of affairs in Boston in the late 1930's, hypothesized that reporting competitors to the police is a reflection of a general policy favoring nonviolence:

> Calling in the police to force out competition has become common in recent years. It has obvious advantages. The competition is disposed of in a legal manner, and the organization need not use violence. In the earlier days of the rackets it was considered the rankest treachery to "squeal" to the police even on one's enemies. That this is being done with increasing frequency today is another indication that business methods are supplanting the old code of gangland.

It is still true, however, that if the technique of betrayal fails, the outsiders are threatened, maimed, or killed. Although Gus Tyler presents no evidence in support of his statement, he probably is correct when he says, "Police are glad to cooperate [with older ethnic groups] because the 'Indian' is a disturbance, a source of violence, a disruption of old ties, a threat to the monthly stipend."

Most threatening of all to the governor of an organized crime "family" are his own underlings, especially when the governor is old and the underlings are young. The charismatic qualities attributed to a leader by his contemporaries are not likely to be attributed to him by the next generation, including his own children. Oldsters are under almost constant threat from the younger generation, and if they are to survive they must organize their defenses. As William Bolitho observed over three decades ago, "The heraldic crest of the underworld is a double cross. The ultimate secret of almost every criminal and gangster is that he is a traitor, willingly, or by force, or just stupidity." The first line of defense used by organized-crime rulers against such double-crossers is the code of conduct we summarized in the previous chapter. The enforcer, the executioner, the gun, the bomb, and various "ball-busting" techniques are parts of the second line of defense. As Richard H. McCleery has said,

Systems of power differ most significantly in the type of intensity of means employed to extract the consent of the governed. . . . Just as responsible democratic government rests on freedom of communication and open access to officials, an authoritarian system of power requires procedures which retain initiative for the ruling class, minimize reciprocity, and prevent the communication of popular values to the ruling elite. *Authoritarian control does not rest basically on the imposition of punitive sanctions. It rests, instead, on the definition, in a system of authority, of a role for the ruler which makes the use of punitive sanctions superfluous.* Thus, the heart of custodial controls in traditional prisons lies in the daily regimentation, routines, and rituals of domination which bend the subjects into a customary posture of silent awe and unthinking acceptance.

A "posture of silent awe and unthinking acceptance" is, after all, what inspires conformity to the criminal law in most members of democratic societies. A "sense of morality," or a "sense of duty," or a "sense of decency" keeps the crime rate low. It is this kind of "sense" which constitutes "consent to be governed" in a democracy. Similarly, in the government of criminal organizations, a "posture of silent awe and unthinking acceptance" is the objective of rulers who would inspire in their subjects a different "sense of morality," "duty," or "decency." The code of honor asks the underlings to be honest, moral, and straightforward in their relationships with the men of high status whose positions of power would be severely threatened should the lower-status men subscribe only to the more general society's moral and legal code. Without honor, "respect," and honesty there could not be, among the underlings, the "posture of silent awe and unthinking acceptance" which enables rulers to acquire vast fortunes through the hard work and even suffering (in the case of imprisonment) of the underlings.

The "respect" accorded bosses and commissioners by underlings is based on fear, but more than fear is involved. Unless a soldier is a complete idiot (which, of course, is sometimes the case), he knows that his boss achieved his high position by using muscle. He knows that some of his friends have been murdered on the boss's orders and he knows that the boss will murder him if he doesn't conform. But ideally, from the perspective of the boss, the soldier does not live in constant fear. He offers "respect," believing, just as the boss would have him do, that men who are honorable incite no occasion for the use of violence. There is talk that the young Detroit lieutenants and soldiers no longer either fear or stand in silent awe of the old dons in their city. If this be true, Detroit is likely to witness an intergenerational war in its Cosa Nostra organization within the next few years. In the terminology used in the previous chapter, three or four underlings have grown up to be "toughs" rather than "right guys." ("You can't argue with the young guys; they just tell you.") These underlings are the sons (one is a son-in-law) of bosses who have respected each other and who have arranged for intermarriage of their sons and daughters. Each of the "heirs apparent," however, seems more interested in power and profits than in peace.

Apparently, the Detroit dons have lost the consent of a powerful segment of the men being governed. When Joseph Profaci, the late boss of a New York "family," lost the consent of some of his underlings in 1960, open war broke out. As the story of this war was told by men testifying before the McClellan Committee, the three Gallo brothers, who are best described as "toughs" rather than honorable soldiers, led an armed revolt which was put down only after "The Old Man," as Profaci was called, died of natural causes in 1962. One theory of the revolt—advanced especially by Raymond V. Martin, then Assistant Chief of Brooklyn South Detectives—maintains that Profaci was awarding lucrative enterprises to his relatives and to older men, while repressing the ambitions of his younger soldiers. Among the latter, according to the McClellan Committee testimony of Ralph Salerno, were the Gallo brothers, Joseph Giorelli, and Carmine Persico, Jr., all of whom had worked for Frank Abbattemarco, who was murdered in November, 1959. The Gallo group expected to be awarded a part of Abbattemarco's operations, but Profaci ruled against them. At first they hoped that a power vacuum would be created by the incarceration of Profaci and his underboss and brother-in-law, Joseph Magliocco, both of whom had been convicted of obstructing justice, on charges growing out of the Apalachin conference. When the convictions were set aside by the appellate courts, the Gallos tried to assert their rights by brute force. In order to announce openly the fact that they had withdrawn their consent to be governed, they kidnapped five of Profaci's men and held them until Profaci agreed to meet their demands. But their demands were not met, despite the honorable agreement. There was an "armed truce" for about six months, with negotiations being conducted by intermediaries. The Commission ruled that the matter was an intra-family dispute, and that other "families" should not interfere.

By August, 1961, Profaci apparently had negotiated long enough. He managed to split the coalition of underlings, while at the same time saving face:

Joe Profaci's final answer was made manifest in August, 1961, when Joseph Giorelli (Joe Jelly) disappeared, and an attempt was made on the life of Larry Gallo. It is not insignificant that the instruments chosen for this purpose were Carmine Persico, Jr., and his cohort of angry young men who were dominated by Nicholas "Jiggs" Forlano and John Scimone. These latter two had been the ones who had previously encouraged the younger element of the Profaci family to rebel.

A proper analysis of this action would indicate that Joe Profaci was seeking to achieve two ends with the same act. He would save face by having revenged the rebellious act of the Gallos, and at the same time by using the dissatisfied young men of the Forlano-Persico faction for this purpose, he could later reward them for obeying the orders of the old man rather than have it appear that he was yielding to their original complaints.

Nevertheless, Profaci's use of an enforcer and executioners did not immediately bring peace to the "family." Between August, 1961, and August, 1963, nine men were killed, three disappeared and presumably were killed, and about fifteen were either wounded or narrowly escaped assassination. The Gallos holed up in a fortress and would have been massacred had they not been protected by the New York City police and the FBI. The economic issues in the dispute never were really settled, but the fighting stopped in 1963.

Giuseppe Magliocco became boss after he actively sought the support of Commission members Angelo Bruno (Philadelphia) and Stefano Magaddino (Buffalo). Later, the Commission deposed Magliocco and gave his boss position and his seat on the Commission to Joseph Colombo.

Even a democratic government must constantly seek to maintain among its members the consent to be governed. Further, even in a democracy, government must constantly seek measures for the control of those members whose "sense of morality" and "decency" does not stop them from violating the criminal law. When an individual citizen's consent to be governed has been lost, as indicated by the fact that he has committed a crime, "force" must be used to coerce conformity. But force usually is not physical control; it is *ex post facto* infliction of pain for deviation. If such intentional infliction of suffering is to be accepted by the recipients and by citizens generally, it must be made "justly," in measures suitable to correcting deviation without stimulating rebellion. Maintaining "consent of the governed," then, requires that punishments for deviation will be accepted as legitimate by those being governed.

This is the basic meaning of "justice" in criminal cases. One who believes that criminals should be dealt with "justly" believes, among other things, that punishments can be inflicted on criminals without great danger of revolt, rebellion, or passive resistance, provided sufficient *advance notice* is given in the form of rules. Especially in the Western societies with long traditions of barring *ex post facto* legislation, elaborate systems for *warning* citizens that nonconformity of certain kinds will have punishment as its consequence stimulate rather docile acceptance of official punishments when they are in fact ordered by the courts and executed by prison officials and others. In other words, democratic states operate on the basic assumption that conformity can be maximized only if the punitive system has a rational base. If punishments were imposed irrationally or capriciously, the citizen would be unable to discern just which rules he is to conform to. Moreover, the infliction of punishments in an apparently arbitrary way would be viewed as "unjust" and would, then, contribute to divisiveness in the society.

An important function of the criminal law, so far as maintaining consent of the governed is concerned, is providing the "advance notice" necessary for justice. The carefully stated and precisely stated prohibitions stipulated in criminal laws give advance notice that wrongdoers will be punished, thus contributing to the maintenance of the consent of the governed even when the latter in fact are punished. In addition, since it is not correct to assume that all criminal laws are perfectly clear, the police are utilized to give additional advance notice that whoever violates a criminal law risks punishment—police discretion often means that the police are to issue warnings that *further violations* will have punishment as a consequence. Judicial discretion has the same function. In the long run, then, the consent of the governed and, thus, a maximum degree of conformity, rests at least in part on a public belief that punishments will be imposed only for deliberate violations of regulations clearly stipulated in advance.

In this regard, the code of the "stand-up guy" is in organized crime the functional equivalent of the criminal law. As indicated, conformity to the code is expected of all members, and severe punishments are meted out to nonconformists. But there is one significant respect in which this code of honor differs significantly from the criminal law of democratic societies: It is unwritten. Since the code is unwritten, it can be said by the rulers to provide for whatever the rulers want, and to prohibit whatever the rulers do not want. The same effect was provided by a Nazi law of June 28, 1935: "Whoever commits an action which the law declares to be punishable or which is deserving of punishment according to the fundamental idea of the penal law and the sound perception of the people, shall be punished. If no determinate penal law is directly applicable to the action, it shall be punished according to the law, the basic idea of which fits it best."

In Cosa Nostra, the uncertainty of the applicability of the unwritten code is illustrated by the case of a somewhat honest soldier who was performing somewhat honestly as a minor official of a labor-union local, despite the fact that the union was controlled by a Cosa Nostra boss. The union's management decided to save money by renting cars for its officials rather than continuing its policy of granting each official an allowance of $150 a month for a car. The minor official, who was making a few dollars a month on his car allowance, told the management to go to hell. A week later he was summoned to the office of the boss, which was far from the union headquarters. He quaked, because he did not associate his defiance of the union management with the summons, For all he knew, he had in some other way displeased his boss. But he was merely questioned about why he defied the order, and after he had explained he was told that he could continue under the car-allowance arrangement. But he then revealed the power of the boss to determine the content of Cosa Nostra "law." He asked, "Joe, am I all right?" By this he meant, "Are you going to beat me up, kill me?" He was assured that he was all right, and he was.

In democratic societies, such vagueness in the criminal code is not permitted. For example, in holding a New Jersey criminal statute void for vagueness under the due-process clause of the Fourteenth Amendment, Justice Pierce Butler said, "No one may be required at the peril of life, liberty, or property to speculate as to the meaning of penal statutes. All are entitled to be informed as to what the State commands or forbids." The rules of the criminal law, and even the rules contained in the procedural manuals of business firms, governmental bureaus, and universities, control the actions of high-status as well as low-status personnel. But the organized criminals' code, being oral, lacks the precision necessary to identifying the violations of high-status personnel who do not want them identified. Note, for example, that the code prohibits interference with the interests of fellows and asks that fellows be loyal to each other. As indicated earlier, this rule is somewhat comparable to the law of larceny, which asks that citizens not interfere with each other's rights to private property. But while the law of larceny is stated precisely, the rule for organized criminals is stated so imprecisely that very few underlings can appreciate the fact that the rulers are actually rule violators.

If an underling is told that he cannot establish a lottery enterprise in a certain part of town because a lottery operation already is being conducted there, he can rationalize the decision as an honorable one that is based on the principle that one should not interfere with the interests of a fellow organized criminal. But when the ruler makes an honorable decision that he henceforth will be a partner of each bookmaker in a certain area, the bookmakers are not quick to note that both the ruler's decision and his action are in violation of the code. In one case, the Cosa Nostra officials of a labor-union local did not even notice that by supporting their boss they violated their own code. The president of the local in some minor way displeased the boss who controlled the local. The boss called a meeting of the remaining officers, told them he was not happy with the president, and asked if they had had any unfavorable experiences with him. One by one the officers each made up some kind of grievance against the president, probably out of fear that the boss would be displeased if they did not concur in his judgment. The president was then told by the boss to resign or be killed. He resigned. This kind of case, without the threat of murder, is not rare outside Cosa Nostra, for executives everywhere are looking for yes-men. The difference is that yes-men have by no means sworn that an attack on one is an attack on all.

Similarly, if one soldier starts competing with another soldier or with a captain, the boss may find it expedient to have him killed, thus enforcing the rule against interfering with another criminal's interests. But in ordering the killing the ruler is by no means being guided by the code saying that one should not interfere with the interests of another. The "law of the land" does not apply to him. The king can do no wrong.

Further, the lack of precision in the code enables the leader to run his "family" organization primarily on the basis of information received from informers, while at the same time enforcing with a gun the idea that informers are the lowest form of life. The role of the buffer, which we described earlier, is partly the role of an informer. The buffer, like the underboss and other couriers, gets information about any defections or suspected defections in the organization from other informers and passes it on to his boss, thus allowing the boss to interfere with the interests of his fellow criminals. The same process occurs at the level of captain. Each soldier is required to be loyal to his captain, and "loyalty" includes keeping the captain informed about any gripes or plots one hears. This form of loyalty is not regarded as informing, principally because it is called "loyalty."

Cosa Nostra rulers' positions of power are also protected by the confederation's judicial system, which has been devised by the rulers to give advance notice that violators of the code will be punished. There are two basic parts to this system, one referring to conflicts in which the disputants are members of the same "family," the other to disputes between men who each report, through a hierarchy of ranks, to a different boss. In either case, the distinction between tort and crime is unclear. One who claims that another is interfering with his criminal interests is at once a plaintiff in a civil suit and a complainant in a criminal case.

If two soldiers working for the same lieutenant are quarreling, it is expected that they will follow the code's admonition to settle their differences quietly, without violence, so as not to antagonize the citizenry. If they cannot come to an agreement, one of them lodges a complaint with their lieutenant, who makes a judgment on the matter. If the lieutenant cannot make a decision, or if the disputants are not satisfied with his decision, the matter is referred to the boss, usually through the underboss or *consigliere*. The accused is sometimes permitted to present his defense, sometimes not, depending on the conclusiveness of the evidence and the seriousness of the charge. The judgment has the function of the warning given to the general public by the criminal law. Thus, it is advance notice to all concerned that henceforth the arrangements will be adjudicated and that all members should conduct themselves accordingly. If one of the parties to the quarrel does not heed the "notice," he is punished or executed on the order of the man making the decision. Only the boss can order an execution. Lieutenants, underbosses, and bosses can all order, and execute, punishments such as a public reprimand, a slap in the face, a roughing up, or a beating.

Reprimands and corporal punishments are administered in the presence of the offender's close friends and associates, as a demonstration of his weakness. Economic sanctions are also involved, through a system of guilt by association—"If he has done something so bad that Joe slaps him, he will bring heat, so I don't want to be a business associate of his." A soldier-bookmaker asked his boss for help in financing a new venture. The boss, learning that the soldier was to put in none of his own money, denied the request. When the soldier asked him for permission to seek financial aid elsewhere, he gave the permission but stipulated that no other boss could be approached: "You belong to me." The soldier, unhappy about this restriction, later made some derogatory remark about his boss's authoritarianism. The boss called him in, slapped him around (with the help of two lieutenants), and told him that such talk had to stop. It stopped.

One soldier got into an adjudication hearing with his boss because of the affairs of two of his nonmember friends. The friends, both crooks, operated a legitimate business through a front man, who got into a dispute with a criminal he thought was a Cosa Nostra member, although he was not. This man threatened to kill the front man, who fled for his life, leaving the business operation in shambles. The soldier's friends then told him about the affair and asked if he could help them. In a casual conversation, the soldier told his lieutenant and his underboss of the situation. Within a few days the underboss ordered the soldier to meet with him, in the presence of the boss. At this meeting, the underboss told the boss the story and then asked if he had any interest in the business run by the front man or any business relationship with the criminal who threatened him. The boss did not. He scolded the soldier for not advising him that he was associating with criminals outside the "family," thus warning him not to repeat the error. The soldier apologized and the hearing was over.

When the disputants work for two different lieutenants in the same "family," the procedure is essentially the same. Each is required to report his problem to his lieutenant. The two lieutenants confer at a meeting called a "sit down," *"argomentazione"* (argumentation), "table," or "carpet," and if they can come to an agreement they issue a notice regarding subsequent arrangements. A Philadelphia soldier found guilty by two lieutenants of striking another soldier was banished from the city for six months, at great financial loss.

If the two lieutenants cannot come to an agreement, they refer the case to their boss. There are no restrictions stemming from the necessity for due process of law. The legitimate criminal law restricts the power of officials, who can inflict no punishment unless it has been specifically prescribed in advance for a particular offense or a particular kind of offender. Thus, for example, banishment recently was held as "beyond the power of the court to inflict" because it had not been stipulated in advance as an appropriate punishment for the behavior in question. But in Cosa Nostra a territorial dispute between two lieutenants was recently settled when the boss simply said to one of them, in the presence of the other, "You give [the other] a piece of the action or you will wind up in the river." This directive instantaneously became "the law."

Occasionally Cosa Nostra men of honor behave like schoolchildren taking a case of alleged playground slander to the teacher and the school principal. As in children's disputes, the issues raised in the process of adjudication surmount the issues raised in the initial beef. One soldier, Joe, heard that another soldier, John, was claiming that Joe was trying to persuade their underboss to dismiss John from his field-man position. Knowing that he had been misunderstood, and knowing that his boss (who was also the boss of John) had heard of the matter, Joe asked his lieutenant to talk with John. The outcome of this meeting was unsatisfactory because, it developed, John believed what he had claimed. John, disturbed by the visit, asked his lieutenant to arrange for him to discuss the matter with the boss. Instead the lieutenant met with Joe and Joe's lieutenant. At this meeting, Joe learned that John had tried to meet with the boss without an OK from the underboss, and he became angry. He asked to see the underboss, and he got an appointment with him. The plot thickens. Now Joe became fearful that John would tattle to the boss that he, Joe, got the appointment with the underboss by telling him he had cleared the meeting with the boss, which was not the case. He expressed this fear at the meeting with the underboss and the two lieutenants. The underboss, in response, complained that he now would have to tell the boss that everything was not OK between Joe and John, while only a week earlier he had told him the little

squabble was over. Joe asked him not to do that. The two lieutenants ordered Joe and John to forget the whole thing and get back
to work. They did.

When members of two different "families" are involved in a dispute or disagreement, the lieutenants refer the case to their respective
bosses if they cannot come to an agreement. The bosses then meet,
reach an agreement, and issue the notice. A New York soldier who
stole from a soldier outside his "family" was excused when two
bosses determined that he did not know the victim was "a friend of
of ours." He was ordered to make restitution. Two bosses settled
another dispute with a ruling that was announced to a lieutenant in
words something like, "You tell [soldier] to stay in his own
territory."

Cosa Nostra's judicial system unquestionably keeps the amount
of violent crime down, just as does the legitimate system of justice.
One old scoundrel made the system seem like a charitable public
service when he said, "You see, these people [police] don't know
the good that we do or else you know what trouble they would have
on their hands, because before trouble starts we sit down and
straighten these things out."

If the two bosses cannot agree, the matter is a very serious one
and it is referred to the Commission, which issues the notice. The
Commission does a land-office business in jurisdictional disputes,
especially those arising in "open territories" like Las Vegas and
Tucson. The decision of the Commission is final. There are two
recent innovations, appearing since about 1960. First, individual
commissioners sometimes are appointed by the Commission to act as
judges and arbitrators of matters not pertaining to their own individual interests. Second, the Commission sometimes appoints a subcommittee to handle a specific matter, be it a case of controversy
or the formality of replacing a deceased or deposed boss. Perhaps
these forms were invented after the Apalachin meeting, in an attempt
to avoid police detection of Commission affairs. The huge Apalachin
crowd, consisting of Commission members and their lieutenants,
would certainly attract the attention of the FBI today. Alternatively,
the forms could have been invented too because each commissioner

feared that while he was away from home attending Commission meetings, a rival boss or an underling would steal part of his empire. One Commission member in 1964 refused to attend meetings for this reason. This dishonorable situation among "men of honor" is not unknown among legitimate businessmen, some of whom refuse to be an industry's representative on a trade-association board because they fear that while they are away from home attending meetings their fellow members will grab their customers.

A notice by the Commission may demand compromise, payment of damages, or withdrawal on the part of one of the litigants. Failure to obey the notice gives the Commission the "right" to order punishments. When only two lieutenants settle a dispute, the lieutenant for whom an offending soldier works orders the punishment of that soldier. Similarly, a boss orders punishments only of members of his own "family," not of a different "family." In other words, it is always a member's own supervisor who orders him punished or executed. The Commission may order the execution of a boss, but a boss himself orders all other executions, sometimes on instructions from the Commission. The boss gives the "contract" for the killing to an enforcer, who enlists the aid of as many men as he needs to carry out the killing. The "contract" ordinarily is let in an informal and seemingly indifferent manner. The boss might say to his lieutenant (who also is to act as enforcer), "I would take care of him if I were you," or "We can't have men like that around," or "When Tony did that, he got hit." If the "contract" is let in this way, the lieutenant selects the men to act as executioners. If the "contract" is let in more precise terms, the boss might select them. In either case, the executioners usually are member of the boss's "family." The attitude has been (and perhaps still is) that a boss or lieutenant does a soldier a favor when he asks him to participate in a killing.

By giving the rulers of the illegal government the power to assist and reward him, then, the member also gives the rulers the right to kill him. This is the basic meaning of "illicit government," when viewed from the perspective of the participants. Because the operations of bookmakers and other low-echelon personnel are illegal, these men cannot call upon the police and courts for prosecution of criminal activities in which they are victims. The strong emphasis in the code on being loyal, on being rational, on being honorable, and on being inconspicuous is an emphasis which gives the rulers a monopoly on violence. The code denies to the individual his right to legitimate use of the coercive power of the state, while at the same time conferring upon his superiors the "right" to use illegitimate power to control him. This principle applies to nonmembers who somehow get "involved" with Cosa Nostra members, but here it gives even soldiers the "right" to punish and kill fellow conspirators. Once you shake hands with the devil, you do as you are told.

A hotel owner involved in some illegal operations not involving Cosa Nostra was being shaken down by men who were not Cosa Nostra citizens. His brother-in-law, who was not involved in any illegalities, happened to be acquainted with three Cosa Nostra soldiers. He asked the Cosa Nostra men to see that the extortion stopped. They did, apparently as a mere favor to their friend. But some time later the extortionist gave the hotel man another whirl. When the soldiers heard about it they killed him, perhaps to show that they were not to be defied. Neither the hotel owner nor his brother-in-law was consulted. A few years later the Cosa Nostra friends killed a man over a matter that was entirely unrelated to the hotel owner. They were indicted for murder. At the trial, the hotel man provided a false alibi for them by saying they were with him at the time of the murder. He had to perjure himself or be killed. "You are one of us."

In another case, a somewhat honest businessman confessed that he was paying off the corrupt official of a labor-union local controlled by a Cosa Nostra boss. At the trial he changed his mind and lied, saying he had never paid off the official. He was indicted for perjury, but before the date of the trial he was murdered. It is a hypothesis that he was killed because the corrupt official or the crooked boss feared that he would now tell the truth, to save himself from imprisonment. In a similar case, two New York longshoremen told a grand jury on November 9, 1966, that a man had lent them money at exorbitant rates. On January 11, 1968, the same men told a Brooklyn court that they would rather risk prison for perjury than testify against the alleged loan shark. They asserted that their grand-jury testimony had been all lies, and they were arrested on perjury charges. One of the men said, "I was told the other night that if I testified I might get hit on the head with a crate."

The fact that the Cosa Nostra code denies participants the right to appeal to legitimate authorities for assistance, while conferring on bosses the power to enforce their own "law," is one of the most insidious aspects of organized crime. Both members and nonmembers of Cosa Nostra become the subjects of a dictatorial government. Especially insidious is the tendency to induce, for a fee, representatives of the legitimate government to subscribe to the Cosa Nostra code. A policeman or political figure who plays a role in organized crime transfers his allegiance from one government to another. Sometimes the allegiance of entire police departments and of all the political figures in a ward are transferred in this way. In "Wincanton," the fictitious name given to a real town of about 75,000 population, studied by John Gardiner and David Olson for the President's Commission, a large proportion of the city's police and political figures were corrupt almost continuously for a period of over thirty years. "Mayors, police chiefs, and many lesser officials were on the payroll of the gambling syndicate, while others received periodic 'gifts' or aid during political campaigns." Corrupt officials, like other organized criminals, both deny and are denied access to the judicial processes of legitimate government, while at the same time condoning, in the name of honor, the coercive power of totalitarian government.

In short, the "men of honor" and "stand-up guys" who have assumed positions of power in the confederation of criminals have done so with the assistance of a code of conduct stipulating that no underling should interfere with their interests, that underlings should not go to the police for protection, that underlings should be "stand-up guys" who go to prison in order that the bosses may amass fortunes. All the processes of government within organized crime are devoted to enforcing the code so that profit can be maximized, and the code, in turn, is the code of a despot bent on securing conformity to his demand that he be left alone to enrich himself at the expense of men who shower him with honor and respect. The leaders are men who have secured their high status and wealth by virtue of a code which gives them exploitive authoritarian power, and they are bent on enforcing the mandates and injunctions of the code so that their power to exploit is maintained.

🎗

The Mafia code of *omertà,* like the Cosa Nostra code and the code of "right guys" everywhere, supports extralegal government by making it seem chivalrous to comply with the wishes of strong men seeking out their own interests in a particular territory. One principle of control in the Sicilian Mafia, as in American organized crime, is deterrence from deviation by threatening certain, swift, uniform, and severe punishment of those who deviate. But use of this principle is secondary. Another principle is cultivation and maintenance of "respect" and an air of deference. The principal means used to develop such deference is not ostentatious displays of wealth or lordly displays of power. On the contrary, it is an exhibition of humility and "understatement" in all social relationships, and especially in relationships of power. This device is often overlooked by American observers because it does not mesh with the conduct of the the "typical" American gangster of the 1920's and early 1930's. But both the Sicilian Mafia and Cosa Nostra have learned a thing or two from upper-class culture, which decries ostentation. A Mafia don in Sicily, the boss of a Cosa Nostra "family," a descendant of the old Italian nobility, and a New England blue blood all have at least one thing in common. They are "above" the petty social rules which demand conspicuous consumption on the part of those who would climb the social ladder.

In the Sicilian Mafia, a man's rank is determined by the amount of respect and fear he can generate, but the man with the clearest halo of respect and fear around him is not distinguishable, in manner of living, from those who fear him. His manner is majestic, but humble. When in 1943 American soldiers met the Mafia boss of the Sicilian area being invaded, they probably expected to find him well-manicured, diamond-studded, and dressed in a $400 silk suit and $85 alligator shoes. They found an old illiterate man, dressed in his shirt sleeves and suspenders, whose whole game seemed to be that of de-emphasizing appearances. He did not change his demeanor even when the Allied soldiers nicknamed him "General Mafia." In almost direct contrast, a bandit enlisted by this Mafia chief to help in a political fight a few years later was a twenty-three-year-old "tough" who came to a meeting bedecked with a calendar wristwatch, a golden belt buckle, and a diamond-solitaire ring. He was said to dress better than a professor or lawyer, and the press referred to him as "the King of Montelepre."

The same kind of understatement on the part of the leaders, and the same kind of contrast with the demeanor of the underlings, is found in American organized crime. Vito Genovese, head of a New York "family" and, before his current incarceration, leader of the Commission, had at the time of the Apalachin meeting in 1957 been invested with charismatic qualities by his followers. He was almost revered, while at the same time being feared, like an Old Testament divine. Even his name had a somewhat sacred quality to his underlings, with the result that Joseph Valachi sometimes referred to him as "a certain party," rather than by name. There was, in short, more than the kind of envy, awe, or even fear commanded by an ordinary immigrant who has accumulated $25 to $30 million. Yet at the time of the Apalachin meeting, Mr. Genovese lived in a modest house in Atlantic Highlands, New Jersey, drove a two-year-old Ford, and owned not more than ten suits, none of which had been purchased for more than about a hundred dollars. On the dusty top of a dresser in his bedroom stood cheap plaster statues of saints. His children and eight grandchildren visited him frequently, and he personally cooked spaghetti for them.

The contrast with the demeanor of underlings who ostentatiously display their new-found wealth is obvious. According to Nicholas Pileggi, the police in one city were unaware of the importance of a man who was in fact a highly placed underboss until they were able to observe his participation in a meeting. First a dozen men, known to be quite high-ranking, arrived in their air-conditioned automobiles, some of them with chauffeurs. Their manners and style of dress were not "flashy," but they were impeccable. After they had been assembled for a few minutes, a small man, dressed in a shiny-seated black suit and carrying a bag of his wife's homemade peppers, entered the room. All those in attendance jumped to their feet and whipped off their hats. The man addressed the group in Italian, haranguing them about their behavior on a particular issue. After speaking for about fifteen minutes, he left the room abruptly and walked to the nearest subway station, where he took the next train home. The meeting broke up upon his departure, the remainder of the group driving off in their expensive automobiles.

Ostentatious display of wealth or power is generally frowned upon in the brotherhood. Big houses such as Joe Barbara's are rare. A *mafioso* may have a substantial fortune tucked away, as a good many have, but the ancient tradition requires him to live an outwardly modest life. He has his Cadillac or Chrysler, bought for cash, and almost always at least one mistress; the number depends on his standing in the brotherhood. Home, however, is often a two-family house with overstuffed furniture, antimacassars on the chairs, five-and-ten ceramics and all the other trappings of a stuffy middle class European household. Here he is the soul of respectability—an affectionate husband, a kind father, usually temperate and a faithful worshiper at his church.

Norman Lewis attributes the fashion of understatement in the demeanor of Sicilian Mafia leaders to linguistic confusion arising out of the similarity between the words *"omertà* and *"umiltà"*—manliness and humility. "Many illiterate Sicilians have combined the two words to produce a hybrid of mixed pagan and Christian significance. The virtuous man is in Mafia fashion 'manly' and silent, and as a Christian humble." The matter probably is not so simple, even in Sicily. Certainly the incidence of great humility among top American rulers is much less than the incidence among Sicilian Mafia leaders in the past. Humble men like the two described above are rare, either inside or outside American criminal organizations. Even Genovese once lived lavishly. When, in 1952, his wife sued him for separation she testified that their house cost $75,000, another $100,000 for renovations, and $250,000 for furnishings.

Our living room was forty feet long. The dining room was exactly the same size as the living room. Our bedroom was twenty-five feet long.

A marble staircase led from the living room to the dining room. A very beautiful nude marble statue was at the foot of the staircase. One wall in the living room took an artist six months to paint. . . . The furniture in the bedroom was imported Chinese teakwood. The bed had a swan back made of lucite. All of our furniture was made to order. We had twenty-four-carat gold and platinum dishes. Our silverware was the best that money could buy. We had parties every weekend. Twenty-five to thirty persons always showed up. Vito insisted that I buy the best champagne—sometimes we even hired entertainers from New York City. We never spent less than five hundred dollars on a party. . . . Vito liked company.

Mr. Genovese denied such weath, saying that the only income he had was from his work as manager of the Colonial Trading Company, a Manhattan salvage firm. Fred J. Cook, the writer, claims that Genovese's subsequent frugality and understatement was a direct consequence of federal probes into the sources of the income his wife said he had: "Genovese realized that there were penalties attached to gaudy display, and he warned his Mafia lieutenants, 'Forget the high living. It'll put you in jail if you're not careful.' For himself, he adopted the pose of a poor and humble suburbanite, cooking his own meals, tidying up his own small house, raking leaves off his lawn when they fell in the fall."

The similarities in the "humble" behavior of some American Cosa Nostra rulers and the typical Sicilian Mafia ruler makes it tempting to conclude that the Americans have merely transplanted a Sicilian behavior pattern, complete with a confusion of manliness and humility. The differences, as indicated by the lavish displays of wealth on the part of other Cosa Nostra leaders, challenge this conclusion. A more plausible explanation can be found in the observation that most Cosa Nostra men have not yet "arrived" in American society. Since their power and positions of high status are not yet secure, they behave more like the newly rich than like the old families constituting the upper class of New England. One can afford to neglect a personal display of power only if his position of power is secure. On the other hand, ostentatious display is a sign that one is only climbing the status ladder, as indicated by the behavior of underlings everywhere.

The leaders of organized crime are following a pattern followed by other Americans, whose methods became smoother, more subtle, and more gentlemanly as they achieved some measure of success:

As American society became more "organized," as the American businessman became more "civilized" and less "buccaneering," so did the American racketeer. And just as there were important changes in the structure of business enterprise, so the "institutionalized" criminal enterprise was transformed too.

But, taken as a group, American rulers of organized crime are still on the way up, as compared with Sicilian Mafia rulers. They are nonjoiners. They once lived in tenement apartments, each in his own territory. But as their illicit businesses have become bureaucratized and the need for personal supervision and control has diminished, they have joined the move of respectable citizens to the suburbs. About a dozen of Detroit's top Cosa Nostra fellows have migrated to fashionable Grosse Pointe, which is favored by such eminent industrialists as Henry Ford II and Walker L. Ciser, President of the Detroit Edison Company. The criminals live quiet lives with their families and do not associate with Mr. Ford and Mr. Ciser. Cosa Nostra members do not participate extensively in the activities of the residential communities where they live, whether they reside in Grosse Pointe, on Long Island, in Westchester County, or in River Forest.

Perhaps the nonparticipation in community government and social affairs is not all a matter of choice. When a boss avoids being judged by the residents of his own suburb, he might be making the most of a situation in which he would not be envied or well liked. Probably some Cosa Nostra rulers are excluded from offices in city government and in the Parent-Teachers' Association, from sailing weekends, and from debutante balls not because they make their living in crime but because they do not have the social graces and social background which make them eligible to participate. It is obvious that a Cosa Nostra member or anyone else who drives a white Cadillac convertible bedecked with pink rabbit-skin upholstery is not going to make it into the upper class. He is trying too hard. As the old leaders attempt to show exclusiveness by means of understatement, the new leaders are as yet excluded by their proclivity for ostentation. But some of them are making the adjustment; they have reached the top of the illegitimate social ladder and are using the wealth and status acquired there to get them near the top of the legitimate social ladder. One New York boss even went to a psychiatrist to try to overcome his inferiority feelings about his inadequacy in social situations. As such feelings are overcome among the rulers —as they gain more power, as they extend their influence to wider and wider circles of economic, social, and political activities—they will attain the self-confidence and poise necessary to refrain from displaying one's wealth to the world.

American leaders are not far away from this condition. They do not have the "humility" that requires them to dress and act like Sicilian peasants, because they have not seized power over Sicilian peasants, as the humble dictators of the Sicilian Mafia have done. But some of them do have the "humility" that requires them to dress and act like American businessmen, rather than like characters in a "B" movie about Chicago gangsters, because they have seized, and are continuing to seize, power from American businessmen. As we will show later, underlings in American organized crime are beginning to follow the bosses because the latter are men of wealth, rather than revering them as divines or fearing their guns. Further, the degree of involvement in illicit businesses is decreasing, while participation in legitimate business is increasing. The danger to America is that respectable businessmen will follow the same men, on the assumption that they are deserving of respect because they are wealthy.

As time goes on, bosses and underlings alike will try to facilitate our support by adopting the system of understatement used by American upper-class citizens, rather than the system of understatement used to impress working-class groups, as was the case with Vito Genovese and, before him, the crime bosses now given the derogatory title, "the mustaches." The Chicago leaders, at least, are well aware of the need for understatement which will permit the boss to blend into the world of respectable businessmen. Federal investigators in June, 1966, reported that Sam Giancana faced a trial before a tribunal composed of the council which he headed before going to jail for a one-year term, beginning June 1, 1965. According to the *Chicago Tribune,* this trial arose because Chicago leaders were irked by Mr. Giancana's lack of humility, his lack of understatement, and the inattention to business stemming from his playboy activities. "In a sense, Giancana will defend himself against charges of having permitted his international playboy activities to interfere with more serious, day to day business of running the underworld organization." This was not the first occasion on which Chicago's council had suggested that Giancana be dumped, and for the same reason. Even the lowly soldier knows that he will be reprimanded or punished in some other way if he attracts attention by prancing into a fancy night club with a dizzy blonde on his arm.

CHAPTER X

Shifting Patterns of Authority and Recruitment

Everybody today is professional.

JOSEPH VALACHI

THE INTERNAL arrangement for governing Cosa Nostra is not democratic. It is authoritarian. There are no general elections. The rights of each "family" member are the rights given him by a dictator who is in an alliance with other dictators. Even a dictator, however, must establish and maintain the consent of the governed, and for that reason alone there always are cracks in the totalitarian monolith. No known process of recruitment and indoctrination will produce a sense of decency and morality—a sense of honor—so deep that there will be absolute obedience to the indoctrinator, even when the indoctrination is supplemented by the threat of death for nonconformists. Yet the Cosa Nostra bosses keep striving for this objective, and the fact that organized crime continues to flourish is evidence that they have come close to achieving it.

The bosses succeed in part because they are controllers of a large business enterprise, as well as the rulers of an illicit government. Perhaps the principal advantage they have over legitimate government officials is an almost unlimited supply of funds to be offered as rewards for effective business behavior. Although democratic governments can penalize disloyal citizens economically, they cannot offer a reward of economic wealth to any citizen who is not disloyal. Totalitarian government, which controls economic and social life as well as political life, can do so. Maybe it is for this reason that young men eagerly seek membership in Cosa Nostra, even if they know that the probability of getting killed on orders from a "stand-up guy," a "man of honor," is high. There are few participants in organized crime who have not at some time lived in fear of their superiors' guns, and "social life" among organized criminals consists at least in part of devising protective devices which amount to insurance against being killed by one's best friends. One of these devices is submissive compliance to the wishes of the ruler.

Yet the fact that a boss heads an organization which is a business as well as a government poses serious administrative problems for him. Most of all, the business character of his enterprise makes it necessary for him to recognize and reward technical competencies. Men with highly prized skills cannot be "ordered" to perform in certain ways, as a dictator demanding absolute obedience would have them do. The patterns of authority, influence, recruitment, decision-making, and communication established for totalitarian government are different from the patterns established for productive and profitable business enterprise.

Authority in organizations can be divided into two major types. One type rests on rank, or simple incumbency in a high-status position. Persons occupying higher ranks initiate rules rather arbitrarily, "for the good of the system," rather than "for the good of the members." These rules are implemented primarily by imposition of punishments for violation. ("I cannot make you do it, but I control the agents of power who can make you wish you had done it.") In a system of rank authority, "membership" is more important than "employment." The old-fashioned policeman was "on duty" twenty-four hours a day, and even now the "working hours" of policemen are less clear than those of factory employees. In systems of this kind, subordinates consent to being governed by persons of higher rank, but they do not necessarily believe that these persons possess superior knowledge. They accept the system because they have been taught that it is their duty to do so and because it is painful to do otherwise. Ideally, judgments of the rationality or morality of action based on orders from above are not to be made. If they are made, they are to be set aside, and the reaction is to be to the *position* of the person giving the command.

The second type of authority is the authority of the "expert." It rests on possession of technical knowledge and skill rather than on rank. Here, the subordinate "believes in" the rules he is expected to follow, as he does in a system of rank, but he defers to the expert knowledge of his superiors because he expects that their knowledge will somehow be used for his personal benefit. The system of "expert authority" is democratic in the sense that the subordinate confers "superiority" on some of his fellows because he is convinced that they can help him. A doctor's orders to his patients, a foreman's instructions for simplifying a work task, and a stock-broker's instructions to his clients are all examples of technical authority.

Both types of authority are likely to be present in any organization. While the system of authority in totalitarian government is ideally one of rank, the system in complex business enterprises is ideally one of expertise. When the two systems get intermingled, as they do in a criminal organization which is both a confederation and a cartel, one cannot be sure that subordinates obey orders because of a sense of duty, because of the fear of consequences of disobedience, because of anticipation of personal benefit, or because of some combination of these.

The history of organized crime since 1931 shows a tendency to shift from a system in which rank authority was dominant to a system in which authority based on expertise is becoming equally important. The trend, then, seems to be away from totalitarian government bent on securing and maintaining conformity to a code, and toward economic enterprise. Currently, however, both the structure and the operations of illicit enterprises point to the indecision and disorder brought about by attempting to maximize both patterns at the same time.

We have seen that the term "button" or "button man" is used to refer to the lowest-echelon workers who also are members of Cosa Nostra "families." Some writers believe that the term developed from the idea that these positions are on the lowest level of a system of rank authority. Men occupying the position carry out the orders of a hierarchy of leaders who merely "push the button." While there is no way of knowing whether or not this derivation is correct, it is clear that the term "soldier," also used to refer to lower-echelon men, symbolizes the worker's obligation to follow orders handed down by men of higher rank. If soldiers did in fact react automatically to orders from above, which would mean that they never got aspirations and ambitions of their own, then a Cosa Nostra "family" would be a perfect example of a rank-oriented system of government.

We know that such perfection is not present, however. In the first place, personal tastes, prejudices, biases, and jealousies get in the way of absolute obedience and loyalty. For example, it is still true that "Neapolitans" and "Sicilians" resent and hate each other, even if the persons in question are actually the third-generation American descendants of Neapolitans and Sicilians. Even legitimate military organizations and similar tightly knit chains of legitimate command operating in multigroup societies like ours are not able to maintain absolute control over the behavior of subordinates. In the second place, and more significantly, systems of "total power" resting on the authority of rank always become something less than "total" at least in part because the authority of the expert cannot be eliminated. I suggested earlier that unofficial governments like the Sicilian Mafia, underground movements, prisoner organizations, and Cosa Nostra arise because the strong official government needs the "expert" illicit services which some of its citizens command. I see no reason why the same process should not occur in illicit governments, with power shifting to the experts that the illicit operation demands.

The rulers of organized crime have from the beginning found it necessary to recognize and reward the special kinds of technical competence possessed by men occupying the various positions making up the organization. When the system of rank authority is dominant, these technical competencies are concerned either with establishing order or with maintaining order. "Autonomy within limits," as Alfred H. Stanton and M. S. Schwartz have named an organizational phenomenon, is granted to indoctrinators, recruiters, and trainers, and to executioners, enforcers, and buffers. When the problem is one of making profits, the rulers must grant some autonomy to occupants of even the low-echelon positions calling for skills such as those of the lottery operator and the bookmaker. When the illicit business becomes big, and when the profits of illicit business are invested in licit businesses run illicitly, there must be some acknowledgment of the authority of the accountant, the lawyer, the corrupter, and the money mover. Where the boss once walked down the street flanked by bodyguards, he now sallies forth surrounded by accountants and lawyers.

Such experts cannot be dictated to about technical procedures by which they are to achieve their tasks, so decisions as to actual work procedures are necessarily left to them. This does not mean that complete autonomy is granted, however. Since the operations of the organization still must be kept secret, conformity to the code of conduct continues to be essential. Autonomy must therefore be limited, even in technical areas. For example, an accountant who is a Cosa Nostra member, or who merely works for a Cosa Nostra member, does not practice the profession of "accounting." He has a different occupation, "illegal accounting." His membership or pseudomembership makes him a "citizen" who must follow the mandates and obey the injunctions of the organization's code. His skills as an accountant, then, must be used in activities of direct interest to, and under the direct control of, a boss. Since a boss has the power of life and death over him, he must be prepared to carry out the boss's orders. The basis of his decision-making is transformed from "technical" or "expert" to "technical within the framework of a system of ranks."

In any organization, the patterns of communications and the pattern of decision-making are closely related to the pattern of authority. The amount and kind of communication among the participants are consistent with the expectations regarding the kind of decision-making at each point. A special pattern of decision-making, in turn, is closely associated with each of the two authority patterns described above. When a principal goal of the organization is security or secrecy, each subordinate has an area or activity to control, and each supervisor has the duty of controlling subordinates. In a sense, the duty of all participants is to be "on duty." Further, when secrecy is a problem, as it has been for organized criminals, possession of highly developed technical skill is not as important as evidence of "rightness" and possession of "muscle," which can be used to coerce conformity. Generally speaking, members of "families" have been expected to place themselves almost completely at the disposal of the rulers, to be used as the latter see fit. In order to maintain the conditions of restriction necessary to protect the ruler's positions of power, and in order to keep operations secret from the police, low-level employees were denied, and still are denied, extensive opportunities to make decisions. Because of the illegal character of organized crime, a leader's fame and fortune can be seriously damaged if improper decisions are made at the lower levels. Decision-making is therefore concentrated at the top of the hierarchy. Although the reference points in the following casual comment are vague, the comment does show something of the degree to which a low-status member is expected to surrender his own will to the authority of his superiors. One soldier is discussing with his lieutenant the troubles of a fellow-soldier who also is in the lieutenant's clique. He reveals both his equality with the soldier ("I can't actually send for you") and the superiority of "them."

He said, "Nobody came to me, nobody is talking. Nobody came to me and said, 'You should do this, and—'." Well, I said, "All right, nobody sent for you." I said, "I can't actually send for you. If they don't send for you, you got to go to them. What do you want me to do? This is my situation. You take your pride, you know what I mean? You don't want to eat. If you don't want to eat— You shove it up your ass. Because it is not a question of you. It's Cosa Nostra."

Sandy Smith, writing for *Life,* has suggested that even a member's position in Cosa Nostra's authority structure might be shifted downward on command from persons high in the hierarchy. Albert Anastasia, Smith says, had in the 1950's made his brother Tony boss of the biggest local of the International Longshoremen's Association. But when Albert was murdered, Tony was reduced to the rank of soldier and assigned to a new Cosa Nostra boss:

The brooding Anastasio was flying to Miami for a few days in the sun. In the seat beside him, as it happened, was an official of a federal law enforcement agency. . . . They talked of what had happened to Albert, and suddenly Tony blurted: "They *gave* me to Gambino!"

"I got to answer to Carlo," he moaned to his astonished companion. "Joe Colozzo told me I'm nothing but a soldier."

"They," of course, were the Cosa Nostra Commissioners, who had put

Anastasio—not to mention his 14,000 union members—under the control of Carlo Gambino, who had taken over the slain Albert's Cosa Nostra Family.

Until now, Joe Colozzo had been just another of Tony Anastasio's gangsters in the Brooklyn longshoremen's union. Now he was Gambino's strongman—and Tony was suddenly nothing.

Communications to the outside world must be "through channels." Organizations concerned with security must be arranged so that the leader, be he army commander, prison warden, chief of police, or boss of a Cosa Nostra "family," can control the messages going to the outside world. If anyone on the inside can make public statements about the organization, anyone can weaken the security control needed by the leader. Further, anyone with access to "the outside" can threaten the leader's rank authority. Communication to the outside must be channeled through the man in charge, and arrangements for minimizing decision-making at the lower levels must be made. In organized crime, lower-echelon men have been permitted to make only those types of decisions, and to make only those communications to the outside, which prior study by the rulers has shown to be of no danger to operational security. A soldier may use his ingenuity to promote the sale of illegal lottery tickets, but he may not expand his territory and he may not advertise in a way that might direct public attention to all illegal bet-taking.

The concentration of decision-making at the top and the stress on communication through channels can be observed in internal communications as well. A key figure here is the buffer, who also plays the role of courier. Although the men playing this role have established such a close relationship with the boss that their pronouncements often are taken as commands, the boss expects them to make a minimum number of decisions about their work. In his affairs with the men on the street, the ideal buffer is a kind of robot who asks questions, carefully observes the conduct of the persons in his charge, and reports rule violations and suspected rule violations, as well as other information, to his governor for action. He then carries the ruler's decisions back to the men at the operating level. Viewed from the perspective of the lower-echelon men, he could be considered a paid "rat," "fink," or "stool pigeon," because his business is that of informer. Yet, paradoxically, he is engaged to report on, among other things, any signs that the men in his charge might be "rats," "finks," or "stool pigeons." Since the activities of Cosa Nostra are illegal, its leaders must be authoritarian, and in order to retain their authoritarian control these leaders must restrict decision-making and control communication channels.

Similarly, the enforcer must be permitted to make a minimum number of nontechnical decisions. Like the buffer, he is expected to behave something like an archetypal traffic policeman, who merely cites violators and leaves any decision-making about guilt to the courts. The enforcer has no authority to punish or to make decisions about punishment. The power to punish is centralized in officers and a Commission which can maintain an overall view of organizational activities. Too many errors would occur if decision-making about infliction of punishments were permitted to occur on the lower levels, where the perspective on organizational activities is rather narrow. As in any bureaucracy, all performance is expected to be *sine ira et studio*. Moreover, if the enforcer were permitted freedom to decide who should be punished or executed, he might decide to have his superiors punished or executed.

This system in which men occupying the enforcer position are prohibited from making decisions about imposing punishments is useful to the top-echelon men who order the punishments. Bureaucratization of judicial affairs gives the lower-echelon men the impression that they are controlled by an impersonal organization, or "system," rather than by an individual, thus minimizing the probability of rebellion or revolt. An execution becomes impersonal when it is known that the enforcer or executioner will be executed if either tries to give the condemned man a "break." It really is not impersonal, however, if a solitary man at the top makes the decision. Confusion is profitably maintained in the minds of lower-echelon men by the custom of calling an organized-crime unit "Cosa Nostra," "the mob," "the organization," "the syndicate," or even "the family." Such terms, like restriction of decision-making among enforcers and executioners, perpetuates the myth that killings and punishments are impersonal. Things might be much different if lower-echelon men stopped calling the unit controlling them a "syndicate" or a "family" and started calling it, for example, "Joseph Profaci's system for extorting from me a part of the profits of my illegal business." The code functions to insure that this change in terminology does not occur. The tendency to punish appears to be the "disinterested" tendency which the Danish sociologist Svend Ranulf found to be a characteristic of the lower middle class. What keeps Cosa Nostra soldiers honorable is in part their failure to observe that the punishments ordered by bosses are in fact the vengeful retaliations of feudal lords. Moreover, the monetary rewards for participation are high. A belief in order is supplemented by an opportunity to become wealthy.

Because the rulers of "families" also are the controllers of the business enterprises of their private governments, they have available to them one important control device not ordinarily available to the heads of legitimate rank-oriented systems such as an army, a police department, or a prison. The device is money. Bosses can offer tremendous financial opportunities to persons who will become subordinate to them and remain subordinate to them, thus increasing their own incomes. One lawyer's income went from about $25,000 a year to about $150,000 a year within three years after he started working for a boss. An expert on organizational behavior, Amitai Etzioni, has pointed out that the means distributed among various organizational positions for control purposes can be exhaustively classified into three analytical categories: physical, material, and symbolic. The application of physical means for control purposes is *coercive power;* the use of material means for control purposes is *utilitarian power;* and the use of symbols, including symbols of prestige and esteem as well as love and acceptance, is *identitive power.* Cosa Nostra bosses use all three kinds of power, as do the administrators of most other organizations. Identitive power is found in inducements to be "right," loyal, and honorable; utilitarian power in the allocation of money, in huge amounts; and coercive power in the allocation of punishments.

In Cosa Nostra, manipulating and balancing the use of these three kinds of power is a complex operation because both governmental operations and business operations are involved. The former requires use of much coercive power and identitive power while the latter, by definition, requires a stress on monetary reward. Of necessity, conformity to the code must be maintained by means of a system of rank authority, with its emphasis on punishments for nonconformity (coercive power). Yet, also of necessity, expertise which contributes to increased profits must be rewarded with money and prestige (utilitarian power and identitive power).

Punishment is a response to deviation from form, and financial reward is a response to furthering organizational ends, in this case the maximizing of profits. Since all members of Cosa Nostra "families" now must be conformists while some of them also are good profit makers, there are bound to be fluctuations between the use of coercion as a response to rule violation (especially violation of rules prohibiting underlings to join with others to take a larger share of the profits) and the use of rewards for making contributions to the flow of profits. These fluctuations make understandable the seemingly strange fact that organized criminals are at once well-integrated into a somewhat impervious society of "honor" while at the same time they maim and kill each other with a frequency unheard of in legitimate organizations.

If one's duty is only to be loyal to a code of conduct, then it is impossible for him to earn rewards for *outstanding* or *extraordinary* performance. He is either loyal or he is not. Thus, a Cosa Nostra soldier who maintains the code of silence cannot logically be rewarded for doing so; he can only be punished for not maintaining it. Yet in at least two respects reward and punishment become confused in this area, just as they do in areas of legitimate behavior. First, a criminal might be rewarded by his ruler for doing his duty under extraordinarily difficult circumstances, such as maintaining silence under protracted questioning by the police. Such "hero awards" are sometimes given by legitimate society to persons who have only done their duty, but under difficult circumstances. For example, a policeman whose duty it is to catch criminals might be rewarded for capturing an especially dangerous or notorious criminal. Second, rewards are given for not having been punished. If one's duty is to be a "stand-up guy," then by definition a "stand-up guy" is one who is not caught being something else. Evidence of *failure* to do as expected, which means that a rule has been violated, is taken to be evidence of *refusal* to do as expected, and it results in punishment for the violator.

Rewards, primarily in the form of a larger share of the profits, cannot be awarded as inducements to *become* a "stand-up guy." That is one's duty. But rewards can be given to persons who *already* are "stand-up guys," as evidenced by the fact that they have not been punished for failing to do their duty. Thus, a soldier who has a number of bad-conduct reports may be barred from the reward of a lottery operation of his own, but a soldier who has no bad-conduct reports has only behaved as he is supposed to have behaved. In either case, the man's destiny is in the hands of his paternalistic boss, who gives him what he wants to give him.

Except in the case of "hero awards," then, increased income, promotions, and symbols of status are allocated by Cosa Nostra bosses for *satisfactory* performance of the duty to conform to the dictates of the code. So far as the code is concerned, the member's duty is to be "on duty," and status symbols are therefore withheld from those who show evidence of not being on duty. As indicated earlier, in the administration of this negative system for evaluating members, publicly administered reprimands and minor punishments are used in accumulating evidence regarding unsatisfactory performance. These actions serve as advance notice that continuation of undesirable behavior will be *more severely* punished by bodily harm or death.

Further, just as the reprimands given by a police department's disciplinary board are viewed by patrolmen as "black marks" against the chances for a pay raise, so indications of a boss's disfavor are viewed by organized criminals as "black marks" against the opportunity for advancement and job security. They are signs that performance with regard to the organization's integrating code has been unsatisfactory and that, therefore, the culprit's profits should not be increased. No matter what the degree of a member's expertise, it is impossible for him to be a "better criminal" than one of his colleagues. He might be wealthier than his colleagues, and he might possess more status symbols than they do, but these are not rewards for being a good criminal who obeys the code. They are rewards for being a good businessman who at the same time is not a bad criminal.

🦋

We are now witnessing the passing of the days when the rulers of organized crime had to devote most of their time and intelligence to insuring that their members were not bad criminals. Either the rulers are securing such a degree of conformity that defection is no longer much of a problem, or they are becoming so respectable, and thereby so insulated from law-enforcement processes, that strict conformity is no longer essential. I believe the latter is true. The United States government has always been strong enough to give dissenters, nonconformists, and criminals certain rights. Now the Cosa Nostra government is beginning to show signs of similar strength. There has been a gradual shift from the use of coercive power to emphasis on the use of the other two types as well. Since governments tend to monopolize coercive power, any shift from coercion to material reward would mean that Cosa Nostra is becoming less like a government and more like a big business, a cartel. This seems to be the case.

During the period of national Prohibition, the illicit governments controlling most persons engaged in the production and distribution of alcohol were ruled primarily by men who, in prison life, would be called "toughs," "hoods," or "gorillas." Wild and somewhat public violence, principally against members of rival gangs, was the order of the day. Further, within individual gangs, executions of nonconformists were sometimes performed almost capriciously in an effort to maintain rank authority. As time has passed, control of organized crime has been shifting to men playing the role prisoners label "merchant," "peddler," or "politician" and to men whose role is similar to the type prisoners call "the real man" or "the right guy." The judicial process functioning on both the "family" level and the Commission level, discussed in the previous chapter, now makes it "illegal" for even a boss to exercise his power totally.

One factor in the shift away from coercive power has been the employment of "outsiders" to occupy street-level positions such as writer and runner. Button men are at the bottom of the Cosa Nostra hierarchy, but they also are managers of men. Because they are managers, they are experts of sorts, and they cannot be ordered to behave in specific technical ways. If the managers of an airplane factory decide to manufacture boats instead of planes, their decision is of little consequence to the assembly-line worker. But if a Cosa Nostra boss were to decide to replace bet-taking with usury, he would first have to obtain some degree of agreement among his soldiers because these men now are part of the management hierarchy. When Cosa Nostra is viewed as a government, soldiers are at the bottom of the status hierarchy. But when the organization is viewed as a money-making business enterprise, soldiers are "works managers" or "foremen." Some of them supervise the work of as many as forty or fifty men, and their activities therefore cannot be dictated, like the activities of an assembly-line worker can be dictated, without danger to profits. Soldiers still can be maimed or executed for being bad criminals, but even such actions weaken the economic enterprise. When Vito Genovese went to prison, at least twenty-seven of the soldiers in his "family" were millionaires. The "old-timers" in Cosa Nostra are now deploring the shift toward an emphasis on money-making rather than on discipline. They complain that the entire enterprise, and individual members as well, have become "commercialized." Quarrels among lower-echelon personnel tend to center as much on money matters as on violations of the norms which the organization holds essential to "decency." A lieutenant who returned from eight years in prison was dismayed to find that he was "only" a lieutenant—his lottery business had been allocated to soldiers and to other lieutenants, so all he had was rank. It took five years and a considerable number of "sit-downs" for him to regain his economic status.

Further, huge investments in licit as well as illicit businesses have made it necessary to create a position called "money mover," outside the system of rank. Men occupying this position cannot be "ordered" in the way an enforcer or executioner can be ordered, or in the way all soldiers could once be ordered. The money mover is a kind of treasurer, but, significantly, he works for the "family," or some part of it, rather than for the boss. He is an expert who goes into a vague kind of partnership with any family member who needs his expertise. In the course of the McClellan Committee hearings, John F. Shanley, then Chief of the Central Investigation Bureau of the New York City Police Department, identified and described the role of the money mover. In doing so, he performed what social scientists call a "functional analysis," which is a way of working backward from observation of function to description of structure. He testified as follows:

The Money Mover. The main objective of these families is the efficient massing of money. Huge amounts of cash from illegal sources pose two problems. Its true ownership must be hidden, and it must be put to work. The greedy overlords consider the need to put the money to work quickly equal in importance to the need to hide its ownership. The money mover provides this service.

Money movers, reasonably skilled in finances, are family members and, although not at policy level in systematized crime, are important and trustworthy. The money mover handles cash for a clique rather than an individual. He may, for instance, handle the Profaci or the Genovese "house." There may be more than one money mover for each family.

The cash is given him through a conduit, and the profits return to the thugs the same way. The money mover knows broadly whose money it is. But, it is probably not possible to go beyond him in tracing the specific origins, as he does not know.

The money mover is apt at insulating himself. He has fury at his service. He has excellent and widespread connections. And he has as his partner an astute, unethical businessman. He and his partner merge two basic abilities: brains and brawn. The partner invests through corporations, other partners, and as an individual. Importing, real estate, trust funds, books, stocks and bonds, are his typical undertakings. Both the money mover and his partner enjoy some return, but the bulk of the profits go to the mob. The object is to invest in legitimate situations, but anywhere a quick buck can be made without too much risk is not overlooked.

Loan sharks often play the role of money mover, and in this regard they have become at least as important as "toughs." Their expertise is needed. Similarly, the experts occupying a "family's" positions for corrupter and corruptee cannot be "ordered," in a rank system of authority, to perform their duties according to a detailed set of procedural rules.

Yet today the system of rank authority is still present, and the activities of men occupying organizational positions for money movers, corrupters, corruptees, soldiers, and all other economic functionaires continue to be closely integrated with the activities of men occupying positions for enforcers, executioners, and other governmental functionaires. The pattern of authority is somewhat of an anachronism. The bosses continue to ask subordinates to give them absolute loyalty, to be "on duty" at all times, to display "respect," and to receive, in return, rewards allocated on a paternalistic basis. By means of the "code of honor," underlings are asked to subordinate all their individual desires to the welfare of the organization. Not too many years ago, such a system of rank authority pervaded the army, the police, prison administration, and similar legitimate organizations concerned with security. By becoming a member of such a hierarchical organization, the individual soldier, policeman, or guard necessarily gave up a good measure of freedom. He could not participate in some activities available to the ordinary citizen; he might be required to live in prescribed housing, to pay his bills promptly, to keep out of bars, to be in bed at a certain time at night. He was required to obey whatever commands his superior officers gave. In legitimate governmental organizations, this system of rank authority is rapidly giving way to authority based on expertise, perhaps because our society's needs for maintaining security have changed. It would be most surprising if it did not also gradually give way in illegitimate governmental organizations, as these organizations gain power and respectability, thus diminishing the need for secrecy.

At least one "family" already seems to have introduced something resembling a democratic legislative process, which is not unexpected when an illicit government is surrounded by the legitimate processes and procedures of a democratic social order. A few years ago a New York "family" agreed to implement, in an "unemployment-insurance" program, the tenet of the Cosa Nostra code asking for loyalty and mutual aid. It was decided, in some kind of legislative process about which nothing is known, that the "family" would compensate any member who goes to jail or prison. The wives and children of any imprisoned member are supported, and the member receives a kind of "bonus" when he is released. A year or two after the decision was made, and implemented by assessment of a "tax," a lieutenant was overheard bragging to his friends, "I introduced that bill." Whether or not the lieutenant was factually correct, and whether or not the legislative process was as formal as the word "bill" implies, the man was revealing his belief that a democratic government process was operating.

If it is to survive, every organization must have an institutionalized process for inducting new members and inculcating them with the values and ways of behaving of the social system. In Cosa Nostra, the process of admitting new members is called "opening the books." It is reasonably certain that the books have been "closed" for about a decade. Taken literally, this would indicate that no new members have been admitted since about the time of the Apalachin conference. It is tempting to take such a literal position, for it carries the assurance that the "family" cartel and confederation organization is on the way out, that an important decline in membership and influence will occur as soon as the current leaders, who tend toward old age, die or are deposed. This is not the case. While it may be true that the "books are closed," it also is true that in some neighborhoods all three of the essential ingredients of an effective recruiting process are in operation: inspiring aspiration for membership, training for membership, and selection for membership.

Some recruits are deliberately sought out and trained on the assumption, implicit or explicit, that without the induction of youngsters the organization will founder. Other recruits, usually mature college graduates, are sought out because they possess the expert skills needed for modern large-scale business operations. One boss has financed the entire college education and law-school education of at least three white Anglo-Saxon Protestants who now serve him, even if they are not members of Cosa Nostra. Most recruits of both kinds must now remain for years in a kind of probationary status because inducting them into a "family" might change the balance of power between "families," thus disturbing the peace. As indicated in Chapter VII, a few members are admitted, despite the fact that the "books are closed," but only if the Commission itself gives a boss explicit permission to induct a specific individual into his "family." The argot terms for induction are "make" and "made": "We will make Joe," "Sam was made in 1952."

The most successful recruitment processes are those which do not appear to be recruiting techniques at all. There are the processes by which membership becomes highly desirable because of the rewards and benefits the prospective members believe it confers on them. Some boys grow up knowing that it is a "good thing" to belong to a certain club or to attend a certain university, and they know it is a "good thing" because men they emulate have or have had membership. Other boys grow up knowing that it is a "good thing" to become a member of a criminal "family," for the same reason. Because activities of Cosa Nostra are illegal, it is necessary for aspirants to abandon some of the values of conventional society as they learn to aspire to membership. They do so because they grow up in social situations in which the desire for membership comes naturally and painlessly. It is still an honor to be taken into the society of "stand-up guys," and, moreover, not all the best things in life are free.

In the 1930's, members were "made" in a rather elaborate oath-swearing ceremony which also was used by the Sicilian Mafia. The ceremony stressed the importance of organizational integrity and, consistently, secrecy. It was preceded by a formal background investigation, including a check on the candidate's credit rating, and formal sponsorship by a member. The sponsor was responsible for the subsequent behavior of his candidate, and each recruit therefore had to swear that he would obey any command given him by his sponsor. Some informants have claimed that up until about the time of the Kefauver hearings each candidate had to kill an older member in order to create a vacancy. This is highly doubtful, however. No informant has said that *he* killed in order to become a member; informants have only "heard about" the practice. The FBI bug of conversations in the office of New England boss Raymond S. L. Patriarca (see p. 158) suggests that an induction ceremony of some kind is still used, but nothing is known about its form. Boys living in the Italian-American neighborhoods of large American cities know there is a concept of membership, however, and many of them live in hope that some day they will be "made."

It has long been known that in a multigroup type of society such as that of the United States, conflicting standards of conduct are possessed by various groups. Discovery of the process leading to the invention of criminal subcultures which conflict with the standards of conventional groups is now the focus of the research of many social scientists. It has for some time been acknowledged that the condition of conflicting standards, which anthropologists and sociologists call "normative conflict," is not distributed evenly through the society. Simply stated, persons growing up in some geographic or social areas have a better chance than do others to come into contact with norms and values which support legitimate activities, in contrast to criminal activities, while in other areas the reverse is true. Individuals who come into intimate association with legitimate values will use legal means of striving for "success," while individuals having such associations with criminal values will use illegitimate means. Henry D. McKay has referred to the acquisition of desires for membership in either noncriminal or criminal groups as an "educational" process, and he has pointed out that in many neighborhoods alternative educational processes are in operation, so that a child may be educated in either conventional or criminal means of achieving success.

Raymond V. Martin, Assistant Chief of Brooklyn South Detectives during the Gallo-Profaci war, has referred to these alternative processes for education in the values of conventional society and the values of the society of organized crime by reporting that in some neighborhoods of South Brooklyn boys grow up under two "flags." One is the flag of the United States, symbolizing conventional institutions, traditions, and culture, and the other is the flag of organized crime, symbolizing traditions quite different from conventional American ones. For Cosa Nostra leaders, recruitment of boys who grow up under the "syndicate flag" is no real problem because the boys have in a sense recruited themselves. Helpful, however, is what Martin calls the "legend" of the importance of Cosa Nostra men in political, economic, and social affairs. A story about the virtues of the members of a social group need not be true in order to be effective; it can be wholly false or it can be an elaboration of some incident that occurred in the past, as most legends are. A "stand-up guy" can be made into a revered hero, even if that "stand-up guy" also kills and "works over" his devoted friends and subordinates. A powerful illicit cartel can, similarly, become so respectable, once it has undermined legitimate political and economic processes, that aspirants do not even have to experience any psychological conflict as they transfer their allegiance from conventional society to criminal society in order to achieve its economic rewards.

In his testimony before the McClellan Committee, Joseph Valachi argued, in effect, that in the 1930's the boys who were to become recruits to Italian-Sicilian "families" of organized criminals trained themselves. As they participated in boys' criminal activities such as burglary, they were observed by the syndicated criminals in the neighborhood, who paid special attention to the behavior of the boys when they were jailed. A boy who revealed nothing about himself or his criminal associates was a likely candidate for membership; other boys were not. Thus, the recruits trained themselves to adhere to a code which put them under the domination of the recruiters. This process is still in operation. It is old-fashioned and inefficient, however. Syndicate members now deliberately set out to help boys obtain skills that will be valuable to the syndicate. These include, especially, personal values about silence, honor, and loyalty—values which make them controllable, as ex-convicts who cannot find legitimate employment are controllable. On the streets of Brooklyn the important attribute sought is the orientation of the "stand-up guy":

Some hoodlums are assigned to recruiting. . . . He learns which kids are good prospects and which are not. Like a telephone-company public-relations man enrolling Amherst seniors or a California airplane-plant personnel manager looking over graduate engineers from M.I.T., he wants the best and the smartest. He also wants the strongest, the meanest, and the most vicious. He starts testing boys at sixteen or seventeen. They are put into teams of six, eight, or ten for training. There are rules to be followed by the trainees and rewards to be won. Mob injunctions begin with *omertà*, the heart of the syndicate code of honor. Silence on pain of death; say nothing, know nothing. Drink if you wish, but don't get drunk. Avoid narcotics; they are all right to sell, no good to use. The rewards include money, status, and release from the yoke of morality. . . . Eventually, the mob men plan burglaries for the recruits. There are techniques to be taught.

A recent study by Irving Spergel confirms the notion that "attitude" is the important feature examined in the recruitment and selection process. This sociologist studied juvenile delinquents in three different neighborhoods of Chicago, one of which was given the ficticious name "Racketville" because organized-crime activities flourish there. In this neighborhood, organized criminal activities such as lotteries, bookmaking, and usury employ a large proportion of the population in the usual bureaucratic structures. The delinquents working in lottery operations were involved primarily through family connections. For example, a boy might drive his uncle's Cadillac to pick up the receipts from a policy writer, or he might be given other opportunities to prepare for organized criminal roles by performing seemingly minor errands. "Such assignments served to put him in a position to do a small favor for the racketeer, thus showing him that he was willing and trustworthy." Usurers were viewed as respectable businessmen in this neighborhood, and they were greatly admired by the delinquents, who emulated them. The delinquents themselves participated in money-lending, and two of them were apprehended for systematic usury activities while still attending school. Spergel concluded, however, that it is more important for an organized-crime aspirant to display evidence that he is a "stand-up guy" than to learn specific criminal skills.

Racketeers placed a premium on smooth and unobtrusive operation of their employees. The undisciplined, trouble-making young "punk" was not acceptable. The primary condition for admission to the racket organization was not necessarily involvement in delinquent acts but training in attitudes and beliefs which would facilitate the smooth operation of the criminal organization. Prior development of specific skills and experiences seemed less necessary than the learning of an underlying illegitimate orientation or point of view conducive to the development of organized crime.

Eight out of ten Racketville delinquents named some aspect of organized crime when asked, "What is the occupation of the adult in your neighborhood whom you most want to be like ten years from now?" Similarly, the delinquents believed that the most important quality in "getting ahead" is "connections," not ability, or good luck, or education. Seven out of ten delinquents chose education as the *least* important factor in achieving success, perhaps indicating a belief that "education" and "connections" are antithetical. I think these boys are factually incorrect. Nowadays, being a "stand-up guy" and having the right "connections" is not enough. The orientation of the boys prepares them only for street-level involvement, not for positions of leadership, which increasingly call for skills learned in colleges and universities. One must be a "stand-up guy" in order to be admitted, but if he is to advance he must have the skills of a purchasing agent, an accountant, a lawyer, an executive. Spergel found, in fact, that significant upper-echelon opportunities in organized crime were not open to the youth of Racketville. While some delinquents engaged in "apprentice racketeer roles on a limited basis," other delinquents eventually became racketeers "without necessarily starting at the bottom."

In legitimate industry, the path from the shop floor to the manager's office is no longer a direct one. Engineering colleges and schools of business administration in America are crowded with the sons of skilled workers and clerks whose advancement has been blocked by the hard wall of technology. Determined that the advancement of their sons shall not be similarly blocked, mechanics and clerks early orient them to the idea that a degree in engineering or business administration is highly desirable. Both Daniel P. Moynihan and Jean Susini have observed that the boys living in areas dominated by organized crime are being given the same kind of orientation, for the simple reason that advancement up the echelons of organized crime now depends on much more than being "honorable" and skilled in burglary, mayhem, or numbers writing. Cosa Nostra members occupying the higher echelons of organized crime are orienting their sons to the value of education, if only as a part of the general move toward respectability. While their daughters still tend to become nuns, they are sending their sons to college to learn business skills, on the assumption that these sons will soon be eligible for "family" membership. One particular college has in its student body an overrepresentation of the sons and other male relatives of Cosa Nostra members. Accounting and business administration are the favorite major subjects.

Not everyone who wants to participate in the business conducted by crime syndicates can do so. One cannot "just decide" to become a member of Cosa Nostra, or to participate in business affairs controlled by a "family," any more than he can "just decide" to become a professional baseball player, a policeman, or a banker. His desires must be matched by his competence, and by the desires of those who control membership in the profession he wants. Until recently, "competence" was judged, as in Racketville, by estimates of loyalty and a certain toughness made evident in the condition of being "right." But the procedures for selecting men to highly desired positions are always more stringent than those for positions which are less desirable. Mr. Martin tells how selection for initial participation operates on the streets of South Brooklyn:

From a safe distance the mob instructors observe the operation [of a burglary] and prepare for a subsequent critique of the job. . . . A team that shows capacity for avoiding trouble is allowed eventually to operate on its own, though it must still get mob clearance on each job. Frightened kids are weeded out, tougher ones move closer to the day when they join the syndicate and achieve the good life.

Again we point out that the skills now needed and sought in the higher echelons of Cosa Nostra are not merely those necessary to "avoiding trouble." Relatively unskilled men will always be needed to conduct street operations, and these men must of necessity be honorable and, thus, exploitable. But because organized crime is becoming increasingly respectable, there is less "trouble" to avoid. The pattern of authority can therefore shift from "rank" to "expertise." The man who relies alone on the old-fashioned virtues of honor and obedience will not go far in the organized crime of the future, because these virtues are not essential when the organization is so powerful that it need not be kept secret. The career of Maier

Suchowljansky (Meyer Lansky)—a poor Russian immigrant who began his work in organized crime as an executioner and now boasts because his enterprise is "bigger than United States Steel"— is not likely to be frequently duplicated in the future. For that matter, even now there are few businessmen, criminal or noncriminal, who possess the untrained organizational genius which enabled Suchowljansky to become the world's most successful money mover and corrupter. United States Steel's assets in 1966 amounted to over $5.5 *billion* dollars, and its profits were $249,238,569, plus or minus a few cents. Identitive power is still prevalent in Cosa Nostra, but we are witnessing a shift from respect for the "tough" or even for the "stand-up guy" to respect for the entrepreneur. Respect for men of rank is still an important control device, but the deference now seems to be as much to "the old man" who is wealthy as to "the old man" who is a patriarch, as much to a company president as to a governor.

In rank-oriented organizations such as old-fashioned armies, police departments, and prisons, management is an end, not a means. Members of such organizations do not produce. They serve. This never has been true of Cosa Nostra, which always has been organized primarily for making profits. Discipline has been a means to an end, not an end in itself. Consistently, profit makers who are not bad criminals have always been accorded higher status than disciplinarians. But this distinction is not clear at the street level of operations, which has been the level at which most recruits have begun work. One young man with the right connections and the right attitudes might be rewarded with a job as a collector of street-level bets, as a courier who picks up and delivers usury monies, or as a truck driver in a cigarette-smuggling operation. If he is ambitious and talented, he may do all three. Another young man may be rewarded with an executioner position, such as "wheel man," "finger man," or "hit man." Both men are either salaried employees or behave as if they were, even if unpaid or paid on a piecework basis. Neither has high status, and neither has necessarily been admitted to membership in Cosa Nostra. But the career-development pattern for the first man is much clearer than the pattern for the second. If either man is admitted to membership, his initial position is likely to involve moneymaking, perhaps at a supervisory level such as book-maker, rather than discipline. On occasion, an executioner may be given a salaried position as bodyguard to his boss, but bodyguards do not ordinarily move up to supervisory positions oriented prin-cipally to discipline, such an enforcer and buffer. Either of the two men may, after years of work as a soldier-bookmaker who shares his profits with his superiors, move up to lieutenant-enforcer, lieutenant-buffer, lieutenant-corrupter, or lieutenant–money mover. The four positions are listed in ascending order of status. The person occupy-ing a high-status money-mover position is self-employed to a greater degree than is the corrupter and, in descending order, the buffer and enforcer. His frontiers of action are wider, and his income is greater.

Men serving as enforcer or buffer have important supervisory roles, but they remain more civil servants than entrepreneurs. The man occupying a corrupter position is not quite a civil servant but he is not an entrepreneur or a producer either—his is a "service occupation" like that of the chief of the Ford Motor Company's public-affairs division. Of the four positions, it is the money mover that most precisely consists of duties, obligations, and rights demand-ing use of the technical skills of the business specialist. It is too soon to generalize about the positions of underboss, boss, and com-missioner because so few men have occupied them. We expect, however, that money mover, with all its requirements for expertise and technical skills, is a better channel into top management than is enforcer, or buffer, simply because top managers must now admin-ister complex business enterprises.

Business firms and other organizations have devised two principal systems for specifying the kind of work which will be rewarded. One is to standardize procedures in explicit sets of rules. In this system, ordinarily called "bureaucracy," members who commit themselves explicitly to form and procedure are rewarded, even if such commit-ment might mean decline of achievement of success measured by some other criterion, such as contribution to profit-making. The "bureaucrat" follows rules which his superiors have devised. In the other system, workers are evaluated on the basis of clearly specified results which they are expected to accomplish. This system encourages ingenuity and, at the same time, "assures the standardization necessary for bureaucratic operations." It is used in "creative bureaucracies," such as advertising agencies, firms of architects, and universities. It also is used in sales firms employing commission agents, who learn that their overall performance is judged on the amount of their sales, the end product, even if one stated criterion for measuring their work performance is conformity to standardized rules of procedure.

Cosa Nostra is in the process of shifting from the first to the second system for evaluating members. The organization which is Cosa Nostra is, thus, becoming "loose," "flexible," and creative, enabling its participants to bob and weave in a fashion unheard of only fifteen years ago. In basketball, coaches have learned that the successful team is one in which each player is permitted to improvise, within a loose organizational framework of "fundamental" positions. In warfare, the old army of ranks and files that marched up Bunker Hill has given way to an army in which each soldier is expected to improvise, as in guerrilla warfare. In basketball and in warfare, the "loose" organization has proved to be highly efficient, primarily because opponents find it difficult to defend against a team whose members appear to be behaving almost randomly. Cosa Nostra's recent emphasis on rewarding profit makers rather than on punishing nonconformists has given the organization a flexibility which, similarly, makes it difficult to defeat. For example, in about three months, New York Cosa Nostra members in the spring of 1965 organized and then operated a multimillion-dollar cigarette-smuggling operation which involved purchase of huge quantities of untaxed cigarettes in North Carolina, truck transportation of the cigarettes to New York, a network of warehouses and wholesalers, and a huge system of retail sellers, including milkmen, vending-machine servicemen, and union shop stewards. Managers of a legitimate firm dealing in legitimate merchandise could not have organized such an enterprise in less than three years. Cosa Nostra struck so quickly and efficiently that the police and other enforcement agencies were rather helpless. Except for intelligence divisions and similar units, police departments still tend to be organized for fighting Napoleon's orderly ranks of disciplined soldiers rather than the guerrillas of North Vietnam. Cosa Nostra leaders have learned a thing or two from the guerrillas.

As organized crime has gained power and respectability by moving out of bootlegging and prostitution and into gambling, usury, and control of legitimate businesses, the need for secrecy and security has decreased and the need for expertise has increased. If this trend continues, the pattern of extreme totalitarian control will change. Even now, neither the multimillionaire boss nor the millionaire soldier is able to handle alone the complicated problems of business organization and finance. In criminal life as in noncriminal life, fewer and fewer jobs are simple and routine. Guerrilla warfare has made it inefficient for an army to recruit dumb but brave men as cannon fodder. Even the police keep talking about "professional training" on the college and university level. Soon there will be no place for high school graduates, let alone high school dropouts, in the higher levels of the military, the police, or Cosa Nostra. As the technical competence of even lower-echelon Cosa Nostra members increases, decision-making will be decentralized and individual freedom of action will expand. There already are signs that each member's frontiers of action are expanding. They probably will continue to expand as organized crime continues to move away from profit and control by violence and toward profit and control by fraud.

Perhaps, however, we should expect a new wave of violence in organized crime before the lines between membership and non-membership become blurred by the increasing need for workers with the kind of business skills which only so-called legitimate society can provide. As the shift to the authority of the expert occurs and, concurrently, as decision-making is decentralized, opportunities for the present unskilled participants to achieve positions of power will decrease. In legitimate life, government officials and others are urging that each individual citizen must be given his rights—as a member of society and as a human being—to justice, to a living wage, to human dignity. Most respectable citizens are now demanding those rights, primarily in the form of opportunities to achieve, and they are rejecting governments which will not or cannot make the opportunities available. We expect that within the next decade the disrespectable citizens who are the underlings of organized crime will similarly demand, from the unofficial governments that rule them, their opportunities to achieve. We can expect them to grow tired of a system which denies equal opportunities to low-status personnel, even if everyone in the system is relatively rich. If these men begin demanding their rights we will witness in the ranks of organized crime rebellions comparable in principle to the current rebellions of Negroes.

CHAPTER XI

Corruption of the Law-Enforcement and Political Systems

An attack on organized crime is an attack on political corruption.

CONGRESSMAN JOSEPH M. MCDADE

COSA NOSTRA functions as an illegal invisible government. However, its political objective is not competition with the established agencies of legitimate government. Unlike the Communist Party, it is not interested in political and economic reform. Its political objective is a negative one: nullification of government.

Nullification is sought at two different levels. At the lower level are the agencies for law enforcement and the administration of criminal justice. When a Cosa Nostra soldier bribes a policeman, a police chief, a prosecutor, a judge, or a license administrator, he does so in an attempt to nullify the law-enforcement process. At the upper level are legislative agencies, including federal and state legislatures as well as city councils and county boards of supervisors. When a "family" boss supports a candidate for political office, he does so in an attempt to deprive honest citizens of their democratic voice, thus nullifying the democratic process.

The two levels are not discrete. If an elected official can be persuaded not to represent the honest citizens of his district on matters pertaining to the interests of organized criminals, he is, at the same time, persuaded that he should help insure that some laws are not enforced, or are enforced selectively. When the "representative" of a district works to prevent the passing of laws which would damage

248

Cosa Nostra but help honest citizens, the political process has been nullified. But when the same "representative" is paid by criminals to block appropriations for law-enforcement agencies which would fight organized crime, to block the promotion of policemen who create "embarrassing incidents" by enforcing antigambling statutes, and to use his political position to insure that dishonest or stupid administrators of criminal justice are appointed, he is being paid to nullify the law-enforcement process. The American Bar Association Report on organized crime concluded, "The largest single factor in the breakdown of law enforcement dealing with organized crime is the corruption and connivance of many public officials." Cosa Nostra members are willing to pay a higher bribe to a United States congressman than to a local policeman. They spend a lot of money foolishly, on things like horses and whores, but when it comes to bribery, which is part of their business, they insist on their dollar's worth.

The Chief Justice of the United States, Earl Warren, like everyone else who is knowledgeable about organized crime, believes that the basic problem of organized crime is a problem of political corruption. At a 1967 conference of law-enforcement officials, the Chief Justice stated that it could be taken as "rule of thumb" that corruption is the basis of organized crime. He went on, "Of course, there has been more than enough [corruption] in police departments, prosecuting agencies and in the courts as well. The weak link in the chain of law enforcement may be one agency in one community and a different one in another, or all may be tainted when it finally spreads to its full proportions." The President's Commission concluded, similarly, "All available data indicate that organized crime flourishes only where it has corrupted local officials." The operations of organized crime should never be referred to as the operations of the "underworld." The activities of Cosa Nostra members are so interwoven with the activities of respectable businessmen and government officials that doing so directs our attention to the wrong places. More than one Cosa Nostra captain is only a telephone call away from a governor's office.

Most metropolitan police departments developed during the late nineteenth century, when government corruption in the United States was most prevalent. Perhaps it is for that reason that police have often been deeply involved in corruption. Investigating bodies, usually created in response to campaigns for "reform," have found extensive corruption every time they have looked for it. Perhaps corruption flourishes because we are indifferent to it most of the time, and perhaps we are indifferent to it most of the time because it flourishes. But the potential harm of corruption is much greater today than it ever has been, simply because nullification of government today means nullification of a broader range of regulatory activity. Only a few years ago a criminal did not have to bribe an official in order to get a liquor license, because the character of the persons selling liquor was not regulated. Now that the scope of government activity is greater than ever before, the power to corrupt government processes affects a greater and greater sphere of the lives of more and more citizens. As the President's Commission said, "As government regulation expands into more and more areas of private and business activity, the power to corrupt affords the corrupter more control over matters affecting the ordinary life of each citizen."

Every Cosa Nostra "family" has in its division of labor at least one position for a corrupter. The person occupying this position bribes, buys, intimidates, threatens, negotiates, and sweet-talks himself into a relationship with police, public officials, and anyone else who might help "family" members maintain immunity from arrest, prosecution, and punishment. The corrupter is not depicted on the "organizational chart" which informants and policemen have sketched out as they have described Cosa Nostra's hierarchy, from commissioner to soldier. It is an essential, but "unofficial," functional position like buffer and money mover. It might be occupied by a person who is a soldier, a lieutenant, an underboss, or even a boss. Frank Costello once held both the position of boss and a position as corrupter in a New York "family." Most frequently, a corrupter position is occupied by the *consigliere* or counselor.

Although tenure in the role of corrupter is not permanent, it tends to be lengthy. Once a corrupter has established his relationships and connections, it is not easy for a boss to assign another person to the position. Moreover, there is a distinct advantage in centralizing corruption functions in a few positions. A soldier who discovers, perhaps accidentally, that a policeman or public official has a weakness which makes him a likely target of corruption is not allowed to make the bribe or exert the influence himself. In the first place, he might botch the job. In the second place, he might simply have located a man who is already on the payroll. The soldier with ideas merely reports them to a corrupter, who can work the potential dishonesty into the broad scheme of things, including his network of corruptees.

Yet the corrupting functions of a "family" are seldom centralized in a single position. In one or, perhaps, two instances, a single corrupter does all the "fixing" for his "family," which means that he is responsible for the political dishonesty of a geographical territory. More commonly, one corrupter takes care of one subdivision of government, such as the police or city hall, while another will be assigned a different subdivision, such as the state alcoholic-beverage commission. A third corrupter might handle the court system by fixing a judge, a clerk of court, a prosecutor, an assistant prosecutor, a probation officer. It depends on who you know, and who knows you. Some "families" have a position for what might be called "chief corrupter." The person occupying this position does not have the connections necessary for all the "family's" corruption, but he has subordinates who do. For example, a soldier who is going to trial might request the help of the chief corrupter, who has been bribing the police for him, who once convinced a reputable businessman to write a favorable letter to the parole board in the soldier's behalf, and who once got a corrupt assessor to reduce the soldier's real-estate taxes by 10 percent. The chief corrupter might in this case immediately discern that the soldier needs the help of a corruptee in a specific court, and he might, accordingly, give the soldier a verbal "letter of recommendation" to that corruptee's corrupter. If the soldier's problem is one of obtaining an illegal liquor license, the chief corrupter merely calls the corrupter dealing with the corruptee in the licensing office, or in the political office controlling the licensing office.

Cosa Nostra members do not use the term "corrupter," of course. They usually refer only to the corruptee. They use expressions something like "Smith is our political front man," or "Smith is our cousin in city hall," or "Smith is the rabbi for the Profaci family," or "Smith is Profaci's beard in the police department." In one neighborhood, where the soldier in charge of all bet-taking operations is the brother-in-law of the corrupt city councilman presumably representing the district, a corruptee is simply called "Frank," which is the councilman's first name.

For every corrupter, there must be at least one corruptee. Most corrupt policemen and public officials have been sought out and wooed to a position of corruptee. Men must be recruited and selected for this position just as they must be recruited and selected for a position such as bookmaker or lieutenant. While the officials occupying corruptee positions are not ordinarily members of Cosa Nostra, their positions are part of Cosa Nostra's division of labor, just as are positions for runner and lay-off man. Occasionally, a corrupter does not have to recruit a public official to a corruptee position because the corrupter's "family" has, with the help of the corrupter, recruited him in advance and put him in office. Most of the corruptees put in office have not been admitted to membership in Cosa Nostra. They are said to be "owned" by Cosa Nostra, which means that if papa says, "Eat your goddamn spinach," they start gulping it down. In 1962 a member of a city council who was "owned" by Cosa Nostra resigned after a meeting with the boss, giving "ill health" as the reason. The boss then picked one of his relatives for the job, but this man withdrew from candidacy when his association with the boss was publicized by alert newspapermen. Another man was later selected by the boss, and this one won the election, despite the fact that he did not meet the residence requirements. This deficiency was discovered, and the man resigned about sixty days after he was elected. The boss then gave the seat to a man who was the partner of a well-known usurer. In the same district, also in 1962, a United States congressman who employed the son-in-law of the boss as his assistant fell out with the boss, who told him to resign. He did so immediately, giving "health of wife" as his reason. The boss selected another man to assume the congressional seat, and his son-in-law stayed on as the new congressman's assistant. In this district, Cosa Nostra also "owns" both judges and the officials who assign criminal cases to judges. About 90 percent of the organized-crime defendants appear before the same few judges. It may properly be said that the entire political district is "owned" by the Cosa Nostra boss. Both law enforcement and democracy have been nullified.

The simplest medium for achieving the domination of a public official is outright bribery. A more subtle but equally effective method is the contribution to a political campaign. Elected officials are keenly aware of the high costs of political campaigns, and they know that re-election depends a great deal on the size of the campaign war chest they can assemble. They welcome financial assistance, and when such assistance comes from Cosa Nostra members, the officials are soon likely to experience at least subtle pressures for corruption. An appointed official, in turn, may well be indebted to an elected official for his position and, thus, susceptible to pressure for corruption put on him by his sponsor. Alternatively, the appointed official may have been given his post as a reward for building up the campaign chest, with the result that he, knowing the tainted source of assistance, puts pressure for corruption on the man that appointed him. None of the parties may think of the relationship between Cosa Nostra influencers and the influenced as one of corruption. It is more likely to be considered merely an "understanding" or a "working relationship" or "one of those things."

One noted political analyst guesses that "the underworld" contributes 15 percent of the costs of local and state political campaigns. Professor Harold D. Lasswell, another noted political analyst, has observed that local cycles of corruption-reform-corruption reflect changing states of accommodation between conflicting interests in "morality," efficiency, and law enforcement on the one hand, and "immorality," demands for jobs and favors, and evasion of law on the other. He argues that as the federal government becomes more deeply implicated in municipal and regional government, these cycles may be transposed to the federal level. While organized crime now pays for protection by political parties, "if legitimate business and other legitimate private interests are willing to pay for or engage in political activity, political parties can afford to sacrifice gamblers, racketeers, and related interests."

Despite extensive contributions to political campaigns by corrupters, most men have to be recruited to a corruptee position after they have assumed public office. The arguments and tactics used are smooth, refined, subtle, and persuasive. A West Coast police official, interviewed by a member of the President's Commission staff, reported the following attempt of a bookmaker to influence him:

These people really work on you. They make it seem too logical—like you are the one that is out of step. This bookie gave me this kind of line: "It's legal at the tracks, isn't it? So why isn't it legal here? It's because of those crooks at the Capitol. They're getting plenty—all drivin' Cads. Look at my customers, some of the biggest guys in town—they don't want you to close me down. If you do they'll just transfer you. Like that last jerk. And even the Judge, what did he do? Fined me a hundred and suspended fifty. Hell, he knows Joe Citizen wants me here, so get smart, be one of the boys, be part of the system. It's a way of life in this town and you're not gonna change it. Tell you what I'll do. I won't give you a nickel; just call in a free bet in the first race every day and you can win or lose, how about it?"

An extraordinarily detailed account of the "line" used on this West Coast policeman was obtained when a Chicago policeman made a tape recording of a corrupter's attempt to recruit him. In this case, which is taken from an annual report by Virgil Peterson, the Executive Director of the Chicago Crime Commission, a boss himself played the role of corrupter. It is possible, however, that he merely assumed the role temporarily, and that the assistant who accompanied him was his regular corrupter.

In September, 1965, Jacob P. Bergbreiter, formerly a lieutenant of the Cook County police force and in charge of the vice squad under former Sheriff Joseph Lohman, was indicted by a Cook County grand jury for having arranged a meeting of himself, Joseph Aiuppa, and Donald Shaw, a detective on the Sheriff's vice-control squad. Mr. Aiuppa, described by Mr. Peterson as "the powerful crime-syndicate rackets boss of Cicero, Illinois," was accused of offering a bribe to Officer Shaw. Aiuppa wanted Shaw to weaken his testimony in an earlier bribery case involving another syndicate member, and to give warnings of impending raids against gambling establishments in Aiuppa's bailiwick.

Mr. Peterson does not report how Bergbreiter and Aiuppa originally approached Officer Shaw, but he does report that Shaw went to the meeting equipped with a tiny radio transmitter strapped under his coat in a shoulder holster. The conversation between the three men was thus transmitted to other officers seated in a nearby car, who tape-recorded it. Officer Shaw was a likely target of corrupters because Kaspar J. Ciapetta (alias John Carr) had been arrested in early 1965 after Shaw reported that Ciapetta had given him a $500 bribe to forget about a Cicero slot-machine raid. If Ciapetta were to remain immune from arrest, someone had to corrupt Officer Shaw, and Bergbreiter and Aiuppa did their best. One part of the conversation went as follows:

AIUPPA. Would you have any objection to helping John Carr get off the hook in court, for a consideration, and, if in so doing, it wouldn't hurt your position as a police officer?

SHAW. I stated that I wouldn't mind helping if I didn't hurt myself as a police officer and I didn't perjure myself in court.

AIUPPA. You won't hurt yourself and you won't have to be in court. Just give the lawyer a loophole in our prosecution.

(Aiuppa then asked Shaw for the details of the incident in which he had arrested Carr for bribery, including information about the manner in which the $500 bribe was paid, and information about whether Officer Shaw's partners had witnessed any part of the transaction.)

AIUPPA. (interrupting) Excuse me. Do you think there is such a crime as playing a slot machine or a pinball machine?

SHAW. By the law there is.

AIUPPA. Wait a minute. The laws are flexible, they are made to bend, just like a big tree standing there. It's made to flex. I agree with this. . . . Let's put it cold. This is your home town. These are your people. Are you going to let an out-of-town guy like O'Mara [head of the Cook County police force vice squad] come in and wrap you around his finger? Like all these Negroes and these demonstrators. Is that any goal to you? To me, to our friends? To our kids? It's the law. It's not right but it's the law.

SHAW. Like I say, it's the law. I get paid to do it.

AIUPPA. All right, all right. Fine. We understand each other. There is several ways to do things. . . .

(Aiuppa then promised Shaw that he would take care of him when Sheriff Richard B. Ogilvie left office, and Bergbreiter assured Shaw that Aiuppa would be around after everyone else was gone. Aiuppa also explained that Shaw's testimony would be nullified by telling the court that the $500 could have been cash for Carr's bond.)

AIUPPA. Every month I will see that there is a C note [$100] or some worldly goods in your mail box. You'll be on the [pay] roll.

SHAW. What do you want from me to be on the roll?

AIUPPA. All I want from you is the information, so that they will not be kicking me with the point of the shoe but the side of the shoe. If you find something out, see something I should know, you think I should know about it, I'll give you a [telephone] number. You follow me?

SHAW. The thing of it is, I would suddenly be out of a job if I stopped making pinches. We can do it like you say and kick you with the side of the shoe and not the toe.

AIUPPA. You will never stop making pinches. If you haven't got an out, you go ahead. I paid for these pigeons.

BERGBREITER. He will give you some good ones.

AIUPPA. Do you follow me?

SHAW. What area are you in?

AIUPPA. When you find out about me, you will see I am a pretty nice guy. All I am interested in is the gambling and the night spots in Cicero. I am not interested in the residential areas. You could go anywhere outside the business district and you will find nothing but a nice area.

BERGBREITER. Shaw, can I give you a little advice, being a boss like I was out there?

SHAW. In vice and gambling?

BERGBREITER. That's right. Do this on your own. This is between the three of us. Don't trust your partner, nobody. (Aiuppa then explained to Shaw that if he ever got into trouble and faced a trial, Aiuppa's money would be there to help him.)

SHAW. Say the [Chicago Police Department] intelligence unit had a game under surveillance for a while and then gave it to us and suddenly it wasn't there any more. They would get wise. They would know someone blew the whistle.

AIUPPA. Fine. The tables would be there. The game would be there, but the money wouldn't be on the table. Do you follow me? I'll never embarrass you, never hurt you. I can be nice to you. . . . I can decorate the mahogany a bit. You know what I mean? See what I mean? I could help with the payments on the new car. I can see that you are taken care of every month. I can see that every month there is a little worldly goods for you. Just like myself. If you walked into a place and saw me there, and your superior said, "Pinch him," I never even met you. Go ahead and pinch me. I go along with the show.

SHAW. I kick you with the side of the shoe.

AIUPPA. Now you're catching on. Are you with me now?

SHAW. I guess.

(Aiuppa then told Shaw that he is not involved in prostitution or narcotics and that it was all right with him if Shaw arrested prostitutes. If the prostitutes were arrested, the casino owners would make more money. Aiuppa then discussed arrangements which would enable Shaw to telephone him about impending raids. He said he would obtain a transcript of Shaw's testimony in the bribery case so that Shaw could study it and avoid giving conflicting testimony when the matter came to trial.)

A few minutes after the conclusion of the tape-recorded conversation, Mr. Peterson reports, Bergbreiter appeared at Officer Shaw's home to give him $500 as a first payment on the total bribe he would get for fixing his testimony in the earlier bribery case. Bergbreiter boasted that he had been on the payroll of "the outfit" while he was supposedly handling vice and gambling as a law-enforcement officer. But about a month after the conversation was recorded, it became evident that information about the bribery case against Aiuppa was being leaked to him by one or more of Shaw's colleagues on the vice squad. In fact, Bergbreiter told Shaw that Aiuppa was aware that a trap had been set for him, and then held no further conversations with the detective. On August 23, 1965, a month before the grand-jury indictments, Sheriff Ogilvie announced that two members of the vice squad were being suspended for having twice refused to take lie-detector tests arranged to determine whether they had leaked investigative secrets to Aiuppa. The *Chicago Sun-Times* editorialized on August 25, 1965:

Two detectives properly have been suspended by Sheriff Richard B. Ogilvie for refusing to take a lie-detector test. Ten members of Ogilvie's force agreed to the tests as part of an investigation into an apparent leak of department secrets to Joseph Aiuppa. . . . As a condition of employment, sheriff's policemen agree to take lie tests whenever ordered to do so. They have a constitutional right to refuse to submit to a test, which cannot provide courtroom proof of guilt. But, as Ogilvie points out, balkers have no constitutional right to go on being a member of a law enforcement agency. . . . During the last session of the Legislature an effort was made to forbid the use of the lie detector as a condition of employment for public or private employees. It passed the House but was turned down by the Senate. The case at hand shows the wisdom of the Senate.

The men working in the organized-crime intelligence divisions of police departments probably know more about police corruptees than anyone else. It was this knowledge, in part, which led police intelligence specialists to establish the Law Enforcement Intelligence Unit, a private organization for exchanging police intelligence information. The chiefs of the Los Angeles and San Francisco police departments noted the need for a central clearinghouse which would handle information on organized crime, and the Federal Bureau of Investigation was asked to provide this service. When the request was denied, LEIU was formed. In its early years, the association consisted of law-enforcement officials representing twenty-six police and sheriff departments in seven western states, but now it has a nationwide membership. Prosecutors, and investigators for agencies such as the New York Waterfront Commission, as well as police, are included. Each member department must maintain a permanent intelligence unit of some kind, even if it consists of only one officer. Unstated, however, is a more important requirement: each participant must be honest and trustworthy, and thus eligible to receive the intelligence information shared by other participants. Because of this requirement, some policemen cannot become members. In fact, the original need for a central intelligence-information clearinghouse arose in part because policemen know they cannot trust just any policeman with information about organized crime, as the Aiuppa incident illustrates. If a policeman in one city calls the police department of another city to report a piece of valuable information about organized-crime activities in either of the two communities, he can never be sure that a corrupt policeman will not answer the telephone. Organized crime, thus, is a major impediment to the establishment of a national clearinghouse for information about organized crime.

After three years of planning and study aimed at developing an automated information-sharing system to serve New York's law-enforcement and correctional agencies, administrators of the New York State Identification and Intelligence System still had not devised a procedure for getting organized-crime information into their computers. In early 1968, Governor Nelson Rockefeller asked for a new study of organized-crime control procedures because it appeared that police and prosecutors would not voluntarily release to each other, through a central agency, the "sensitive" information they had assembled about organized crime. As Murray Kempton, columnist for the *New York World Telegram,* said in 1966, "The trouble, of course, is that cops are in business for themselves, instead of being a government like the Mafia. . . . It was the narrow parochial concerns of competition that guaranteed the triumph of John D. Rockefeller over the oil industry." Speaking of the incorruptible District Attorney of New York County, Frank S. Hogan, one state official told a reporter, "When it gets right down to it, I just don't know whether Hogan is going to let N.Y.S.I.I.S. see the sensitive kind of stuff he's got in his files, especially when there's a possibility it might fall into the hands of a corrupt sheriff or police chief at the other end of the state." There also were indications that the New York State Police had reservations about making its organized-crime files available. Organized crime, thus, is a major impediment to the free exchange of police intelligence information about organized crime.

To overcome these impediments, the Law Enforcement Intelligence Unit carefully screens its participants and introduces honest policemen to each other. As a result, each LEIU member can confidently telephone his fellow members in other police departments when he has relevant organized-crime information, rather than making official calls to police departments. However, if the information developed by an organized-crime intelligence unit falls into the hands of policemen outside the unit but within the same department, it is likely to fall into the hands of Cosa Nostra. It is part of the corrupter's duties to see that it does. Some intelligence-unit directors even believe it foolhardy to pass sensitive information up to their chief of police, let alone to their mayor, city council, or prosecuting attorney. It is not beyond the realm of possibility that some directors of intelligence units are corruptees, but if they are, they are not members of LEIU. The association is designed to fight corruptees as well as corrupters and other organized criminals.

The President's Commission noted the effective work of the Intelligence Division of the Los Angeles Police Department and concluded that honesty of local and state officials at least in part accounted for the effectiveness:

Competence and dedication of the department has thus accounted, in part, for the present law-enforcement control of organized crime in Los Angeles. The absence of serious political-corruption problems has also played a major role. This is accounted for, in part, by the traditions of the state dating back to former Governor Earl Warren and the wide use of civil service.

Cosa Nostra, like the President's Commission, respects the integrity of the Los Angeles Police Department. Most Cosa Nostra members also routinely assume that the FBI operates as a team, with very few weak spots. They know, or believe, by way of contrast, that most police departments do not present a solid front against organized crime. For one thing, the FBI can immediately fire any agent who doesn't seem to be dedicated to the objectives and methods of the Bureau, or who lets his comrades down. FBI agents are not protected by civil-service regulations. While such regulations operate to select and retain good policemen in Los Angeles, they also operate to keep bums, incompetents, and suspected criminals in other police departments. In an extreme case, a policeman who saw his partner murdered in cold blood by a Cosa Nostra member was later offered a bribe on the condition that he agree that he saw nothing. The briber's assumption, obviously, was that there is no bond whatever—moral, legal, professional, or personal—between policemen.

The services provided Cosa Nostra by corruptees are many and varied. Most commonly, the crimes committed by corrupt officials are perpetrated in order to facilitate the perpetration of crimes by others. For example, a criminal employed by a police department might, for a fee, issue another criminal an illegal and unofficial "license" to take bets in a particular neighborhood. Often both the corruptee and the corrupter are "general contractors" who farm out some of their work and profits to "subcontractors." Just as a legitimate building contractor obtains a legitimate building permit which licenses an electrical or plumbing subcontractor to proceed with work on a building, a corrupter buys a general illegal permit to violate the law. Like the general contractor, he then permits persons who will bring him the most profits to operate under his permit. And just as the permit monies coming to the honest official of a building and construction department are distributed to the employees and higher officials as part of their salaries, so the fees paid to a corruptee are spread around among both underlings and superiors.

The *New York Post* revealed in 1960 that corrupt New York police had systematized the issuing and policing of illegal licenses granted to Cosa Nostra members operating illegal lotteries. Each spot where illegal lottery tickets were sold had to be on "the pad," which was a police-approved list of locations. Of course, each spot also had to be on the approved list of the Cosa Nostra soldier operating the lottery. Payments to the police were made by the owners of each spot, not by the soldier himself. Each policeman on the beat collected $2 daily from each spot in his area. The two men in the squad car patrolling the area collected $35 weekly from each spot. Detectives, sergeants, lieutenants, and officials of precincts, divisions, borough commands, vice squads, and gambling squads, and officials from police headquarters sent their own special pick-up men to collect fees totaling about $2000 a month. The minimum cost for operating a spot on "full pad," meaning that its operator was immune from arrest by policemen on any level, was about $2500 a month. It should be noted that in this operation the police were in effect issuing each other illegal licenses to issue illegal licenses to violate the law.

In the spring of 1968 a witness before a New York grand jury refused to comment when asked if he had ever told his Cosa Nostra lieutenant that it was costing the lieutenant $600 a month "for police protection" of the lieutenant's lottery operations in East Harlem. In a press interview, a spokesman for the New York Police Department also refused to comment on the question.

Sandy Smith, who is better informed on organized-crime matters than any other journalist in the country, has an uncanny knack for getting his hands on transcripts of bugged conversations between Cosa Nostra members. In a recent issue of *Life,* Mr. Smith told of a dinner-table conversation between two New Jersey members of the Genovese "family." "Also at the table," Mr. Smith says, "was an informant for a law-enforcement agency. . . ." The two men discussed many things, including murders and bet-taking. They complained bitterly that "a top-level officer in the New Jersey State Police," as Smith called one crook, was greedily requesting that payoffs to him totaling $7250 a month be *doubled* during the tourist season. The two Cosa Nostra men, at least one of whom is a lieutenant, blamed themselves for having personally picked their greedy corruptee and then arranging for another corruptee, a politician, to promote him to his high position in the State Police.

Once policemen have been bribed into issuing crime-committing licenses, they tend to get sucked into conducting themselves as if their licensees were honest and upright citizens. They become friends with their licensees and do legal favors for them even without being bribed. The following story was recently told by the Executive Director of the Chicago Crime Commission:

On April 12, 1966, State Police officers in a small town near Elgin, Illinois, arrested Rocco Salvatore, the bodyguard and chauffeur of crime syndicate leader Sam Battaglia, on speeding charges. When the case was called for trial two weeks later in a court in Carpentersville, Sergeant Dominic Cimino of the Melrose Park Police Department appeared instead of Salvatore. Cimino pleaded with the court that Salvatore deserved a "break" because of his excellent character and reputation and needed his driver's license in his business. On August 9, 1966, the Chicago Crime Commission directed a letter to Chief of Police Anthony Iosca of Melrose Park in which it was stated: "Salvatore's 'business' is acting as chauffeur and bodyguard for hoodlum Sam Battaglia with whom he has been associated for many years and in whose Oak Park home Salvatore is known to have lived in the past. The disturbing element in this matter is that a law enforcement officer would appear in a traffic case pleading for a defendant to be given a 'break' when the traffic incident happened so many miles away from the community in which the officer is stationed, and further to go on record vouching for the character and reputation of a man such as Salvatore." On November 10, 1966, Chief of Police Iosca advised the Crime Commission that following an investigation, "Sergeant Cimino has been suspended by me for a period of five days for conduct unbecoming an officer."

On November 5, 1967, Anthony Iosca, Chief of Police of Melrose Park, died. Three weeks later, on November 27, 1967, the Board of Trustees of Melrose Park named forty-six-year-old Dominic R. Cimino as the new chief of police of the suburb at a salary of $10,680 a year. Shortly after his appointment, publicity was given to the new chief's frequent meetings with Charles (Chuck) Nicoletti, a notorious crime syndicate muscleman and terrorist. News accounts related that Chief Cimino was observed conferring with Nicoletti almost daily in Slicker Sam's saloon at 1911 Rice Street in Melrose Park, a place owned by Sam (Slick) Rosa and his wife, Zena. Rosa, a golfing partner of Sam Giancana and Jackie Cerone, formerly worked in the Capone gang's floating crap game and has been arrested for gambling violations.

The "favors" police do for organized criminals are sometimes returned in kind. A city official had a prostitute in his house while his wife was away. The whore stole a fur coat and the official noted its absence. He called a trusted police official, explained the situation, and said it would be embarrassing if the coat were still missing when his wife returned. The police official called on a dozen prostitutes, with no success. He then revealed his plight to a Cosa Nostra lieutenant, keeping the name of the city official confidential. The lieutenant returned the coat two days later but the police official kept it for another two days, then "explained" to the city official that diligent and delicate detective work was necessary for its retrieval.

In the extreme, a significant proportion of the functionaries of the legislative, judicial, and executive branches of a local government become corruptees who derive their income from shares of the illegal contracts negotiated by corrupters for the privilege of violating the law. This was somewhat the case in "Wincanton," the fictitious name given to a real community studied by John A. Gardiner for the President's Commission. It also has been somewhat the case in Jackson County, which includes Kansas City, Missouri. In 1966, a reform group of candidates tried to break the stranglehold which Cosa Nostra had on the county government. The presiding county commissioner, who led the reform ticket, said:

I believe that the national crime syndicate has more political influence here than in almost any other county in the country. It controls some county officials and it considers the county government its bastion. The issue in this election is whether the people rule or the Mafia rules.

Sandy Smith's "informant" revealed to *Life* that Cosa Nostra similarly had almost total control of Long Branch, a town of about 26,000 in New Jersey. Anthony Russo bragged that in this town Cosa Nostra had fixed elections and maneuvered the ouster of a city manager. "What we got in Long Branch is everything," Mr. Russo said. "Police we got. Councilmen we got, too. We're gonna make millions."

But producing such extensive corruption is neither necessary nor economical. Adequate control of enforcement policy can be obtained by corruption of a few key individuals who for a fee or a favor undermine and nullify the day-to-day work of honest policemen. Within police departments, the "vice-squad pattern" was used as an instrument of corruption for so many years that it has been labeled a "classic technique." Police action against organized criminals is centralized in the vice squad, and policemen not assigned to that unit must refer organized-crime matters to it. Only the members of the vice squad need be corrupt. When this pattern prevails, the bet-taker, among others, need not worry about the neighborhood police —they have no authority over him. Even if the neighborhood police are corrupt and demand bribes, he does not fear them. After all, the "vice-squad pattern" was invented in part to insure that corrupt neighborhood policemen are cut out of their rightful share of the graft.

More indirect than the "vice-squad pattern" is the simple practice of inducing a legislator or city councilman to oppose legislation which would give police the manpower or tools they need to conduct the lengthy investigations necessary for the successful prosecution of criminal conspiracies. It is as easy for a corrupt legislator to argue, in the name of civil liberties, that the police should not be equipped with computerized information-retrieval systems or with electronic surveillance devices as it is for honest legislators, genuinely concerned for civil liberties, to do so. Although the influence of Cosa Nostra clearly reaches into our state and national legislative chambers, the organization has not yet mustered a majority in any of these chambers. But then it has never needed a majority.

The intricate relations between the syndicate and law-enforcement officers is illustrated by the results of a 1963 investigation—by the Chicago Crime Commission—of the innocent fact that the president of an appliance firm gave a Chicago police detective and his wife all-expense-paid trips to a Norge Company convention in Spain. The president had won six such tickets in a routine sales contest, and it was his right to give them to whomever he wished. But a study of the relations between the appliance firm (Moeller Brothers Company) and other firms and persons suggested that something was fishy. In the first place, the secretary of the appliance firm was also an officer in two finance companies that did quite a business with usurers, bet-takers, and gamblers. In the second place, the secretary's brother was the secretary of a fourth finance company doing a similar business. (This man, Fiore Buccieri, was said by Sandy Smith, writing for *Life,* to have participated in the torture and murdering of another member of the Chicago "outfit.") In the third place, the president of the appliance firm was also president of one of the finance companies. In the fourth place, the president and secretary-treasurer of one of the finance companies were former policemen, and two of its major stockholders were politicians. And in the fifth place, one of the six tickets was given to Felix Alderisio, described by the Executive Director of the Chicago Crime Commission as a "syndicate big-wig" and an "infamous gangster." The following list of companies and officers was assembled from the 1961 and 1963 reports of the Executive Director. The phrases in quotation marks and parentheses are his.

Moeller Brothers Company
   President: James Bianco
   Secretary: Frank Buccieri ("reputed syndicate gambler")
B and B Finance Company
   President: James Bianco
   Secretary: Fiore Buccieri ("syndicate hoodlum" and "a pal of Tony
      Accardo and other Capone mobsters")
Frontier Finance Corporation
   President: John H. Scherping ("retired Chicago police captain")

Vice President: Frank Buccieri
Secretary-Treasurer: Michael B. Tenore ("former Cook County deputy sheriff")
Associates (each had $20,000 invested in the company):
Carl A. Schroeder ("former Chicago Postmaster")
Edward F. Moore ("former Republican Cook County Chairman and member of the Chicago Transit Authority")

Post Finance Corporation
President: Frank Buccieri
Secretary: Michael B. Tenore

The Executive Director of the Chicago Crime Commission goes on to say that James Bianco gave tickets to Frank Buccieri and Michael Tenore as well as to Detective and Mrs. Charles Malek and Felix Alderisio. Detective Malek said he did not know who his traveling companions were to be, insisted that he did not recognize Alderisio and Buccieri until the plane was about to land in Spain, and denied that he associated with these men during the trip. In view of this testimony, no disciplinary action was taken by the Chicago Police Department against Officer Malek, who in 1960 also had to defend himself against corruption charges that were not substantiated.

Corruptees are not the minor actors in all the crimes they commit, as is the case when they issue crime-committing licenses. In another form of corruption highly relevant to organized crime, two criminals, one of them a governmental official, conspire to cheat the citizens the official represents. In some cities, for example, Cosa Nostra groups holding garbage-collecting franchises charge the citizens, say, two dollars a month more than an honest firm would charge, then pay one of the dollars to an official for the privilege of holding the franchise. In other cases, the partnership for extortion is even more obvious. For example, a member of a state legislature conspired with a Cosa Nostra member to shake down night-club owners, promising immunity from prosecution for violation of alcoholic-beverage-control laws to these owners who paid a fee. The owners did not bribe the legislator; they simply paid the Cosa Nostra member, who threatened them with legal harassment if they did not pay, and called on his silent partner for help whenever he needed it. Had the legislator (or a policeman or other enforcement official) threatened the harassment himself, the night-club owners would have found it necessary to think of themselves as both criminals (bribery) and victims when they paid the fee. But the Cosa Nostra man's service as an intermediary enabled them to conceive of themselves only as the victims of extortion.

Crime-committing licenses are also issued by court officials, in the form of immunity from prosecution or conviction. As G. Robert Blakey, the nation's leading expert on the legal aspects of organized-crime prosecution, has said, "Useful as corrupt police may be, no dollar of corruption buys as much real protection as the dollar which directly or indirectly influences the public prosecutor or one of his trusted assistants." After all, the prosecutor makes the crucial decision as to whether the suspect shall be prosecuted or not. The Kefauver Committee reported in some detail on the operations of William O'Dwyer, one-time District Attorney of Kings County, New York, and then concluded:

[Mr. O'Dwyer failed to take] effective action against the top echelons of the gambling, narcotics, waterfront, murder, or bookmaking rackets. His defense of public officials who were derelict in their duties, and his actions in investigation of corruption, and his failure to follow up concrete evidence of organized crime, particularly in the case of Murder, Inc., and the waterfront, have contributed to the growth of organized crime, racketeering, and gangsterism in New York City.

Professor Joseph Goldstein reports that in one jurisdiction, during a six-month period, criminal prosecutions were initiated against only 25 out of 600 persons arrested for gambling (about 4 percent). During the same period there were 80 raids on alleged gambling operations, accounting for about 580 of the 600 gambling arrests. Professor Goldstein uses the low ratio of prosecution to arrest as an index of police harassment of known bet-takers, whereby officers tour the city and search on sight, because of prior information or such telltale actions as carrying a paper bag. This interpretation seems to overlook the possibility that a goodly proportion of the 80 raids might have been "tipover raids" in which one or more corrupt policemen destroy the effectiveness of the raid by perpetrating planned illegalities which will cause even honest prosecutors and judges to dismiss the defendants on the grounds that their constitutional rights have been violated. This is a common practice. The interpretation also overlooks the possibility that the prosecutor, judge, or some other court official was a corruptee who sold immunity for a fee. Of 11,158 gambling arrests made in Cook County (Chicago), Illinois, in 1963, 76 percent were dismissed. The proportion of prosecutions thus was much higher than in Goldstein's jurisdiction. Further, of the 2,678 persons prosecuted, 1,818 (68 percent) were convicted (about 16 percent of the arrests). But only 17 jail terms were imposed, and only four of the jail sentences were for terms longer than thirty days. When Thomas Aurelio, newly nominated for a judgeship on New York's Supreme Court bench, pledged undying loyalty to Frank Costello, then boss of what is now the Genovese "family," he perverted his office and all it stands for.

On December 3, 1962, George Ammeratto, who described himself to arresting officers as a "self-employed bookie," got into an argument in a Chicago-area bar. A patron cuffed him. According to the Director of the Chicago Crime Commission, the following scenario then took place. Mr. Ammeratto left the tavern and returned a short time later brandishing a revolver. When the female owner of the bar tried to take the weapon away from him, he hit her on the head with it, knocking her unconscious. He waved the gun at the patrons and said he was going to "get that guy," meaning the man with whom he had argued and scuffled. A bystander tried to creep up behind the bookie and take his gun away, but the bookie wrestled the gun free and shot him in the chest. The wounded man staggered out to the street and collapsed. The bookie pursued him and shot him again, in the back. The assailant then got into his car and fled. The presiding trial judge found the defendant not guilty of murder or manslaughter. Apparently accepting the defendant's argument that both shots were accidental, the judge found Ammeratto guilty of involuntary manslaughter and sentenced him to five years on probation, with the first ninety days to be spent in the Cook County jail. The Chicago Crime Commission assailed the disposition in this case as a "travesty of justice," and the Executive Director of the Commission reported it as "one of the more flagrant miscarriages of justice in the Cook County Criminal Court in 1963."

If a Cosa Nostra member is so unfortunate as to be convicted and sent to jail or prison, corruptees sometimes provide an additional service by making his stay as comfortable as possible under the circumstances. It is probable, however, that the proportion of corruptees in the prison service is much less than in police departments and court systems. Within two months after Chicago's Sam Giancana was committed to the Cook County jail on a contempt charge stemming from his refusal to give testimony before a grand jury, two jail guards were discharged for doing his laundry, and another guard was discharged when a polygraph test revealed that he was untruthful when he denied having received gratuities from Mr. Giancana or one of his friends. The warden stated that Giancana's underwear and socks had been laundered as a special favor to him at least seven times in about a month. It was rumored that Giancana's cell door was left unlocked at night, enabling him to stroll around the jail and to watch television long after the 10:00 P.M. curfew.

The FBI summaries of some of the bugged conversations occurring in the office of Raymond L. S. Patriarca and subsequently released to the public via the *Providence Journal* (May 20, 1967) reported several cases of corruption and hinted at many others (see p. 120). The following were the most direct observations:

Patriarca said that he was contacting [name blanked out] in an effort to obtain the parole of Lee Santanielle and Lawrence Baiena. (4/16/63)

Raimondi then mentioned that he at one time was very wealthy and, because of his habit of helping friends financially, he has lost most of his money. He pointed out that at one time an individual, name not mentioned, was given an order to kill somebody. While completing the murder, he was observed by a witness. Later, on another job, probably murder, he was picked up and identified by the witness in the first murder. A payoff of $5,000.00 was necessary to "square the rap away." $5,000.00 was furnished to a Lt. Dunn (phonetic) for this purpose and the charge was dropped. The individual was released and the following day he also was murdered. This resulted in the loss of $5,000.00 to Raimondi. (10/26/64)

Roy French, a horse trainer, contacted Angiulo [Patriarca's underboss] through an intermediary requesting assistance to obtain a license as a horse trainer at the Rhode Island tracks. Patriarca indicated he would assist in this. (1/25/65)

Joe Modica, Boston, Mass. contacted Patriarca specifically concerning the Berkshire Downs Race Track in which Raymond Patriarca allegedly has a financial interest. Patriarca told Modica to contact his friend who is allegedly extremely close to Attorney General Edward W. Brooke of Massachusetts and have him arrange to release the $100,000 bond that is being held by the Massachusetts Court in connection with civil suits that have been heard in Massachusetts courts. (1/25/65)

Henry Tameleo advised he contacted George Kattar and reiterated to Kattar that in order to operate he "must have the State." Kattar told him that he has arranged to pay-off the State Police and that he would furnish Tameleo the identities and the amounts paid to individual members of the State Police. This apparently refers to a gambling operation that Kattar will open in Biddeford, Maine, which was previously reported. The Boston Office is conducting an investigation relative to this matter. It appeared that "Blackie" (last name unknown) who owns the club had been tipped off by members of the State Police that a game was to be held. In view of this, the opening of the operation had been temporarily discontinued. (1/28/65)

A *Saturday Evening Post* article reporting on this bug, and other things, on November 18, 1967, concluded that the Patriarca "family" had the following officials, among others, "in the bag": a high-ranking state official, a police chief, two licensing officials, a high-ranking court administrator, and "a handful of powerful state senators and representatives." The article also contains the following remarkable paragraph:

The "bug" transcript reveals that pay-offs to politicians are much more subtle and usually take the form of campaign contributions. In the transcript Patriarca complained bitterly that he had been rebuffed in several attempts to induce Massachusetts ex-Lieutenant Governor Francis S. Bellotti to accept $100,000 in Cosa Nostra money for his campaigns for governor and for attorney general last year. Bellotti's honesty went unrewarded. Piqued by his refusal, the mob spread the word that he had taken mob money, and these rumors were a major factor in Democrat Bellotti's defeat in both campaigns. The "bug" transcript (or the Patriarca Papers, as they are called) established that the going rate for politicians in New England is $100,000.

After this paragraph had appeared, Mr. Bellotti gave public thanks to its author for clearing his name. But the "remarkable" thing about the paragraph lies in the fact that those parts of the bug transcript which the court released to the public contain no reference whatever to Bellotti and no indication that Patriarca even hinted about what the paragraph states he "complained bitterly" about.

Corrupters nullify the law-enforcement and political processes primarily by outright bribery and other rationally designed forms of "influence" such as contributions to political campaigns and promises to deliver the votes in a particular area. One city councilman complained to his chief of police about the breakup of a large lottery enterprise—"That raid cost me 2000 votes." But corrupters also establish unwitting allies who are victims, not corruptees or fellow conspirators. For example, a governor or even the president of the United States might grant a pardon to a convicted Cosa Nostra member, thus becoming an ally in the attempt to nullify the law-enforcement process. But such elected executives tend to sign whatever is put before them by their trusteed assistants, and the trusted assistants might put before them a pardon application which has been endorsed by an important political figure who has been or can be of political help to the executive—the chairman of a metropolitan county Democratic party, the chairman of a state Republican committee, the speaker of a state house of representatives. These political figures are not necessarily corruptees either; they might simply be trying to help an important friend help a friend help a poor unfortunate prisoner. Only someone very low in the political hierarchy need be a corruptee; the remaining men might be victims. Nevertheless, all the principals, and all their assistants, are unwitting allies of the sort deliberately sought by Cosa Nostra.

In 1963 the United States District Court in Chicago issued a preliminary injunction ordering that when Sam Giancana was playing golf there must be at least one foursome of golfers between Mr. Giancana and the FBI agents who were keeping him under surveillance. On appeal the injunction order was stayed, on the ground that there can be no judiciary supervision over the executive branch of government. Shortly after Giancana filed his petition for the injunction, United States Representative Roland W. Libonati introduced a bill which would make it a crime under the laws of the United States for a federal agent to violate the civil rights of a person during an investigation or surveillance. Libonati had moved up from the Illinois Senate to the U.S. House of Representatives, where he sat on the Judiciary Committee. During a Washington press interview, Congressman Libotani denied that his proposed bill was designed to aid Giancana. The Kefauver Committee earlier said that Libonati, a close associate of Al Capone, "spearheaded the opposition to reform legislation proposed by the Chicago Crime Commission and Governor Stevenson and backed by the bar." Libonati resigned as congressman when Giancana told him to do so.

Respectable bankers have become unwitting allies. Most of the securities stolen in the United States during the last two decades are lying safely in the vaults of respectable banks, hypothecated for legitimate loans. Cosa Nostra members buy, steal, or extort stolen securities from the burglars and robbers into whose possession they have illegally fallen. Sometimes, in fact, they themselves make the arrangements for the original theft. They then employ a front man (often a victim of loan-sharking) to take the securities to a bank and offer them as the basis for a legitimate loan. Just as government executives tend to look into the character of the person asking a minor political favor, rather than into the details of the favor itself, bankers have tended to look more at the character of the potential borrower than at the securities he offers to hypothecate. Some bankers are crooked. But few bankers know that they have issued millions of dollars worth of legitimate loans on pledges of stolen securities. Once the transaction has been completed, Cosa Nostra only has to pay the interest, again through a front man, in order to use the clean money for the purpose of corrupting the very governmental and business systems which keep the bankers alive.

Cosa Nostra members also seek, and find, unwitting allies in civil libertarians. For example, Cosa Nostra members were wildly enthusiastic about the "invasion of privacy" position taken in 1967 by United States Attorney General Clark and the American Civil Liberties Union with reference to legalization of wire tapping and electronic surveillance. There is no evidence that any member of ACLU has been corrupted by Cosa Nostra. But it is impossible to determine from the contents of some antibugging speeches whether the speaker represents civil libertarians or organized criminals. Cosa Nostra members prefer it that way.

There is no connection between the Communist Party and Cosa Nostra, which is oriented to making money rather than to political ideology. Communist nations, in fact, are efficient organized-crime repressers. While "friends of ours" have allies or counterparts in most of the nations of the world, none of these nations are behind the Iron Curtain. Nevertheless, Cosa Nostra members seek Communist allies. They applaud when Communists lash out at their common enemies—the FBI, other law-enforcement groups, and investigating committees that behave as if they were the sole guardians of the nation's internal security. A Cosa Nostra member does not care whether the system of government is democratic, communistic, or fascistic so long as he can persuade its officials to let him remain immune from the criminal law. Some Americans tend to see a Communist under every rock. They should be assured that each rock-covered Communist is accompanied by at least two organized criminals, who are holding down the rock and forcing the Communist to promise that he will insure their immunity if they let him up.

We have already indicated that Cosa Nostra members have been quite successful in seeking and obtaining unwitting allies in the Italian-American community. They have had phenomenal success in promoting the notion that "They hate all of us because we are Italian," when really they should say, "They hate a few of us because we are crooks, regardless of race, creed, or place of national origin." Figuratively speaking, a criminal of Italian descent slips between two respectable citizens of Italian descent, locks arms, and cries, "Look, they are calling the three of us criminals." According to Nicholas Pileggi, The Grand Council of Columbia Associations in Civil Service once forced the New York City Board of Education to correct a social-studies textbook which stated "a small percentage of Italians became notorious racketeers and gamblers" upon their arrival in New York. Similarly, when Edgar Croswell was chosen as inspector general to clean up corruption in the New York Sanitation

Department, the Uniformed Sanitation Men's Association of New York City, a union made up largely of Italian-Americans, threatened a citywide garbage collection slowdown because they thought the choice of Croswell was a "slur on Italian-Americans." Croswell was the New York State Police sergeant that uncovered the Apalachin Cosa Nostra meeting in November, 1957. Mr. Pileggi acknowledges the propriety of Italian-American groups organized to smite smears, but he deplores "Mafia censorship leagues," groups which do not protest against Cosa Nostra itself but against "every book with an Italian villain, every television drama with an Italian crook, every newspaper mention of the Mafia, Cosa Nostra, Camorra, or Unione Siciliana." He singles out Americans of Italian Descent (formerly called The American-Italian Anti-Defamation League) as *"Numero Uno"* among such image-watching societies. Too few Italian-Americans have come to the obvious and logical conclusion that men with names like Gambino, Giancana, and Marcello are giving them a bad name. Instead, they have been duped into concluding that men with names like Andreoli, Piersante, Salerno, and Siragusa are giving Italian-Americans a bad name because they keep pointing out that Gambino, Giancana, and Marcello are crime promoters.

Some of Cosa Nostra's unwitting allies have been seduced by nothing less than rational "public-relations" schemes. One boss in 1965 employed a legitimate public-relations firm to improve his "family's" image. More indirectly, even Cosa Nostra crimes are selected with public relations in mind. Nobody likes a child molester, a pimp, or a dope dealer, and we tend to conclude that a criminal who is not involved in loitering around schoolyards, prostitution, or narcotics selling can't be all bad, even if he admits to every other kind of crime. Even more indirectly, Cosa Nostra members attempt to improve "public relations" by attaching themselves to that which is popular and "in" at the time. In the 1930's it was prize fighting and prize fighters; in the 1940's it was Hollywood and movie actors; in the 1950's it was Las Vegas and night-club singers; now it is suburbia and corporation executives. Next it might be think tanks, astronauts, and space scientists. Cosa Nostra members love the Knights of Columbus and similar charitable organizations. Frank Costello of New York City once ran a dinner for the Salvation Army and more than twenty judges showed up. The Dean of Planning and Development for Brandeis University has reported that Meyer Lansky has been an "occasional donor of small gifts" to the University.

Cosa Nostra pays some policemen to ignore crime. However, the mere fact that a policeman or other official overlooks bet-taking or some other form of organized crime activity by no means suggests that he is on the payroll of the criminal organization. He might be involved in any of three different organizational conditions favorable to a program of nonenforcement.

First, the policeman could be saddled with a nonenforcement policy formulated by a corrupt official above him in the organizational hierarchy of his department. In this situation, his choices are to become corrupt himself, to resign in disgust, or to remain in public work and do what he can. The honest policeman in a corrupt system has a time of it, but he holds his chin up high, even when he is transferred to a punishment beat, demoted, or given unpleasant duties. His complaints, like the complaints of citizens observing the same crimes he observes, might be fruitless because the person hearing the complaint (a police commissioner, a prosecutor, a mayor, a member of the city council) may himself be playing the role of corruptee. The police chief of one large city was formerly the doorman at crap games run by Cosa Nostra men. In one "investigation" of municipal corruption, the "prosecutor" announced that any citizen who came forward with evidence of bribery would be prosecuted for participating in such unlawful conduct. After studying the relationships between organized crime and the urban poor, a group of twenty-three Republican members of the United States House of Representatives concluded that the basic problem really is one of political corruption.

A war on organized crime is inseparable from a war on political corruption. In this fact may lie hidden the reason why it is so difficult for political leadership to wage a comprehensive war on organized crime— for to do so would be to risk severe political consequences. A tacit alliance between organized crime and some local public officials has a far more devastating effect on society and the urban poor than merely permitting organized crime to practice its vices. In the broader sense corruption of local public officials inevitably results in a breakdown of public respect for authority. In recent years—indeed recent weeks—much has been said about a deplorable loss of morality among segments of the urban poor in America's cities. But to whom are the people to look for standards of honesty and virtue if they cannot look to their local public officials? What is the lesson taught to today's young men and women when members of their local public community choose to cooperate with (or choose conveniently not to see) organized crime? . . .

When a "general soreness against the world" erupts into massive violence in America's cities there are many causes—but a principal catalyst is a disrespect for authority bred by corruption in public officials. The willingness of many more local and national officials to be indifferent toward it inevitably feeds the sense of desperation of the urban poor.

Essentially the same position was taken by the National Advisory Commission on Civil Disorders. After investigating many incidents of Negro rioting, this body assigned some of the blame for such incidents to organized crime. In discussing Newark, New Jersey, for example, the Commission observed: "The Mafia was reputed to control much of organized crime." More generally, the Commission noted that poverty, violence, and organized crime activities combine to produce great cynicism about the idea that success is to be achieved by legitimate means:

With the father absent and the mother working, many ghetto children spend the bulk of their time on the streets—the streets of a crime-ridden, violence-prone and povery-stricken world. The image of success in this world is not that of the "solid citizen," the responsible husband and father, but rather that of the "hustler" who takes care of himself by exploiting others. The dope sellers and the numbers runners are the "successful" men because their earnings far outstrip those men who try to climb the economic ladder in honest ways.

Young people in the ghetto are acutely conscious of a system which appears to offer rewards to those who illegally exploit others, and failure to those who struggle under traditional responsibilities. Under these circumstances, many adopt exploitation and the "hustle" as a way of life, disclaiming both work and marriage in favor of casual and temporary liaisons. This pattern reinforces itself from one generation to the next, creating a "culture of poverty" and an ingrained cynicism about society and its institutions.

The indifference of officials feeds "the sense of desperation" and

"cynicism" of policemen as well as the urban poor. Success as a corrupter is determined by the ability to find or place key corruptees
at every level of government having anything to do with law enforcement. Earl Johnson, Jr., formerly a special attorney in the
Organized Crime and Racketeering Section of the United States Department of Justice, has pointed out that such diversified corruption
"tends to thwart any intensive effort against the organization by one
dedicated man or group of men located in one or two departments."
Cosa Nostra is safe in Chicago as long as the relevant city, county,
and state departments do not all become honest at the same time.
That is pretty safe indeed. Moreover, in such circumstances the
morale of the personnel in all agencies is likely to be low. Johnson
has put the matter succinctly and well:

> Every member of each agency finds it easier to excuse his own yield-
> ing to organization pressure when he feels that his own efforts to oppose
> the law against a criminal organization would be of no avail, since so
> many others in law enforcement serve the organization. The more that
> have been corrupted, the easier it is to corrupt the remainder.

Second, community indifference to organized crime sometimes
makes police and other officials look corrupt when in fact such
officials are doing the best they can, which is not very much, with
the manpower and resources provided them. In this situation, the
community might be openly opposed to the activities of organized
criminals, but not enough to pay for detecting, arresting, prosecuting,
and incarcerating them. One weak link in the chain is sufficient. For
example, if the prosecutor or his close assistants are honest but
nevertheless inefficient, there is no need for any official to be dishonest. When a Cosa Nostra boss contributes to political campaigns
that he does not control, he contributes to all candidates, just in case.
Because he wants to win, his slogan is "May the best man lose."
Inefficiency of public officials is one of his weapons, and he is by no
means a member of any citizens' committee which would have the
community pay its prosecutor a salary such that capable lawyers
would be attracted to the post.

It should be noted, however, that Cosa Nostra members are decidedly effective in getting laws enforced when it is to their advantage

to do so. Irving Spergel found that in a Chicago neighborhood where organized crime thrives, the sale of drugs on a wholesale level was approved by the adults, but the same persons were strongly opposed to the retail distribution of narcotics, especially in the immediate neighborhood. "In previous years, when drug-selling had been permitted in the neighborhood, the racketeers themselves were 'hurt' when their own sons and nephews in certain instances succumbed to the use of drugs. Drug-selling was now prohibited in the area. Racketeers had even gone to the extreme of setting the police on the trail of small-time peddlers who would not obey their injunctions."

Few communities are willing to spend the money essential to an efficient anti-organized-crime program staffed by competent officials. For example, when Cosa Nostra recently pitted its resources against the resources of a large and efficient prosecutor's office in a narcotics case, the criminals almost drained the prosecutor dry. The defendants spent about $500,000 on trial expenses, including the fees of eighteen lawyers who dragged the proceedings out for six months before a mistrial was declared. The new trial took three more months and cost the defendants and their backers another $250,000. Justice was done. But most prosecutors simply cannot afford that much justice. Even the prosecutors for wealthy counties cannot afford it very often. They must bargain and negotiate with criminals. Thus, they frequently must exchange the time and expense of a trial for a plea of guilty to a minor offense, or they must bargain for a guilty plea in exchange for a promise of a light sentence or a suspended sentence. There are not enough court personnel to do otherwise. If the overworked court personnel did not bargain, court calendars would be hopelessly swamped within a few weeks. Even with bargaining, one New York court recently closed down all its civil procedures for a month, to give it time to catch up with the criminal-case calendar.

The police, similarly, are rarely given the money and manpower necessary to combat organized crime effectively. As a consequence, they appear to be more inefficient and corrupt than they are. Some police departments consider themselves successful merely because they have survived. Most significantly, organized-crime specialists are unanimous in their belief that a rational intelligence program is essential to effective long-range action against Cosa Nostra. But under the current restricted budgets, and with corruptees serving as intelligence agents for organized criminals, Cosa Nostra knows more about the activities of policemen than policemen know about Cosa Nostra. Statutes similar to the Jencks Act (see p. 120) make it mandatory that even honest police and other officials reveal many of their secrets to Cosa Nostra.

Merely keeping one Cosa Nostra member under surveillance for twenty-four hours a day takes an extraordinary amount of police time. A decent surveillance requires two men per shift. What with sick leave, days off, holidays, and vacations, about twenty-five policemen must work full time to keep a suspect under surveillance for 365 days. Taxpayers are not certain they can afford such "frills." Cosa Nostra can afford them—policemen, suspected informants, and men selected for execution are kept under twenty-four-hour surveillance. For that matter, Cosa Nostra keeps most of its members under surveillance most of the time. Similarly, taxpayers now complain loudly that they do not see enough uniformed policemen on the street, but strategic intelligence, tactical intelligence, and counter-intelligence all use manpower in ways not visible to street watchers. Moreover, men working on problems of strategic intelligence, especially, do not really know what they are looking for until something they have written turns out to be valuable. As an authority on the use of intelligence in foreign policy decisions has said, "It is impossible to set precise limits upon the scope and kinds of information needed in the strategic intelligence process." Accordingly, it is difficult to measure the "efficiency" or "effectiveness" of an intelligence worker. Perhaps it is for this reason that city councils and state governments are inclined to believe that police intelligence work costs too much. Intelligence officers in police departments make few arrests, never issue traffic citations, and rarely help old ladies across busy streets.

Most cities do not have intelligence units in their police departments. Any information gleaned about the activities of "Cosa Nostra" therefore tends to be information about bookmakers and writers who are not even members of the organization. Occasionally an ordinary detective is asked to ferret out information about the "higher-ups" in bet-taking, but this is like asking a small-town hardware store clerk to find out all he can about the workings of United States Steel. The Army, Navy, and Air Force would be at a distinct disadvantage in protecting the country from an enemy or potential enemy if they did not maintain effective intelligence services. "In a similar fashion, a police department in any major city is helpless in coping with organized crime without the help of an efficient intelligence unit." O. W. Wilson, Chicago's former Police Commissioner, whose writings on police administration tend to be taken as "the word" by police officials all over the world, agrees:

> In all but small departments, the chief finds it difficult to ascertain vice and organized-crime conditions in his community and the integrity of his force except by using an intelligence unit working directly under him or an assistant chief. . . . The intelligence unit is concerned with the nature of the criminal organization rather than with its individual criminal acts. . . .

Even the intelligence units of big-city police departments are hopelessly understaffed, assuming that the nation should know as much about Cosa Nostra as it knows about, say, Cuba. For example, the New York City Police Department has 27,000 officers, of whom 96 are assigned to the Criminal Investigation Bureau, which deals with the investigation, but not arrest and prosecution, of organized criminals. This works out to less than one-third of one percent. In Chicago, 95 out of 10,000 police officers are assigned to the Criminal Intelligence Division, which is responsible for carrying its investigations through to arrest and trial. The Los Angeles Police Department also assigns about one percent of all its police officers to the Intelligence Division, which neither has criminal investigative responsibility nor makes arrests—51 out of 5177. In the entire country, only six prosecutors have assigned men to concentrate their work on organized-crime cases. Continuity of command is a variable too. Most Cosa Nostra bosses have been in office longer than have most directors of police intelligence units. One boss has been in command almost as long as J. Edgar Hoover.

Third, some police and other officials are tolerant of organized crime because important members of their community demand that they be tolerant of it, not because someone pays them to do so. The niggardliness of communities with respect to budgets for police departments and other agencies of criminal justice is a symptom of community indifference, not a cause of it. Even when "the public" is on its best behavior, it demands police and political action against organized crime only sporadically, usually when some sensational disclosure reveals "intolerable" violence or corruption caused by organized crime. As the President's Commission concluded,

> Politicians will not act unless the public so demands; but much of the urban public wants the services provided by organized crime and does not wish to disrupt the system that provides these services. And much of the public does not see or understand the effects of organized crime in society.

Governor John McKeithen of Louisiana is a good example of the "politicians" the Commission mentions. This governor will order the state police into action against bet-taking only when it becomes "flagrant or notorious." Generally speaking, this means that action is taken only when someone of significance complains in a loud, firm voice. The governor knows it does not pay to be overzealous. Referring to a former superintendent of the Louisiana State Police he said:

> Look at Grevemberg. He cracked down on gambling. He was tough. He went around with a flashlight and an ax, busting up little honky-tonk places. Do you know where he placed when he ran for governor? *Fifth!*

In such circumstances it might be said that the entire community or society is corrupt, in the sense that it tolerates activities which it has previously declared to be immoral and illegal. In 1961 a nationwide television documentary program showed ten policemen entering or leaving a bookmaking establishment, presumably to make bets or to receive pay-offs. A police captain has commented as follows:

> There are so many millions of people in this country, and about half of them play the number pool. We all know it's going on. Why, one of those three men at the desk outside my office can play a number for you any time. He just calls up the office. The number pool isn't considered such a serious thing. The only bad thing is that it's run by men who don't want to work. As long as it is kept quiet, the cop can't

complain. We might say, "For God's sake, don't write them under my nose. Go in the back street." The police have to see that it doesn't become too open. Of course, if an officer accepts money to let them do business, that's a very serious thing.

Such indifference can, of course, readily lead to corruption. It doesn't take a genius to determine that he can become wealthy if he stops chasing bet-takers into back streets and lets them operate in the open and under his nose. United States Representative Joseph M. McDade of Pennsylvania, however, stresses the notion that indifference is itself a form of corruption:

> It does not require many on the take to allow organized crime to flourish, but it takes some few wherever organized crime does flourish— and it takes many more who are doing nothing illegal but who practice the corruption of indifference.
> We are easily shocked by indifference to corruption. We should be equally shocked by the corruption of indifference.

Although indifference to law violation of any kind may be considered a kind of corruption, much apparent inactivity among police and other criminal justice administrators is neither indifference nor corruption. We have already noted that if the courts are not to be hopelessly swamped with trials, court personnel must bargain with criminals. Judge Charles Breitel of the New York Court of Appeals has recently written, "If every policeman, every prosecutor, and every post-sentence agency performed his or its responsibility in strict accordance to the rules of law, precisely and narrowly laid down, the criminal law would be ordered but intolerable."

The police dealing with organized crime must, like other police and like prosecutors and judges, engage in selective nonenforcement. This practice might become the occasion for bribery, leading to additional nonenforcement, but bribery is not necessarily part of it. Police are asked to arrest all criminals and, generally, to "enforce the law." Just as clearly, they also are asked to take no action with respect to many law violations. They are not necessarily either corrupt or indifferent, then, when they seemingly ignore crimes committed under their noses.

No modern community or nation could possibly give the police enough manpower to "enforce the law," even if it wanted it enforced. The police must necessarily make judgments about which conduct is in fact criminal and about which criminal incidents are "grave" enough to call for arrest. And even if police were somehow allocated all the money and manpower necessary to "enforcing the law," there still would be strong pressure for selective nonenforcement because full enforcement would cast an unbearable burden on other public agencies. If a community could somehow arrange for unlimited manpower in all its agencies of criminal justice, significant citizens nevertheless would exert strong pressures for selective nonenforcement because this practice is essential both to efficient police work and to justice.

When criminal activity involves a "willing buyer" and a "willing seller," as is the case with much organized crime, there are few complainants. Moreover, Cosa Nostra intimidates its victims so effectively they dare not complain. A New York law makes it a felony to lend money at more than 25 percent annual interest. It was adopted in 1965, after the State Investigation Commission showed that loan-sharking is an important Cosa Nostra activity in the state. Yet today a New York Cosa Nostra member is more likely to be hurt in an automobile accident than be convicted of usury. Because victims are warned that they will be murdered if they ask the police for protection, the police must themselves discover usury and other organized crimes, without much help from the public, just as they must themselves discover most traffic violations. And even when the police discover organized crime activity they find it difficult to obtain convictions because witnesses are afraid to come forward. They ask their community leaders for permission to develop substitute witnesses—in the form of wire taps and electronic bugs—but the leaders are reluctant to provide such efficient substitutes, just as they are reluctant to authorize traffic policemen to use radar and other electronic equipment as substitutes for witnesses in traffic cases.

It is sometimes said that police do not enforce gambling laws because they do not have enough manpower to ferret out gambling violations. This assertion is misleading. Discovery of gambling might be difficult because it occurs everywhere, but discovery of bet-taking does not take much manpower or diligent detective work. Even a sleepy policeman can observe men paying short visits to a store or some other spot at all hours of the day or night. Most policemen don't need to be given much in-service training before they become educated to know that activity of this kind is presumptive evidence of a brothel, an illegal saloon, or a bet-taking operation. Newspapermen and other alert citizens know where a neighborhood's bookmakers are located, and so do the police. But newspapermen and irate individual citizens who "expose" bookmaking tend to ignore the organizational, political, and budgetary pressures for honest negotiations with bet-takers, who appear to be gamblers when they are not. The police cannot ignore these pressures.

Occasionally an irate citizen publishes a list of the bet-taking establishments in his city and infers that police who do not admit that they know about the establishments are either inefficient or corrupt. Such lists often are embarrassing even to honest policemen, who cannot publicly admit that taxpayers in fact employ them as much to negotiate with criminals as to "enforce the law." The police are really asked to keep the crime rate tolerable by making "deals" with criminals. But when the police or other administrators of criminal justice make "deals" by explicitly or implicitly negotiating with criminals, the process is called "corruption," even if no money changes hands. The police therefore cannot make speeches about it. On the other hand, when officials of our Department of State engage in an identical process while dealing with Russia or Red China, the process is called "negotiation" or "diplomacy."

Just as State Department officials often have good reasons for ignoring a foreign nation's violations of a treaty, the police often have good reasons for overlooking bet-taking and similar offenses. For example, they might ignore the crimes of small fry in the hope that they will catch a shark. Some bet-taking establishments are kept under surveillance for months and even years in the hope that the Cosa Nostra member in charge of it will somehow get involved. Police, as a matter of policy, sacrifice arrests of writers and walking books in the hope that managers, supervisors, and financiers will, sooner or later, make a mistake. Viewed naively, the problem is one of money. Surveillance of a bet-taking establishment is horribly expensive. As we just indicated, intelligence work of the kind that keeps the police informed about the workings of Cosa Nostra and its members is even more expensive. It is so expensive that it tends to be neglected, even in large police departments. This means that the police must wait for a long, long time for a Cosa Nostra lieutenant or boss to make a mistake that will lead to a good pinch.

More indirectly, police also ignore bet-taking and other crimes because the police serve on the front line of diplomacy between those citizens who want the laws enforced and those who do not. For example, widespread community support for illegal gambling requires that the police decide what constitutes an "appropriate level" of law enforcement. This means that the policeman must serve as a buffer between divergent social interests with their conflicting standards of conduct. William F. Whyte came to this conclusion long ago. After studying the relationships among the police, the organized criminals, the residents of an Italian neighborhood in an eastern city, and the "good people" of the same city, he observed that the police are required by their community to play an "elaborate game of make-believe."

Often police are asked to take action when gambling is "commercial" in nature but not when it is "social." This presents impossible problems because some forms of "social" gambling, such as church bingo, look exactly like "commercial" gambling. It also presents problems because some forms of gambling are either "commercial" or "social" depending on who is looking at it. The men involved in a poker game at a country club usually know each other, while the men gathered for a crap game in a ghetto apartment do not. When the police investigate the latter, the fact that the men do not know each other might be taken as evidence that the gambling is not "social" and is, therefore, subject to enforcement. On the other hand, the police know a great deal more about ghetto life and the values of working-class men than do most citizens, and for that reason they may conclude that the crap game is "social" even if the participants do not know each other, much to the consternation of the country-club poker players. As another alternative, police experience might indicate that ghetto crap games often end in fights, sometimes resulting in homicide, while illegal bet-taking and middle-class gambling do not. Accordingly, they might define a ghetto crap game as "commercial" and, thus, *really* illegal, only because doing so serves to prevent assault and homicide.

All illegal bet-taking is "commercial" if it is backed by lay-off men, but discerning the lay-off operation is difficult, even for police. It is surprising how many policemen know nothing about lay-off operations. One policeman excused his ignorance in such matters by telling me, "I never gamble myself." Further, even if police know about lay-off operations, they have difficulty getting evidence of it in specific cases, especially when they are prohibited from tapping the telephones used in the lay-off business. They define the operation as "social" until such time as they can get solid evidence of the "commercial" participation of "higher-ups." In doing so, they can rightfully view themselves as honest law-enforcement officers while at the same time permitting law violations to go virtually unchecked.

The police also seem to overlook some organized-crime activities in an honest attempt to reduce the profit stemming from such activities. The enormous profits in bookmaking, lotteries, usury, and narcotics importation stem in part from the fact that the operations are illegal. If the demand is constant, and if there is no competition between legal and illegal means for meeting the demand, then the profits to illicit dealers remain constant. A state lottery, such as the one recently introduced in New York, is no competition to the numbers operator if it is played in a sterile atmosphere in which the gambler has to declare himself a kind of gambling addict to an upright citizen of the community. After all, the store clerk or hotel cashier selling my legal lottery ticket might be my child's Sunday-school teacher. New York is now trying to give numbers operators a little competition by selling its lottery tickets at news stands; it offers improved odds for persons who are now foolish enough to make a 1 to 500 bet when the correct odds, for *gambling*, are 1 to 1000.

The President's Commission observed that illicit suppliers of gambling opportunities are protected by the ban of the criminal law itself, and the Commission concluded, "The use of the criminal sanction serves to raise the stakes, for while the risk becomes greater, so do the prospects of reward." The same conclusion can readily be drawn about the effects of enforcement crackdowns. Mr. Whyte long ago stated, "Since competition in illegal activities leads to violence, it is in the interest of the [police] department to cooperate with the racket organization in eliminating competition." By the same token, it can be concluded that if the police reduce the risks of bet-taking, the increase in the number of bet-takers will reduce individual profits to such a low level that no one will be able to make a decent living taking bets. But this conclusion overlooks the fact that illegal bet-taking has been *monopolized* by Cosa Nostra through the use of violence. Police must understand that as long as Cosa Nostra thrives there will be no significant competition to drive individual profits down.

It is true, however, that if the police suddenly were to put nine-tenths of a city's bookmakers in jail, the remaining tenth would make fortunes unless the demand for bookmaker's services were somehow altered. For over twenty years Alfred R. Lindesmith has been arguing that narcotic-drug use would diminish if the enormous profits in narcotic distribution were diminished by legalizing sales, under controlled conditions. This argument assumes, basically, that the importers, distributors, and dealers to some extent *create* the demand, because of the profits involved. Such an argument has not been used extensively in reference to other sets of willing buyers and sellers—the bet-takers and the gamblers, the usurers and the borrowers. The extent to which bet-takers and usurers create a need for their services is unknown. Their very presence to some extent creates the demand for their services, of course. Communities certainly do little to reduce the demand. Honest policemen who try to regulate the demanded sales and services, rather than trying to suppress them, are likely to be viewed as corruptees rather than as the diplomats they are.

In times of crisis, usually arising from loud complaints about corruption, it is difficult for the police to retain their roles as diplomats. They then must function as law-enforcement officers, thereby shaking up the whole community. An insistent complaint disturbs the conditions of peace which the police have unofficially and perhaps even honestly arranged between those who want to gamble and those who want gambling eradicated. When bet-taking establishments are being closed down in a spasm of reform, police are likely to hear even respectable citizens ask them, "Why don't you stop chasing gamblers and go out and catch some criminals?" One pious old crook, who could in no sense be considered "respectable," put it this way: "There is not a book operating in [neighborhood] today, but I wonder how many wives have been raped." The same idea was recently expressed by United States Representative Cornelius E. Gallagher of New Jersey. As a member of a Congressional Committee which was examining the federal effort against organized crime, Congressman Gallagher suggested that he might favor the legalization of gambling, then addressed William A. Kolar, Director of the Internal Revenue Service's Intelligence Division as follows: "You could get out of the Mafia business, and we could perhaps pay more attention to some of the greater problems, which is the breakdown of law and order on the streets. Organized crime does not embrace murder and rape and mugging and robberies and this sort of thing." A little over a year after Congressman Gallagher made this statement, a team of *Life* magazine reporters said he was "a man who time and time again has served as a tool and collaborator of a Cosa Nostra gang lord." Gallagher categorically denied the charge.

Unfortunately, the diplomatic role of the police and other officials is not explicitly recognized by Cosa Nostra bosses and commissioners. An official who gratuitously uses his office to help a Cosa Nostra member endangers his life as well as his career, just as does an official who accepts a Cosa Nostra bribe. Some government workers undoubtedly have done a few gratuitous favors for Cosa Nostra or even accepted a few bribes and then severed all connections with the organization. But the rule seems to be that one who shakes hands with the devil becomes the devil's partner. This is what law-enforcement officers mean when they say that an official is "owned" by Cosa Nostra even if he is not a member.

A state official shut his eyes to the criminal record of a Cosa Nostra soldier and issued a liquor license to him. No bribe was involved. Within a year he was informed that if he did not act favorably on another criminal's application for a license, the first transaction would be exposed. He issued the second license and soon found himself with other criminal applicants. He then made the best of a bad situation by successfully negotiating for bribes. Soon he was up to his armpits in corruption, but he was never convicted. He was discovered, arrested, and indicted, but he was murdered before the trial took place. Another "fixed" officeholder lived to describe a similar experience:

I forgot that those gangsters are animals. When I gave them my hand, they began nibbling at my fingertips. Before I knew it, they had swallowed my arm and were gnawing on my shoulder.

The process is a general one. A policeman who overlooks a minor bet-taking violation by a Cosa Nostra member can hardly turn back. Even if the violation is overlooked diplomatically, in the interests of community peace and harmony, the policeman's life is henceforth in danger. He is "in," and he must play. The fundamental principle evoked here with a vengeance is well known to philanthropists, executives, administrators of foreign aid, and do-gooders everywhere: No good deed goes unpunished.

CHAPTER XII

Search, Destroy, and Appease

We are gnawing away at one or two heads of a many-headed Hydra, without knowing with certainty where the other heads are, or where the rest of the body extends.

POLICE COMMISSIONER CHARLES R. THOM

THE ECONOMIC and social affairs of the United States are being seriously disrupted by Cosa Nostra, but neither lawmakers nor law enforcers have been able to develop penal legislation which would eliminate the organization or even seriously curtail its activities. Experts in the United States Congress, in the Department of Justice, and in various police and investigative agencies have been unable to propose a criminal-law remedy which would be at once practical and Constitutional. Those who would bell the cat have found it difficult to go much beyond the proposition that organized criminals should be prosecuted as if they were not organized.

The prevailing notion seems to be that stricter enforcement of existing criminal laws would do the trick, especially if the police were authorized to use the electronic tools they desperately need as substitutes for the potential witnesses Cosa Nostra intimidates or kills. But in reality this proposition merely asks that we keep on doing what we have been trying to do since the days of Prohibition—seek out and destroy organized criminals one by one. This traditional approach, if conducted with vigor, certainly would spook Cosa Nostra members and decrease individual profits. In the long run, however, Cosa Nostra would simply meet it with vigorous countermeasures of the sort that also are traditional.

When the president or vice president of a large legitimate corporation dies or retires, a dozen men are waiting in the wings to take his place. While the new incumbent might not have the skills of the old one, this loss to the corporation is only temporary. In an effective bureaucracy, no man is indispensable. Cosa Nostra is such a bureaucracy. Even if its members could all be individually prosecured and sent off to prison, the *positions* held by these members would remain. For each vacant Cosa Nostra membership position, there are at least a hundred applicants. Incarceration of members disrupts the organization only for the time needed to obtain replacements. Thus, for example, the imprisonment of one New York "family" boss, Vito Genovese, has had no discernible effect on the amount of crime committed by his "family."

If, by some miracle, a nationwide police crackdown on large numbers of Cosa Nostra members could be maneuvered Constitutionally, the organization might be disrupted for as long as twenty years. Nevertheless, the measure would be a "temporary" one, even if the period of quiescence lasted for fifty years. Premier Mussolini used dictatorial methods to squash members of the Sicilian Mafia in the 1930's, but the organization was thriving again within a decade. In the summer of 1966, Dr. Angelo Mangano, deputy police chief of Palermo, announced that once again the Sicilian courts and police had "broken the back of this criminal association." We predict that the organization will rise from its hospital bed, broken back notwithstanding, if its whole skeleton is not destroyed. G. Robert Blakey has pointed out that the killing of Jesse ended the James gang, but the deportation of Charles Luciano merely resulted in the passing of the leadership to Frank Costello.

It seems reasonable to expect that a vigorous program that focused on enforcement of existing criminal laws, rather than on attacking the structure of organized crime, would be met with increased legal evasive tactics. Cosa Nostra leaders rarely violate, directly, the laws prohibiting bet-taking, usury, extortion, murder, and other crimes that are organized. Their most common offense is *conspiracy* to commit such crimes. But prosecutors currently find it very difficult to prove conspiracies, simply because Cosa Nostra members conspire with each other, and with outsiders, to eliminate or hide traces that could be used as legal evidence of a conspiracy. They conspire with members of their "family" to assassinate any witnesses who might come forward with testimony regarding the original conspiracies. But they also hire, legitimately, bevies of lawyers and accountants to insure that other forms of evidence regarding their conspiracies and other crimes cannot be assembled by police and prosecutors or, if assembled, can be legally suppressed. Directors of police intelligence units across the nation can only watch Cosa Nostra's leaders, hoping they will make the mistake of violating some traditional criminal law such as the one prohibiting extortion, the one prohibiting fraud, or the one prohibiting income-tax evasion. As the tempo of police action against individual bet-takers, usurers, extortionists, frauds, and income-tax evaders is increased, Cosa Nostra leaders will merely employ more and better lawyers and accountants to help them decrease the number of mistakes.

It also seems reasonable to expect that more vigorous prosecution of individual organized criminals will stimulate more vigorous *illegal* evasive action on the part of Cosa Nostra. Any campaign to imprison persons working in the bet-taking business, for example, is not likely to have any significant effect on Cosa Nostra leaders who have already purchased immunity from the law-enforcement process. Moreover, if the demand for illegal gambling services remains constant, imprisonment or deterrence of large numbers of individual bet-takers will increase the profits of those men who have corrupted our law-enforcement and political systems, thus enabling them to escape arrest and imprisonment. Cosa Nostra bosses who are immune from arrest are not afraid of police crackdowns. On the contrary, being immune, they welcome any official action which will eliminate competitors who are not immune. The increased profits going to these men as a consequence of a vigorous campaign to eliminate individual organized criminals would enable them to buy an even greater degree of immunity. This has been the pattern since 1931, and there is no reason to believe that the fundamental character of the pattern will change unless the pattern itself is attacked.

One common proposal for attacking the pattern of action and reaction suggests, as the economist Thomas C. Schelling has done, that the Cosa Nostra organization be damaged by inflicting damage on its economic base. One way to damage that economic base is to reduce the organization's profits by legalizing gambling. Competition from respectable bet-takers would, the idea goes, reduce the enormous profits now being used by Cosa Nostra members to steal the nation. Moreover, the idea continues, even if the monopoly on bet-taking now held by Cosa Nostra is not completely eliminated by repeal of laws prohibiting gambling, repeal would reduce the amount of profit accruing from the current gambling market. This reduction, in turn, would reduce the funds available to Cosa Nostra for corruption purposes. While the idea has great merit, to be discussed below, there are five things wrong with it.

First, the proposal follows the "Kinsey principle" regarding the criminalization of conduct. Some years ago, Professor Alfred Kinsey and his associates discovered that Americans were participating in an enormous number of violations of the laws regulating sexual conduct. They proposed that the laws therefore should be repealed. They could have proposed, with equal logic, that the laws be enforced. Certainly the morality of those who originally formulated the laws would dictate that the laws be enforced or, at least, kept on the books as a sign of an ideal morality expected of all men. With reference to gambling, it is easy to observe existing laws being violated with great frequency, and it is easy to propose that, therefore, gambling ought not to be a crime. My own inclinations are in this direction. It is difficult to see why it would be any more immoral to place legal bets at a downtown store than it is to place bets at a race track. But perhaps it is immoral to make legal bets at the race track, too. If one takes the position that all gambling is immoral, as many persons do, then the fact that the first bastions fell when on-track betting was legalized is no basis for arguing that the remaining bastions ought to fall. Unfortunately, perhaps, the standards of morality set by legal codes in America tend to be viewed as the *only* standards of morality, where in an ideal world they would always be considered as examples of the *minimal* level beneath which no decent man should fall. Should we abolish the laws making the providing of illicit services a crime, some of the current buyers certainly would be converted into sellers unless restrictions of some kind were imposed. The margin is thin. Men who consider themselves respectable and who are considered respectable by the leaders of their communities stand side by side with criminals when they patronize illicit businesses.

Second, both technical skill and huge amounts of capital are needed to conduct a profitable bet-taking enterprise, legal or illegal. At the moment, most of the Americans possessing both the skill and the capital necessary to establishing legal bet-taking enterprises are crooks. Since World War II, we have witnessed four major experiences with legalized bet-taking—in Nevada, in Cuba, in the Bahamas, and in England. In all four cases, Cosa Nostra members and their associates moved in. When bet-taking is legal, the proportion of profit usually is regulated by law, but the opportunities to cheat are great. When three or four race tracks operate in a state, the racing commission can quite effectively police each of them. But when hundreds of gambling establishments are in operation, as in Nevada, only nominal controls can be administered. Until quite recently, the hidden owners of four Las Vegas casinos alone were cheating tax collectors by drawing off profits amounting to a million dollars a month before totaling up their profits officially, a process called "skimming." Following an inquiry into this kind of crime, the Nevada Gaming Commission announced that it simply could not afford the manpower needed to place an inspector in the counting room of each casino. More recently, computer control of the calculation of winnings has been introduced at one small Las Vegas casino, on an experimental basis. Gamblers and the government are both cheated when criminals are behind legalized bet-taking. Inspectors cannot be everywhere at once, even if they are computerized, and when they are out of sight the gambler is likely to be treated to all the crooked tricks favored by card sharks and tin horns everywhere. Most Nevada bet-takers seem to be opposed to cheating the customer because widespread cheating, if discovered, would drive the pigeons away. Based on the conduct of the managers of one casino that recently went bankrupt soon after it was found to be using crooked dice, the rule seems to be that one should cheat the customer only when necessary. Were legal bet-taking parlors to spring up in American cities like gasoline stations and liquor stores, the probability would be high that they would be controlled by the same persons who now control illegal bet-taking.

Third, the total amount of profit in bet-taking probably would increase if gambling were legalized. It is true that bet-taking is now enormously profitable in part because it is illegal. But were it to be legalized, the amount of gambling surely would increase, thus offsetting the diminished amount of profit on each transaction. If a government agency itself operated the enterprises this might not be true, simply because government-operated bet-taking enterprises seem unable to compete with illegal ones. The Spartan decor of state-owned liquor stores has been generalized to the entire operation of the New Hampshire and New York legalized lotteries, making them unattractive and uninteresting. In New York, at least, a legal lottery has made only a tiny dent in the illegal bet-taking business. I have played roulette with the government officials legally operating a casino in Switzerland, and my hunch is that the only game that could be duller would be one operated by American civil servants.

Fourth, there is no assurance that legalizing gambling would decrease the profits of organized criminals, even if the measure completely dried up all of their profits from bet-taking. After all, when the manufacture, distribution, and retail sale of alcohol was legalized after the period of prohibition, the organized criminals went into bet-taking. Should Cosa Nostra's profits be reduced by legalization of bet-taking, the organization might corrupt some other area of activity. They might even step up their extortionist business, becoming more like the Sicilian Mafia.

Fifth, the proposal to legalize gambling simply is not practical because of the relationships between federal, state, and local American governments. Should illegal bet-taking be sharply curtailed in New York by competition from legalized bet-taking, the criminal bet-takers would merely move to Pennsylvania, New Jersey, or Quebec. The federal government cannot legalize gambling everywhere. Even if a state legalized gambling, some of its citizens might insist on a local option, with the result that some counties and cities would continue to provide income for criminal bet-takers, just as some "dry" counties and cities now provide income for bootleggers.

The greatest evils of contemporary illegal bet-taking arise from the lay-off operation. This is the system for taking the gambling out of bet-taking, and it is the operation which makes organization essential. It follows that the greatest evils of bet-taking could be eliminated by eliminating illegal lay-off betting. Should a state legalize gambling, perhaps a partnership between free enterprise and government could be arranged, with free-enterprise merchants providing the setting for gambling while civil servants conducted the lay-off operation from the state capitol. The resources of a state, thus, would provide the backing for "mom and pop" bet-takers across the state, and the state would reap the profits now reserved mostly for persons high in the hierarchy of Cosa Nostra. It is not inconceivable that the federal, state, or local government might similarly go into competition with usurers, providing short-term loans for desperate persons with no collateral except their bodies. Universities already provide such loans to needy students.

Despite moral and practical limitations, the proposal to curtail organized crime by legalizing gambling has great theoretical merit. It is a reasonable alternative to the current law-enforcement approach, which is oriented to the traditional notion that individual criminals must be detected, arrested, and prosecuted. In the last analysis, what law-enforcement agencies want to know, and need to know, is that a suspect's behavior has been in violation of a specified criminal law. Even the "organized-crime" sections of large metropolitan police departments must be concerned more with accumulating evidence that an individual violated a law than with the structure and functioning of the businesses or other organizations in which that individual participates. Accumulation of data on the economic, political, and social bases of Cosa Nostra—what the CIA and similar agencies call "strategic intelligence"—has not been of much concern to law-enforcement agencies. Professors might show that ordinary crime is rooted in the economic, political, and social organization of the society in which it occurs, but policemen cannot be concerned with the effects of these remote influences on an individual burglar. Similarly, organized crime may be rooted in the citizens' demand for its illegal goods and services, but policemen cannot worry about such matters when confronted with a case of bribery, extortion, or murder. In the long run, however, social problems can be eliminated only if their causes are eliminated. Piracy did not disappear because of strict police action; it disappeared because the advent of the steamship made piracy unprofitable. Cosa Nostra bosses did not get out of the whore-house business because of police crackdowns; they got out because, due to changes in immigration trends, a decrease in the number of unattached men and an increased number of willing women in large cities reduced the demand for whore houses. Organized crime of other varieties will not disappear until similar structural changes occur.

We believe that organized crime will not be curtailed, whether or not gambling is legalized, until we have learned a lot more about it, and about its place in the economic and political affairs of American society. This, of course, amounts to the usual proposal for further study. Such study must be "practical" in the sense that it is oriented to the framework of the criminal law, thus giving policemen and prosecutors a handle on the problem. Yet it also must be oriented to the acquisition of knowledge of a kind not now in the files of law-enforcement and investigative agencies. We propose that social scientists, systems engineers, law-enforcement personnel, and legislators work together, probably in a new agency within the United States Department of Justice, to specify in detail the formal and informal structures of the illicit governments and businesses traditionally lumped together as "organized crime."

Implicit in this proposal is the suggestion that a cadre of policemen be broadly trained for organized-crime work. The training of modern military leaders goes far beyond preparation to lead men in battle. The modern soldier is much more than a warrior. His leaders must have backgrounds in governmental administration, economics, international trade, foreign cultures and languages, diplomacy, espionage, and counterespionage. By way of contrast, the men dealing with organized crime in America are still being prepared for direct combat, if they are being prepared at all. The policemen and prosecutors who specialize in organized crime have more or less just fallen into their specialization, then trained themselves to do their best. It is high time that some policemen be trained as organized-crime specialists, and that their training include general studies of the kind now necessary for military leadership. This, we think, is the real basis of pleas for more and better intelligence work on the part of law-enforcement agencies. William J. Keating, formerly an Assistant District Attorney in New York City, has deplored the absence of any comprehensive body of information about what he calls "the enemy." In noting this fault, and in using the "enemy" terminology, he acknowledges the fact that police work and police training, like warfare and military training, can no longer be what they used to be.

In defending the public against the underworld, neither prosecutors' offices nor police departments see fit to compile facts about the enemy. . . . The reason for the general lack of data . . . is the indifference of law-enforcement agencies toward conducting intelligence operations in the underworld. . . . Crime in our country is fought almost entirely on a complaint basis, after the horse is stolen, and preventive criminology is practiced only by one or two police departments and two or three well-staffed, privately financed citizens' anticrime commissions.

The study group made up of "modern policemen" and others oriented to questions of strategic intelligence will not have an easy task. Defining illicit businesses in organizational terms, compiling strategic intelligence data, and making systems analyses of illicit operations will be much more difficult than identifying the formal and informal structures of large legitimate corporations.

Studies conducted by this group should be oriented to the task of making "organized crime" illegal. While the United States Constitution will continue to make it extremely difficult to formulate legislation of this kind, compiling and analyzing strategic intelligence information as if it were to be used in support of legislation which would outlaw organized criminals' behavior will focus attention on the Constitutional problems and other legal problems which must be solved if organized crime is to be controlled. Not until we have specified precisely and in detail the structures of illicit criminal organizations will legislatures be able to proceed with the enactment of one or both of two kinds of criminal laws that have been under consideration for at least a decade.

One kind of criminal law, proposed especially by the framers of the Model Penal Code and the Model Sentencing Act (to be discussed below), would specify that a person committing a crime while occupying a position in an illicit division of labor (i.e., "organized crime" or "Cosa Nostra") shall be subject to different procedures in criminal-law administration than a person committing the same crime while not participating in such a division of labor. A second kind of criminal law, proposed especially by United States Senator John L. McClellan, would specify that development of and participation in an illicit division of labor (i.e., "organized crime" or "Cosa Nostra") is a crime. Both these legislative proposals require precise definition of the phrases in parentheses, and we will show later how both of them have floundered because such definitions have not been provided.

The fact is that "organized crime," as such, is not now against the law. It is not against the criminal law for an individual or group of individuals rationally to plan, establish, develop, and administer an organization designed for the perpetration of crime. Neither is it against the law for a person to participate in such an organization. What is against the law is bet-taking, usury, smuggling and selling narcotics and untaxed liquor, extortion, murder, and conspiracy to commit these and other specific crimes. Because "organized crime" is merely a social category, rather than a legal category, police and other governmental agencies cannot even routinely compile information on it, as they do for other categories of crime, such as larceny, burglary, and automobile theft. Even if our proposed study did not result in Constitutional legislation, it would serve the important purpose of reorganizing and expanding the organized-crime files of law-enforcement agencies. Careful legislative studies of, say, "homicide in America" can be undertaken because police routinely maintain files on homicide. But attempts to conduct comparable studies of "organized crime in America," our most serious crime problem, lead to frustration because, not being a legal category, there is no reason for police routinely to assemble information on the subject. As indicated, police and prosecutors must be primarily concerned with violations of specific criminal laws. Whether an individual's specific crime is described in social terms as "organized crime," "property crime," "dishonorable crime," "nasty crime," or some other type of crime not specified in the criminal law is not of much relevance to them.

This is more than "a problem of definition." It is a fact of life which permits directors of businesses dealing in illicit goods and services to remain immune from arrest, prosecution, and imprisonment unless they themselves can be caught violating specific criminal laws such as those prohibiting bet-taking, usury, bribery, or the sale of narcotics. It is the problem of organized crime. None of the laws enacted for the regulation of legitimate businesses or cartels can be applied. None of the laws enacted for the regulation of membership in either legitimate organizations (labor unions) or illegitimate organizations (Communist Party) can be applied either. "Organized crime" thrives because it is not crime.

Stated in different terms, if "organized crime" is to be controlled by traditional methods, legislatures must in the long run be able to define it as precisely as burglary, automobile theft, and murder are now defined in criminal statutes. Once defined, the behavior involved conceivably could be prohibited by criminal law, as behavior defined as burglary is now prohibited. Were that the case, law-enforcement agencies could bring offenders to trial for committing organized crime, not merely for committing the crimes that are organized, such as bet-taking. Considerable assistance in this process can be obtained from men skilled in the theory of social organization and the techniques of systems analysis.

The United States Supreme Court has characterized as "the first essential of due process of law" that "the terms of a penal statute creating a new offense must be sufficiently explicit to inform those who are subject under it what conduct will render them liable to those penalties." Because "organized crime" obviously involves organization, what is needed as a basis for legal control is detailed and precise specification, by social scientists, engineers, and anyone else with a knowledge of systems, of the formal and informal structures of illicit businesses and governments. In the last decade alone there have been thousands of studies of legitimate organizations. Variations in the effectiveness and efficiency of different kinds of divisions of labor and in the conditions under which these arise, persist, and change have been studied in many settings, ranging from broad administrative systems to specific factories, firms, hospitals, and prisons. The theory, techniques, and research results from these studies of formal and informal divisions of labor would be directly applicable to illicit enterprises if even the most rudimentary scientific data on them were collected and systematized.

Moreover, "systems-analysis" corporations have in the last five years begun to show considerable interest in the organizational arrangements designed for law enforcement and the administration of justice. Defense-research corporations, looking for new ways to serve their country while still turning a profit, are increasingly going into the business of crime control. For example, defense-research outfits in California and in New York have made, and are making, careful analyses of the judicial process, from arrest to recidivism, and "systems models" of this process have been constructed. Similar work was done by the Science and Technology Task Force of the President's Commission. Such attempts at systematization have been undertaken, by and large, with a view to cost accounting, to improving data-gathering procedures, and to maximizing the flow of information about what happens to criminals after they commit their crimes. If an efficient model of the judicial process can be constructed, and if relevant data can be stored in a central location, then almost instant help can be given to agents with a need to know about the criminal case histories of individuals, about trends in crime rates, and about the economic and social costs of crime. It is somewhat paradoxical to observe, in the light of this development, that the systems approach has not been utilized in the study of criminal organization itself. The only attempts to date have been the tentative analysis I made for the President's Commission and a small preliminary analysis by the Matson Research Corporation, also done under contract with the President's Commission.

The difficulty of defining undesirable conduct for purposes of outlawing or even understanding it is well illustrated in the discussion of gambling by the President's Commission. The Commission distinguished between "casual social gambling" or "private gambling" and gambling activity which "is a highly organized illicit business, involving large and sometimes national organizations dealing in billions of dollars a year." After making this traditional kind of distinction, the Commission went on to recommend that the criminal law and law-enforcement processes be re-examined with a view to relieving "private gambling and religious fund-raising enterprises" from criminal penalties, "while seeking to bring the law to bear more effectively on the organized gambling promoter." "This," the Commission continues, "should be accomplished by legislative definition rather than by the haphazard and uneven application of police or prosecutorial discretion." But the Commission gave no clues about what might be an appropriate "legislative definition" of the "highly organized illicit businesses" and the "organized gambling promoters" it would control. The Commission here seemed to assume that everyone knows the difference between organized crime and other crime, and it gave no help whatever to legislative bodies which would outlaw the former.

In another place the Commission got closer to the heart of the problem, but even here the assumption seemed to be that common-sense terms like "illegal business" could adequately be used in the technical world of law. In its attempt to distinguish street workers in bet-taking operations from office supervisors and other management personnel, the Commission merely coughed, honked, and blew its nose. It recommended: "Federal and state legislation should be enacted to provide for extended prison terms where the evidence, presentence report, or sentence hearing shows that a felony was committed as part of a continuing illegal business in which the convicted offender occupied a supervisory or other management position." It should be noted that the proposed legislation would not outlaw organized crime. It would subject to long prison terms those men who committed a crime, such as bet-taking, while acting as managers of "continuing illegal businesses." But many such managers do not take bets, and they do not commit any other traditional crimes except conspiracy. Even if they did, how would a court go about establishing that the defendant (1) was a manager of (2) a continuing illegal business? In the form it is stated, the Commission's recommendation does not even differentiate any felonies committed by Boss Carlo Gambino from any felonies committed by a whorehouse madam.

On a single page, the Commission used the phrase "organized crime" or "organized criminal activity" fourteen times without ever indicating precisely what was being discussed. It even used the phrase "organized crime" in a legal sense, despite the fact that, as indicated, "organized crime" is not against the law. For example, the Commission recommended that witnesses be protected "during the pendency of organized-crime litigation," but it did not specify what kind of litigation was being considered. A prosecution for extortion, after all, is "extortion-litigation," a prosecution for violating an anti-gambling statute is "gambling litigation," and a prosecution for "conspiracy to murder" is "conspiracy litigation" or even "murder litigation." The Commission also mentioned local witnesses "who fear organized-crime reprisal," but it did not state how such reprisal differs from the reprisal of any crook who is out to take private vengeance against one who bears witness against him.

The Model Penal Code also glosses over the most difficult task confronting those who would control organized crime, that of stating in legal terms just what organized crime is. This proposed Code has a provision which could be used as the basis for imposing heavier penalties on organized criminals than on ordinary criminals, but it avoids the difficult task of defining just what it is that is to be deterred by lengthy prison terms. Article 7, Section 7.03 provides that a court may sentence a person who has been convicted of a felony to an extended term of imprisonment if "the defendant is a professional criminal whose commitment for an extended term is necessary for protection of the public." But a "professional criminal" may be a sneak thief, a pickpocket, a confidence man, or even an automobile thief who has never been a member of an illicit organization and never engaged in any of the activities ordinarily considered "organized crime." Defining "professional" for the purpose of framing precise criminal statutes is almost as difficult as defining "organized crime." Article 7 can hardly be said to advance our knowledge or efforts at control by going on to provide:

The Court shall not make such a finding unless the defendant is over twenty-one years of age and: (a) the circumstances of the crime show that the defendant has knowingly devoted himself to criminal activity as a major source of livelihood; or (*b*) the defendant has substantial income or resources not explained to be derived from a source other than criminal activity.

The first clause would be extremely difficult to prove in the case of a Cosa Nostra boss, for such bosses make it a point to commit no crime except conspiracies, which are extremely difficult to prove. Again, the device does not differentiate Carlo Gambino from the madam or even from the solitary drug addict who makes his living stealing cameras and radios from parked automobiles. The second clause would apply or not apply to an organized (or other) criminal depending upon the definition of "substantial."

The Model Sentencing Act also avoids the issue. Unlike the Model Penal Code, however, the Act at least gets us on the right track. This proposed legislation stipulates that a thirty-year prison term shall be imposed on any felon who is so dangerous that the public must be protected from him, and whose felony was committed as part of a continuing criminal activity in concert with one or more persons. The legislation would leave to the discretion of prosecutors and judges the question of whether the felon is in fact "dangerous." But all felons are dangerous, by definition. More important, the only definition of organized crime really suggested is "continuing criminal activity in concert," and this sounds like two or more homosexuals practicing their trade in Carnegie Hall. Together, the two criteria apply to members of check-passing rings as well as to Cosa Nostra bosses. "Continuing criminal activity" is vague but not impossible to measure. "In concert" requires precise specification of organizational ("systemic") variables.

Legislators have gone to psychiatrists for help in defining terms like "sexual psychopath" and "irresistible impulse," but they have not gone to organization specialists for help with phrases like "in concert," "illegal business," "highly organized illicit business," and "organized crime." The analytic definitions provided by such specialists might not be any better than the psychiatric ramblings about "psychopaths" and "mental disease," but they certainly would be better than the common-sense ideas about organization now being used as weapons against Cosa Nostra. Viewed from one perspective, the anthropological, sociological, business-administration, and systems-analysis disciplines are devoted exclusively to determining what phrases like "in concert" stand for, just as the psychiatric profession is devoted to determining what "psychopathy" means.

It is reasonable to expect law-enforcement agencies to establish "organized-crime squads" even if legislatures have not defined "organized crime" precisely enough to be used in a Constitutional statute. Generally speaking, such police squads or units are charged with enforcement of specific criminal laws, such as those pertaining to bet-taking, usury, and prostitution. The social definition is adequate and useful to administrators who must make decisions about the allocation of law-enforcement personnel and resources. Yet the practice of establishing organized-crime units in police departments in this manner unfortunately enables law-enforcement personnel to avoid the difficult task of determining what "organized crime" is all about. Moreover, it leads to strange and varying conceptions of what organized crime is.

Suppose, for example, that a police chief establishes an "organized-crime squad," a "vice squad," and a "narcotics squad," assigning to each of these units the duty of enforcing specified laws. The probability is high that the personnel in these units would not consider as "organized crime" the criminal behavior prosecuted by the vice squad and the narcotics squad. Further, if the organized-crime squad is asked to investigate "rings" (another kind of organization vaguely defined) of check passers and juvenile automobile thieves, these activities are likely to be included in the departmental conception of organized crime.

When a police department has no organized-crime unit, the vagaries of vagueness become compounded. The lack of precision enables Cosa Nostra leaders to remain immune from arrest. Equally important, it also enables law-enforcement agencies to ignore Cosa Nostra and other organized-crime units if they wish to do so, because any change in policy is not reflected in a set of statistics. Even experienced police officers disagree on the incidence of organized crime in their communities, mostly because they don't know what they are talking about. If a policeman tells a colleague that he has been working on a case of "organized crime," he might mean, or be understood to mean, that he has been investigating a forgery or shoplifting ring, a troupe of pickpockets, an illicit bet-taking operation, or even a conspiracy among Cosa Nostra members to commit murder.

Vagueness of this kind may be illustrated with reference to "racketeering," which is a favorite occupation of Cosa Nostra members. "Racketeering" is a more serious, and more dangerous, activity than is simple extortion because it is *organized* extortion. Yet neither the criminal law nor its administrators give us many good clues as to how to go about determining whether extortion is organized or not. The United States Department of Justice has even found it necessary to differentiate between "organized crime" and "racketeering," probably because the activities of the personnel in its "Organized Crime and Racketeering Section" are assigned by reference to their duty to investigate and prosecute violations of specified federal statutes. Tacking "racketeering" onto the title helps members of Congressional appropriations committees understand that the Section is doing something worthwhile.

A number of the experts who testified before the McClellan Committee were of the opinion that legislation should be aimed either at outlawing Cosa Nostra itself, or at outlawing membership in it. Senator McClellan steered the hearings in this direction, and he later drafted a Senate bill consistent with it. This bill is the most significant attempt to outlaw organized crime that has ever been made, but it fell of its own weight, for Constitutional reasons. It will be discussed below. The problem was precisely identified for the Committee by O. W. Wilson, then Superintendent of the Chicago Police Department: "The hard-to-realize fact is that we have not legislated it to be a crime to engage in that activity which we have come to refer to as 'organized crime' and it follows that there are no meaningful sanctions to be imposed."

George C. Edwards, then Police Commissioner of Detroit, might not have heard his colleague Mr. Wilson, who appeared before the Committee a day after Mr. Edwards. If he did hear him, he ignored what he heard and advocated the vague terminology used in the Model Sentencing Act. Mr. Edwards was, prior to becoming Police Commissioner, a member of the Supreme Court of Michigan, which is the highest court in that state. In the context of the prior testimony, it is clear that Senator McClellan used "racketeer" as a synonym for "Mafia member" when he asked Mr. Edwards how he would establish the fact that persons are racketeers except by showing "that they are members of an organization dedicated to crime, or habitual offenders, repetitious offenders." Unfortunately, the question was garbled and, moreover, lumped three kinds of offenders together. The response also was garbled.

MR. EDWARDS: I was a member of a group of judges that wrestled with this problem for about five years, Senator. We didn't find all the answers we wanted, but we found some that we thought might at least be worth printing. We put out a model sentencing act . . . and one of the provisions is that a judge may take into account, in sentencing, a presentence report which indicates that a man has a substantial sum of financial means available to him with no known legal source by which he can account for it.

I think this would be quite a thing, because it would differentiate a great many of these people from the beginner or the unorganized criminal who flows through the courts in far greater number than these people do, and who properly, I think, should be treated on a very different basis.

THE CHAIRMAN: You would have to establish in some way—you would have to have some formula, some criteria to establish the fact that they were professional racketeers.

MR. EDWARDS: Multiple conviction, Senator—the times of crimes—because these folks deal in specific types of racketeering; income which cannot be legally accounted for. These are at least three areas in which presentence reports could bring before the judge a considerable amount of information upon which he could base the finding that this was a racketeer whom he was sentencing.

Commissioner Edwards did not explain what he meant by "times of crimes." It appears, however, that he meant to say "*types* of crimes." If he did, this criterion is useless. We need to know precisely how a racketeer or organized criminal differs from other criminals. The Commissioner's other two criteria are, similarly, clearly useless for distinguishing organized criminals from others. Moreover, a probation officer writing a presentence report would need all the resources of the Intelligence Division of the Internal Revenue Service if he were to come up with relevant information about unexplained income. If a probation officer asked the Internal Revenue Service if they had such information, the answer clearly would be "no." If IRS agents could show that a man had "income which cannot legally be accounted for," they would clap him in jail or, at least, begin their own investigation.

Senator McClellan knew he was trying to get information which would enable him to do what Superintendent Wilson implicitly recommended that he do, even if Commissioner Edwards did not. In his opening statement at the hearings, the Senator said, "I have in mind a statute to deal directly with and to prohibit membership in such a criminal and secret organization as Cosa Nostra." He picked up this theme again in a discussion with the Committee's first witness, Attorney General Robert F. Kennedy:

I am thinking of making it a crime, making it illegal to belong to a secret society or organization or association, whatever term we want to give it, where allegiance is taken that assumes disloyalty, an individual pledges disloyalty to the Constitution and laws of the United States. In other words, where there is a conspiracy at the time of entering the organization to violate laws, to permit crime, to pursue an enterprise of crime against the laws of the country, to make that act of joining or taking the pledge or taking the oath to commit these things, and to provide protection to others of the organization who do not commit these acts, to make that a crime.

I know it will have some problems, Constitutional problems maybe, but to me it seems that we have established the fact, and I think we all know it, that such an organization exists, that we might be able to enact some law striking directly at the source. There is where the source is, the organization. That is why it can be so effective—because it is organized. Why it can be so effective is because they agree and conspire to go beyond the laws, to violate the laws, to disregard them, to obstruct law enforcement right from the beginning. We should strike directly with some statutes, strike directly at the membership, at the incipiency of the offense, so to speak. . . .

Attorney General Kennedy responded that there are "certain Constitutional problems" in such legislation but said, "Obviously, we are most sympathetic to the objective, which would be very, very helpful if we can work out the Constitutional problems. I think that is what we should devote our attention to." Senator McClellan continued, "I am not saying at the moment that it can be done Constitutionally, but if it can be I think it might be one of the important pieces of legislation that could come out of these hearings."

Another organized-crime expert, Joseph Valachi, wholeheartedly agreed with the Senator. In fact, the following exchange indicates that Mr. Valachi might have planted in the Senator's mind the idea of outlawing membership in Cosa Nostra. At a minimum, the minds of the two experts thought as one.

THE CHAIRMAN. But I asked you a question when I conferred with you out at the jail. I think it was last Tuesday afternoon. I asked you what you thought that Congress might do, and what we might do to combat this organization or this kind of criminal syndicate, and you answered me, and do you want to tell me again what you said then?

MR. VALACHI. Yes, I was hoping that you or Congress, and I don't understand too much, but talking to you Senators, I understand that you would come up with some law so as to make it a penalty or a felony or whatever you may want to call it, to belong to this organization.

THE CHAIRMAN. In other words, outlaw the organization, and make it a crime to even belong to it?

MR. VALACHI. That is right. That is what I asked.

THE CHAIRMAN. Now, I had not suggested that to you, and I don't know whether anyone had or not. When I asked you the question, what you thought we could do—

MR. VALACHI. That is right.

THE CHAIRMAN. You then are saying here today, after having given your testimony, and you have much more to give, that you would like to see this organization, this Cosa Nostra destroyed.

MR. VALACHI. Yes, and I will ask you again the same question—if you make such a law, I would be a happy man.

THE CHAIRMAN. What is that?

MR. VALACHI. If you Senators make such a law, so it would be a crime just to belong to it, I will be a happy man.

We also would be happy if Congress would make it a crime "just to belong to it." But, as our prior discussion has indicated, a Congress cannot pass such a law until "it" has been identified in such a way that Cosa Nostra and other organizations devoted to organized crime can readily be distinguished from other organizations, criminal or not.

The prior efforts of social scientists to define categories of crime in nonlegal terms are not very helpful in the task of precisely identifying the division of labor which is organized crime, for two reasons. First, one who would define organized crime precisely enough to outlaw the category of behavior itself must be concerned with formal and informal structure. It is the necessity for this concern that puts organized crime in the scholarly domain of systems analysts and other organizational specialists. Second, categories such as "white-collar crime" and "crime against property" can be defined without specific reference to the attitudes and values of the criminals involved, even if nice problems of "criminal intent" arise. This is not true of organized crime, where the rules, agreements, and understandings forming the foundation of social structure appear among the individual participants as attitudes. As a man participates in the Cosa Nostra division of labor rationally designed to maximize the profits from crime, he subscribes to an organizational code of such character that it is possible to say that he is engaged in a "continuous" or "self-perpetuating" conspiracy. Whether a person is properly labeled an "organized criminal" depends in part on whether he exhibits the antilegal attitudes which accompany his adherence to the code of conduct.

Organization experts must begin where the McClellan Committee hearings left off. The social category "organized crime" is being used as if it were a legal category, thus hindering both the understanding and control of a serious economic, political, and social problem. In the past, social categories of crime—such as "crimes against the person," "crimes against property," and "sex offenses"—have been invented to help summarize and make sense of legal categories. Now we are faced with the task of outlawing a social category of behavior because it consists of more than the legal categories it started out to describe.

The sociological work on the identification of "white-collar crime" can be used to illustrate both the advantages and disadvantages of dealing with a social category of crime rather than with the specific crimes involved. The late Professor Edwin H. Sutherland invented the "white-collar crime" concept, and he defined white-collar crimes as crimes committed by persons of respectability and high social status in the course of their occupations. This definition has had an important effect on criminological theory because it called attention to offenders and offenses frequently overlooked by persons studying crime. It was customary, for example, to attribute criminality to social and personal pathologies. Invention of the "white-collar crime" concept challenged this kind of theory by identifying a category of criminals who are "persons of respectability and high social status," and, hence, not the victims of personal and social pathologies.

The President's Commission and President Johnson himself deplored the rising incidence of white-collar crime, just as they deplored the rising incidence of organized crime. Nevertheless, an accurate measure of the frequency of white-collar crime has never been made, and it could be made only with great difficulty. The concept is defined with reference to the social status of offenders, rather than by reference to the legal categories of crime (such as fraud, embezzlement, and abortion) which are sometimes committed by persons of "respectability and high social status" in the course of their occupations. Because "white-collar crime" is not a crime, statistics on the phenomenon cannot be routinely compiled by law-enforcement agencies or by quasi-law-enforcement agencies such as the Interstate Commerce Commission. Moreover, "respectability and high social status" would not be easy to measure, even by law-enforcement agencies interested in making a serious attempt to determine who is a white-collar criminal and who is not. The data compiled by police agencies are data about specific offenses such as fraud, abortion, and violations of various statutes regulating business and professional practices, not about "white-collar crime."

The similarity to the problem of organized crime is obvious. A significant difference is this: Organized criminals, to a much greater extent than white-collar criminals, directly corrupt police and other officials to insure that they can violate the law with impunity. Some of the laws against white-collar business practices are not meant to be enforced, and they are violated frequently. But if this is corruption at all, it is very different from the corruption induced by Cosa Nostra bribes. White-collar criminals are not organized for corruption, and only occasionally are they organized for crime. And even when they are organized for crime, they do not kill witnesses or potential witnesses against them.

Another illustration of the advantages and problems of combining specific types of crimes into social categories is found in my own work on "criminal violation of financial trust." This term was invented upon discovering, in connection with a study of embezzlers, that some men sentenced to prison for "embezzlement" had in fact committed some other offense, and that some men sentenced for forgery, larceny by bailee, and confidence game had in fact committed embezzlement. The new social category of crime avoided the error of extending a legal concept beyond its legal meaning, e.g., calling all the behavior "embezzlement." At the same time, it both provided a rigorous definition of the behavior being studied and suggested that traditional crime categories could be grouped in a useful way. Like "white-collar crime," the social category was invented for research purposes, rather than for purposes of control, something like categories such as "crimes against the person" were invented years ago. But, also like "white-collar crime," the fact that the category is not a legal one makes it all but impossible to assemble data on the incidence of the criminal behavior included in it.

The problem of specifying the characteristic of organized crime is much more difficult than the problem of identifying white-collar crime and the criminal violation of financial trust. Except that members of Cosa Nostra are all Italians or of Italian descent, organized *criminals* do not have personal characteristics in common, as do white-collar criminals. Neither do organized *crimes,* ranging from bet-taking to murder, have a characteristic in common, as do crimes involving violation of positions of financial trust which were accepted in good faith. Moreover, both white-collar crime and the criminal violation of financial trust usually are perpetrated by individuals, not organizations, and hence they are subject to control by traditional methods. This is not the case with organized crime. The behavior in which we are interested involves some but not all criminal conspiracies, some but not all cases of illegal bet-taking, some but not all cases of assault and murder, some but not all cases of prostitution and bootlegging, some but not all cases of burglary, larceny, and robbery, and some but not all cases of almost any other kind of crime. If the title of a unit such as the "Organized Crime and Racketeering Section" of the United States Department of Justice is to have as much relevance as the title of units such as the "Anti-Trust Division," the nature of the unit's legal involvement with all these forms of crime must be spelled out in statutes. Antitrust divisions of federal, state, and local governments prosecute violations of antitrust laws, but organized-crime sections do not prosecute violations of organized-crime laws.

It is helpful to specify, in a preliminary way, that an organized crime is any crime committed by a person occupying a position in an established division of labor designed for the commission of crime. This preliminary statement tells us that any organized criminal's activities are coordinated with the activities of other criminals by means of rules, in the way the activities of a cashier in a retail firm are coordinated with the activities of a stockroom clerk, a sales person, and an accountant. It also tells us that each organized criminal occupies a position in a set of positions which exist independently of the incumbents. Each has his criminal obligations, duties, and rights specified for him in much the way a civil servant's obligations, duties, and rights are specified in a job description and other sets of rules.

But we need to know what each position is, how the positions are related to each other, and how they, as a set or system, differ from legitimate systems and from illegitimate systems (such as juvenile gangs) which are not organized crime. The discussion in our previous chapters identifies some of the formal and informal positions in the system and gives clues as to interrelationships between them. But differentiating the organization which is "organized crime," or even Cosa Nostra, from other organizations is a different matter. Saying, as we have just done, that organized crime "is an established division of labor designated for the commission of crime" helps a little but not much. This definition does not differentiate between the division of labor making up small working groups of criminals, the division of labor making up the structure of small illicit businesses such as policy wheels, and the division of labor characterizing an illicit cartel and confederation like Cosa Nostra. Only the latter is organized crime in the traditional sense of the term, and it is the latter which must be controlled if we are to keep criminals from nullifying the democratic process. But the deficiency in definition must remain until much more is known about the structures of each of these kinds of criminal systems.

The proceedings of a recent series of meetings of some of the nation's leading authorities on organized crime provides some important clues in this regard. These Oyster Bay Conferences on Combating Organized Crime were sponsored by Governor Rockefeller of New York. The participants did not set out specifically to study the structure of illicit organizations. They have just begun to perceive organized crime as a social system. Nevertheless, they have identified a configuration of three positions in the criminal division of labor that might, upon further study, be found to be unique to the criminal organization in question. One of the three is the position of "fixer," or corrupter, the second is the position of corruptee, and the third is enforcer. We have discussed each of these positions individually. The focus now is on their configuration.

The members of the Conference Group did not use the terms "corrupter," "corruptee," and "enforcer," but they hinted at them by listing various characteristics of organized crime. In one publication they named the following as the characteristics of the "most highly developed forms" of organized crime: (1) totalitarian organization; (2) immunity and protection from the law through professional advice or fear or corruption, or all, in order to insure continuance of their activities; (3) permanency and form; (4) activities which are highly profitable, relatively low in risk, and based on human weakness; (5) use of fear against members of the organization, the victims, and, often, members of the public; (6) continued attempt to subvert legitimate government; (7) insularity of leadership from criminal acts; and (8) rigid discipline in a hierarchy of ranks.

In another publication the Conference Group made the following seven statements about the characteristics of the type of organization which it is working to combat: (1) Organized crime is a *business venture*. (2) The principal tool of organized crime is *muscle*. (3) Organized crime seeks out every opportunity to *corrupt or have influence* on anyone in government who can or may in the future be able to do favors for organized crime. (4) *Insulation* serves to separate the leaders of organized crime from illegal activities which they direct. (5) *Discipline* of a quasi-military character. (6) An interest in *public relations*. (7) A *way of life* in which members receive services which outsiders either do not receive or receive from legitimate sources.

These lists of identifying items do not characterize organized crime in all of its manifestations, and they are not unique to organized crime. Moreover, some of them refer to the attitudes and values of participating members, some to modes of operation, some to objectives, and some to the divisions of labor, the structure, of illicit governments and businesses. The latter is of most relevance, because, as indicated, structure means organization, and information about organization obviously is needed for control of organized crime. By emphasizing "immunity," "protection," "corruption," and "low risk," the Conference Group suggested that two positions essential to the structure of illicit business are corrupter and corruptee. While some small working groups of criminals also possess these positions, such groups can operate without them for long periods of time. The business of bet-taking and selling illicit products and services cannot. The position of corrupter is as essential to an illicit business as the position of negotiator is to a labor union.

Next, the Conference Group's stress on "totalitarian organization," "fear," "rigid discipline," and "muscle" suggests that the structure of the organized-crime organization necessarily contains a position for enforcer. As we suggested earlier, any person occupying an enforcer position is a penal administrator analogous to a prison warden or the man charged with making the arrangements for imposing the death penalty. This position is critical because its presence indicates that the illicit organization in question has the character of a government as well as the character of a business. Although the division of labor for small working groups of criminals sometimes contains the corrupter and corruptee positions, it does not contain the enforcer position. The members of organizations such as pickpocket troupes, check-passing rings, and juvenile gangs are likely to take punitive action against any member who holds out more than his share of the spoils, or who betrays the group to the police. But these groups have not been rationally organized in advance to enforce specific rules prohibiting organizational dishonesty and organizational disloyalty. They do not, among other things, recruit persons to, or train persons for, a well-established enforcer position. They are not governments. The members of a gypsy band that engages in a wide variety of criminal activities are likely to censure, condemn, and in other ways punish a participant who cheats his fellows or informs the police about their crimes. It might be that gypsies have positions for enforcers. It is clear, however, that they do not have positions for corrupters and corruptees. Their structure, thus, is not the structure of Cosa Nostra.

We believe that only the illicit division of labor customarily called "organized crime" and now called "Cosa Nostra" contains a position to be occupied permanently or temporarily by persons whose duty it is to secure immunity from the law by bribing or otherwise illegally influencing public officials (corrupter), a position to be occupied permanently or temporarily by persons whose duty it is to be so influenced (corruptee), and a position to be occupied permanently or temporarily by persons whose duty it is to maintain organizational integration by making arrangements for penalizing, maiming, and killing members who do not conform to organizational "law" (enforcer).

Like the conclusions of the Oyster Bay Conferences on Combating Organized Crime, a United States Senate bill drafted by one of the nation's leading legislative experts on organized crime, Senator McClellan, implicitly emphasizes the great relevance of the configuration of corrupter, corruptee, and enforcer. We have already reported Senator McClellan's conclusion that anyone occupying an organizational position for committing crime should be specified by law as a criminal. In a legislative attempt to implement this conclusion, he in a roundabout way noted that the relevant organizational positions of this kind are those linked with positions rationally designed for corruption and coercion. The Senator's position is found in Senate Bill 2187, coauthored by Senator Frank J. Lausche and introduced in the 89th Congress on June 24, 1965—"A Bill to Outlaw the Mafia and Other Organized Crime Syndicates." The bill was reintroduced in the 90th Congress (1967–1968) as Senate Bill 678. Despite its title, this statute is designed to outlaw *membership* in specified types of organizations. Although the bill probably never will become law—Attorneys General Nicholas deB. Katzenbach and Ramsey Clark both raised very damaging questions about its Constitutionality—its theoretical value should not be overlooked. The preamble to the bill, called "Findings and Declaration of Fact," attempts to describe in precise legal terms the characteristics of the organizations in which membership would be outlawed. The attempt flounders because there is confusion of organizational structure, organizational goals, and values of members of the organization. Nevertheless, the second, fourth, and fifth points outlined below validate our conclusion that description of organizational structure, including, especially, description of corrupter, corruptee, and enforcer positions, is essential to understanding and controlling organized crime.

First, the preamble defines the objectives of the organizations in which membership shall be a felony: "There exist in the United States organizations, including societies and syndicates, one of which is known as the Mafia, which have as their primary objective the disrespect for constituted law and order."

Second, the preamble describes the types of crime the members of the organizations perpetrate as they express their disrespect for constituted law and order. These are the types of offenses customarily called "organized crime": "The members of such organizations are recruited for the purpose of carrying on gambling, prostitution, traffic in narcotic drugs, labor racketeering, extortion, and commercial-type crimes generally, all of which are in violation of the criminal laws of the United States and of the several states."

Third, the preamble acknowledges that members of such organizations share a code of conduct, one essential part of which is secrecy about membership and about organizational structure: "These organizations, such as the Mafia, are conducted under their own code of ethics which is without respect for moral principles, law, and order. . . . Secrecy as to membership and authority within such organizations is a cardinal principle." It is somewhat of a contradiction to specify that the value system of an organization is devoid of "respect for moral principles, law, and order," because an organization is, by definition, an orderly arrangement of positions. Further, as we have shown, members of criminal organizations place a great deal of stress on honor and honesty in their dealings with each other, a form of "moral principle." The framers of the bill obviously here had in mind specific *kinds* of moral principles, such as those proscribing *all* murders, not just some of them.

Fourth, the preamble recognizes the essential alliance between such organizations and the public officials whose civic duty it is to prevent and repress crime: "The existence of these organizations is made easier through use of bribery and corruption of certain public officials." In the terminology we have been using, the organizations include corrupter and corruptee positions for which men are recruited and trained.

Fifth, the authors of the bill explicitly recognize that a coercive system of justice is used in an attempt to maximize conformity to organizational authority and ethics: "Discipline and authority within such organizations are maintained by means of drastic retaliation, usually murder, and . . . similar methods are employed to coerce nonmembers." At least one position for an enforcer of organizational order is a part of the division of labor.

Our preliminary legal definition of an organized crime implied that the process of identifying a defendant as an "organized criminal" clearly must be concerned with identifying his participation "in an established division of labor designed for commission of crime." In view of the fact that a configuration of positions for corrupter, corruptee, and enforcer seems to be uniquely characteristic of this division of labor, the preliminary definition can now be refined. *An organized crime is any crime committed by a person occupying, in an established division of labor, a position designed for the commission of crime,* providing *that such division of labor also includes at least one position for a corrupter, one position for a corruptee, and one position for an enforcer.* This statement might not contain the precision necessary for specifying in a statute that it is a certain kind of division of labor, of organization, which is illegal. Nevertheless, the statement is more precise than the organized-crime concepts currently being used. Moreover, it directs attention to three critical positions which legislative experts should be able to define as precisely as they have defined "larceny," "robbery," and "taking indecent liberties with a minor." Even if the entire organization cannot as yet be outlawed, it could be seriously disrupted by vigorous prosecution of any person occupying one of its corrupter, corruptee, or enforcer positions.

The President's Commission accepted my conclusion that the configuration of corrupter, corruptee, and enforcer is both essential to and unique to the organization which is organized crime. However, this body made no recommendation for legislation which would outlaw the organization itself, or any part of it. Building on the work I did as a consultant, the Commission concluded that organized crime can be distinguished from other kinds of criminal activity by the "element of corruption" and the "element of enforcement":

There are at least two aspects of organized crime that characterize it as a unique form of criminal activity. The first is the element of corruption. The second is the element of enforcement, which is necessary for the maintenance of both internal discipline and the regularity of business transactions. In the hierarchy of organized crime there are positions for people fulfilling both of these functions. But neither is essential to the long-term operation of other types of criminal groups. . . . Organized-crime groups . . . are believed to contain one or more fixed positions for "enforcers," whose duty it is to maintain organizational integrity by arranging for the maiming and killing of recalcitrant members. And there is a position for a "corrupter," whose function is to establish relationships with those public officials and other influential persons whose assistance is necessary to achieve the organization's goals. By including these positions within its organization, each criminal cartel, or "family," becomes a government as well as a business.

It should not by any means be concluded that illicit organizations consist of *only* the three positions described as corrupter, corruptee, and enforcer. Dozens of other positions are integrated with these three to make up an illicit business and government. The formal structure has only been sketched out, and much less is known about the informal structure and even the operational processes of illicit enterprises than is known about legitimate organizations of comparable size. A common assumption seems to be that "everybody knows" how a business or government is organized and therefore how it operates, whether that organization is dealing in an outlawed commodity or not. But "everybody" does not know about the formal and informal divisions of labor of even legitimate business enterprises and governmental units, let alone illegitimate ones.

We have not been deluded into believing that a law making it a crime to belong to an illicit organization could easily be enforced. Cosa Nostra does not keep membership rolls, and it does not issue membership cards or any other form of tangible evidence as to membership which would be accepted by the courts under the current rules of evidence. Ralph Salerno, a leading police authority on organized crime, has criticized the McClellan-Lausche Bill, saying "It would appear to be at least premature to declare a course of action to be illegal without any substantial standard which can be applied to prove that such a course of action has indeed been taken by an individual." Attorney General Ramsey Clark, similarly, stated his concern for the questions of proof involved in the enforcement of the proposed statute. But statements of concern for "the problem of proof" are in actuality merely restatements of concern for "the problem of organized crime." Police and other law-enforcement agents, including Mr. Salerno and Mr. Clark, know beyond any reasonable or moral doubt that men whose names they can recall at the drop of a hat are members of "Cosa Nostra," "the syndicate," "the organization." The "problem of organized crime" persists because no one has as yet devised a scheme for transforming such definite knowledge into the kinds of legal knowledge which can be used by the police and courts to attack the structural foundations of the organization itself. The President's Commission in its general report stated "the problem" in consistent, but more general terms.

Our system of justice deliberately sacrifices much in efficiency and even in effectiveness in order to preserve local autonomy and to protect the individual. Sometimes it may seem to sacrifice too much. For example, the American system was not designed with Cosa Nostra-type criminal organizations in mind, and it has been notably unsuccessful to date in preventing such organizations from preying on society.

The United States Constitution is in effect designed to insure this less-than-optimal efficiency and effectiveness in the criminal-justice process. It is highly probable that any enforcement action taken under any law similar to the McClellan-Lausche Bill would be declared unconstitutional. When United States Representative Charles Weltner in 1966 introduced a bill (H.R. 12302) which would reconstitute the Subversive Activities Control Board as a "Criminal Conspiracies Control Board" he was attempting to attack Cosa Nostra as well as the Communist Party and the Ku Klux Klan. Under the Weltner Bill, a board would make determination that organizations are "criminal conspiracies" and that individuals are members of such organizations. Vern Countryman, Professor of Law at Harvard and Chairman of the Massachusetts Committee to Abolish the House Un-American Activities Committee, easily found in the bill a half-dozen serious threats to those freedoms of speech, belief, and association which the First Amendment forbids Congress to abridge.

Most of, if not all, these threats stem from the fact that the Weltner Bill would, among other things, have a board, not a court, determine whether an organization has "as its purpose the planned, continued, and consistent execution of acts which violate the criminal statutes of the United States," and whether an individual is a member of the organization. These provisions would clearly circumvent the Constitutional guarantees regarding criminal trials. The following comments, drawn as a conclusion from a detailed study of the prosecution of an organized-crime case, were made with reference to "racketeering enterprises," but they could just as well have been made about organized crime in general.

The [racketeering] activities *per se* do not elicit moral disapproval, and it becomes necessary to whip up moral fervor through the use of criminal sanctions and widespread publicity. In effect, criminal prosecution becomes a political weapon in various types of conflict situations. These observations are clearly seen in the recent legislative-committee attacks on business-unionism and in Kennedy's crusade against the Teamster leader. The increasing use of legislative committees presents a novel form of law enforcement to the American scene. There are no clearly defined procedures regulating committee actions, and there exists only a vaguely formulated criterion for assessing the power of Congressional investigations and the rights of witnesses.

As indicated, however, we believe that even now a criminal court (not a board or a legislative committee) could as Constitutionally find a defendant to be an "organized criminal" as it can Constitutionally find a defendant to be a "child molester," a "sexual psychopath," a "casual social gambler," a "professional criminal," a "dangerous offender," or a "racketeer." All such terms have vague referents, presenting judges and juries with difficult problems of proof. But with proper and detailed legislative definition, criminal courts could as Constitutionally find men guilty of "organized crime" as they Constitutionally find men guilty of "burglary" and "robbery."

Should Cosa Nostra be outlawed in New York, in some other state, or even in the entire nation, its members undoubtedly would soon find loopholes in the law. Moreover, as indicated, impossibly difficult Constitutional questions are involved in such legislation. Despite these obstacles, attempts to formulate precise laws would serve the useful purpose of forcing investigators to ask organizational questions, rather than traditional questions oriented to the task of putting individual criminals in jail or prison. If we start asking questions about the structure and operations of Cosa Nostra, we will at least start assembling more intelligence information about the organization itself, and about its economic and political bases, as well as about the personnel who participate in it. This information could then be used to attack the organization even if it could not be effectively outlawed.

Moreover, if the organization can be acknowledged at the legislative level, we might be able to deal with it informally but officially on the state and national levels without any "attack." Our State Department and Department of Defense rightfully engage in negotiations with cold-war and hot-war enemies. Once Cosa Nostra has been precisely identified as a unit, in somewhat the way the Soviet Union and Cuba are identified as units, then there can be "tacit or explicit understandings analogous to what in the military field would be called limitation of war, the control of armament, and the development of spheres of influence."

Similarly, in the regulation of legitimate corporations engaged in interstate commerce there can be negotiations, appeasement, and accommodation because "the other side" is clearly identifiable to the government officials responsible for the regulation. In criminal statutes pertaining to legitimate corporations, the behavior prohibited is not clearly defined, and even the enterprises to be regulated change continually. Professor Sanford Kadish of the University of California Law School has observed that implicit in the legislative scheme for regulating legitimate economic enterprises "is the conception of the criminal sanction as a last resort to be used selectively and discriminately when all other sanctions fail." If Cosa Nostra were precisely defined, perhaps this conception of a proper regulatory scheme could be used with reference to it.

We agree with the notion implied by Kadish and explicitly stated by Thomas C. Schelling that "a little cold-blooded appeasement is not necessarily a bad thing." This ideology is especially valuable when "our side" is losing, as it is losing to Cosa Nostra. But establishing diplomatic or accommodating relations with America's crime syndicate is impossible because this "enemy" or "side" has not been precisely identified and acknowledged as an organization. In the organized-crime field, appeasement, accommodation, resistance, and punishment are now more readily available to the criminals than to the noncriminals, principally because the "respectables" have found no acknowledged organizational officials with whom to negotiate.

At present, local officials do negotiate with local members of Cosa Nostra, often in haphazard and corrupt fashion, and with little or no knowledge of the organizational implications of their transactions. But no state or federal agency has ever come to an understanding with Cosa Nostra's Commission in the way the Department of State has come to an understanding with the Kremlin. It is highly unlikely, but not inconceivable, that Cosa Nostra would agree to give up its political involvements and its illegal operation of legitimate businesses, which in combination threaten to undermine the whole nation, if it could be assured that it will be permitted to keep the profits, after payment of taxes, on bet-taking.

Such an agreement on the part of Cosa Nostra's leaders would automatically eliminate two of the three critical positions in the organization's structure—corrupter and corruptee. And the assurance guaranteed by government officials would further eliminate the third key position, enforcer. In addition, by entering into such an agreement, Cosa Nostra's bosses would necessarily have to acknowledge that their organization is indeed an organization. Such acknowledgement would subject the organization to reasonable government regulations such as those pertaining to all corporations. In Schelling's words:

Just as in war one may hope that the enemy government remains intact, thus assuring that there is an authority to negotiate with and to discipline the enemy troops themselves, maybe in the war on crime it is better that there be a "command and control" system intact on the other side.

Notes

PREFACE

PAGE

ix Jennings quote: Dean Jennings, *We Only Kill Each Other: The Life and Bad Times of Bugsy Siegel,* Englewood Cliffs, N.J.: Prentice-Hall, 1968, p. 28.

xiii Kennedy quote: *Hearings Before the Permanent Subcommittee on Investigations of the Senate Committee on Governmental Operations* (McClellan Committee), 88th Congress, 1st Session, 1963, p. 16.

CHAPTER I: TROUBLE

PAGE

1 Johnson quote: "Special Message on Crime," March 9, 1966. *Congressional Record,* Vol. 112, p. 5397.

4 When organized crime embarks: Earl Johnson, Jr., "Organized Crime: Challenge to the American Legal System," *Journal of Criminal Law, Criminology and Police Science,* 53: 399–425, December, 1962, and 54: 1–29, 127–145, January and March, 1963. At p. 406.

4 Organized crime will put a man: Ralph Salerno, quoted by Charles Grutzner, *The New York Times,* January 21, 1967, p. 65.

4 Dolci comments and quote: Danilo Dolci, "Mafia-Client Politics," *Saturday Review,* July 6, 1968, pp. 10–13 ff. At p. 10.

6 If organized criminals paid: *Task Force Report: Organized Crime,* U.S. President's Commission on Law Enforcement and Administration of Justice, Washington: Government Printing Office, 1967, p. 1.

6 Statistics on Internal Revenue Service assessments: Testimony of Sheldon S. Cohen, Commissioner of Internal Revenue, *Hearings Before the Subcommittee on Administrative Practice and Procedure of the Senate Committee on the Judiciary,* 89th Congress, 1st Session, Part 3, 1965, p. 1119.

6 New York tax statistics: Morris Weintraub, *A Report on Bootlegging of Cigarettes in the City and State of New York,* January, 1966; *The Bootlegging of Cigarettes Is a National Problem,* October, 1966; and, with Roger Kaufman, *Bootlegged Cigarettes: New York's Costly Problem and Its Solution,* January, 1967; mimeographed papers prepared for the Wholesale Tobacco Distributors of New York, Inc.

7   President's Commission quote: *Task Force Report: Organized Crime,* *op. cit.,* p. 24.

7   Kennedy quote: Robert F. Kennedy, *The Enemy Within,* New York: Harper & Row, 1960, p. 265.

CHAPTER II: FROM MAFIA TO COSA NOSTRA

PAGE

8   President's Commission quote: *Task Force Report: Organized Crime,* U.S. President's Commission on Law Enforcement and Administration of Justice, Washington: Government Printing Office, 1967, p. 24.

9   Kefauver Committee quote: Special Committee to Investigate Organized Crime in Interstate Commerce (Kefauver Committee), *Third Interim Report,* U.S. Senate Report No. 307, 82nd Congress, 1st Session, 1951, p. 150.

10   No single individual or coalition: J. Edgar Hoover, *FBI Law Enforcement Bulletin,* January, 1962. The quotation is reproduced in Earl Johnson, Jr., "Organized Crime: Challenge to the American Legal System," Part I—"Organized Crime: The Nature of Its Threat, the Reasons for Its Survival," *Journal of Criminal Law, Criminology and Police Science,* 53: 399–425, December, 1962. At p. 401, note 12.

10   La Cosa Nostra is a criminal fraternity: Testimony of J. Edgar Hoover, *Hearings Before the Subcommittee on Departments of State, Justice, and Commerce, the Judiciary, and Related Agencies Appropriations of the House Committee on Appropriations,* 89th Congress, 2nd Session, 1966, p. 272.

11   Anti-Defamation League law suit: *The New York Times,* May 18 and December 9, 1967.

11   Mary Sansone quote: *The New York Times,* April 3, 1968. The *New York Daily News* reported on March 27, 1968, that many members of the association's Board of Directors had resigned, but this report turned out to be false.

11   A campaign to discourage identification: Charles Grutzner, *The New York Times,* May 12, 1967.

11   Salerno statement, I think the: quoted by Grutzner, *loc. cit.*

12   Salerno statement, I'm not your kind: quoted by Charles Grutzner, *The New York Times,* January 21, 1967, p. 65.

12   Rao quote: *Hearings Before the Permanent Subcommittee on Investigations of the Senate Committee on Governmental Operations* (McClellan Committee), 88th Congress, 1st Session, 1963, pp. 317–318.

14   Turkus quote: Burton B. Turkus and Sid Feder, *Murder, Inc., The Story of "The Syndicate,"* New York: Permabooks, 1952, p. 98.

15   March and Simon suggestion: James G. March and Herbert A. Simon, *Organizations,* New York: Wiley, 1958, pp. 129–131.

16   But during the last decade: See, e.g., Edwin H. Sutherland and Donald

R. Cressey, *Principles of Criminology,* Seventh Edition, Philadelphia: Lippincott, 1966.

16 Tyler quote: Gus Tyler, "The Roots of Organized Crime," *Crime and Delinquency,* 8: 325–338, October 1962, p. 334.

16 Recent work in the sociology of deviance: See, e.g., Howard S. Becker, *Outsiders: Studies in the Sociology of Deviance,* New York: Free Press, 1963.

17 This name: *A Theory of Organized Crime Control: A Preliminary Statement,* mimeographed paper prepared by the technical staff and consultants of the New York State Identification and Intelligence System, May, 1966, p. 9.

17 McClellan Committee excerpt: *McClellan Committee Hearings, op. cit.,* p. 93.

18 Mike and Pete bug: *The Voices of Organized Crime,* an educational tape prepared by the New York State Joint Legislative Committee on Crime: Its Causes, Control, and Effect on Society, 1968.

20 Of which the New York Mafia: Hank Messick, *The Silent Syndicate,* New York: Macmillan, 1967, p. 56.

20 All of these terms: *A Theory of Organized Crime Control, op. cit.,* p. 10.

21 Messick quote: *op. cit.,* p. 287.

23 Hoover quote: J. Edgar Hoover, "The FBI's War on Organized Crime," *U.S. News and World Report,* Vol. 60, No. 16, April 18, 1966, pp. 102–104.

23 Raymond S. L. Patriarca bug: *The Providence Journal,* May 20, 1967, p. 4.

24 Herskovitz quote: Melville J. Herskovitz, *Man and His Works,* New York: Alfred A. Knopf, 1956, p. 499.

26 Willie and Mike bug: *The Voices of Organized Crime, op. cit.*

27 An overall inventory: Robert T. Anderson, "From Mafia to Cosa Nostra," *American Journal of Sociology,* 61: 302–310, November, 1965, p. 304.

27 Lewis statement: Norman Lewis, *The Honored Society,* New York: G. P. Putnam's Sons, 1964, especially p. 84.

28 Barzini quote: Luigi Barzini, *The Italians,* New York: Atheneum, 1964, pp. 259–260.

28 Lewis quote: *op. cit.,* pp. 43–45.

CHAPTER III: WAR, PEACE, AND PEACEFUL COEXISTENCE

PAGE

29 Mundt quote: *Hearings Before the Permanent Subcommittee on Investigations of the Senate Committee on Governmental Operations* (McClellan Committee), 88th Congress, 1st Session, 1963, p. 171.

29   Udy statement: S. J. Udy, Jr., "The Comparative Analysis of Organizations," Chap. 16 in James G. March, Editor, *Handbook of Organizations*, Chicago: Rand McNally, 1965, p. 687.

30   Loose, ephemeral, and highly insecure: David W. Maurer, *Whiz Mob: A Correlation of the Technical Argot of Pickpockets with Their Behavior Pattern*, Gainesville, Florida: American Dialect Society Publication No. 24, 1955, p. 84.

32   Mike and Willie bug: *The Voices of Organized Crime*, an educational tape prepared by the New York State Joint Legislative Committee on Crime: Its Causes, Control, and Effect on Society, 1968.

38   Pasley description: Fred D. Pasley, *Al Capone: The Biography of a Self-Made Man*, New York: Garden City Publishing Company, 1930, pp. 139–148, 241.

39   Join up with him: Testimony of LaVern J. Duffy, Committee Staff Member, before the McClellan Committee, *op. cit.*, p. 168.

40   Now the war is nationwide: Duffy, *op. cit.*, p. 172.

41   He will give up anything: Testimony of Joseph Valachi before the McClellan Committee, *op. cit.*, p. 198.

41   Valachi quote, we were in war: *op. cit.*, p. 193.

41   Valachi quote, naturally about five days: *op. cit.*, p. 212.

43   Turkus argument: Burton B. Turkus and Sid Feder, *Murder, Inc.: The Story of "The Syndicate,"* New York: Permabooks, 1951, pp. 97–98.
      McClellan Committee excerpt: *McClellan Committee Hearings, op. cit.*, pp. 278–279.

44   Turkus quote, the chief difference: *op. cit.*, p. 87.

44   Turkus quote, an outfit runs on its own: *op. cit.*, p. 95.

47   Whyte quote: William Foote Whyte, *Street Corner Society*, Chicago: University of Chicago Press, 1943 (Enlarged Edition, 1955), p. 112.

48   Took control of the policy: Whyte, *op. cit.*, p. 115.

48   McClellan Committee excerpt: *McClellan Committee Hearings, op. cit.*, p. 575.

48   Edwards quote: *Ibid.*, p. 426.

49   The date can be fixed: Hank Messick, *The Silent Syndicate*, New York: Macmillan, 1967, pp. 141–142.

50   Turkus report on meeting: Turkus and Feder, *op. cit.*, p. 110.

50   It was quickly realized: Turkus and Feder, *op. cit.*, pp. 111–112.

51   Not one top boss: Turkus and Feder, *op. cit.*, p. 113.

52   Assorted New Jersey operations: Turkus and Feder, *op. cit.*, pp. 106–107.

52   Valachi quote: *McClellan Committee Hearings, op. cit.*, p. 159.

53   There is a guy: Quoted by Dean Jennings, *We Only Kill Each Other: The Life and Bad Times of Bugsy Siegel*, Englewood Cliffs, N.J.: Prentice-Hall, 1968, p. 56.

CHAPTER IV: EDUCATING THE PUBLIC

PAGE

54　Barkham quote: John Barkham, writing for the *Saturday Review* Syndicate and quoted on the dust jacket of John L. McClellan, *Crime Without Punishment*, New York: Duell, Sloan and Pearce, 1962.

54　Kefauver Committee quote: Special Committee to Investigate Crime in Interstate Commerce (Kefauver Committee), *Third Interim Report*, U.S. Senate Report No. 307, 82nd Congress, 1st Session, 1951, p. 174.

54　Task Force quote: *Task Force Report: Organized Crime*, U.S. President's Commission on Law Enforcement and Administration of Justice, Washington: Government Printing Office, 1967, pp. 15–16.

55　Davis quote: J. Richard Davis, "Things I Couldn't Tell Till Now," *Collier's*, July 22, July 29, August 12, August 19, and August 26, 1939. The quote is from pp. 35–36 of the August 19 issue.

56　Kefauver Committee quote: Kefauver Committee, *op. cit.*, p. 150.

56　Found it difficult: *Ibid.*, p. 149.

57　Italian police report: Charles Grutzner, *The New York Times*, January 2, 1968.

58　McClellan quote: *Crime Without Punishment, op. cit.*, p. 119.

58　Federal agencies alone: *Hearing Before a Subcommittee of the House of Representatives Committee on Government Operations*, 90th Congress, 1st Session, 1967, p. 20.

60　Kennedy quote: *Hearings Before the Permanent Subcommittee on Investigations of the Senate Committee on Governmental Operations* (McClellan Committee), 88th Congress, 1st Session, 1963, pp. 6–8.

61　Chief Justice quotes: Earl Warren, "Address," *Proceedings of the First National Conference on Crime Control, Washington*, March 28–29, 1967, Washington: Government Printing Office, 1967, pp. 7–8.

62　The White House press release is reproduced in *Hearings Before a Subcommittee of the House of Representatives Committee on Government Operations, op. cit.*, pp. 12–13.

62　The Memorandum is reproduced *ibid.*, p. 13.

63　Clark statement: *The New York Times*, May 19, 1967, p. 23.

64　Information about special "strike forces": *The New York Times*, November 26, 1967, p. 38.

64　Clark newspaper column and Hoover quote: Ramsey Clark, "U.S. Cracking the Cosa Nostra," *New York Daily Column and The New York Knickerbocker*, July 10, 1968, p. 1.

65　Ruth quote: Henry S. Ruth, Jr., "Why Organized Crime Thrives," *Annals of the American Academy of Political and Social Science*, 374: 113–122, November, 1967. At p. 119.

66   President's Commission statements: *Task Force Report: Organized Crime, op. cit.*, pp. 10–11.

67   Schelling quote: Thomas C. Schelling, "Economic Analysis of Organized Crime," Appendix D, *Task Force Report: Organized Crime, op. cit.*, p. 114.

69   Warren quote: *op. cit.*, p. 8.

69   Peterson quote: *Associated Press* dispatch, March 29, 1967.

70   Federal official quote: Ed Cony column, *Wall Street Journal*, November 18, 1963, p. 1.

CHAPTER V: DEMAND, SUPPLY, AND PROFIT

PAGE

72   Lippmann quote: Walter Lippmann, "The Underworld: A Stultified Conscience," *Forum*, 85: 65–69, February, 1931.

72   Lippmann observation: Walter Lippmann, "Underworld: Our Secret Servant," *Forum*, 85: 1–4, January, 1931.

74   Kefauver Committee quote: Special Committee to Investigate Crime in Interstate Commerce (Kefauver Committee), *Third Interim Report*, U.S. Senate Report No. 307, 82nd Congress, 1951, p. 37.

76   Thom quote: Charles R. Thom, *Statement Before the New York Commission of Investigation on April 22, 1960* (mimeographed), p. 2.

77   The same degree of complicity: William J. Duffy, "Organized Crime— Illegal Activities," Chapter in S. A. Yefsky, Editor, *Law Enforcement Science and Technology*, Washington: Thompson Book Company, 1967, pp. 30–32. At p. 30.

78   Study of embezzlers: Donald R. Cressey, *Other People's Money*, New York: Free Press, 1953.

78   Marcus indictment and Corallo sentence: *The New York Times*, December 19, 1967; *San Francisco Chronicle*, July 27, 1968.

79   Marcus and Corallo histories: Sandy Smith and William Lambert, "The Mob," *Life*, January 5, 1968, pp. 44–51; *The New York Times*, December 19 and 22, 1967.

79   Smith and Lambert quote: *loc. cit.*, p. 48.

79   Bonfondeo indictment: *The New York Times*, May 8, 1968.

80   Contractor's testimony: *The New York Times*, June 12, 1968.

82   New York State Commission of Investigation statement: *An Investigation of the Loan-Shark Racket*, Albany: State Printing Office, April, 1965, pp. 11–12.

86   Dom and Jack bug: *The Voices of Organized Crime*, an educational tape prepared by the New York State Joint Legislative Committee on Crime: Its Causes, Control and Effect on Society, 1968.

91   Frank Sacco information: Ed Cony column, *Wall Street Journal*, November 18, 1963, p. 1.

91 Morgenthau quote: *Ibid.*

91 Information of San Francisco operations: Alan G. Sutter, "The World of the Righteous Dope Fiend," *Issues in Criminology,* 2: 177–122, Fall, 1966.

93 Information on Lord Clive: Virgil Peterson, "Rackets in America," *Journal of Criminal Law, Criminology and Police Science,* 49: 583–589, March-April, 1959. At p. 583.

98 Information on the indictment of the vice president: *The New York Times,* April 4, 1968, p. 40.

99 Kennedy quote: *Hearings Before the Permanent Subcommittee on Investigations of the Senate Committee on Government Operations,* 88th Congress, 1st Session, 1963, p. 12.

100 Statistics on business interests: Select Committee on Improper Activities in the Labor or Management Field, *Final Report,* U.S. Senate Report No. 1139, 86th Congress, 1960, pp. 487–488.

100 Identification of specific business interests: Peter D. Andreoli, "Organized Crime Enterprises—Legal," Chapter in S. A. Yefsky, Editor, *Law Enforcement Science and Technology, op. cit.,* pp. 21–27.

101 Whyte quote: William Foote Whyte, *Street Corner Society,* Chicago: University of Chicago Press, 1943 (Enlarged Edition, 1955), p. 146.

102 Andreoli quote: *op. cit.,* p. 24.

103 New York Court of Appeals cases: *People vs. Kaiser,* 21 N. Y. 2d 86 (1967).

104 Information on Joseph Di Varco: Virgil W. Peterson, *A Report on Chicago Crime for 1958,* Chicago: Chicago Crime Commission, 1959, p. 35.

104 Johnson statement: Earl Johnson, Jr., "Organized Crime: Challenge to the American Legal System; Part I—Organized Crime: The Nature of Its Threat, the Reasons for Its Survival," *Journal of Criminal Law, Criminology and Police Science,* 53: 399–425, December, 1962. At p. 408.

105 New York fraud story: *The New York Times,* July 11, 1968.

106 Delivered it to: Virgil W. Peterson, *A Report on Chicago Crime for 1961,* Chicago: Chicago Crime Commission, 1962, p. 41. Mr. Peterson's report for 1966 discusses the trials of the principals.

106 Information on Dioguardi: *The New York Times,* December 12, 1967, and January 8, 1968.

106 President's Commission quote: *Task Force Report: Organized Crime,* U.S. President's Commission on Law Enforcement and Administration of Justice, Washington: Government Printing Office, 1967, p. 4.

107 Information on Dioguardi and Corallo: Andreoli, *op. cit.,* p. 24.

108 McClellan quote: John L. McClellan, *Crime Without Punishment,* New York: Duell, Soan and Pearce, 1962, p. 210.

CHAPTER VI: THE STRUCTURAL SKELETON

PAGE

109   Bryce quote: James Bryce, *The American Commonwealth*, London: Macmillan, 1889, Vol. II, p. 204.

116   Mike and Pete bug: *The Voices of Organized Crime*, an educational tape prepared by the New York State Joint Legislative Committee on Crime: Its Causes, Control and Effect on Society, 1968.

120   Ramsey Clark assertions: *The New York Times*, May 19, 1967, p. 23; and *The New York Times*, November 23, 1966, p. 24.

120   Information on the airtels: *The Providence Journal*, May 20, 1967, p. 1.

120   American Bar Association statement: American Bar Association Project on Minimum Standards for Criminal Justice, *Standards Relating to Electronic Surveillance*, Tentative Draft, New York: Institute of Judicial Administration, 1968, pp. 53–54.

121   The question of who will decide: *Kolod v. United States*, 390 U.S. 136; Association of American Law Schools, Committee on Supreme Court Decisions, Docket No. 133, April 25, 1968.

121   Blakey quote and airtel analysis: Testimony of G. Robert Blakey, *Hearings Before the Subcommittee on Criminal Laws and Procedures of the Senate Committee on the Judiciary*, 90th Congress, 1st Session, July 11, 1967, pp. 932–1010. At pp. 937–939. The ten airtels are reproduced at pp. 942–954. They also appear in *Standards Relating to Electronic Surveillance, op. cit.*, pp. 54–58.

126   The documentation for the Cosa Nostra position of each man mentioned has been provided by the compilers of *Standards Relating to Electronic Surveillance, op. cit.* pp. 57–58.

135   In New York in 1960: Ted Poston, "The Numbers Racket," *New York Post*, February 29–March 10, 1960. Reproduced in Gus Tyler, Editor, *Organized Crime in America, A Book of Readings,* Ann Arbor: University of Michigan Press, 1962, pp. 260–274.

136   Chicago writers' strike: *Chicago Daily Times*, February 23, 1938.

138   Clearing House quote: Harold R. Danforth and James D. Horan, "Fixing the Clearinghouse," from *The D.A.'s Man*, New York: Crown Publishers, 1957. Reproduced in Gus Tyler, *op. cit.*, pp. 274–281. At p. 279.

CHAPTER VII: ORIGINS OF THE AUTHORITY STRUCTURE

PAGE

141   Anderson quote: Robert T. Anderson, "From Mafia to Cosa Nostra," *American Journal of Sociology*, 71: 302–310, November, 1965. At p. 310.

141   Cultural elements: Felix M. Keesing, *Cultural Anthropology*, New York: Rinehart, 1958, p. 121.

142   Anderson demonstration: *op. cit.*, p. 310.

142   A book published in 1900: Antonio Cutrera, *La Mafia e i mafiosi: origini e manifestazioni studio di sociologia criminale*, Palermo: Alberto Reber, 1900, pp. 118–122, 132–141. See also Francis Marion Crawford, *Southern Italy and Sicily and the Rulers of the South*, London: Macmillan, 1900, Vol. II, pp. 333–385. This report on the Mafia draws heavily on Cutrera's work.

143   Anderson quote: *op. cit.*, p. 308.

143   Barzini quotes: Luigi Barzini, *The Italians*, New York: Atheneum, 1964, pp. 260, 261–262.

145   Mosca quote: Gaetano Mosca, "Mafia," *Encyclopedia of the Social Sciences*, New York: Macmillan, 1933, Vol. X, p. 36.

145   Valachi quote: *Hearings Before the Permanent Subcommittee on Investigations of the Senate Committee on Government Operations* (McClellan Committee), 88th Congress, 1st Session, September 27, 1963, p. 88.

150   The evidence from current studies: Herbert J. Gans, *The Urban Villagers*, New York: Free Press, 1962, Chap. 3.

153   The FBI believes: Charles Grutzner, "The Mafia: Joe Bonanno Returns as Kingpin and Chief Profiteer," *New York Times News Service*, printed in *The Ventura County (California) Star-Free Press*, May 14, 1967, p. B-7.

156   Grutzner quote: Charles Grutzner, "New York to Montreal: A Million Dollar Narcotics Pipeline," *op. cit.*, May 15, 1967, p. B-4.

156   Information on Ridgewood shootings: *The New York Times*, April 6, 1966.

157   New York police said: Grutzner, *op. cit.*, May 15, 1967.

157   Among those killed later: *The New York Times*, November 12, 1967; March 19, April 3, and April 5, 1968.

159   Accumulate henchmen: Barzini, *op. cit.*, p. 260.

161   In a campaign: Charles Siragusa (as told to Robert Weidrich), *The Trail of the Poppy: Behind the Mask of the Mafia*, Englewood Cliffs, N.J.: Prentice-Hall, 1966, pp. 3–32.

CHAPTER VIII: THE CODE

PAGE

162   Wickersham Commission quote: National Commission on Law Observance and Enforcement (Wickersham Commission), Vol. 12, *Report on the Cost of Crime*, Washington: Government Printing Office, 1931, p. 7.

163   Hoebel's study: E. Adamson Hoebel, *The Law of Primitive Man: A*

Study in Comparative Legal Dynamics, Cambridge: Harvard University Press, 1954.

165   Radcliffe-Brown description: A. R. Radcliffe-Brown, *Method in Social Anthropology,* Chicago: University of Chicago Press, 1958, p. 26.

168   1892 statement: Ed Reid, *Mafia,* New York: New American Library, 1964, p. 31, summarizing rules appearing in *The Chambers Journal,* 1892.

168   1900 statement: Antonio Cutrera, *La Mafia e i mafiosi: origini e manifestazioni, studio di sociologia criminale,* Palermo: Alberto Reber, 1900, pp. 132–141. Cited by Robert T. Anderson, "From Mafia to Cosa Nostra," *American Journal of Sociology,* 61: 302–310, November, 1965. At p. 308.

168   Tyler statement: Gus Tyler, *Organized Crime in America: A Book of Readings,* Ann Arbor: University of Michigan Press, 1962, p. 333.

169   Mosca report: Gaetano Mosca, *Encyclopedia of the Social Sciences,* Vol. X, New York: Macmillan, 1933, p. 36.

169   Barzini quote: Luigi Barzini, *The Italians,* New York: Atheneum, 1964, pp. 253–254.

170   Mori quote: Cesare Mori, *The Last Struggle with the Mafia,* London: Putnam, 1933, pp. 39–40.

171   The norms said by: Paul J. Gillette and Eugene Tillinger, *Inside the Ku Klux Klan,* New York: Pyramid Books, 1965; Tan Jee Bah, "Secret Societies in Singapore," *FBI Law Enforcement Bulletin,* 34: 7–16, January, 1965.

172   Karski argument: Jan Karski, *Story of a Secret State,* Kingsport, Tenn.: Kingsport Press, 1944.

172   Bloch statement: Herbert A. Bloch, "The Gambling Business: An American Paradox," *Crime and Delinquency,* 8: 355–364, October, 1962.

174   One summary of the many descriptions: Gresham M. Sykes and Sheldon L. Messinger, "The Inmate Social System," Chap. I in Richard A. Cloward, Donald R. Cressey, George H. Grosser, Richard Mc-Cleery, Lloyd E. Ohlin, Gresham M. Sykes, and Sheldon R. Messinger, *Theoretical Studies in Social Organization of the Prison,* New York: Social Science Research Council, 1960, pp. 5–9.

174   Elsewhere I have shortened: Edwin H. Sutherland and Donald R. Cressey, *Principles of Criminology,* Seventh Edition, Philadelphia: Lippincott, 1966, pp. 559–560.

175   John Irwin and I: John Irwin and Donald R. Cressey, "Thieves, Convicts, and the Inmate Culture," *Social Problems,* 10: 142–155, Fall, 1962.

176   Tyler quote: *op. cit.,* pp. 408–409.

177   Soldier Mike bug: *The Voices of Organized Crime,* an educational tape prepared by the New York State Joint Legislative Committee on Crime: Its Causes, Control and Effect on Society, 1968.

178 Strong and Schrag suggestions: Samuel M. Strong, "Social Types in a Minority Group," *American Journal of Sociology*, 48: 563–573, March, 1943; Clarence Schrag, "Leadership Among Prison Inmates," *American Sociological Review*, 19: 37–42, February, 1954; and "A Preliminary Criminal Typology," *Pacific Sociological Review*, 4: 11–16, Spring, 1961.

179 Dutch Schultz was ugly: J. Richard Davis, "Things I Couldn't Tell Till Now," *Collier's,* July 22, July 29, August 5, August 12, August 19, and August 26, 1939. The quote is from p. 9 of the July 22 section.

180 Martin description: Raymond V. Martin, *Revolt in the Mafia,* New York: Duell, Sloan and Pearce, 1963.

180 One of the Gallo brothers: *New York Daily News,* May 24, 1959.

180 Mike, Pete, and Larry bug: *The Voices of Organized Crime, op. cit.*

183 Salerno quote: New York State Commission of Investigation, *An Investigation of the Loan Shark Racket,* Albany: State Printing Office, 1965.

184 Pasley quote: Fred D. Pasley, *Al Capone: The Biography of a Self-Made Man,* New York: Garden City Publishing Company, 1930, p. 67.

184 A *right guy* is always loyal: Sykes and Messinger, *op. cit.,* pp. 10–11.

CHAPTER IX: SOME FUNCTIONS OF THE CODE

PAGE

186 Kefauver Committee quote: Special Senate Committee to Investigate Organized Crime in Interstate Commerce (Kefauver Committee), *Second Interim Report,* 82nd Congress, 1st Session, 1951, p. 4.

189 But while Giancana: *Chicago Tribune,* June 5, 1966.

189 But in May, 1967: *Santa Barbara News-Press,* May 10, 1967, p. C-8.

189 Officials explained that: Testimony of Joseph F. Morris, *Hearings Before the Permanent Subcommittee on Investigations of the Senate Committee on Government Operations* (McClellan Committee), 88th Congress, 1st Session, October 11, 1963, p. 502.

190 Cassese quote: *The New York Times,* August 15, 1966.

191 Policeman and Mike bug: *The Voices of Organized Crime,* an educational tape prepared by the New York State Joint Legislative Committee on Crime: Its Causes, Control and Effect on Society, 1968.

194 Kennedy quote: *McClellan Committee Hearings, op. cit.,* p. 25.

195 President's Commission quotes: *Task Force Report: Organized Crime,* U.S. President's Commission on Law Enforcement and Administration of Justice, Washington: Government Printing Office, 1967, pp. 1 and 19.

196 McDade quote, the warlords of this cycle: Joseph M. McDade, "Study of Organized Crime and the Urban Poor," *Congressional Record,* Vol. 113, No. 139, August 29, 1967.

196 McDade quote, we are losing ground: Joseph M. McDade, *Organized Crime and the Urban Poor,* address before the National Civil Liberties Clearing House, Washington, October 12, 1967 (mimeographed), p. 2.

197   We believe that one part: McDade, *op. cit.*, p. 3.

197   *Wall Street Journal:* Nicholas Gage column, *The Wall Street Journal*, October 26, 1967.

198   Powell quote, I am against numbers: *The New York Times*, January 4, 1960.

198   Powell quote, at this time: *The New York Times*, January 7, 1960.

198   Powell quote, every Negro lottery operator: *The New York Times*, January 10, 1960.

198   *The New York Times* estimated: January 6 and 11, 1960.

199   Whyte quote: William Foote Whyte, *Street Corner Society*, Chicago: University of Chicago Press, 1943 (Enlarged Edition, 1955), p. 130.

199   Tyler quote: Gus Tyler, Editor, *Organized Crime in America: A Book of Readings*, Ann Arbor: University of Michigan Press, 1962, p. 336.

199   Bolitho quote: William Bolitho, "The Natural History of Graft," *The Survey*, 63: 138–140ff., April, 1931.

200   McCleery quote: Richard H. McCleery, "The Governmental Process and Informal Social Control," Chap. IV in Donald R. Cressey, Editor, *The Prison: Studies in Institutional Organization and Change*, New York: Holt, Rinehart and Winston, 1961, pp. 153–154. Italics added.

202   Joe Profaci's final answer: Testimony of Ralph F. Salerno, *McClellan Committee Hearings, op. cit.*, p. 377.

204   Whoever commits an action: Quoted by Lawrence Preuss, "Punishment by Analogy in Nationalist Socialist Penal Law," *Journal of Criminal Law and Criminology*, 26: 847, March-April, 1936.

205   Butler quote: *Lanzetta vs. New Jersey*, 306 U.S. 451 (1939).

209   Beyond the power of the court: *State vs. Doughtie*, 237 N.C. 368, 74 S.E. 2nd 922 (1953).

213   I was told the other night: *The New York Times*, January 12, 1968.

213   Gardiner and Olson quote: John A. Gardiner, with the assistance of David J. Olson, "Wincanton: The Politics of Corruption," *Task Force Report: Organized Crime, op. cit.*, Appendix B, pp. 61–79. At p. 62.

215   According to Pileggi: Nicholas Pileggi, "The Lying, Thieving, Murdering, Upper-Middle-Class Respectable Crook," *Esquire*, January, 1966, pp. 50–52, ff.

216   Ostentatious display: Frederic Sondern, Jr., *Brotherhood of Evil: The Mafia*, New York: Farrar, Straus and Cudahy, 1959, p. 55.

216   Many illiterate Sicilians: Norman Lewis, *The Honored Society*, New York: G. P. Putnam's Sons, 1964, p. 37.

216   Our living room: Quoted by Fred J. Cook, *The Secret Rulers: Criminal Syndicates and How They Control the U.S. Underworld*, New York: Duell, Sloan and Pearce, 1966, p. 338.

217   Cook quote: *op. cit.*, p. 339.

218   As American society: Daniel Bell, "Crime as an American Way of Life," *Antioch Review*, 13: 131–154, June, 1953. At p. 131.

220   In a sense, Giancana: *Chicago Tribune*, June 5, 1966.

CHAPTER X: SHIFTING PATTERNS OF AUTHORITY AND RECRUITMENT

PAGE

221 Valachi quote: *Hearings Before the Permanent Subcommittee on Investigations of the Senate Committee on Government Operations* (McClellan Committee), 88th Congress, 1st Session, October 9, 1963, p. 356.

224 "Autonomy within limits": Alfred H. Stanton and M. S. Schwartz, *The Mental Hospital,* New York: Basic Books, 1954, pp. 260–267.

226 Smith quote: Sandy Smith, "Mobsters in the Marketplace—Money, Muscle, Murder," *Life,* September 8, 1967, pp. 98–104. At p. 102.

229 The tendency to punish: Svend Ranulf, *Moral Indignation and Middle Class Psychology,* Copenhagen: Levin and Munksgaard, 1938.

229 The application of physical: Amitai Etzioni, "Organizational Control Structure," Chap. 15 in James G. March, Editor, *Handbook of Organizations,* Chicago: Rand McNally, 1965, pp. 650–651.

234 Shanley testimony: *McClellan Committee Hearings, op. cit.,* p. 70.

238 McKay has referred: Henry D. McKay, "The Neighborhood and Child Conduct," *Annals of the American Academy of Political and Social Science,* 261: 32–42, January, 1949.

238 One is the flag: Raymond V. Martin, *Revolt in the Mafia,* New York: Duell, Sloan and Pearce, 1963, p. 60.

239 Some hoodlums are assigned: Martin, *op. cit.,* pp. 61–62.

240 Such assignments served: Irving Spergel, *Racketville, Slumtown, Haulburg,* Chicago: University of Chicago Press, 1964, p. 30.

240 Spergel quote, racketeers placed a premium: *op. cit.,* pp. 35–36.

241 Spergel found, in fact: *op. cit.,* p. 31.

241 Both Moynihan and Susini: Daniel P. Moynihan, "The Private Government of Crime," *Reporter,* July 6, 1961, pp. 14–20; Jean Susini, "La Bureaucratization du Crime," *Revue de Science Criminelle et Droit Pénal Comparé,* 21: 116–128, 1966.

242 Martin quote: *op. cit.,* p. 62.

245 Assures the standardization: Peter M. Blau, *Bureaucracy in Modern Society,* New York: Random House, 1956, p. 66.

CHAPTER XI: CORRUPTION OF THE LAW-ENFORCEMENT AND POLITICAL SYSTEMS

PAGE

248 McDade quote: Joseph M. McDade, "Study of Organized Crime and the Urban Poor," *Congressional Record,* Vol. 113, No. 139, August 29, 1967.

249   American Bar Association quote: American Bar Association, *Report on Organized Crime and Law Enforcement,* 1952, p. 16.

249   Warren quote: Earl Warren, "Address," *Proceedings of the First National Conference on Crime Control,* Washington, March 28–29, 1967, pp. 7–13. At p. 9.

250   President's Commission quotes: *Task Force Report: Organized Crime,* U.S. President's Commission on Law Enforcement and Administration of Justice, Washington: Government Printing Office, 1967, p. 6.

253   One noted political analyst: Alexander Heard, *The Costs of Democracy,* Chapel Hill: University of North Carolina Press, 1960, pp. 154–168.

253   Lasswell quote: Harold D. Lasswell and Arnold A. Rogow, *Power, Corruption and Rectitude,* Englewood Cliffs, N.J.: Prentice-Hall, 1963, pp. 79–80.

254   These people really work on you: *Task Force Report: The Police,* U.S. President's Commission on Law Enforcement and Administration of Justice, Washington: Government Printing Office, 1967, p. 209.

254   The powerful crime syndicate: Virgil W. Peterson, *A Report on Chicago Crime for 1965,* Chicago: Crime Commission, 1966, p. 70.

255   Aiuppa-Shaw-Bergbreiter transcript: *Ibid.*

259   Kempton quote: Murray Kempton, "Our Betters—The Mafia," *New York World Telegram,* April 21, 1966.

259   Speaking of the incorruptible: quoted by David Burnham, writing in *The New York Times,* January 15, 1968.

260   President's Commission quote: *Task Force Report: Organized Crime, op. cit.,* p. 12.

261   The *New York Post* revealed: Ted Poston, "The Numbers Racket," *New York Post,* February 29–March 10, 1960.

261   In the spring of 1968: *The New York Times,* April 24, 1968, p. 74.

262   Smith quotes: Sandy Smith, "The Fix," *Life,* September 1, 1967, pp. 22–23, 42–45. At p. 44.

262   The following story: Virgil W. Peterson, *A Report on Chicago Crime for 1967,* Chicago: *Chicago Crime Commission,* 1968, pp. 88–89.

263   This was somewhat the case: John A. Gardiner, with the assistance of David J. Olson, "Wincanton: The Politics of Corruption," Appendix B in *Task Force Report: Organized Crime, op. cit.,* pp. 61–79.

264   County commissioner quote: *Kansas City Star,* July 20, 1966.

264   Russo quote: Smith, *op. cit.,* p. 45.

265   Chicago Police detective story and Executive Director quotes: Virgil W. Peterson, *A Report on Chicago Crime for 1963,* Chicago: Chicago Crime Commission 1964, pp. 52–53.

267   Blakey quote: G. Robert Blakey, "Organized Crime and Corruption Practices," chapter in S. A. Yefsky, Editor, *Law Enforcement Science and Technology,* Washington: Thompson Book Company, 1967, pp. 15–20. At p. 17.

267 Kefauver Committee quote: Senate Special Committee to Investigate Organized Crime in Interstate Commerce (Kefauver Committee), *Third Interim Report*, 82nd Congress, 1st Session, 1951, p 125.

267 During the same period: Joseph Goldstein, "Police Discretion Not to Invoke the Criminal Process: Low Visibility Decisions in the Administration of Justice," *Yale Law Journal*, 59: 543–594, March, 1960. At p. 584.

268 The Chicago Crime Commission assailed: Peterson, *A Report on Chicago Crime for 1963, op. cit.*, pp. 14–15.

269 It was rumored that: Peterson, *A Report on Chicago Crime for 1965, op. cit.*, p. 49.

270 The "bug" transcript reveals: Bill Davidson, "The Mafia: How It Bleeds New England," *The Saturday Evening Post*, November 18, 1967, pp. 27–31. At p. 28.

272 During a Washington press interview: Peterson, *A Report on Chicago Crime for 1963, op. cit.*, pp. 45–47.

272 Kefauver Committee quote: *Third Interim Report, op. cit.*, p. 59.

273 Nicholas Pileggi, "How We Italians Discovered America and Kept It Pure, With Lots of Swell People," *Esquire*, June, 1968, pp. 80–82.

275 The Dean of Planning: *Wall Street Journal*, January 18, 1968.

275 A war on organized crime: McDade, *op. cit.,*

276 National Advisory Commission quotes: *Report of the National Advisory Commission on Civil Disorders*, New York: Bantam Books, 1968, pp. 59, 262.

277 Johnson quotes: Earl Johnson, Jr., "Organized Crime: Challenge to the American Legal System; Part I—Organized Crime: The Nature of Its Threat, the Reasons for Its Survival," *Journal of Criminal Law, Criminology and Police Science*, 53: 399–425, December, 1962. At p. 422.

278 In previous years: Irving Spergel, *Racketville, Slumtown, Haulburg*, Chicago: University of Chicago Press, 1964, p. 34.

279 It is impossible: Harry H. Ransom, *Central Intelligence and National Security*, Cambridge: Harvard University Press, 1959, p. 12.

280 In a similar fashion: Virgil W. Peterson, *A Report on Chicago Crime for 1956*, Chicago: Chicago Crime Commission, 1957, pp. 23–24.

280 Wilson quote: O. W. Wilson, *Police Administration*, New York: McGraw-Hill, 1950, pp. 67–68.

281 President's Commission quote: *Task Force Reports Organized Crime, op. cit.*, pp. 15–16.

281 McKeithen statement: Quoted in *Life*, September 8, 1967, p. 94.

281 In 1961, a nationwide: "Challenge to Morality," essay in the *Christian Science Monitor*, January 9, 1963, p. 9; and Dwight S. Strong, "New England: The Refined Yankees in Organized Crime," *Annals of the American Academy of Political and Social Science*, 347: 40–50, May, 1963.

281   A police captain has commented: Quoted by William Foote Whyte, *Street Corner Society,* Chicago: University of Chicago Press, 1943 (Enlarged Edition, 1955), p. 137.

282   McDade quote: Joseph M. McDade, *Organized Crime and the Urban Poor,* address before the National Civil Liberties Clearing House, Washington, October 12, 1967 (mimeographed), p. 3.

282   Breitel quote: Charles Breitel, "Controls in Criminal Law Enforcement," *University of Chicago Law Review,* 27: 427, 1960.

285   Whyte came to this conclusion: *op. cit.,* p. 138.

286   President's Commision quote: *Task Force Reports The Courts,* U.S. President's Commission on Law Enforcement and Administration of Justice, Washington: Government Printing Office, 1967, p. 100.

287   Whyte quote: *op. cit.,* p. 139.

287   For over twenty years: Alfred R. Lindesmith, *Opiate Addiction,* Bloomington, Ind.: Principia Press 1947; and *The Addict and the Law,* Bloomington, Ind.: Indiana University Press, 1965.

288   Gallagher quote: *Hearings Before a Subcommittee of the House Committee on Government Operations,* 90th Congress, 1st Session, 1967, p. 111.

288   *Life* quote: Russell Sackett, Sandy Smith and William Lambert, "The Congressman and the Hoodlum," *Life,* August 9, 1968, pp. 20–27. At p. 20.

289   I forgot those gangsters: Quoted by Sandy Smith and William Lambert, "The Mob Finds a 'Patsy' in a Mayor's Inner Circle," *Life,* January 5, 1968, pp. 44–51. At p. 49.

CHAPTER XII: SEARCH, DESTROY, AND APPEASE

PAGE

290   Thom quote: Charles R. Thom, Commissioner of Police of Suffolk County, N.Y., *Statement Before the New York State Commission of Investigation on April 22, 1960* (mimeographed), p. 3.

291   In the summer of 1966: Reuters dispatch carried by the *Newark News,* June 19, 1966.

291   Blakey has pointed out: G. Robert Blakey, *Brief of Amici Curiae Urging Affirmation,* Ralph Berger v. The People of the State of New York, Supreme Court of the United States, No. 615, October term, 1966, p. 23; and "Organized Crime in the United States," *Current History,* 52: 327–333, June, 1967.

292   As the economist: Thomas C. Schelling, "Economic Analysis of Organized Crime," Appendix D, *Task Force Report: Organized Crime,* U.S. President's Commission on Law Enforcement and Administration of Justice, Washington: Government Printing Office, 1967, pp. 114–126.

293   Some years ago: Alfred C. Kinsey, Wardell B. Pomeroy, and Clyde E.

Martin, *Sexual Behavior in the Human Male,* Philadelphia: W. B. Saunders, 1948.

294   More recently, computer control: *The New York Times,* January 14, 1968.

298   Keating quote: William J. Keating with Richard Carter, *The Man Who Rocked the Boat,* New York: Harper & Row, 1956, pp. 87–88.

301   The only attempts to date: Donald R. Cressey, "The Functions and Structure of Criminal Syndicates," Appendix A, *Task Force Report: Organized Crime, op. cit.,* pp. 25–60; and *Plan for Operations Research Study of Organized Crime in the United States,* Technical Memorandum to National Crime Commission, Matson Research Corporation, Project 66–110, September 20, 1966.

301   The Commission distinguished: *Task Force Report: The Courts,* U.S. President's Commission on Law Enforcement and Administration of Justice, Washington: Government Printing Office, 1967, pp. 99–110.

302   It recommended: *Task Force Report: Organized Crime, op. cit.,* p. 19.

303   Model Penal Code quote: Proposed Official Draft, 1962.

304   This proposed legislation: National Council on Crime and Delinquency, *Model Sentencing Act,* Article 3, Sections 5-b and 5-c, 1963.

306   Wilson quote: *Hearings Before the Permanent Subcommittee on Investigations of the Senate Committee on Government Operations* (McClellan Committee), 88th Congress, 1st Session, 1963, p. 493.

307   Edwards statement: *Ibid.,* pp. 423–424.

308   In his opening statement: *Ibid.,* p. 3.

308   McClellan quote: *Ibid.,* p. 20.

309   McClellan Committee excerpt: *Ibid.,* p. 120.

311   The late Professor: Edwin H. Sutherland, *White Collar Crime,* New York: Dryden, 1949.

312   Another illustration: Donald R. Cressey, *Other People's Money,* Glencoe, Ill.: Free Press, 1953, pp. 19–22.

314   In one publication: *Combating Organized Crime,* Report of the 1965 Oyster Bay, New York, Conferences on Combating Organized Crime, Albany: Office of the Counsel to the Governor, 1965, pp. 19–24.

315   In another publication: *A Theory of Organized Crime Control: A Preliminary Statement,* mimeographed paper prepared by the technical staff and consultants of the New York State Identification and Intelligence System, May, 1966, pp. 18–24.

319   President's Commission quote: *Task Force Report: Organized Crime, op. cit.,* p. 8.

320   Salerno quote: Ralph F. Salerno, "Syndicated Personnel Structure," in S. A. Yefsky, Editor, *Law Enforcement Science and Technology,* Washington: Thompson Book Company, 1967, pp. 9–14. At p. 9.

320   Attorney General Clark: *Hearings Before the Subcommittee on Criminal Laws and Procedures of the Senate Committee on the Judiciary,* 90th Congress, 1st Session, 1967, p. 83.

321   President's Commission quote: *The Challenge of Crime in a Free* · *Society,* Report of the President's Commission of Law Enforcement and Administration of Justice, Washington: Government Printing Office, 1967, p. 7.

321   Vern Countryman: *The Worker* (New York City), May 22, 1966.

321   The racketeering activities: Alan G. Sutter, *The Combination Racket in Union Insurance: Analysis of Emergent Crime and Social Power,* unpublished master's thesis, Department of Sociology, University of California (Berkeley), 1963, pp. 139–140.

323   Tacit or explicit understandings: Schelling, *op. cit.,* p. 123.

323   Kadish quote: Sanford H. Kadish, "Some Observations on the Use of Criminal Sanctions in Enforcing Economic Regulations," *University of Chicago Law Review,* 30: 423–449, Spring, 1963. At p. 426.

323   Schelling quote: *op. cit.,* p. 123.

324   Schelling quote: *op. cit.,* p. 122.

Glossary

Administration. Synonym for *Commission,* Cosa Nostra's judicial board, and for *Inner Circle, Roundtable.*

American way. A condition of peaceful coexistence, rather than of violence, between rival groups participating in organized-crime activities.

Amico. Friend, member.

Amico nostro. Friend of ours, member.

Area man. The person in charge of the organized-crime activities in a section, made up of several "districts," of a city.

Argomentazione. See *sit-down.*

Arm. Synonym for *Cosa Nostra,* used, especially, in upstate New York.

Avvocato. Literally, advocate, counsel. A member of the *Commission.* Synonym for *chairman.* Each *avvocato* represents one or more "families."

Bag. A package of diluted heroin weighing about five grains. Synonym for *balloon, pack.*

Balloon. See *bag.*

Bank. The headquarters of an illegal lottery. Synonym for *main office.*

Banker. The operator of an illegal lottery. Synonym for *manager, owner.*

Beard. A corrupt official. Synonym for *cousin, rabbi, front.* See *corruptee.*

Big bag. A package of diluted heroin weighing about two grams.

Big lay-off man. A bet-taker who accepts bets from an area's bet-takers, all of whom have, previously, reinsured some of the bets accepted by bookmakers. Synonym for *large lay-off man.*

Big six. The collectivity of eight men, each of whom was a specialist, controlling organized crime activities in the New York metropolitan area in the 1930s.

Big-time dealer. A narcotics dealer who purchases his wares from an

343

importer or from a bulk distributor. Used principally in the western United States with reference to what is elsewhere called *kilo man*.

Black Hand. Synonym for *Mafia*. Popular in the United States at the turn of the century and still used occasionally as a synonym for *Cosa Nostra*.

Bleeder. A lottery ticket whose purchaser has bet that he can guess the last two digits of a three-digit number to be determined by chance.

Board. A judicial and decision-making body composed of representatives from each of the Cosa Nostra units in a city. Used especially in Detroit, Chicago, New York City. Synonym for *council, high court*.

Bolita. Illegal lottery. Used especially in Spanish-speaking communities. See *numbers, policy*.

Books are closed. Commission ruling stipulating that no new members may be admitted to Cosa Nostra.

Bookmaker. The employer or financial backer of *solicitors,* who sell illegal bets on the outcome of horse races and athletic contests. Synonym for *handbook, handbook operator*.

Bootlegger. A person engaged in the illegal manufacture, smuggling, or sale of a commodity. Usually used with reference to alcohol, but also used with reference to other untaxed items such as narcotic drugs and cigarettes.

Boss. The head of a geographically based Cosa Nostra "family." Synonym for *capofamiglia, don, old man, rappresente, skipper*. See *capo*.

Boss of bosses. The chairman, president, or perceived leader of a group consisting of all the bosses in a territory. Popular in the 1930s; now rare.

Boxed number. A lottery ticket whose purchaser has bet that he can guess, in any combination, the digits of a three-digit number to be determined by chance. The ticket specifies that the bettor has guessed, for example, that the number will be 8-7-1, 7-8-1, 1-8-7, 1-7-8, 8-1-7, or 7-1-8. Synonym for *combination number*.

Brotherhood. Synonym for *Cosa Nostra*.

Bug. Any electronic device used for eavesdropping. Ordinarily, the overheard conversation is recorded.

Buffer. A *Cosa Nostra* position designed to insure that neither Cosa Nostra members nor outsiders have direct access to a Cosa Nostra official or to knowledge of the official's activities. Also, the person occupying such a position.

Button, button man. See *soldier.*

Bust out. The final phase of bankruptcy fraud. After purchasing goods on credit, a dishonest businessman busts out by selling them at cost (or below cost) and then declaring bankruptcy.

Capo. Used interchangeably to refer either to the highest-level position in a Cosa Nostra "family" authority structure (*boss*) or to the third-level position in the authority structure (*lieutenant*).

Capodecina. Literally, head of ten. See *lieutenant, caporegime.*

Capofamiglia. See *boss.*

Caporegime. See *lieutenant.*

Captain. Synonym for *capo.*

Captains of industry. Bosses. Used in 1928 to refer to a body which would now be called the *Commission.*

Carpet. See *sit-down.*

Castellammarese War. 1930–1931 armed conflict between two factions of Italian and Sicilian criminals living in the United States. One of the factions was made up primarily of men coming from the Castellammare del Golfo area of Sicily.

Chairman. See *avvocato.*

Chairman of the board. The highest-ranking member of a *board* or *council.* Used especially in Detroit.

Chief corrupter. The member of a Cosa Nostra *"family"* charged with coordinating that "family's" attempts to bribe or in some other way influence governmental officials.

Circle. The men owing allegiance to a *lieutenant.* Synonym for *clique, nostra brigata.* Also, a synonym for *"family."*

Clearinghouse. Any establishment or system maintained to reinsure the bets taken by *bookmakers.* Synonym for *master book.* See *lay-off.*

Cleveland Syndicate. An association of non-Italian organized criminals.

Clique. A geographically based unit of Cosa Nostra, resembling a "*family.*" Synonym for *circle, nostra brigata.*

Close the books. See *books are closed.*

Code of honor. The "all for one and one for all" principle of the Sicilian Mafia.

Combination, combine. A synonym for *Cosa Nostra,* used especially in the early 1930s.

Combination number. See *boxed number.*

Comeback man. A person who makes large legitimate bets at the race track in an attempt to change the amount to be paid out (odds) on a winning ticket should a designated horse win.

Commission. The nine- to twelve-man judicial and decision-making body serving Cosa Nostra's twenty-four known American "families." Synonym for *Administration, Grand Council, High Commission, Inner Circle, Roundtable.*

Compare. Godfather, sponsor.

Consigliere. See *counselor.*

Consigliere of Six. Council consisting of the *bosses* of the six "families" operating in the New York metropolitan area. Synonym for *grievance committee.*

Consiglio d'Amministrazione. Synonym for *Commission.*

Consiglio direttivo. See *counselor.* Used with reference to the Sicilian Mafia.

Consorteria. A regional alliance of Sicilian Mafia units.

Contract. A decision to murder a specific person.

Controller. In illegal lotteries, the man supervising the persons selling the lottery tickets. Synonym for *field man.*

Corruptee. A position designed to assist Cosa Nostra members nullify the law-enforcement process and the democratic political process. Also, the person occupying such a position.

Corrupter. A position occupied by Cosa Nostra members whose duty it is to buy or in some other way insure immunity from the law-enforcement process.

Cosa Nostra. A nationwide cartel and confederation of criminals, all of whom are Italian or Sicilian or of Italian-Sicilian descent, who have banded together into "families" for fellowship, and for the sale of illegal goods and services. Synonym for *Brotherhood, Mob, Syndicate, Arm, People, Fratellanza, Friends.*

Cosca (plural *cosche*). A local alliance of Sicilian Mafia units.

Council. See *board.*

Council of Six. See *Consigliere of Six.*

Counselor. A staff adviser to a *boss* and his *underboss.* Synonym for *consigliere, consiglio direttivo.*

Cousin. See *beard, corruptee.*

Cut number. In illegal lotteries, a number for which the standard pay-off (odds) has been reduced.

Dealer. A retailer of narcotics.

Deck man. The narcotics operator who sells the commodity to street *dealers.*

District man. The supervisor of the organized-crime workers in a few square blocks of Chicago.

Don. Patriarch. Also, the leader of a *council.* Also, synonym for *boss.*

Drop. A fixed location, often a lunch stand or bar, where the sellers of illegal lottery tickets turn in the day's receipts.

Drop man. The person receiving each day's receipts from sellers of illegal lottery tickets.

Elder statesman. In Detroit, a *board* or *council* member.

Elected boss. In Detroit, leader of the *board* or *council.* Synonym for *don, chairman of the board.*

Enforcer. A Cosa Nostra executive position occupied, usually temporarily, by a person whose duty is to make the arrangements for carrying out the judicial decisions of his superiors.

Executioner. A *soldier* who executes the orders for inflicting punishment or death given him by an *enforcer* in his *"family."*

"Family." Geographically based Cosa Nostra administrative, judicial, and membership unit. The members of a *"family"* need not be blood relatives. Also, synonym for *Cosa Nostra.*

Field man. See *controller.*

Financial backers. Title given Cosa Nostra supervisors by organized criminals employed by or franchised by them.

Finger man. One who locates a Cosa Nostra member or nonmember whose punishment or death has been ordered by a *boss,* a *council,* or the *Commission,* and arranged by an *enforcer.* One variety of *executioner.*

Fix. The process of bribing or in some other way insuring immunity

from the law-enforcement process. Also, the person who ar-
ranges the bribe. Also, any illegal process used to influence the
outcome of a horse race or athletic contest.

Fratellanza. See *Cosa Nostra.*

Friend, friend of ours. Member of Cosa Nostra. See *amico, amico nostro.*

Friends, friends of ours. Synonym for *Cosa Nostra.* Also, plural of
friend.

Front. A nonmember of Cosa Nostra who acts on behalf of one or
more Cosa Nostra members so as to conceal the latter's interests in a legitimate business or activity. Also, a legal enterprise which conceals an illegal one. ("That lunch stand is a
front for a bookie.") Also, a corrupt official and, in this sense,
a synonym for *beard, cousin, rabbi.* See *corruptee.*

Gallo-Profaci War. A 1961–1962 sidewalk war between two factions
of the Brooklyn-based Profaci *"family."*

Gig. A wager that the bettor can guess which number, varying from
one-digit to five-digit, will appear by chance.

Goner. A person doomed to death.

Good fellow. See *soldier.*

Goon. A bodyguard or *executioner* whose duty it is to intimidate
others by physical appearance and threat of violence.

Grand Council. Synonym for *Commission.* Also, the judicial body
made up of Sicilian Mafia leaders.

Greaser. Old-fashioned Sicilian Mafia member operating in the
United States during the Prohibition era. Synonym for *handlebar,
mustache Pete.*

Grievance Committee. Synonym for *Consigliere of Six.*

Group leader. See *section chief.*

Guys, the guys. Members. Similar in meaning to *friends* and *friends
of ours* but also used with reference to a specific working group
or task force.

Handbook, handbook operator. See *bookmaker.*

Handlebar. See *greaser.*

Head. See *lieutenant, capo.*

High Commission. See *Commission.*

High court. Synonym, in Detroit, for *board.*

Hijack. Process of robbing a conveyer of illegal goods.

Hit. A murder. Also, a winning ticket in an illegal lottery.

Hit man. One who murders on orders from a *boss,* a *council,* or the *Commission.* One variety of *executioner.* See *finger man, wheel man.*

Holding the cream. A process whereby the street worker in an illegal bet-taking operation hides from his supervisor those bets which he believes to be sure losers, thereby booking the "sure thing" bets himself.

Hole. Woman, prostitute.

Honor. A condition of loyalty to a *boss,* to a "family," and to *Cosa Nostra.*

Horse Room. An illegal bet-taking establishment designed in such a way that gamblers may make bets, at track odds, just before the running of each race.

Hot. Stolen. Also, a gun that has been used in a murder.

Humility. An attitude and appearance rationally exhibited by a Cosa Nostra leader in an attempt to underplay the extent of his power.

Hustle. Illegal or marginally legal ways of making a living without holding a regular job. Most frequently used with reference to narcotics dealing, pimping, prostitution.

Independent. A bet-taker or lottery operator who is not a member of Cosa Nostra but who pays a Cosa Nostra member a royalty for permission to do business.

Indian. Nonmember of Cosa Nostra who is engaged in illicit bet-taking, usury, narcotics wholesaling, or some other organized-crime activity.

Inner Circle. See *Commission.*

Ins. Those illicit horse-racing bets which will be paid off, with the money bet on the losers, should certain horses win. The *outs* (losing bets) must balance the *ins* (winning bets) if the *bookmaker* is to have a *middle* (a sure thing). See *outs.*

Juice. Usury. Also, interest on usurious loans. See *vigorish.*

Kid. Man of inferior status, often someone's son or younger brother, regardless of his age.

Kilo man. Cosa Nostra member who buys heroin from the importer in bulk lots weighing not less than one kilogram.

Knock down the business. The process of selling bets on horse races and athletic contests on a commission basis or in partnership with a Cosa Nostra member.

Large lay-off man. See *big lay-off man.*

Law. Police, policeman.

Lay-off. The process by which the acceptor of illegal bets himself bets some of the funds gambled with him.

Lay-off man. One who receives a *lay-off* bet made by a *bookmaker.*

Lay-off room. A *bookmaker*'s headquarters.

Leader. A lottery ticket whose purchaser has bet that he can guess the first digit of a three-digit number to be determined by chance.

Lieutenant. Position on the third level in the hierarchical authority structure of Cosa Nostra "families." Synonym for *capodecina, head.* See *capo.*

Loan shark. One who makes loans at usurious (or exhorbitant) rates and uses force or the threat of force to collect them. Synonym for *shylock, shell.*

Loan-sharking. Usury.

Made. Induction to Cosa Nostra membership. ("He was made in 1957.")

Mafia. Sicilian underground alliance between numerous local bands organized to perpetrate extortion. Sometimes used in the United States as a synonym for *Cosa Nostra.* Synonym for *Società degli amici.*

Mafia Grand Council. Judicial and decision-making body made up of leaders of the Sicilian Mafia.

Mafie. Local Sicilian bands organized to perpetrate extortion.

Main office. See *bank.*

Manager. See *banker.*

Master book. See *clearinghouse.*

Member. An Italian, Sicilian, or person of Italian or Sicilian descent, who in a ceremony has been declared a participant in the affairs of a Cosa Nostra *"family."* See *amico, friend, made.*

Men of honor. Members of the Sicilian *Mafia.* Rarely, members of *Cosa Nostra.*

Men of respect. Synonym for *men of honor.* Used more frequently in the United States than *men of honor.*

Middle. A betting arrangement in which a gambler or bet-taker cannot lose.

Mob. See *Cosa Nostra.*

Money mover. *"Family"* investment counselor and broker who invests funds, often in legitimate enterprises, for the members of his organization.

Mustache, Mustache Pete. See *greaser.*

Muscle. Force or the threat of force.

Nostra brigata. See *circle.*

Numbers. Illegal lotteries in which customers bet that they can guess which number, usually from three to five digits, will be determined by chance. In some forms, the number is randomly allocated to the purchaser rather than selected by him. Also called number pool, *policy, bolita.*

Numbers operator. The owner or manager of an illegal lottery.

Old man. See *boss.*

Omertà. A combination of manliness, honor, and humility.

Onorata Società (Honored Society). Synonym for the Sicilian *Mafia.* Used only occasionally in the United States.

On the gamble. An arrangement whereby the seller of illegal lottery tickets finances his own operation, paying winners from his own profits. A man on the gamble pays a fixed fee or a percentage of profits to his supervisor for territorial rights.

Open area, Open territory. Western and Southern regions of the United States in which no specific *"family"* has exclusive rights to gambling, usury, or other organized crime activities.

Open the books. Declaration by the Commission that Cosa Nostra "families" are eligible to induct new members. See *books are closed.*

Operator. A man engaged in one or more of the various organizational positions essential to conducting illicit businesses.

Organization. The Chicago enterprise engaged in the selling of illicit services and goods, and including non-Italians as well as Italians. Synonym for *outfit.*

Ounce man. The person on the fourth level in the hierarchy of illicit businessmen who import, distribute, and sell narcotics.

Outfit. See *organization.*

Outs. Those illicit horse-racing bets which can be used to pay off winning bets, should a specific horse win. See *Ins.*

Owner. See *banker.*

Pack. See *bag.*

Pad. A list of illicit lottery sales locations whose operators have bribed the police to insure immunity from arrest. See *spot.*

Paper local. A fictitious labor union created explicitly to engage in illicit competition with a legitimate union or to extort money from small businessmen.

Patsy. A dupe, victim of fraud.

Pick-up man. See *writer.*

Piece man. In the Western United States, the person on the fourth or fifth level in the narcotics business. See *ounce man.*

Piece of work. A murder done on contract. See *contract.*

People. See *Cosa Nostra.*

Policy. See *numbers.*

Policy writer. See *writer.*

Polizza. Slip indicating the number a gambler has chosen or been assigned in an illegal lottery.

Proposed. A man who has been invited to become a member of *Cosa Nostra* and who in most respects is treated as a member until such time as the books are open to membership.

Punk. A low-status person, especially a young man who attempts to influence others by force or threat of force.

Pusher. Politicians' and newspapermens' term for *dealers.* Rarely used by *dealers.*

Purge Day. September 11, 1931. The day Salvatore Maranzano and other Prohibition era gangsters were slain, thus ending the *Castellammarese War.*

Quarter-kilo man. The person on the third level in the hierarchy of illicit businessmen who import, distribute, and sell narcotics.

Rabbi. See *beard, corruptee.*

Raise. To elevate a *boss* to a position on the Commission.

Rappresente. See *boss.*

Regime. The organization of men reporting to a *lieutenant.*

Rehash. A form of bankruptcy fraud. See *bust out.*

Repeater. In an illicit lottery, a number with identical digits such as 6-6-6-6-6. When the number has three digits, *repeater* is a synonym for *triples* and *trips.*

Respect. An attitude of deference, based principally on fear.

Right. A condition of honesty, loyalty, manliness, and rationality, said to characterize the best criminals. ("Joe is right.")

Right guy. A man who is *right.* Synonym for *stand-up guy.*

Roundtable. See *Commission.*

Runner. In illicit lotteries, the man who sells the lottery ticket to the bettor—a synonym for *writer.* In bookmaking, the man who collects bets and makes pay-offs to the customers of a *telephone solicitor.* In narcotics distribution, and in other operations, a courier.

Scam. Bankruptcy fraud. See *bust out, rehash.*

Section chief. A *soldier* in charge of a portion of a *lieutenant's* operations. Synonym for *group leader.*

Single action. In illicit lotteries, a bet that the gambler can guess all three digits of a three-digit number to be determined by chance, and also that he can guess each individual digit. For example, the gambler makes separate bets that the first digit will be 3, that the second digit will be 7, that the third digit will be 4, and that the total number will be 3-7-4.

Shell. See *loan shark.*

Shylock, shy. See *loan shark.*

Sit-Down. A meeting between two or more Cosa Nostra officials who attempt to settle a dispute over territory, proceeds, or some personal matter. Synonym for *argomentazione, carpet, table.*

Six for five. Type of small loan obtained from a usurer. For each five dollars borrowed for one week, the borrower repays six dollars.

Skipper. See *boss.*

Società degli amici. See *Mafia.*

Soldier. The lowest-level position in the Cosa Nostra authority structure. Synonym for *button, good fellow, wise guy.*

Solicitor. A person who accepts for his *bookmaker* illicit bets on the outcome of horse races or of athletic contests.

Sottocapo. See *underboss.*

Spoon man. In West Coast narcotics distribution, the fourth man down in the business hierarchy beginning at the top with importer and descending to the street-level *dealer.*

Sportsman. Newspaper term for gambler and for criminal bet-taker.

Spot. A location at which illegal lottery tickets are sold.

Stand-up guy. See *right guy.*

Stationary solicitor. A solicitor who accepts bets at a fixed location such as a newsstand or factory floor.

Stop the clock. To declare that no interest shall be due on a usurious loan for a fixed period of time, or until further notice.

Street man. In Chicago, a man at the lowest level in the hierarchy of the *organization.*

Substation. The place of business of a numbers lottery *field man.* Synonym for *turn-in station.*

Syndicate. See *Cosa Nostra.*

Table. See *sit-down.*

Tap. An electronic device (wire tap) used to overhear telephone conversations.

Telephone solicitor. A *solicitor* who accepts bets only by telephone.

Tipover raid. A police raid on gambling establishment conducted in such a way that the civil rights of the suspects are violated, thus insuring that they will not be convicted.

Traveling book, traveling solicitor. A *solicitor* who walks a fixed route on which he accepts bets. Synonym for *walking book.*

Treasury number. A lottery in which the winning number is determined by the published figures on the daily United States Treasury cash balance.

Triple, trips. In illicit lotteries using three-digit numbers, synonym for *repeater.*

Turn-in station. See *substation.*

Underboss. The position of second rank in the hierarchical authority structure of Cosa Nostra "families." A deputy *boss.* Synonym for *sottocapo.*

Unione, Unione Siciliana. A Prohibition era organization of American-Sicilians devoted primarily to the manufacture, distribution, and sale of illicit alcohol. A forerunner of *Cosa Nostra.*

Usury. The loaning of money at interest rates higher than those permitted by law or, when there is no stipulated maximum legal interest rate, the loaning of money at exhorbitant rates.

Vigorish. The interest on a usurious loan. Generally, profits.

Walking book. See *traveling book.*

Walking writer. See *writer.*

Wheel. In an illicit lottery, the operating unit in which money bet by losers is used to pay off the holders of winning tickets.

Wheel man. One who drives the automobile used in the execution of a murder ordered by a *boss,* a *council,* or the *Commission.* Generally, a chauffer who drives a car used in the perpetration of a crime. See *finger man, hit man.*

Wise guy. Synonym for *button* and *soldier* and, also, for *right guy* and *stand-up guy.*

Writer. The person who sells illicit lottery tickets to bettors. Synonym for *pick-up man, policy writer, walking writer.*

Index

357

75 76 77 78 79 80   12 11 10 9 8 7